ASEAN Ventures of Western Guangdong Enterprises

Modern China Series

ASEAN Ventures of Western Guangdong Enterprises

Tu Yulong

North American Business Press

ASEAN Ventures of Western Guangdong Enterprises

ISBN: 978-1-948915-37-3

NORTH
AMERICAN BUSINESS
P R E S S

North American Business Press
Atlanta, Georgia
Miami, Florida
New York, New York
Toronto, Canada

FIRST PRINTING, 2025

About Modern China Series

As one of the oldest civilizations globally, China has emerged as a "new world" by embracing its essence and heritage and linking them to viable economic strategies. In the last 25 years, China has made tremendous strides. The country and its people have every right to take pride in these accomplishments. Many Chinese leaders and intellectuals anticipate continuing growth with these successes. Furthermore, China's plans and strategies are often based on this premise.

The U.S. has a tremendous interest in the Chinese economy and business environment. China has emerged as a global superpower, and scholars and businesspeople in the U.S. are keenly interested in learning how this will affect them and how to do business with China. In response to growing interest from international and Asian scholars, North American Business Press is pleased to announce our Modern China Series (MCS) books. It is the first book series about modern China in the U.S., garnering tremendous interest in the U.S. and worldwide. With our first book set to reach stores in September 2011, this initiative aims to foster relationships between NABP and Chinese scholars. They desire to promote their academic and applied business writings to the rest of the world.

We have experienced an overwhelming demand for the Modern China Series from authors who wish to publish in the series and readers who are eager to read the books. The books have been viewed by thousands of people from the U.S. and the rest of the world. There are currently ten books published in the series, and we have a couple of dozen books under consideration for the series.

We have published books on several areas revolving around the Chinese business environment. We have a few that focus on the best practices in marketing in China; some are compared to "best practices" in doing business in China, and a few are on the outlook of the Chinese economy. The market for the Modern China Series is enormous. There are tens of thousands of scholars who are keenly interested in the continued growth of the Chinese economy and its implications for the business world. Even more significant are the millions of businesspeople interested in the impact that China will continue to have on the global economy. It is difficult to pinpoint the exact demand for the series, but it is enormous.

We have big plans to grow the Modern China Series. It can be one of the most significant economic/business series ever produced. We are very selective about the books we add to the collection. Still, we encourage scholars who believe they have unique and exciting perspectives on China to submit their book manuscripts. From the readers' perspective, we are committed to producing high-quality books regularly, so readers can expect a steady stream of insightful books to be published for many years to come.

This initiative is headed by Dr. Robert Tian, a renowned researcher and academic. He spearheads our efforts to partner with foreign authors and administer the day-to-day operations of this series. Dr. Tian, the Vice-President of North American Business Press and Editor of this series, spends much of his time in Beijing, Shanghai, and other Chinese cities, focusing on developing and managing our interests with authors and universities. Below is the list of the books we have published:

Enterprise Strategy: New Horizon, authored by Zhang Xiuyu

Governance of Private Enterprises in Modern China, authored by Zhong Qin

The Art of War and Enterprise Strategy Management, authored by Fu Shouzhi

Marketing Issues in Modern China, edited by Robert Guang Tian et al.

The Footprints of the Academician, authored by Fu Zhouzhi

Marketing and Economics in Modern China (I) edited by Xiaoguang Qi et al.

Marketing and Economics in Modern China (II) edited by Wang Tianjin et al.

An Islamic Heritage in China, authored by Ma Zhanming

China Environmental Anthropology, authored by Wang Tianjin, Tian Guang, and Ma Jianfu

Can China Rule the New World? authored by Tian Guang and Chen Gang

Critiques on Pan-marketization authored by Li Cunlin, Liu Hongfei, and Tian Guang

Economic and Business Anthropology in China, edited by Xiaoguang Qi and Tian Guang
China-Mongolia Economic Corridor authored by Eerdun Taoketao, Zhang Zhe, Wang Gang, and Wei Lisi
Anthropology of Chinese Foodways, authored by Tian Guang and Chen Gang
Urbanization of Rural China, authored by Li Taohong
Child Rearing in Rural China by Jiang Youchun and Yang Yunyi
Belt and Road vs. China and World by Tian Guang and Chen Gang
Modernization of China by Tian Guang, Luo Kanglong and Chen Qian
Abnormal School Behaviors: China vs. South Korea by Yu Yanyan
China in the Xi Jinping Era by Shu Xiaohui, Li Yangkuo and Tian Guang
Shi Zhengyi and Chinese Ethnological Economics by Tian Guang and Zhong Ni
Decoding Entrepreneurial Vision by Fan Xiaoping
Huaihua International Inland Port by Shu Xiaohui, Hou Tengteng and Tian Guang
Tourism and Sustainable Development in China by Guo Yan
ASEAN Ventures of Western Guangdong Enterprises by Tu Yulong

Table of Contents

Preface

Against the backdrop of in-depth adjustments in economic globalization and the accelerated advancement of regional economic integration, the Association of Southeast Asian Nations (ASEAN), with its continuously growing economic vitality, vast market space, and close geoeconomic ties with China, has become a core destination for Chinese small and medium-sized enterprises (SMEs) to "go global." As one of China's southwestern gateways connecting with ASEAN, the western Guangdong region's SMEs, leveraging their unique geographical advantages and distinctive industrial foundations, possess inherent potential to participate in the ASEAN industrial chain division of labor. However, constrained by issues such as insufficient scale and strength, inefficient resource allocation, and a lack of international experience, they generally face the practical dilemma of "wanting to go but not being able to go steadily, wanting to enter but not being able to get in". Addressing the pain points of Western Guangdong's SMEs in their internationalization efforts in ASEAN, transforming regional advantages into competitive advantages, and achieving "precision going global" under cooperation frameworks such as the RCEP has become a crucial issue in current regional economic development and SME transformation.

The book "ASEAN Ventures of Western Guandong Enterprises" is based on this era proposition. With "problem orientation - empirical analysis - countermeasure construction" as the logical main line, it is divided into four parts and fifteen chapters, namely "Current Development Status of ASEAN Countries," "Ecosystem of Western Guangdong Enterprises," and "Diagnosis and Optimization Plan for Key Obstacles in the Internationalization of Western Guangdong Enterprises in ASEAN," systematically presenting the overall picture and breakthrough paths of the internationalization of western Guangdong SMEs in ASEAN. The book abandons generalized theoretical discussions, focuses on the specific regional pairing of "western Guangdong - ASEAN," and constructs a progressive and interlocking research system from the macro environment to micro subjects, from current situation scanning to problem diagnosis, and then to scheme design, providing practical references for government departments in formulating policies, SMEs in planning their going-global paths, and academic circles in carrying out related research.

The structure of the book consists of four major parts and 13 chapters, among which:

Part One, Current Development Status of ASEAN Countries, aims to understand the external environment for internationalization. This section, covering three chapters, establishes a "cognitive framework" for Western Guangdong SMEs to comprehend the ASEAN market and clarifies the opportunities and differences in the external environment. Chapter 1, The Process of ASEAN Economic Integration, explains the process of ASEAN economic integration; Chapter 2, Differentiated Analysis of ASEAN Member States, analyzes the disparities among the ten ASEAN countries from the angles of infrastructure and business environment, providing a basis for enterprises to develop "one country, one policy" approaches; Chapter 3, New Opportunities for China - ASEAN Cooperation, interprets benefits such as tariff reductions and rules of origin under the RCEP framework, examines new avenues like facilitation of SME cooperation, strengthening supply chain resilience, and collaboration in green and digital economies, helping enterprises identify entry points for cooperation.

Part Two examines Western Guangdong SMEs from a micro perspective, highlighting their advantages and weaknesses. Chapter 4 discusses the "pyramid-shaped" scale structure, operational challenges like "resource dependence + low-cost competition," and suggests differentiated strategies. Chapter 5 details resource dependence across three dimensions: natural, policy, and market. Chapter 6 identifies conditions for ASEAN-oriented internationalization, while Chapter 7 assesses the current state, potential, and gaps in this internationalization.

Part Three, Case studies. It consists of five chapters, spanning from Chapter 8 to Chapter 12, which will be conducted on "4 large enterprises + 1 small and medium-sized enterprise". The four large enterprises (Guolian Aquatic, Yuehai Foodstuff, Linxiao Pump Industry, and Wen's Group) cover the advantageous industries in western Guangdong, and one small and medium-sized enterprise (Hongzhi Technology) aligns with the main structure of regional enterprises. Each chapter corresponds to an enterprise case, presenting the experiences and specific difficulties of enterprises in internationalization through the experiences of typical enterprises in the selected industries.

Part Four covers strategies for enterprises in western Guangdong to internationalize and expand into ASEAN, including a Diagnosis of Key Obstacles in the Internationalization of Western Guangdong Enterprises in ASEAN. This systematically identifies nine core obstacles, such as high talent turnover, difficulties in localized production management, a lack of brand certification, and insufficient risk prevention and control. It also presents Optimization Plans for the internationalization of these enterprises, proposing nine key strategies to overcome obstacles. These include building an industry-education integration ecosystem for talent development, creating a supply chain support network for localized production, and promoting cross-border e-commerce linkage on the brand side, as detailed in Chapter 13.

This book is not only a systematic summary of the internationalization practice of Western Guangdong SMEs in ASEAN but also a beneficial exploration of the "precision going global" model of China's regional SMEs. It is expected to provide intellectual support for promoting industrial synergy between western Guangdong and ASEAN, and helping SMEs achieve high-quality development.

Acknowledgment

The completion of this book would not have been possible without the support of many individuals. I want to thank all the authors of the referenced academic literature, whose intellectual contributions provided a solid foundation for this research. Thanks to Chen Peiyi, Liang Ning, Li Yuxi, Li Minxia, and Abudula Nisaguli from the Department of Human Resource Management at Lingnan Normal University for collecting and processing the relevant cases and data. I am grateful to the editorial team for their thorough proofreading, which reviewed every word to improve the content. I also appreciate the case companies for generously sharing their practical materials, which added real-world examples to the theories. Additionally, I want to thank my colleagues for their professional discussions and my family for their unwavering support. Your companionship and trust have been essential motivators in completing this work. Thanks also to the funding support from the Guangdong Provincial Philosophy and Social Sciences Planning Project (No. GD22CGL270) and the Zhanjiang Municipal Philosophy and Social Sciences Planning Project (No. ZJ24YB23).

Chapter 1
The Process of ASEAN Economic Integration

This chapter primarily outlines the process of ASEAN economic integration, which dates back to the late 1960s. Following the establishment of ASEAN, a series of agreements and initiatives were implemented, gaining momentum especially after the 1990s and laying the foundation for regional economic integration.

Development History

The process of ASEAN economic integration dates back to the late 1960s. In 1967, five countries—Indonesia, Malaysia, the Philippines, Singapore, and Thailand—founded the Association of Southeast Asian Nations (ASEAN) with the original aim of promoting regional peace and stability. Economic cooperation was gradually incorporated as a key agenda item. In the early stages, ASEAN's economic collaboration primarily focused on basic areas, such as trade facilitation and limited industrial cooperation. In 1977, ASEAN signed the Agreement on ASEAN Preferential Trading Arrangements, aimed at promoting trade among member states by reducing tariffs and eliminating non-tariff barriers. The implementation of this agreement marked a significant step in regional economic cooperation, with the list of goods eligible for ASEAN preferential tariff treatment continuously expanding—from 71 items at its inception on January 1, 1978, to 12,783 items by the end of 1987.

In the 1990s, with the strengthening trend of global economic integration, ASEAN accelerated its pace of economic integration. In 1992, ASEAN leaders met in Singapore. They decided to establish the ASEAN Free Trade Area (AFTA) to achieve regional trade liberalization by 2008, progressively reducing tariffs and non-tariff barriers, and promoting the free flow of goods, services, and investment. This initiative significantly boosted intra-ASEAN trade and laid a solid foundation for regional economic integration. In the subsequent development process, ASEAN continued to refine its economic cooperation framework, introducing a series of critical cooperative initiatives and agreements.

Since the 21st century, ASEAN has made more remarkable progress in economic integration. In 2003, ASEAN leaders adopted the ASEAN Economic Community (AEC) Blueprint, which explicitly set the goal of establishing the ASEAN Economic Community by 2020. This initiative aims to create a single market and production base characterized by the free flow of goods, services, investment, skilled labor, and capital, thereby enhancing ASEAN's economic competitiveness and appeal. To achieve this goal, ASEAN has engaged in in-depth cooperation across multiple areas, including trade liberalization, investment facilitation, financial integration, and connectivity development. In terms of trade liberalization, ASEAN has continuously expanded the range of zero-tariff goods, streamlined customs procedures, and improved trade facilitation. In investment facilitation, efforts have been made to refine investment policies and regulations, establish investment promotion agencies, and attract more foreign direct investment. In financial integration, ASEAN has promoted interconnectivity within regional financial markets, strengthened financial regulatory cooperation, and enhanced the stability and efficiency of the financial system.

Current Status

1. ASEAN Free Trade Area (AFTA)

After years of development, the ASEAN Free Trade Area has achieved remarkable results. Currently, the degree of trade liberalization within ASEAN is relatively high, with most goods now subject to zero tariffs. According to data from the ASEAN Secretariat, as of 2024, the proportion of intra-ASEAN trade to its total external trade has continued to rise, reaching approximately 25%. The implementation of zero-tariff policies has reduced production costs for businesses and promoted the integration of regional industrial and supply chains. Many companies have established production bases across different ASEAN countries, leveraging each nation's resource advantages and industrial characteristics to facilitate division of labor and collaboration. This has enhanced production efficiency and product competitiveness. For instance, in the electronics industry, Malaysia possesses technological and talent advantages in semiconductor manufacturing, while Vietnam boasts abundant labor resources for electronic assembly. Through cooperation, businesses in these two countries have formed a complete industrial chain spanning from chip manufacturing to product assembly.

2. Regional Comprehensive Economic Partnership (RCEP)

In November 2020, the ten ASEAN member states, along with China, Japan, South Korea, Australia, and New Zealand—15 Asia-Pacific countries in total—officially signed the Regional Comprehensive Economic Partnership (RCEP). This marks another significant achievement for ASEAN in the field of regional economic cooperation. RCEP officially entered into force on January 1, 2022, covering a wide range of areas, including trade in goods, trade in services, investment, and rules of origin. It aims to establish a unified regional market by reducing tariffs and non-tariff barriers. Since its implementation, RCEP has further expanded ASEAN's market size and economic influence. In terms of trade in goods, RCEP stipulates that over 90% of trade in goods among member countries will eventually achieve zero tariffs, which will significantly boost regional trade growth. According to projections by relevant research institutions, by 2030, regional trade volume is expected to increase by approximately $2 trillion as a result of RCEP implementation. In the areas of trade in services and investment, RCEP also provides member countries with more open and facilitated market access conditions, promoting the liberalization and facilitation of regional trade in services and investment.

3. Other Cooperation Mechanisms

In addition to AFTA and RCEP, ASEAN has also actively participated in and promoted the development of other regional economic cooperation mechanisms. For example, the ASEAN Plus Three (10+3) cooperation mechanism (involving China, Japan, and South Korea) plays a significant role in economic collaboration in East Asia. This mechanism covers cooperation in various areas such as trade, investment, finance, energy, and the environment. Through regular leaders' meetings, ministerial conferences, and senior officials' meetings, it facilitates discussions on significant issues in regional economic cooperation, aligns positions among members, and advances the process of regional economic integration. In terms of financial cooperation, the Chiang Mai Initiative Multilateralization (CMIM) under the 10+3 framework provides an essential financial safety net for countries in the region. By establishing a regional foreign exchange reserve pool, it enhances the ability of member states to respond to financial risks. The East Asia Summit (EAS) is another key regional cooperation platform in which ASEAN plays a central role. Led by ASEAN, the EAS includes the ten ASEAN member states as well as China, Japan, South Korea, the United States, Russia, Australia, New Zealand, and India. The summit plays an active role in promoting regional economic cooperation, security dialogue, and collaboration, offering a high-level platform for exchange and cooperation among countries. It contributes to the coordinated development of regional economic integration and political-security cooperation.

4. Summary

The ASEAN economic integration process has achieved remarkable results in the past, laying a solid foundation for future development. However, it still faces several challenges. For instance, significant disparities exist among member states in terms of economic development levels, industrial structures, and policies and regulations, which may affect the implementation effectiveness and pace of integration measures. Reforms in areas such as market openness, intellectual property protection, and labor standards in some countries need further deepening to meet the requirements of regional economic integration. Additionally, external factors such as global trade protectionism and geopolitical conflicts may also adversely impact the ASEAN economic integration process. Therefore, in its future development, ASEAN must fully leverage its coordinating and leading role. By strengthening policy communication, deepening reforms, and enhancing the level of cooperation, it can overcome various difficulties and challenges, continually advancing the process of economic integration.

Industrial Development Landscape

1. Manufacturing Industry

The manufacturing sector is one of ASEAN's key industries and holds significant importance in the regional economy. In 2022, manufacturing investments reached USD 61.7 billion, accounting for 28% of ASEAN's total FDI. Electronics represented 70% of the announced greenfield investments in manufacturing, with semiconductors and electronic components making up 27%. Battery-related investments grew by 656%, reaching USD 8.4 billion and accounting for 23%. Each ASEAN country has distinct advantages in the manufacturing sector.

Vietnam possesses strong competitiveness in labor-intensive industries such as garment manufacturing and electronics assembly. Leveraging its abundant and low-cost labor force, Vietnam has attracted numerous international apparel brands and electronics companies to set up production facilities. Many well-known sportswear brands have garment production lines in Vietnam, giving the country a notable share in global apparel exports. In electronics assembly, Vietnam provides extensive assembly services for major companies like Apple and Samsung, gradually forming a complete electronics assembly supply chain, with supporting industries also growing rapidly.

Malaysia has a well-developed presence in sectors such as electronics, electrical goods, and chemicals. The country boasts advanced manufacturing technology and a comprehensive supporting ecosystem in electronics, making it one of the world's key semiconductor production and packaging bases. Malaysia's semiconductor industry plays a vital role in the global supply chain, with internationally recognized product quality and production efficiency. In the chemical sector, Malaysia utilizes its abundant oil and natural gas resources to develop industries such as petrochemicals and specialty chemicals, producing a variety of high-value-added chemical products.

Indonesia focuses mainly on resource-processing industries such as petrochemicals and steel. The country is rich in natural resources, including oil, natural gas, coal, and metal minerals, which provide ample raw materials for resource-based manufacturing. Through continuous technological and equipment upgrades, Indonesia's petrochemical industry has improved both product quality and production efficiency, allowing it to meet domestic demand and export to neighboring countries. In steel production, Indonesia is enhancing technological innovation and expanding production capacity, gradually increasing self-sufficiency in steel products and building competitiveness in the international market.

Development Trends As global industries relocate and supply chains reconfigure, ASEAN's manufacturing sector is moving toward higher value-added, smarter, and greener production. On one hand, ASEAN will attract more investment in high-tech manufacturing—such as semiconductors and new energy vehicles—to move up the value chain. The global semiconductor industry is undergoing rapid development and geographic shift. With its strategic location, labor resources, and favorable policies, ASEAN has drawn significant investment from semiconductor firms and is poised to make further breakthroughs in semiconductor manufacturing and design. The new energy vehicle industry is also expanding rapidly. ASEAN countries are actively introducing policies to attract investments in vehicle and component manufacturing, aiming to build a complete NEV supply chain.

On the other hand, manufacturing companies are placing greater emphasis on environmental protection and sustainable development. They are adopting advanced production technologies and equipment to reduce energy consumption and environmental pollution. For instance, some firms are introducing innovative manufacturing equipment and industrial IoT technologies to automate and intelligently manage production processes. This improves both efficiency and product quality while reducing labor costs and resource waste. In terms of environmental protection, companies are implementing green manufacturing processes, enhancing waste treatment, and promoting resource recycling to minimize negative environmental impact.

2. Electronics Industry

The electronics industry is one of the key pillars of ASEAN's manufacturing sector. In recent years, ASEAN's role in the global electronics supply chain has continued to strengthen, attracting substantial investment from international electronics companies. Vietnam, for example, has emerged as a significant global electronics manufacturing hub, leveraging its abundant labor force, low production costs, and favorable investment policies. Many leading electronics firms—such as Samsung, Intel, and Foxconn—have established large-scale production facilities in Vietnam. Samsung's investment in Vietnam exceeds USD 17 billion, and its Vietnamese factories produce mobile phones, tablets, and other electronic devices that are sold worldwide. Vietnam's electronics industry has not only created numerous local job opportunities but also spurred the growth of supporting industries, forming a relatively complete electronics supply chain.

Malaysia also possesses strong capabilities in the electronics sector, particularly in semiconductor manufacturing. With advanced semiconductor production technologies and a highly skilled workforce, Malaysia has attracted many international semiconductor companies. Major players such as Infineon and NXP have established R&D and manufacturing bases in the country. Malaysia's semiconductor industry covers multiple segments, including chip design, manufacturing, packaging, and testing, with products widely used in electronics, automotive electronics, and communications.

Additionally, countries such as Thailand and Singapore have also developed their electronics industries. Thailand holds certain advantages in the manufacturing of electronic components, while Singapore excels in electronics R&D and high-end manufacturing.

2.1 Automotive Industry

ASEAN's automotive industry has experienced rapid growth in recent years, gradually becoming one of the region's key economic drivers. Indonesia is ASEAN's most significant automotive producer and consumer market, with its automotive industry primarily focused on motorcycles and passenger vehicles. The Indonesian government has introduced a series of policies to encourage the development of the automotive sector, attracting numerous international automotive brands to invest and establish production facilities in the country. For instance, Japanese automakers such as Toyota, Honda, and Suzuki hold significant market shares in Indonesia and have established comprehensive production and sales networks in the country. At the same time, local automotive companies like Astra International continue to grow and enhance their technological capabilities and production capacity through partnerships with international brands.

Thailand is also a significant automotive production and export base in ASEAN, often referred to as the "Detroit of Southeast Asia." Thailand's automotive industry boasts a high localization rate and a well-developed supporting ecosystem for auto parts. Many international automakers have set up production bases in Thailand, not only to meet local demand but also to export vehicles in large quantities to other markets. For example, vehicles produced in Thailand by brands such as Ford, General Motors, and Mazda are exported to other ASEAN countries as well as to markets like Australia and New Zealand. The Thai government is also actively promoting the development of the electric vehicle (EV) industry, implementing policies to encourage companies to research, develop, and produce EVs, thereby increasing the adoption of electric vehicles domestically.

2.2 Other Manufacturing Industries

In addition to the electronics and automotive sectors, ASEAN has also achieved notable development in other manufacturing industries. In the textile and garment industry, countries such as Cambodia and Vietnam possess strong competitiveness. Cambodia, with its abundant labor resources and relatively low labor costs, has attracted significant investment from international textile and apparel companies. Cambodia's textile and garment products are primarily exported to markets such as the United States and the European Union, making it a crucial industry for the country's export earnings. Vietnam's textile and garment industry has also experienced rapid growth. In recent years, it has continuously improved product quality and technological capabilities, gradually shifting from pure processing and manufacturing toward independent design and brand development.

In the furniture manufacturing sector, Malaysia and Indonesia are the leading producers and exporters within ASEAN. Malaysian furniture is renowned for its high quality and innovative design, with products exported to numerous countries and regions worldwide. Malaysia benefits from abundant timber resources and holds advantages in wood processing technology. Indonesia's furniture manufacturing industry is also well-developed, with products gaining market recognition for their natural materials and unique craftsmanship. Furthermore, ASEAN has considerable scale and growth potential in other manufacturing areas such as plastic products and metal goods.

3. Services Sector

3.1 Tourism Industry

Tourism is a vital component of ASEAN's services sector and serves as a pillar industry for many countries in the region. ASEAN member states are endowed with abundant tourism resources, including beautiful beaches, ancient cultural heritage sites, and unique natural landscapes, which attract a large number of domestic and international visitors. Thailand is one of the most popular tourist destinations in ASEAN, with world-renowned attractions such as the Grand Palace in Bangkok, the stunning beaches of Phuket, and the ancient city of Chiang Mai. The Thai government places high importance on the development of tourism, continuously improving tourism infrastructure, enhancing service quality, and launching various promotional campaigns. In 2023, Thailand received over 25 million international tourist arrivals, making tourism a primary source of revenue for the country.

Indonesia's Bali is known as the" Island of Paradise", attracting numerous visitors with its enchanting beaches, rich culture, and distinctive religious landscapes. The Indonesian government actively promotes the diversified development of tourism, expanding beyond Bali to develop other destinations such as Borobudur in Java and Lake Toba in Sumatra. Singapore, with its modern urban scenery, diverse shopping and culinary experiences, and efficient transportation system, has established itself as a key tourism hub in Southeast Asia. Attractions like Gardens by the Bay and Sentosa Island draw a significant number of tourists. Additionally, other famous tourist spots in ASEAN include Langkawi in Malaysia, Boracay in the Philippines, and Ha Long Bay in Vietnam. The tourism industry plays a vital role in the economic development of these countries.

3.2 Financial Services Industry

The financial and banking sector remains the largest recipient of FDI in ASEAN, reaching USD 63 billion in 2022 with a growth rate of 3.6%. As the financial hub of ASEAN, Singapore boasts a well-developed financial market system and a diverse range of financial products, holding a significant position in the international financial landscape.

The Singapore Exchange is one of Asia’s major securities markets, attracting numerous domestic and international companies for listing and financing. Many global financial institutions have established regional headquarters or branches in Singapore to conduct various financial activities. Its financial derivatives market is also highly active, offering investors a wide array of investment options. Additionally, Singapore holds a leading position in areas such as wealth management and private banking, attracting a concentration of global financial institutions.

Malaysia's financial services industry is also relatively developed, with Kuala Lumpur serving as an essential financial center in Southeast Asia. The country's banking, insurance, and securities sectors are well-established, offering a rich variety of financial products and services. The Malaysian government encourages financial innovation and promotes digital transformation within financial institutions to enhance the efficiency and accessibility of financial services.

Furthermore, the financial services industries in countries such as Thailand and Indonesia continue to develop. Through measures including strengthened financial regulatory reforms and increased market openness, these countries are enhancing the competitiveness of their financial sectors. In terms of regional financial cooperation, ASEAN member states have improved coordination in financial supervision, promoted the integration of regional payment systems, and facilitated the optimal allocation of financial resources.

Development Trends: With the advancement of ASEAN economic integration, the financial services sector is expected to become more integrated and liberalized. ASEAN countries will enhance cooperation in financial regulation, promote interconnectivity among financial markets, and facilitate cross-border financial activities.

3.3 Other Service Industries

In the logistics services sector, ASEAN benefits from its strategic geographical location, serving as a vital transportation hub that connects Asia, Europe, and Oceania. The Port of Singapore is one of the busiest ports in the world, attracting substantial cargo traffic due to its highly efficient operations and advanced port facilities. Other major ports in ASEAN, such as Port Klang in Malaysia and Laem Chabang Port in Thailand, also provide strong support for regional trade and logistics development. ASEAN countries continue to strengthen logistics infrastructure, enhance the level of informatization in logistics, reduce logistics costs, and promote efficient regional logistics operations.

In the information technology (IT) services sector, countries such as Singapore and Malaysia possess certain advantages in areas including software development, IT consulting, and data processing. Singapore's IT services industry emphasizes innovation and high-end services, demonstrating strong performance in application development for fintech, artificial intelligence, and big data. Malaysia's IT services sector is also growing rapidly, improving its capabilities and standards through measures such as cultivating specialized talent and attracting foreign investment.

Furthermore, ASEAN has also made progress in areas such as education and healthcare services. Several member states offer competitive educational and medical services within the region, attracting students and patients from neighboring countries for study and treatment.

4. Agriculture

ASEAN is one of the world's important agricultural production and export regions, endowed with abundant agricultural resources and favorable climate conditions. In terms of food crops, Thailand and Vietnam are major global exporters of rice. Thailand's fragrant rice is renowned worldwide for its unique taste and quality, exported to numerous countries and regions. The Thai government implements agricultural subsidy policies and promotes advanced cultivation techniques to enhance rice yield and quality. Vietnam has seen rapid development in its rice industry in recent years, ranking among the world's top rice exporters. Vietnam focuses on optimizing rice cultivation structures, improving processing and packaging standards, and strengthening the competitiveness of its rice in the international market.

In the realm of economic crops, Indonesia and Malaysia are the world's largest producers and exporters of palm oil. Palm oil is widely used in food, cosmetics, biofuels, and other industries, with substantial market demand. Indonesia and Malaysia possess extensive palm plantations and maintain their dominant position in the global palm oil market by continuously expanding cultivation areas, improving planting techniques, and enhancing processing efficiency.

Additionally, the Philippines is a significant global exporter of bananas, known for their high quality and excellent taste, making them highly sought after in international markets. Thailand plays a significant role in rubber production, ranking among the world's top countries in both output and export volume. Thailand's rubber industry encompasses planting, processing, trade, and other segments, forming a relatively complete industrial chain.

To enhance agricultural productivity and competitiveness, ASEAN countries are actively promoting agricultural modernization. Many nations are increasing investment in agricultural technology and adopting advanced cultivation and breeding techniques, such as precision farming, greenhouse cultivation, and innovative animal husbandry. In Thailand, some large farms utilize drones for field monitoring and pesticide spraying, improving the precision and efficiency of agricultural production. At the same time, ASEAN countries are emphasizing sustainable agricultural development, with a focus on strengthening the protection and rational use of agricultural resources. In the palm oil sector, Indonesia and Malaysia are implementing sustainable palm oil certification programs, encouraging plantations to adopt environmentally friendly cultivation and management practices to reduce environmental damage.

Furthermore, ASEAN has enhanced regional cooperation in agriculture by sharing agricultural technologies and experiences, as well as promoting trade collaboration in agricultural products, thereby fostering synergistic development in regional agriculture. For example, ASEAN countries have established an agricultural product trade information platform to help businesses stay informed about market trends and trade policies, facilitating the flow of agricultural goods. In agricultural technology cooperation, research institutions and universities across member states have strengthened exchanges and collaboration, jointly conducting agricultural research projects to enhance innovation capabilities in agricultural science and technology.

5. Emerging Industries

5.1 Digital Economy

ASEAN places high importance on the digital economy and has formulated a series of overall plans and layouts, such as the 《ASEAN Digital Masterplan 2025》, the 《ASEAN Digital Economy Framework Agreement (DEFA)》, and 《ASEAN 2045: Our Shared Future》. In December 2023, ASEAN launched the DEFA agenda, aiming to accelerate the development of the digital economy at the regional integration level through a legally binding cooperation agreement. This initiative covers nine key areas: promoting digital trade, cross-border e-commerce, e-payment and e-invoicing, digital identity and authentication, cybersecurity, cross-border data flow and data protection, competition policy, cooperation in emerging fields, and talent mobility. The launch of this agenda provides a more solid institutional guarantee for the development of ASEAN's digital economy, clarifies the direction and priorities of cooperation among member states in the digital economy field, and promotes policy coordination and harmonization in related areas.

The digital economy in ASEAN is developing rapidly and has become a new engine for economic growth. With the continuous increase in internet penetration rates and the widespread use of smartphones, the digital consumer market in the ASEAN region continues to expand. Sectors such as e-commerce, digital finance, and digital content are experiencing vigorous growth. According to the 《2024 ASEAN Digital Economy Report》 jointly released by Google, Temasek, and Bain & Company in November 2024, the total value of digital economic goods transactions in ASEAN countries is projected to reach USD 263 billion in 2024, a year-on-year increase of 15%. The e-commerce industry has undergone a transformation and experienced unprecedented growth. The electronic payment market in six countries—Singapore, Malaysia, Thailand, Indonesia, Vietnam, and the Philippines—has reached USD 220 billion, accounting for over 80% of the e-commerce market in ASEAN. Five key digital sectors—e-commerce, online media, food delivery, online travel booking, and digital financial services—as well as four emerging digital sectors—health tech, software services, Web3, and edtech—have demonstrated outstanding performance and continued expansion.

Singapore, as ASEAN's financial center and technology hub, holds a leading advantage in areas such as digital finance and blockchain. The country actively seizes new development opportunities brought by the Fourth Industrial Revolution, focusing on advancing national digital transformation and development. Efforts are primarily concentrated in four areas: digital governance, digital industries, digital trade, and digital living, to comprehensively enhance digital technology and economic competitiveness and build a "Smart Nation." According to the 《2023 Singapore Digital Economy Report》, digital trade accounted for 17.3% of its GDP in 2022, a significant increase from 13% in 2017. The contribution of Singapore's digital economy to the overall economy nearly doubled over five years, rising from approximately USD 58 billion to about USD 106 billion in value-added contributions. The information and communication sector contributed around USD 33 billion, while other sectors contributed approximately USD 73 billion through digitalization. Since 2017, the compound annual growth rate of Singapore's digital economy has been about 12.9%, three to four times the average GDP growth rate during the same period. In 2024, Singapore achieved a historic breakthrough, ranking first in the Global Digital Competitiveness Ranking released by the International Institute for Management Development (IMD) in Lausanne, Switzerland.

Malaysia focuses on promoting the digital economy through high-tech industries. The government has taken active measures to encourage digital infrastructure construction, guiding enterprises through policies and investments to invest in high-tech, high-value-added sectors, and aiming to build a regional digital hub for artificial intelligence and semiconductor industries. In 2021, the Malaysian government formulated and implemented the 《Malaysia Digital Plan》, proposing strategies to promote digital transformation in the public sector, enhance economic competitiveness through digitalization, develop digital infrastructure, establish an inclusive digital society, and create a secure digital environment. The plan includes three strategies and six main initiatives to create favorable conditions for digital economic development. In 2022, Malaysia launched a digital initiative focusing on nine areas, including digital tourism, digital trade, digital agriculture, and digital finance. The initiative aims to enhance competitiveness in the global digital revolution and digital economy through three measures: promoting the adoption of digital technologies, supporting local tech enterprises, and attracting high-value digital investments. Since 2020, the digital economy's contribution to Malaysia's GDP has remained above 20%. The government expects this contribution to reach 25.5% by 2025.

Indonesia implements multiple measures to accelerate digital economic growth. In December 2023, the Indonesian government released the 《National Strategy for Digital Economic Development 2030》 white paper, building on the 《Digital Indonesia Roadmap 2021–2024》, to guide the country's digital transformation. The government has increased investments in 5G networks, cloud computing, and data centers, aiming to improve internet penetration rates, enhance digital infrastructure, and actively cultivate digital talent aligned with industrial development. Through these measures, Indonesia has fostered vigorous growth in e-commerce, which has become a core driver of the digital economy. Additionally, digital financial services in Indonesia are flourishing. According to the 《2024–2045 Payment System Blueprint》, the Central Bank of Indonesia intends to integrate 91.3 million unbanked individuals and 92.9 million micro, small, and medium enterprises into the digital economy and financial system through digital transformation. As ASEAN's largest economy, Indonesia accounts for about 40% of the region's digital economy, with significant potential for further growth. The Ministry of Trade estimates that Indonesia's digital economy will grow from USD 146 billion in 2025 to USD 366 billion by 2030, contributing approximately 18% to GDP.

Vietnam introduces a new digital roadmap to promote digital economic development. The Vietnamese government has launched multiple initiatives to accelerate the digital economy. In 2022, it issued the 《National Strategy for Digital Economy and Digital Society towards 2025 with a Vision to 2030》, focusing on developing information technology, nurturing digital economy enterprises and products, building unified digital platforms across various industries, and providing basic digital skills training to 70% of the labor force. In 2024, Vietnam accelerated the issuance of 5G licenses and aims to achieve 99% population coverage by 2030. In recent years, driven by e-commerce and online tourism, Vietnam's total digital economic transaction value has maintained double-digit growth. The digital economy accounted for 16.5% of GDP in 2023 and increased to nearly 19% in 2024. The government aims to raise the digital economy's share across all industries and fields to at least 10% by 2025 and double that by 2030. The contribution of the digital economy to GDP is targeted to reach 20% by 2025 and 30% by 2030. According to assessments by international organizations, Vietnam's digital economy has a high growth rate of about 20% annually, approximately three times the GDP growth rate, with e-commerce growth ranking first among ASEAN countries. The government strives to be among the top three ASEAN countries in the digital economy sector.

Thailand promotes the digital economy by improving policies and legal frameworks. In February 2015, the Thai government introduced the "Digital Thailand" concept, followed by the 20-year "Thailand 4.0" strategy in 2016. It has accelerated the formulation and improvement of laws and regulations related to the digital economy, such as the 《Electronic Transactions Act》 and the 《Digital Economy and Society Development Act》, providing a favorable legal environment for digital economic development. Initiatives like the digital economy development roadmap and the first and second phases of the "National E-Commerce Development Action Plan" have introduced a series of policy measures for target industries in the digital economy. These include accelerating digital infrastructure construction, encouraging the adoption of digital technologies, increasing investment in digital industries, and reducing taxes for the digital transformation of small and medium-sized enterprises. Through these measures, Thailand's digital economy has experienced rapid growth. Currently, the growth rate of Thailand's digital economy is more than twice that of its GDP. The digital economy is expected to grow from USD 30 billion in 2021 to USD 57 billion by 2025, accounting for 30% of GDP by 2030.

The Philippines promotes comprehensive digital transformation. Currently, the country has about 90 million internet users, with an overall internet penetration rate of nearly 90%. Its goal is to increase the digital economy's share of GDP to over 10% by 2025. Cambodia, Myanmar, and Laos are also rolling out digital initiatives to varying degrees, actively integrating into the wave of digital economic development.

Future Trends

With the advancement of the China-ASEAN Free Trade Area 3.0 upgrade, deeper integration and innovative applications are expected in areas such as cross-border payments and digital finance, computing infrastructure and AI empowerment, power infrastructure, and communications. This will also drive demand for related hardware, software, and services, including chips, semiconductors, equipment, finance, and legal support. Potential future cooperation projects include

5G networks, optical cable communications, data centers, cloud services, cross-border RMB payments, blockchain, digital currencies, fintech, AI + large model platforms, AI + 5G + smart factories, and AI applications in agriculture, healthcare, and education. Digital technology will further penetrate traditional industries in ASEAN countries, promoting industrial digital transformation and enhancing efficiency and competitiveness. Meanwhile, ASEAN countries will strengthen cooperation in digital technology R&D and talent cultivation to address the challenges brought by digital economic development jointly.

1. Green Economy

ASEAN has established initiatives such as the 《ASEAN Economic Community Circular Economy Framework》, 《ASEAN Strategy for Carbon Neutrality》, and 《ASEAN 2045: Our Shared Future》, demonstrating its commitment to fostering environmentally sustainable economic growth. In May 2025, the 46th ASEAN Summit adopted the Kuala Lumpur Declaration under the theme 《ASEAN 2045: Our Shared Future》, calling for collective efforts to cultivate a green ASEAN and promote regional sustainable development objectives. This initiative aims to unlock economic opportunities, such as attracting foreign investment in green industries, adopting globally trusted standards, and leveraging regional green strengths to ensure sustainable, resilient, and inclusive economic integration. The strategic goals for green development will be achieved through ten specific actions: Creating a supportive environment to unlock the potential of the green economy; Improving resilience through climate change adaptation and speeding up decarbonization of regional supply chains; Strengthening a fair and inclusive energy transition; Promoting sustainable practices in extractive industries; Supporting sustainable agriculture and forest management; Encouraging sustainable and inclusive tourism; Utilizing sustainable finance and investment; Advancing blue economy cooperation as a new driver for inclusive and sustainable growth; Raising awareness and empowering ASEAN businesses, regulators, financial institutions, and policymakers in the green transition; Ensuring energy security, affordability, and sustainability; and Promoting sustainable, green, and smart mobility.

These plans and objectives provide comprehensive and detailed guidance for ASEAN's green economic development, driving the transition to a green economy at all levels. ASEAN member states have actively engaged in cooperation in areas such as renewable energy, sustainable agriculture, and green tourism, achieving notable results. Under the Belt and Road Initiative, China and ASEAN have explored and established a series of green development cooperation mechanisms, which have significantly promoted the low-carbon transition and high-quality development of the regional economy. In 2023, the bilateral trade volume of green products exceeded USD 48 billion, representing a more than fivefold increase compared to 2015.

ASEAN member states have actively cooperated in areas such as renewable energy, sustainable agriculture, and green tourism, achieving notable results. Under the Belt and Road Initiative, China and ASEAN have explored the establishment of various green development cooperation mechanisms, significantly promoting low-carbon transition and high-quality development in the regional economy. In 2023, bilateral trade in green products exceeded USD 48 billion, a more than fivefold increase compared to 2015.

2. Renewable Energy

The ASEAN region is rich in renewable energy resources, including solar, wind, hydro, and geothermal power. In recent years, countries have intensified efforts to develop and utilize these resources. Indonesia, with its abundant solar, wind, and hydropower potential, is vigorously developing its renewable energy industry. In 2022, the value of international investment projects in renewable energy in Indonesia reached a significant scale and continues to grow. Malaysia has also made progress in renewable energy, actively promoting the construction of solar and wind power projects to increase the share of renewables in its energy mix. Several countries have achieved results in hydropower development, providing clean electricity for regional energy supply. However, there are gradients in technology diffusion. For example, Chinese photovoltaic modules accounted for 62% of new installed capacity in ASEAN (2022 data), but market penetration varies significantly among countries—exceeding 75% in Vietnam but below 30% in the Philippines.

3. Sustainable Agriculture

Malaysia has relatively mature sustainable agriculture practices, promoting models such as organic farming and eco-friendly aquaculture. In organic agriculture, Malaysia has established a comprehensive certification system for organic products, encouraging farmers to adopt organic cultivation methods, reduce the use of chemical pesticides and fertilizers, and produce high-quality organic agricultural products for both domestic and international markets. Eco-friendly aquaculture emphasizes animal welfare and environmental protection, improving breeding efficiency and product quality through scientific management. Thailand is also actively promoting sustainable agriculture by introducing advanced technologies such as precision farming and water-saving irrigation to enhance agricultural productivity while reducing resource waste and environmental pollution.

4. Green Tourism

Green tourism projects in Thailand are increasingly attracting visitor attention, including eco-resorts and environmentally friendly tourist attractions. Some eco-resorts are constructed using sustainable materials and utilize renewable energy sources such as solar and wind power to minimize environmental impact while offering tourists opportunities to connect with nature and experience ecological culture. Environmentally conscious tourist sites focus on preserving local ecosystems and cultural heritage, guiding visitors toward sustainable tourism activities. Cambodia, in developing its tourism industry, also emphasizes the protection of world cultural heritage sites like Angkor Wat. Through measures such as rational tourism route planning and visitor number control, it strives to balance tourism development with environmental conservation.

The digital economy layout under the upgraded China-ASEAN Free Trade Area 3.0 is expected to promote deep integration and innovative applications in areas such as smart agriculture, new energy and its infrastructure, new energy vehicles and green transportation industry chains, and green finance. This will also drive demand for related equipment manufacturing, financial services, legal services, and other hardware, software, and services. Potential future cooperation projects include deep processing of agricultural products, photovoltaics, new energy vehicles, new energy materials, and cross-border green finance applications.

As global attention to climate change continues to increase, ASEAN will further intensify investments and cooperation in the green economy sector, accelerate the energy transition, and raise the proportion of renewable energy in energy consumption. Industries such as sustainable agriculture and green tourism will be more widely promoted and developed. In contrast, green finance will provide strong support for the growth of green industries, driving ASEAN's economy toward green and sustainable development.

Chapter 2
Differentiation of ASEAN Members

The ten ASEAN countries exhibit significant disparities in infrastructure development and business environments due to differences in economic foundations, geographical conditions, and development paths. This differentiated pattern directly impacts regional resource allocation efficiency and international capital deployment strategies. Infrastructure analysis focuses on transportation, communication, and energy sectors, while business environment evaluation examines policy openness, workforce quality, and market access barriers. These differences provide practical foundations for enterprises in western Guangdong to formulate differentiated internationalization strategies.

Infrastructure comparison

Vietnam

1. Transportation: In recent years, Vietnam has made significant progress in transportation infrastructure development, with the continuous expansion of road networks and the steady advancement in expressway construction. However, the overall transportation system still faces challenges, particularly concerning substandard road conditions in remote areas that urgently require improvement. Regarding rail transport, aging railway lines remain a prominent issue, necessitating enhancements in both operational speed and efficiency.

2. Communications: Vietnam is accelerating the issuance of 5G licenses, aiming to achieve 5G network coverage for 99% of its population by 2030. While internet penetration continues to grow and communication infrastructure keeps improving, there remains a gap in network speed and stability compared to developed countries.

3. Energy: Vietnam continues to increase investment in energy infrastructure construction, actively explores and develops oil and gas resources, and vigorously develops renewable energy power generation facilities, such as solar power stations and wind farms. However, energy

supply is still under certain pressure during peak electricity consumption periods.

Thailand

1. Transportation: Thailand boasts a well-developed transportation infrastructure with a nationwide highway network that ensures efficient connectivity between major cities. Bangkok, home to a modern international airport, stands as one of Southeast Asia's key aviation hubs with thriving air transport services. The country's railway system continues to undergo upgrades and renovations, steadily improving both capacity and service quality.

2. Communication: Thailand is the first country in ASEAN to achieve 5G commercialization. Up to now, the number of 5G base stations has exceeded 40,000, covering nearly 90% of the country. The high-quality communication network provides strong support for the digital economy and the digital transformation of various industries.

3. Energy: Thailand has a complete energy infrastructure and a diversified energy supply system, covering natural gas, oil, coal, and renewable energy. The energy supply is relatively stable and can meet the needs of domestic economic development and people's livelihood.

Indonesia

1. Transportation: Indonesia has been ramping up investments in transportation infrastructure, building a network of highways and cross-sea bridges. However, its island-dotted geography presents significant challenges in connecting remote islands and underdeveloped regions, with the transportation systems' connectivity and accessibility needing further enhancement. Major cities face particularly severe traffic congestion issues.

2. Telecommunications: Indonesia is ramping up investments in 5G networks, cloud computing, and data centers to boost digital infrastructure development. Industry leader IOH is driving the nation's digital transformation through its 5G+AI strategy, with plans to launch Indonesia's first Indonesian-language large language model. However, network coverage and communication quality still need improvement in some remote areas.

3. Energy: Indonesia is rich in energy resources, but the distribution of energy infrastructure is uneven, and the stability of energy supply in

some areas is insufficient. The government is vigorously strengthening the construction of energy infrastructure to improve the capacity and reliability of energy supply.

Singapore

1. Transportation: Singapore boasts a world-class transportation infrastructure. Changi Airport has been consistently ranked among the world's best airports for years, with air routes connecting global destinations. Its advanced port facilities establish it as a central shipping hub worldwide. The city's internal transportation system operates efficiently and conveniently, featuring extensive subway and bus networks that effectively alleviate traffic congestion.

2. Communications: Singapore has the world's leading communications infrastructure, with high-speed and stable network coverage across the country, providing solid support for the digital economy and technological innovation. It is at the forefront of 5G network construction and application in the world.

3. Energy: Singapore has a sound energy infrastructure and a stable and reliable energy supply. Through diversified energy procurement channels and advanced energy management systems, energy is used efficiently, and supply is secure.

Malaysia

1. Transportation: Malaysia boasts a well-developed transportation infrastructure, with road and rail networks connecting major cities and regions. The country is home to multiple international airports, ensuring efficient air travel. Its well-developed port facilities have significantly boosted foreign trade. However, some remote areas still require further improvements in transportation infrastructure.

2. Communications: Malaysia's communication network covers the entire country with a high internet penetration rate. The government is actively promoting digital infrastructure development to enhance network speed and stability, thereby supporting the growth of the digital economy. Progress is being made in 5G network construction.

3. Energy: Malaysia has a well-developed energy infrastructure and a relatively stable energy supply. It has a diversified energy supply system, including oil, natural gas, coal, and renewable energy. The government

attaches great importance to sustainable energy development and increases investment in renewable energy projects.

The Philippines

1. Transportation: The Philippines' transportation infrastructure continues to improve, though challenges persist. Major cities face severe traffic congestion, while road and rail networks require expansion in both coverage and capacity. While aviation is well-developed with multiple international airports, domestic flight connectivity and service quality still have room for enhancement.

2. Communication: The Philippines' communication network coverage is gradually expanding, but there is a gap in network speed and stability compared with other ASEAN countries. In remote areas, the problem of insufficient network coverage is more prominent.

3. Energy: The energy infrastructure of the Philippines is relatively weak, and there is some pressure on energy supply. The government has increased investment in energy infrastructure construction and actively developed renewable energy to alleviate the contradiction between energy supply and demand.

Cambodia

1. Transportation: In recent years, Cambodia has made significant efforts to improve its transportation infrastructure by investing heavily in road construction. Major highways, including national roads, have been renovated and newly built, which has enhanced domestic transport efficiency to some extent. However, the road network in rural and remote areas remains sparse with poor conditions, making some roads impassable during rainy seasons. Regarding railways, there are only two main lines that are outdated, slow-moving, and lack systematic maintenance and upgrades. Their limited freight capacity struggles to meet the growing demands of trade logistics.

2. Telecommunications: Cambodia has actively introduced foreign investment and advanced technologies to boost its communication infrastructure. 4G networks have achieved basic coverage in urban areas, with several major cities having launched 5G pilot projects. However, rural regions still face inadequate network coverage, unstable signals, and slow speeds that fail to meet emerging demands like remote work and

online education. This situation highlights a significant gap compared to neighboring countries with more developed communication infrastructure.

3. Energy: Cambodia has been actively developing renewable energy projects, including hydropower, solar, and wind power. While significant progress has been made in hydropower construction, these initiatives have created new growth drivers for the nation's energy supply. However, rapid industrial expansion has outpaced energy demand, resulting in substantial power shortages and unstable grid operations. Frequent blackouts have become a recurring issue, particularly during dry seasons when hydropower generation declines, exacerbating energy shortages that severely disrupt normal business operations.

Laos

1. Transportation: Laos has vigorously developed road construction, and the opening of the China-Laos Railway has dramatically improved its transportation convenience and regional connectivity. It not only strengthened domestic connections between the north and south but also established railway freight channels with countries like China. However, road construction still faces several shortcomings, including a low density of domestic roads, substandard road grades in some areas, and high costs and difficulties in maintaining roads in complex terrain regions, which affect transportation efficiency.

2. Telecommunications: In the telecommunications sector, Laos has been actively advancing network infrastructure development. 4G networks have gradually become widespread in major cities and economic zones, with the number of internet users continuing to grow. However, communication base stations in remote mountainous areas suffer from insufficient coverage, weak or even non-existent network signals, and subpar network quality and stability. The low penetration rate of high-speed network services remains a challenge, hindering the rapid development of the digital economy.

3. Energy: Laos boasts abundant hydropower resources, with hydropower development becoming a key focus in its energy infrastructure. The commissioning of numerous hydropower projects has transformed the country from an electricity importer to an exporter. However, the energy transmission network remains underdeveloped, with limited grid coverage—particularly in rural areas where electricity access

still needs improvement. Additionally, the power dispatch and distribution management system is not yet mature, making it prone to operational issues during power scheduling and allocation processes.

Burma

1. Transportation: Myanmar is committed to improving its transportation infrastructure, with road construction progressing steadily and major highways undergoing upgrades. However, the overall road network remains underdeveloped, featuring uneven quality standards. Rural areas predominantly rely on dirt roads or low-grade highways that face significant challenges during rainy seasons. Regarding railways, aging tracks, inconsistent rail standards, slow train speeds, and limited transport capacity have failed to meet the logistics demands of economic development.

2. Telecommunications: With economic liberalization, Myanmar's communication sector has become increasingly vibrant. 4G networks now cover major cities, and the number of internet users continues to grow. However, the late start in infrastructure development has resulted in limited coverage, slow speeds, and poor stability. Remote areas face severe service gaps, while outdated equipment and technology continue to hinder digital economy growth.

3. Energy: Myanmar possesses abundant oil and gas resources, yet its energy development and utilization remain underdeveloped. The country faces weak energy infrastructure, unstable power supply, and frequent blackouts. Outdated exploration and extraction technologies, aging pipelines, and severe energy waste hinder the energy industry's ability to support rapid domestic economic growth effectively.

Brunei

1. Transportation: Brunei's relatively small land area has resulted in concentrated transportation infrastructure development. Roads serve as the primary mode of transport, with a well-developed national road network connecting major towns. However, due to limited territorial space, railway transportation hasn't seen significant expansion. Air travel mainly relies on international airports, primarily linking key cities in neighboring countries and regions, resulting in a relatively limited range of transportation options.

2. Telecommunications: Brunei's communication infrastructure is well-developed, with 4G networks covering the entire country and 5G deployment in progress. The network offers excellent speed and stability, supported by high internet penetration rates. While service quality meets daily communication needs for both residents and businesses, there remains room for improvement in technological innovation and digital economy development compared to some developed countries.

3. Energy: Brunei's economy is anchored by abundant oil and gas reserves, supported by mature extraction technologies and stable self-sufficiency in energy supply. While prioritizing energy efficiency improvements and waste reduction in its utilization, the nation faces challenges due to its relatively homogeneous economic structure and heavy reliance on energy-intensive industries. Progress in diversifying energy sectors and developing renewable energy resources remains relatively slow.

Summary: ASEAN's ten member states exhibit significant tiered disparities in transportation, communication, and energy infrastructure. In transportation, the first tier—Singapore and Malaysia—achieves comprehensive efficiency through smart ports and well-developed road networks. The second tier (Thailand, Indonesia, Vietnam, Philippines) demonstrates "strong core but weak periphery" characteristics, with Vietnam and Indonesia leveraging manufacturing relocation to enhance port infrastructure. At the same time, the Philippines faces transportation gaps due to fiscal constraints. The third tier (Cambodia, Laos, Myanmar) suffers from underdeveloped transport systems. Brunei, despite its small land area, relies primarily on highways with full coverage and good road conditions. However, it has not developed railways extensively and remains dependent on international airports with limited flight routes.

In the telecommunications sector, Singapore and Malaysia demonstrate high 5G penetration rates (with Malaysia reaching 92%), leading in both technology and coverage. The second tier is steadily advancing 5G infrastructure development, with basic communication services meeting current demands. Third-tier countries like Brunei achieve full 4G coverage while making steady progress in 5G deployment. Their network speeds remain stable but lack technological innovation, whereas Cambodia and Laos face challenges in both coverage expansion and speed enhancement.

In the energy sector, Singapore and Malaysia demonstrate efficient and diversified energy utilization. The second tier focuses on supporting industrial development through complementary energy infrastructure. In the third tier, Brunei has achieved self-sufficiency in energy supply through abundant oil and gas resources while prioritizing efficiency improvements. However, its economic reliance on these resources has slowed progress in energy diversification and renewable energy development. Meanwhile, Myanmar and Laos face challenges of insufficient energy supply and structural homogeneity in their energy systems.

Comparison of Business Environments

Singapore

1. Policy: Singapore's government has long adhered to a free-market economy policy, maintaining exceptional stability that fosters a stable and predictable business environment. In terms of taxation, the corporate income tax rate stands at 17%, with tiered preferential rates ranging from 0% to 15% for eligible enterprises. To attract cross-border investments and promote industrial diversification, the government has introduced a series of incentives, including the Regional Headquarters Scheme, Pioneer Manufacturing Program, and Global Traders Scheme. In the digital economy sector, regulations such as the Payment Services Act and Personal Data Protection Act regulate market operations while actively advancing digital finance and e-payment services. Innovative digital enterprises are supported through R&D subsidies and tax relief measures.

2. Workforce: Singapore's workforce boasts world-class qualifications, supported by an internationally integrated education system that has produced a large number of English-proficient professionals with specialized expertise across sectors, including finance, technology, and biomedicine. The highly flexible labor market features 32% foreign employees, enabling companies to efficiently recruit local and international talent according to their operational needs, effectively meeting the staffing demands for various projects and business expansions.

3. Market Access: Singapore's market access is recognized as one of the most lenient globally, with virtually no universal industry restrictions.

Only the Significant Investment Review Act (SIRA) imposes a reporting system for equity changes in "critical sectors" such as telecommunications and energy. Foreign investors are free to purchase non-residential properties, and foreign enterprises enjoy unrestricted participation in land transactions. Under the Protocol between the Government of the People's Republic of China and the Government of the Republic of Singapore on Further Upgrading the Free Trade Agreement, effective December 31, 2024, Singapore has committed to imposing no restrictions on most manufacturing investments except for a few industries like beer, tobacco, and drawn steel. Restrictions on professional personnel's shareholding ratios and control rights have been eliminated in construction services, as well as specialized engineering fields, including machinery, aviation, and marine engineering. High-level openness commitments have been made in environmental protection, international shipping, professional services (excluding legal), and commercial services. A comprehensive and transparent legal framework ensures complete protection of corporate rights and interests, with explicit legal provisions governing every stage from company establishment to operations.

Thailand

1. Policy Framework: The Thai government has implemented a series of business-friendly policies to support enterprise development actively. In investment promotion, it has established multiple Special Economic Zones and industrial parks, such as the Eastern Economic Corridor (EEC), offering preferential policies to target industries. For instance, electric vehicle supply chain enterprises enjoy "8 years tax exemption + 5 years at half rate" benefits. To accelerate digital infrastructure development, policies have been introduced to expand nationwide 5G network coverage. Enterprises adopting digital technologies receive exceptional funding support for digital transformation, while increased investments in digital industries are channeled through dedicated digital economy funds. Tax incentives are also provided to eligible SMEs for a specified period to reduce corporate income tax burdens during the digital transition. With strong policy stability and execution, the government ensures effective implementation through the Investment Promotion Board (BOI), guaranteeing tangible benefits for businesses.

2. Workforce: Thailand boasts a highly skilled workforce with abundant skilled workers and technical professionals. Its well-developed vocational education system has cultivated numerous practical talents for pillar industries such as manufacturing and tourism. Taking the automotive industry as an example, industrial workers possess extensive practical experience and specialized skills, enabling them to operate advanced equipment proficiently. The flexible labor market allows enterprises to adjust workforce sizes according to seasonal fluctuations, project cycles, and other factors, employing workers through short-term contracts, part-time positions, and other flexible arrangements to meet diverse employment demands across various industries and businesses.

3. Market Access: Thailand maintains a flexible market access environment with minimal restrictions on foreign investment. The government actively attracts foreign capital by opening multiple sectors, including manufacturing, agriculture, and services, to foreign enterprises. While the Foreign Investment Promotion Act imposes certain equity ownership limits in specific industries, it permits 100% foreign ownership in encouraged sectors such as high-tech industries and new energy sectors. Additionally, Thailand's comprehensive legal framework—including commercial law, contract law, and intellectual property law—ensures businesses' legitimate rights and interests, creating a favorable legal environment for foreign companies to operate in the country.

Malaysia

1. Policy Framework: To drive economic diversification and industrial upgrading, the Malaysian government has implemented a series of attractive policies. In terms of tax incentives, emerging industries and strategic priority sectors receive varying levels of tax reductions and preferential treatment. For instance, Johor State offers 80% capital expenditure credits to electric vehicle component manufacturers with corporate income tax rates as low as 5%. Regarding industrial support measures, encouraged sectors like semiconductors and medical devices not only enjoy unrestricted equity access but also benefit from R&D subsidies, helping enterprises enhance innovation capabilities and global competitiveness. These policies demonstrate strong coherence and stability, with the government regularly reviewing and adjusting them to align with economic trends and actual business needs.

2. Workforce: Malaysia's workforce demonstrates strong qualifications, with a high English proficiency rate that facilitates operations and communication for multinational corporations. The country boasts a skilled workforce of engineers and technicians in specialized technical fields, particularly in the semiconductor industry, where highly skilled workers account for 27.3% of the workforce. The labor market maintains flexibility, enabling companies to recruit qualified personnel through formal channels like labor agencies and job markets. The government actively promotes labor market reforms, implementing policies that encourage businesses to adopt flexible employment models.

3. Market Access: Malaysia operates under a sector-specific licensing system. In the banking sector, foreign ownership limits range from 30% to 70% depending on specific circumstances, while the wholesale and retail sectors allow 100% foreign ownership based on license conditions. For encouraged industries like semiconductors and medical devices, foreign investors enjoy unrestricted equity participation. Furthermore, through regional cooperation mechanisms such as the Singapore Industrial and Commercial Zone (SIJORI), Singapore capital is permitted to hold stakes in local manufacturing projects, thereby circumventing land approval restrictions and creating additional market access pathways for foreign enterprises. A robust legal framework ensures businesses have clear guidelines for market entry, operations, and dispute resolution, effectively safeguarding the legitimate rights of foreign companies.

Vietnam

1. Policy: The Vietnamese government has implemented a series of preferential policies to attract foreign investment and boost economic development. In terms of taxation, the Haiphong Special Economic Zone offers a 10% corporate income tax rate for high-tech enterprises. Regarding industrial policies, detailed catalogs of encouraged, restricted, and prohibited industries have been established to meet the development needs of different sectors. The new Investment Law, enacted in 2025, lists green energy and electronic information industries as encouraged sectors, providing enterprises with land use incentives and financial support. Additionally, to promote digital transformation, companies adopting digital technologies receive tax reductions and technical training assistance. These policies are continuously adjusted and optimized to

adapt to evolving economic conditions and international competition environments.

2. Labor Force: Vietnam boasts abundant and cost-effective labor resources, with manufacturing workers earning monthly salaries ranging from $200 to $300. The flexible labor market allows enterprises to adjust workforce hiring and layoffs according to order volumes and production cycles. However, the current workforce quality remains uneven, particularly in high-end manufacturing and high-tech sectors where skilled professionals are relatively scarce. To address this, the Vietnamese government has significantly increased investments in vocational education and training programs, collaborating with enterprises to implement targeted talent development initiatives. These efforts aim to enhance overall workforce competence and meet the growing demand for skilled personnel in industrial upgrading processes.

3. Market Access: Vietnam implements a three-tier access control system with a clearly defined market entry list. Foreign investment is prohibited in 25 sectors, including arms manufacturing and news gathering. At the same time, 58 industries, such as insurance and telecommunications, are conditionally open to foreign capital, with foreign ownership limits generally capped at 49%. However, encouraged industries offer more flexible entry requirements. By leveraging the RCEP's rules of origin, Vietnam provides foreign enterprises with advantages in regional supply chain integration. Companies can enjoy tariff reductions by accumulating regional value shares in raw material procurement and product assembly processes, attracting numerous foreign firms. For instance, Samsung relocated 20% of its smartphone production capacity to Bac Ninh Province. The legal framework continues to improve, offering foreign enterprises fundamental legal safeguards for establishment, operation, and intellectual property protection.

Indonesia

1. Policy: To boost economic growth and attract foreign investment, the Indonesian government has implemented proactive measures. In resource development, capitalizing on its 22% global nickel reserves, it attracted the China Nonferrous Metal Mining Group (Qingshan Group) to invest $6 billion in a stainless steel industrial park. To encourage new energy industry chain development, tax breaks and land incentives were

provided to related enterprises, resulting in a 45% FDI increase in this sector by 2024. Through the "Positive Investment List", foreign investment is permitted in 100% sectors except for six major categories. To support SMEs, regulations require cooperation between foreign enterprises and local MSMEs (Micro, Small, and Medium Enterprises) across 106 industries, along with technology transfer or local procurement quotas to drive domestic industrial growth. These policies demonstrate foresight and specificity, continuously being refined as the economy evolves.

2. Labor Force: Indonesia boasts abundant labor resources, with manufacturing workers earning monthly salaries ranging from $200 to $250. However, the labor market flexibility needs improvement, as there are specific legal procedures and restrictions regarding hiring and firing workers. The overall workforce quality requires enhancement. Despite its large population base, there remains a gap compared to developed countries in terms of skills training and educational quality. Nevertheless, the government has launched the "1 Million Skilled Workers Training Program," focusing on cultivating talents in fields such as nickel processing and new energy to meet the demand for high-quality labor in industrial development.

3. Market Access: Indonesia primarily adopts a positive list approach. The *Positive Investment List* specifies sectors open to foreign investment, permitting 100% foreign ownership in most industries except a few designated sectors. While the qualification review and approval processes for foreign enterprises are relatively standardized, administrative inefficiencies persist with lengthy approval timelines. In specific sectors like mining, although foreign investment is permitted, stringent thresholds exist regarding mining rights acquisition and environmental compliance requirements. Although the legal framework continues to improve, implementation gaps in specific regulations hinder the adequate protection of foreign enterprises' legitimate rights and interests.

The Philippines

1. Policy: The Philippine government has actively promoted economic development by introducing a series of business-friendly policies. In terms of taxation, PEZA-certified enterprises enjoy full tariff exemptions on

imported environmental protection equipment, while export companies using direct flights between China and the Philippines can receive 12% freight subsidies. Regarding industrial policy, substantial support is given to the digital economy and export-oriented industries. The 2025 Foreign Investment Access Amendment allows foreign investors to hold up to 60% equity in Manila's retail sector (requiring annual investment ≥$5 million), removes foreign ownership caps in K-12 education, and permits wholly foreign-owned entities in renewable energy, medical R&D, and digital payment platforms. These policies are continuously adjusted to meet economic development needs, aiming to attract more foreign investment and drive industrial upgrading.

2. Workforce: The Philippines boasts a unique advantage in its workforce, with over 80% English proficiency. This gives it a competitive edge in sectors like service outsourcing and call centers. The BPO industry employs 1.5 million workers there, while labor costs are merely 60% of India's. The flexible labor market allows companies to adjust workforce sizes according to business needs. However, manufacturing sectors face challenges due to relatively low skill levels among workers and a shortage of specialized technical talent, requiring enterprises to invest more in training programs to enhance employee competencies.

3. Market Access: The Philippines has been progressively easing its market access policies. The 2025 Foreign Investment Access Amendment Act has relaxed foreign investment restrictions in sectors such as retail, education, and renewable energy. However, key areas, including land ownership, mass media, and mineral resources, remain off-limits for wholly foreign-owned enterprises. The telecommunications sector imposes a 40% foreign ownership cap with mandatory local board representation. Through regional trade agreements like the Regional Comprehensive Economic Partnership (RCEP), the country leverages rules of origin to boost exports of electronic components to Japan, South Korea, and other markets, securing tariff reductions that create import-export opportunities for foreign companies. While the legal framework is relatively robust, bureaucratic red tape and administrative inefficiencies persist in implementation, hindering market entry and operations for foreign enterprises.

Cambodia

1. Policy Framework: To attract foreign investment and boost economic growth, the Cambodian government has established a favorable policy environment. In terms of taxation, export processing zones offer full exemption from corporate income tax, which proves particularly attractive to export-oriented manufacturing enterprises. Regarding industrial policies, labor-intensive sectors such as garment production and electronics assembly receive strong support, with 100% foreign investment permitted. To advance infrastructure development and industrial growth, the government actively collaborates with international organizations and foreign governments to introduce capital and technology. However, policy stability remains an issue, with irregularities in land policy implementation and frequent property rights disputes affecting corporate investment confidence.

2. Workforce: Cambodia's workforce is young and cost-effective, with a median age of 28. Manufacturing workers earn monthly salaries ranging from \$180 to \$208. However, the overall workforce quality remains subpar, as the gross enrollment rate in higher education stands at only 18%. In high-tech industries, there is a heavy reliance on foreign technical workers. The labor market demonstrates high flexibility, allowing companies to hire or dismiss workers easily. Yet due to poor workforce stability, strike rates reach 18%, significantly increasing operational and management costs for businesses.

3. Market Access: The Cambodian market has relatively low entry barriers, with only a few sectors, such as narcotics, cultural heritage development, and others, prohibited from foreign investment, while most industries remain open to foreign entities. Regarding land access, foreigners can acquire land through trust companies, provided they meet financial requirements such as a net capital ratio of ≥150%, with trust service fees ranging from 0.2% to 0.3% of the land value. For instance, China Tianyuan Pet acquired land in Phnom Penh Province through a trust arrangement to establish a production base. However, practical implementation faces hidden barriers, including unclear land ownership and irregular policy enforcement, which have caused an average project delay of 12 months for foreign-funded projects, thereby affecting market access convenience. Although the legal system is continuously improving, gaps remain between domestic practices and international standards in

resolving commercial disputes and protecting intellectual property rights, impacting the safeguarding of legitimate rights and interests for foreign enterprises.

Laos

1. Policy Framework: To drive economic growth, the Lao government has implemented proactive policies. In the energy sector, the Mekong River Hydropower Project generates over 10 billion kWh annually, with electricity exports to Thailand and Vietnam accounting for 8% of GDP. The government provides policy support for hydropower development projects. Infrastructure improvements, notably the China-Laos Railway that reduced freight transit time between Vientiane and Kunming to 24 hours while cutting logistics costs by 40%, have been actively promoted alongside supportive policies to attract corporate investments. However, industrial policies remain restrictive: mining and agriculture require local joint ventures (foreign ownership ≤49%), and hydropower projects demand special government approval. Compounding these challenges, Laos' fragile economy faces a public debt-to-GDP ratio of 78% and the kip currency has depreciated 12% this year, creating difficulties in balancing foreign investment attraction with economic stability maintenance.

2. Labor Market: Laos boasts relatively low labor costs, with manufacturing workers earning approximately $168 per month. However, the workforce's skill level remains subpar, as technical workers heavily rely on foreign expertise. With 60% of the population engaged in agriculture, there's a notable shortage of skilled industrial workers and specialized professionals. The inflexible labor market poses challenges for companies in recruitment, training, and workforce management. Nevertheless, major projects like the China-Laos Railway and hydropower initiatives have created numerous temporary jobs while providing opportunities for vocational skills development. This has prompted the government to prioritize vocational education and workforce quality enhancement programs.

3. Market Access: Laos' market access policies impose strict restrictions in specific sectors. Resource-intensive industries such as mining and agriculture require local joint ventures with limited foreign ownership stakes. While infrastructure development and energy projects welcome foreign investment, the approval process remains cumbersome

due to complex interdepartmental coordination and lengthy timelines. Legal safeguards for market access remain underdeveloped, with loopholes in corporate registration, operations, and intellectual property protection that hinder foreign enterprises' entry and long-term growth. However, opportunities arising from infrastructure projects like the China-Laos Railway are driving the gradual relaxation of market access policies in logistics and trade-related service sectors.

Burma

1. Policy: The Myanmar government has implemented groundbreaking measures to drive economic development and industrial transformation. In 2024, the revised Investment Law now permits 100% foreign ownership in manufacturing sectors, creating favorable conditions for attracting foreign investment, such as the China National Building Materials Group's cement plant project. In the energy sector, the China-Myanmar oil and gas pipeline delivers 12 billion cubic meters of gas annually, with the government providing policy support for related industries. However, domestic political instability following the 2021 military coup and subsequent Western sanctions led to a 35% year-on-year decline in FDI in 2024. This severely undermines policy stability and implementation effectiveness, leaving the government facing significant challenges in balancing domestic governance with foreign investment attraction strategies.

2. Labor Force: Myanmar's workforce enjoys low labor costs, with manufacturing workers earning approximately $150 per month, making it suitable for developing labor-intensive industries. However, the workforce generally lacks high educational attainment and professional training, resulting in low productivity in manufacturing operations. The limited flexibility of the labor market poses challenges for companies in recruitment and management, including issues like incomplete labor regulations and unregulated union organizations. Additionally, political instability leads to significant labor mobility, further disrupting normal business operations.

3. Market Access: Myanmar has relaxed market access in sectors such as manufacturing, allowing 100% foreign ownership, which provides opportunities for foreign enterprises to enter. However, in infrastructure, there is insufficient power supply (only 10% of the population has access

to the grid nationwide), Yangon Ports' throughput is less than 1% of Singapore's, and an underdeveloped transportation and communication infrastructure increases operational costs for businesses and limits the attractiveness of market access. In terms of legal safeguards, the legal system remains incomplete, with over 40% of foreign-funded projects involved in property rights disputes, and an imperfect commercial dispute resolution mechanism that affects the legitimate rights and interests of foreign enterprises and investment confidence. Nevertheless, leveraging the opportunity presented by the China-Myanmar Economic Corridor with planned investments exceeding $20 billion, market access is expected to further improve in related projects and industries involving cooperation with <term_0> China.

Brunei

1. Policy Framework: The Brunei government primarily focuses on energy sector development through comprehensive policies. With a corporate income tax rate of 0% for oil and gas enterprises, this tax incentive has attracted global energy giants like Shell and BP to establish regional hubs. In terms of regional trade policies, tariff exemptions for ASEAN intra-regional trade have reduced supply chain costs by 10% compared to Malaysia, significantly boosting intra-regional trade. However, insufficient support exists in non-oil and gas sectors, where foreign ownership limits in retail and financial industries are capped at 51%, hindering foreign investment and industrial diversification. These policies demonstrate limited effectiveness in driving economic diversification, highlighting the need for enhanced policy frameworks supporting non-energy industries.

2. Labor Market: Foreign workers constitute 40% of Brunei's workforce, with technical positions heavily reliant on external recruitment. The country's limited population and constrained labor resources, coupled with an overemphasis on energy-related training programs, have resulted in insufficient talent reserves outside the oil and gas sector. The labor market lacks flexibility, as the government mandates companies to employ at least 30% local staff to meet quotas, restricting corporate autonomy in staffing decisions. While salaries in the energy industry remain competitive, limited job opportunities in non-oil sectors fail to attract qualified professionals effectively.

3. Market Access: Brunei's energy sector maintains relatively relaxed market access, allowing 100% foreign ownership. However, in other industries such as retail and finance, foreign equity participation faces restrictions due to the limited market size (with only 460,000 local consumers), which constrains corporate development. The legal framework for market access remains relatively simplistic, lacking detailed provisions in commercial operations and intellectual property protection that adequately safeguard foreign enterprises' legitimate rights. Due to both market constraints and policy limitations, foreign companies generally show low willingness to enter Brunei's market, resulting in limited appeal of its market access policies.

Summary: In terms of policy frameworks, first-tier economies like Singapore and Malaysia maintain open and diversified policies. Brunei, however, has prioritized energy sector development by offering a 0% corporate income tax for oil and gas companies to attract industry giants such as Shell. While ASEAN's intra-regional tariff-free trade agreements reduce supply chain costs by 10% compared to Malaysia, its insufficient support for non-oil sectors and foreign ownership restrictions fall short of second-tier economies' "industry-specific policies" (e.g., Vietnam's manufacturing incentives) and Singapore's comprehensive liberalization approach. Third-tier economies like Cambodia and Laos demonstrate even less developed policy frameworks.

In terms of workforce development, Singapore and Malaysia boast highly skilled labor forces with flexible markets. Brunei's foreign employees account for 40% of the workforce, while technical positions rely heavily on external recruitment. Due to its small population and focus on cultivating talent in energy sectors, Brunei faces a shortage of non-oil professionals and is constrained by the "30% local employee quota" policy. This makes its labor flexibility less competitive compared to second-tier countries like Thailand and Indonesia (which have ample manufacturing workforce reserves). In contrast, third-tier nations generally grapple with overall low-skilled workforce challenges.

In terms of market access, Brunei's energy sector allows 100% foreign investment, while imposing restrictions in sectors like retail and finance. Its small market of 460,000 people and an underdeveloped legal framework reduce foreign investment appeal. This contrasts with Singapore's approach: "full-sector openness with robust legal safeguards," the second tier's "key sector opening (e.g., Vietnam's manufacturing industry)," and the third tier's "small market size with high entry barriers." Overall, the business environments of these ten countries are influenced by their economic foundations and industrial positioning. To enhance regional business synergy, they need to optimize policies, cultivate talent, and relax market access regulations.

Chapter 3
China-ASEAN Cooperation

The implementation of the Regional Comprehensive Economic Partnership (RCEP) has injected strong momentum into the economic and trade cooperation between China and ASEAN. This chapter analyzes the opportunities for relevant industries based on the relevant rules of RCEP.

As the world's largest free trade agreement, RCEP has created unprecedented policy dividends for China and the ten ASEAN countries through multiple mechanisms such as unified rules, reduced barriers, and promotion of factor flows.

1. Tariff reductions under RCEP. In the field of goods trade, the tariff reduction arrangements under RCEP have formed a comprehensive preferential network. After the agreement takes effect, over 90% of goods trade between China and ASEAN will ultimately achieve zero tariffs, with the tariff reduction process being implemented in a stepwise manner to accommodate the capacity of countries at different development levels. Taking electromechanical products as an example, Chinese exports of smartphones and integrated circuits to ASEAN received an average tariff reduction of 12% in the first year after the agreement took effect. In 2024, exports of related products increased by 23% year-on-year, with Vietnam's imports of electronic components from China growing by 31%, highlighting the synergistic effects of industrial chains. Agricultural trade has also benefited significantly. Through optimized rules of origin, China's exports of temperate fruits to ASEAN countries such as Thailand and Malaysia saw customs clearance efficiency improve by 40%, with export value exceeding $8 billion in 2024—an 18% increase compared to pre-RCEP levels.

2. Rules of Origin Accumulation. The rules of origin accumulation have become a key engine driving the deep integration of industrial chains. Under this rule, the added value of products within the RCEP region can be cumulatively calculated, enabling more goods to meet origin criteria. Consequently, Chinese automobile enterprises have gained substantial operational advantages in localized production in ASEAN. For instance,

after a homegrown brand's factory in Thailand adopted engines from China and transmissions from Malaysia, its regional added value ratio for vehicles increased from 52% to 68%, successfully benefiting from intra-ASEAN tariff preferences. Exports to Indonesia and the Philippines saw a 57% year-on-year growth in 2024. The synergistic effects in the electronics industry are even more pronounced. By integrating regional resources such as domestic display panels, Singaporean chips, and Thai connectors, Chinese-funded electronic assembly plants in Vietnam have increased their product compliance rate with RCEP origin requirements from 65% to 92%, resulting in annual tariff cost savings of over $30 million.

3. Open Commitments in Service Trade. The open commitments in service trade have opened up new space for bilateral cooperation. RCEP has established higher-level opening arrangements than previous free trade agreements in over 20 service sectors, including finance, telecommunications, and logistics. The specific service trade commitment reduction schedules between China and ASEAN cover a broader range of sectors and higher levels of openness. In the financial services sector, China, Singapore, and Malaysia have achieved relaxed market access in banking, securities, insurance, and other fields. By 2024, China's exports of financial services to ASEAN reached $4.5 billion, marking a 35% year-on-year increase, with cross-border payments and wealth management services leading the growth momentum. Breakthroughs in digital services are particularly remarkable. The agreement's negative list management model, which permits cross-border data flows, has reduced operational costs for Chinese internet companies in ASEAN by 25%. A short video platform in Indonesia saw its user payment rate rise by 12 percentage points compared to pre-RCEP levels, with annual revenue growing by over 60%.

4. Upgrading of investment rules. The RCEP adopts a negative list model to regulate investment access, with China and ASEAN countries reducing their investment barriers by an average of 30%, particularly in sectors such as manufacturing and infrastructure, where openness has significantly increased. In 2024, China's direct investment flows to ASEAN reached $18 billion, including 89% and 67% year-on-year growth in investments in Vietnam's new energy vehicle industry and Indonesia's nickel ore processing industry, respectively. Meanwhile, ASEAN's

investment in China also showed diversification trends: Singapore added 28 regional headquarters in China, mainly concentrated in biomedicine and green technology fields; while Thai and Malaysian enterprises increased investments in agricultural processing and electronic component industries in central-western China, with actual annual investment reaching $7.2 billion, setting a new record. The improvement of the investment dispute settlement mechanism has boosted investor confidence, as the Investor-State Dispute Settlement (ISDS) clause under RCEP provides more efficient relief channels for enterprises. The number of related investment arbitration cases decreased by 40% in 2024 compared to previous years, reflecting the role of institutional safeguards in improving the investment environment.

Opportunities for ASEAN Cooperation

1. SME cooperation has received facilitation support. The Regional Comprehensive Economic Partnership (RCEP) has established a dedicated SME chapter, lowering the threshold for SMEs to participate in regional trade through measures such as simplifying customs procedures, providing trade financing facilities, and establishing information-sharing platforms. The "Cross-border E-commerce Support Program for SMEs" jointly launched by China and ASEAN has reduced the average export clearance time for small and medium-sized enterprises from 5 days to 2 days. In 2024, SMEs accounted for 68% of China's cross-border e-commerce exports to ASEAN, representing a 15 percentage point increase from pre-RCEP levels. Regarding standard mutual recognition, China and ASEAN have achieved technical standard alignment in 12 industries, including toys and textiles, reducing product certification costs for SMEs by 30%-50%. A garment company in Guangdong saw its exports to Cambodia and Laos surge by 200% after obtaining unified ASEAN standard certifications.

2. Enhanced resilience of regional supply chains. The agreement has enhanced the risk-resistance of regional industrial chains through measures such as strengthening customs cooperation, simplifying the certificate of origin process, and establishing a trade remedy cooperation mechanism. Against the backdrop of multiple shocks to global supply chains in 2024, China-ASEAN intermediate goods trade volume

maintained a 19% growth rate, rising to 62% of bilateral total trade, demonstrating the close interconnection of industrial chains. In key industries such as automotive and electronics, enterprises from both sides optimized supply chain layouts through RCEP rules. A specific automotive group increased the capacity utilization rate of its Thai parts factory from 65% to 88%, reduced inventory turnover days by 12 days, and significantly enhanced its ability to cope with market fluctuations.

3. Green economic cooperation has become a new growth area under the RCEP framework. The environmental provisions included in the agreement have promoted bilateral cooperation in areas such as clean energy and low-carbon technologies. The "Regional Green Industry Development Roadmap," jointly formulated by China and ASEAN countries, has facilitated policy coordination in sectors such as photovoltaics, wind power, and energy storage. In 2024, China's exports of new energy products to ASEAN reached $32 billion, with exports of photovoltaic modules and electric vehicle charging piles increasing by 75% and 120%, respectively. The scale of green investment has rapidly expanded, with the first phase of the "Regional Low-Carbon Development Fund" jointly established by China and ASEAN raising $10 billion to prioritize renewable energy projects in Indonesia, the Philippines, and other countries. Chinese enterprises participated in Vietnam's offshore wind power projects and Malaysia's solar power station projects, achieving an annual new installed capacity of 3.2 gigawatts, which boosted ASEAN's renewable energy share by 1.5 percentage points.

The policy dividends under the RCEP framework are reshaping the spatial landscape of China-ASEAN cooperation. Both sides are transitioning from traditional trade complementarity to deeper integration across industrial, supply, and value chains, and upgrading from a focus on goods trade to coordinated development involving goods, services, and investment. As the implementation of the agreement deepens, China and ASEAN are expected to forge closer cooperative relationships in emerging fields such as the digital economy, green economy, and high-end manufacturing. Together, they will create the world's most dynamic economic and trade cooperation zone, injecting lasting momentum into regional economic integration.

The entry into force and implementation of the Regional Comprehensive Economic Partnership (RCEP) has injected strong impetus into economic and trade cooperation between China and ASEAN, and has brought unprecedented development opportunities to the western Guangdong region (the four cities of Zhanjiang, Maoming, Yangjiang, and Yunfu), which is located at China's southwest gateway. As China's "bridgehead" connecting with ASEAN, western Guangdong, relying on its unique geographical advantages, characteristic industrial foundations, and policy dividends, has shown distinct features of "precision docking and complementary advantages" in its cooperation with ASEAN under the RCEP framework. On the basis of the original content, this chapter focuses on adding specific practices and opportunities of the western Guangdong region in areas such as tariff reductions, rules of origin, trade in services, and investment cooperation, and reveals how enterprises in western Guangdong can rely on the dividends of the agreement to transform regional resource advantages into international competitive advantages in ASEAN.

Business Opportunities for Enterprises in Western Guangdong

1. Tariff Dividends from ASEAN

Western Guangdong is an important agricultural production base in Guangdong Province. Characteristic agricultural products such as Zhanjiang prawns, Maoming lychees, Yangjiang longans, and Yunfu southern medicines have natural competitiveness in the ASEAN market. Tariff reductions have further highlighted the cost-performance advantages of these "Western Guangdong flavors" in the ASEAN market. Taking Zhanjiang prawns as an example, before the entry into force of RCEP, exported frozen prawns from Zhanjiang to Vietnam were subject to a 10% tariff. After the agreement took effect in 2022, the tariff has gradually been reduced to zero. In 2024, the export value of aquatic products from Zhanjiang to ASEAN reached 3 billion yuan, a year-on-year increase of 45%, of which exports to Vietnam accounted for over 60%. Maoming's lychee processing enterprises have also benefited significantly. The tariff on their exported lychee cans to Thailand was 8% before RCEP came into effect, and it has dropped to 2% in 2024, with zero tariff expected to be achieved in 2025. This has driven the export value of Maoming's lychee cans to ASEAN to increase from 120 million yuan in

2022 to 380 million yuan in 2024, a growth rate of 217%. The "precision services" provided by customs authorities in Western Guangdong have further amplified the tariff dividends. Maoming Customs launched an "immediate declaration and review" model during the peak lychee export season (June-July each year). Relying on self-service printing and online pre-review, it has enabled the "instant collection" of certificates of origin. During the 2024 lychee season, it issued 48 RCEP certificates of origin for enterprises, helping them reduce tariffs by over 5 million yuan. Zhanjiang Customs has established a "green channel for aquatic product exports" and implemented "7×24-hour" customs clearance services for frozen prawns. In 2024, the customs clearance time for Zhanjiang prawns exported to ASEAN was shortened from an average of 3 days to 1.5 days, and logistics costs were reduced by 12%.

Yangjiang, known as the "Capital of Chinese Hardware Knives and Scissors", produces 1.2 billion knives and scissors annually, accounting for 25% of the national output, with 80% of civilian knives and scissors relying on exports, and ASEAN being one of its core markets. Before RCEP came into effect, Yangjiang's knives and scissors exported to Malaysia were subject to a 5% tariff, and to Indonesia a 7% tariff. After the agreement took effect, these products have been gradually reduced in tariffs according to the "5-year gradient tariff reduction" plan. In 2024, the tariffs have dropped to 2% and 3% respectively, with zero tariffs expected to be achieved in 2028. Yangjiang enterprises have achieved "both volume and price increases" through tariff reductions. Taking a medium-sized knife and scissors enterprise in Yangjiang as an example, the unit price of its civilian scissors exported to Malaysia was 8 yuan per piece in 2023. After tariff reductions, the unit price dropped to 7.8 yuan per piece (including tax) in 2024, but sales volume increased from 500,000 pieces to 800,000 pieces, and net profit increased by 30% instead. In addition, Yangjiang hardware enterprises have flexibly adopted the "dual certificate selection" strategy: for the Thai market, where zero tariffs have been achieved, they choose RCEP certificates; for the Philippine market, where phased tariff reductions are still needed, they continue to use China-ASEAN certificates to further optimize costs. In 2024, the export value of Yangjiang hardware to ASEAN reached 3 billion yuan, a year-on-year increase of 38%, of which exports under RCEP accounted for over 60%.

Zhanjiang and Maoming have developed port-vicinity petrochemical industries relying on their port advantages. Maoming Petrochemical has an annual crude oil processing capacity of 20 million tons, and the Zhanjiang Donghai Island Petrochemical Industrial Park has formed a complete industrial chain of "crude oil - plastic pellets - plastic products". Before RCEP came into effect, exports of downstream petrochemical products (such as plastic pellets and coatings) from Western Guangdong to ASEAN were subject to 3%-5% tariffs. After the agreement took effect, these products were included in the "rapid tariff reduction list". In 2024, the tariffs have dropped to 1%-2%, and zero tariffs will be achieved in 2025. The practice of a medium-sized petrochemical enterprise in Maoming is quite representative. The plastic pellets produced by this enterprise are mainly supplied to food packaging enterprises in Indonesia and Vietnam. In 2023, its export value was 80 million yuan, with tariff costs accounting for 4%. In 2024, the tariff dropped to 1.5%, and the export value increased to 120 million yuan. The cost reduction drove the order volume to increase by 50%. Downstream enterprises of Zhanjiang Petrochemical have used tariff dividends to expand into high-end ASEAN markets. Their environmentally friendly coatings exported to Singapore under RCEP have seen tariffs drop from 5% to 2%. In 2024, the export value exceeded 50 million yuan, successfully entering the supply chain of large-scale construction projects in Singapore.

2. Opportunities for "Supply Chain Restructuring"

The RCEP's rules of origin cumulation allow the cumulative calculation of added value of products within the region, which provides key support for enterprises in western Guangdong to integrate resources from ASEAN and optimize their supply chain layouts. By engaging in raw material procurement and production collaboration under the "China + ASEAN" model, enterprises in western Guangdong can not only more easily meet the rules of origin standards but also reduce their reliance on a single market and enhance supply chain resilience.

Zhanjiang Guolian Aquatic Products is a leading Chinese aquatic product processing enterprise, and its pre-prepared shrimp dishes (such as shrimp slides and shrimp dumplings) are in strong demand in the ASEAN market. Before the implementation of the rules of origin cumulation, if Guolian Aquatic Products used Chinese-produced shrimp meat, Thai-produced seasonings, and Vietnamese-produced packaging materials for its pre-prepared dishes, the proportion of regional added value needed to reach 40% to enjoy tariff preferences. After the implementation of the rules, the added value from the three places can be calculated cumulatively, and the regional proportion increased from 52% to 68%, easily meeting the standards. Relying on this rule, Guolian Aquatic Products has restructured its supply chain: it purchases white shrimp raw materials from Vietnam (accounting for 30%), imports spices from Thailand (accounting for 15%), conducts deep processing in Zhanjiang factories, and finally exports to Indonesia and Malaysia. In 2024, the export value of pre-prepared dishes under this model reached 280 million yuan, a year-on-year increase of 57%, and tariff costs were reduced by more than 3 million yuan. In addition, Guolian Aquatic Products also established a raw material procurement center in Vietnam. In 2024, the amount of raw materials purchased from ASEAN reached 150 million yuan, accounting for 25% of the total procurement volume, and the stability of the supply chain was significantly improved.

Yangjiang hardware enterprises have long faced the problem of relying on imports for core components (such as high-end steel and precision bearings). The RCEP rules of origin cumulation provide them with a new solution. A medium-sized hardware enterprise in Yangjiang that produces industrial-grade knives originally used German steel (accounting for 40% of costs), with the proportion of regional added value being only 35%, which made it unable to enjoy ASEAN tariff preferences. After the implementation of the rules, the enterprise switched to using Malaysian-produced steel (accounting for 35% of costs) and Thai-produced bearings (accounting for 10% of costs), completed assembly in Yangjiang, and the proportion of regional added value increased to 62%, successfully meeting the RCEP rules of origin requirements. This adjustment not only allowed the products to enjoy zero tariffs in ASEAN but also reduced costs. In 2024, the order volume of industrial knives exported to Indonesia by this enterprise increased by 80%, with export value reaching 60 million yuan and gross profit margin increasing by five percentage points. According to data from the Yangjiang Hardware Industry Association, in 2024, 30% of Yangjiang hardware enterprises integrated ASEAN resources through the rules of origin cumulation, with an average cost reduction of 8% and a 20% improvement in supply chain response speed.

Maoming plastic packaging enterprises mainly produce food packaging films and plastic turnover boxes, with raw materials mainly being polyethylene, which originally relied on domestic procurement (accounting for 90%), resulting in a low proportion of regional added value. After the entry into force of RCEP, enterprises began to purchase polyethylene from Malaysia and Singapore (accounting for 40%), mixed with domestic raw materials, and the proportion of regional added value increased from 45% to 70%, successfully obtaining the RCEP certificate of origin. A Maoming plastic factory exported 80 million yuan worth of food packaging films to Vietnam through this model in 2024, with tariffs reduced from 5% to 2%. At the same time, due to the lower price of ASEAN raw material procurement compared to domestic prices, costs were further reduced by 3%, and net profit increased by 25%. In addition, enterprises have also established "raw material mutual supply" cooperation with Indonesian plastic processing enterprises, exporting Maoming-produced plastic particles to Indonesia (enjoying zero tariffs) while importing recycled plastics from Indonesia (with costs 15% lower), forming a closed-loop supply chain with "two-way flow".

3. The breakthrough in Port-Related Services and Digital Economy

The opening commitments of RCEP in areas such as finance, logistics, and digital services have provided new space for Western Guangdong's service industry to connect with ASEAN. Relying on its port advantages, Western Guangdong develops port-related logistics and expands cross-border e-commerce with the help of digital technologies, showing an upgrading trend of "from basic services to high-end collaboration" in service trade cooperation with ASEAN. Zhanjiang Port is the largest comprehensive port in southwest China. After the entry into force of RCEP, relying on the "customs cooperation" provisions in the agreement, Zhanjiang Port has established a "single window" customs clearance collaboration with ASEAN ports (such as Laem Chabang Port in Thailand and Ho Chi Minh Port in Vietnam). In 2024, the cargo clearance time from Zhanjiang Port to ASEAN was shortened from 24 hours to 4 hours, and the container detention time was reduced from 48 hours to 24 hours. To meet the transportation needs of ASEAN's fresh agricultural products,

Zhanjiang Port has further improved cold chain supporting facilities: in 2024, the capacity of cold chain container yards was increased to 1,000 (doubled compared with 2022), and a direct cold chain route from "Zhanjiang to Bangkok" was opened (twice a week), reducing the loss rate of Maoming lychees and Zhanjiang prawns exported to ASEAN from 8% to 3%. In 2024, the cargo volume of Zhanjiang Port's ASEAN routes reached 18 million tons, accounting for 35% of the port's total cargo volume, of which cold chain goods accounted for more than 20%, driving the growth of Western Guangdong's agricultural product exports to ASEAN by 45%. The negative list management model for cross-border data flow allowed by RCEP has reduced the cost for small and medium-sized enterprises in Western Guangdong to expand into the ASEAN market through cross-border e-commerce. Zhanjiang, Maoming, and Yangjiang have successively established cross-border e-commerce comprehensive test zones. In 2024, the export volume of cross-border e-commerce from Western Guangdong to ASEAN reached 3.5 billion yuan, a year-on-year increase of 60%, of which small and medium-sized enterprises accounted for 68%.

The practice of an aquatic product cross-border e-commerce enterprise in Zhanjiang is quite representative. The enterprise settled in Shopee Vietnam, selling pre-made dishes (such as instant shrimp slides and grilled fish). With the help of RCEP cross-border data flow rules, it realized "localized Vietnamese customer service + real-time logistics data docking". In 2024, its sales reached 80 million yuan, and the customer complaint rate dropped from 20% to 5%. A lychee processing enterprise in Maoming promoted lychee dried fruits and lychee cans through TikTok live streaming. In 2024, the live streaming GMV in the ASEAN market reached 30 million yuan, and the brand awareness was significantly improved. In addition, the government of Western Guangdong has built an "ASEAN Cross-border E-commerce Service Platform" to provide one-stop services such as tariff inquiry, logistics price comparison, and overseas warehouse docking. In 2024, the platform served more than 500 enterprises, helping them reduce operating costs by 15%, and the average order fulfillment time was shortened from 7 days to 3 days.

The opening commitments of RCEP in the financial services field have provided opportunities for Western Guangdong's banks to expand their ASEAN business. Local financial institutions such as Zhanjiang

Bank and Maoming Rural Commercial Bank, relying on the "New Western Land-Sea Corridor" policy, have launched products such as "ASEAN cross-border payment" and "export credit insurance financing" to help enterprises in Western Guangdong reduce financing costs and avoid exchange rate risks. In 2024, Zhanjiang Bank launched the "RCEP ASEAN Loan", providing small and medium-sized enterprises exporting to ASEAN with a maximum credit loan of 5 million yuan, with an interest rate 1.5 percentage points lower than ordinary loans. It issued more than 200 million yuan in loans throughout the year, supporting 300 enterprises to expand into the ASEAN market. Maoming Rural Commercial Bank cooperated with DBS Bank of Singapore to launch "cross-border RMB settlement" services. In 2024, it handled more than 1 billion yuan of ASEAN cross-border RMB settlement business, helping enterprises avoid exchange rate fluctuation risks and reduce exchange costs by 8%.

4. The "ASEAN Localization" Layout

The RCEP adopts a negative list model to regulate investment access, reducing the average investment barriers between China and ASEAN by 30%. The degree of opening up is significantly enhanced, especially in fields such as manufacturing and infrastructure. Seizing this opportunity, enterprises in western Guangdong have upgraded from "product export to industrial landing" by establishing factories, conducting mergers and acquisitions, and carrying out technical cooperation in ASEAN, thereby reducing the risks of trade barriers and getting closer to local market demands. To avoid import quota restrictions in some ASEAN countries, Zhanjiang aquatic enterprises have begun to set up processing bases in Vietnam and Thailand. A medium-sized aquatic enterprise in Zhanjiang invested 50 million yuan in 2023 to build a frozen shrimp processing plant in Ba Ria-Vung Tau Province, Vietnam. Taking advantage of the local cheap labor (monthly salary is about 200 US dollars, only 50% of that in Zhanjiang) and tariff advantages, the plant produces frozen shrimp and directly supplies the local and surrounding markets in Vietnam. In 2024, the plant's production capacity reached 10,000 tons, with an output value of 80 million yuan, and the cost was 20% lower than that of domestic exports. Another aquatic enterprise in Zhanjiang quickly obtained local market channels by acquiring a Thai aquatic processing plant. In 2024, the enterprise acquired a processing plant in Rayong Province, Thailand (with an annual production capacity of 5,000 tons). With the help of the original customer network, it introduced pre-made dishes such as shrimp slides and fish balls produced in Zhanjiang into Thai chain channels such as 7-11 and Big C. In 2024, the sales volume reached 60 million yuan, marking the successful entry into the high-end pre-made food market in Thailand.

To enhance the competitiveness of high-end products, Yangjiang hardware enterprises have started to lay out R&D centers in ASEAN. A large hardware enterprise in Yangjiang invested 30 million yuan in 2024 to establish an R&D center in Penang, Malaysia, focusing on the research and development of industrial-grade cutting tools and intelligent kitchenware. Utilizing the advantages of technical talents in Malaysia (the monthly salary of engineers is about 4,000 yuan, 30% lower than that in China) and its proximity to the ASEAN market, it has developed products suitable for the industrial needs of ASEAN. In 2024, the intelligent kitchen knives developed by this center achieved sales of 50 million yuan in the ASEAN market, with a gross profit margin exceeding 30%. In addition, Yangjiang hardware enterprises have expanded the ASEAN market through the "technology output + local production" model. An enterprise in Yangjiang cooperated with an Indonesian hardware manufacturer, providing industrial cutting tool production technology and supplying core components, while the Indonesian manufacturer was responsible for localized production and sales. In 2024, the cooperative sales volume reached 30 million yuan, and the Yangjiang enterprise obtained more than 10 million yuan from technical royalties and component sales revenue.

Western Guangdong has a certain foundation in green energy fields such as photovoltaic and wind power. The green economy cooperation under the RCEP framework provides opportunities for new energy enterprises in western Guangdong to connect with the ASEAN market. A photovoltaic enterprise in Zhanjiang cooperated with a Vietnamese enterprise in 2024 to build a 100-megawatt photovoltaic power station in southern Vietnam. Taking advantage of Vietnam's solar energy resources and the RCEP's preferential policies for green investment, the total investment of the project is 500 million yuan, with an estimated annual power generation of 120 million kilowatt-hours and annual sales of 80 million yuan. A wind power enterprise in Maoming entered the ASEAN market through technical cooperation. The enterprise cooperated with a Malaysian wind power developer, providing wind power blade production technology and supplying core components. In 2024, the cooperative project achieved sales of 60 million yuan, with technical service fees accounting for 15%. In addition, relying on the "China-ASEAN Green Industry Development Fund", western Guangdong supported more than 5 ASEAN green projects in 2024, with a total investment of 1 billion yuan, promoting the precise connection between western Guangdong's green technologies and the market demands of ASEAN.

5. Policy Empowerment

To help enterprises in Western Guangdong better seize the opportunities brought by RCEP, the four cities in Western Guangdong and Guangdong Province have introduced a series of supporting policies, providing guarantees in terms of financial subsidies, platform construction, talent training, etc., and building a "policy bridge" for cooperation between Western Guangdong and ASEAN. Guangdong Province provides support of "50 yuan per ton + 50% premium subsidy" to Western Guangdong enterprises exporting to ASEAN. In 2024, enterprises in Western Guangdong received a total of 280 million yuan in subsidies, covering 1,200 enterprises. Zhanjiang offers a 10% R&D subsidy to aquatic product enterprises exporting pre-made dishes to ASEAN. In 2024, over 30 million yuan in subsidies were distributed, supporting 20 enterprises in developing customized products for ASEAN. Maoming provides a 50% subsidy for cold chain logistics costs incurred by lychee processing enterprises exporting to ASEAN. In 2024, the subsidy exceeded 5 million yuan, reducing enterprises' logistics costs by 20%. Western Guangdong has actively organized or participated in events such as the "China-ASEAN Expo" and the "China (Yunfu, Guangdong) - RCEP Industrial Cooperation Conference". In 2024, enterprises in Western Guangdong reached more than 200 ASEAN cooperation intentions through these platforms, with a signed contract amount of 5 billion yuan. Zhanjiang has built the "ASEAN Aquatic Product Processing Park", where enterprises enjoy policies such as "50% reduction in land rent and 'two-year exemption and three-year halving' of taxes". In 2024, it attracted 15 ASEAN investment projects with a total investment of 2 billion yuan. Yangjiang has established the "ASEAN Hardware Industrial Park". In 2024, the export volume of enterprises in the park to ASEAN reached 1.5 billion yuan, accounting for 50% of Yangjiang's total hardware exports to

ASEAN. Under the guidance of local governments, Western Guangdong has collaborated with universities such as Guangdong Ocean University and Maoming University to set up 定向班 (targeted classes) in majors like "ASEAN Minor Languages", "International Trade", and "Cross-border E-commerce". In 2024, over 1,000 ASEAN-oriented international talents were trained, alleviating the talent shortage problem for enterprises. Zhanjiang organized the "ASEAN Business Training Course", which trained over 500 enterprise leaders in 2024, covering content such as RCEP rule interpretation, ASEAN market research, and cross-border legal risk prevention and control, helping enterprises enhance their international capabilities.

The entry into force and implementation of RCEP has opened a "new window" for cooperation between Western Guangdong and ASEAN. From the cost advantages brought by tariff reductions, to the supply chain restructuring driven by rules of origin, and to the in-depth upgrading of service trade and investment cooperation, enterprises in Western Guangdong are relying on the dividends of the agreement to gradually realize the transformation from "product export" to "industrial landing" and from "passive order taking" to "active layout". In the future, Western Guangdong needs to further focus on the following directions: first, deepen the precise connection between characteristic industries and the ASEAN market, such as promoting the localization of advantageous products in ASEAN, including pre-made aquatic products, hardware knives and scissors, and green energy; second, strengthen the construction of supply chain resilience, reduce dependence on a single market through the integration of "China + ASEAN" resources; third, improve the precision of policy empowerment, and provide more efficient services for enterprises in addressing pain points in tariff declaration, origin certification, cross-border financing, etc. It is believed that with the continuous promotion of RCEP, Western Guangdong will become a "new growth pole" for cooperation between China and ASEAN, injecting Western Guangdong's strength into regional economic integration.

Chapter 4
Scale Stratification and Operational Characteristics

Western Guangdong serves as a crucial node for the Guangdong-Hong Kong-Macao Greater Bay Area to extend its reach to the Beibu Gulf Economic Zone. The small and medium-sized enterprise (SME) sector in Western Guangdong is not only the "capillary network" of the regional economy, but also a core vehicle for connecting with the international market of the Association of Southeast Asian Nations (ASEAN). Based on a sampling survey of 236 enterprises (selected from 187,000 enterprises in four cities of Western Guangdong), 32 enterprise forums, and 124 in-depth interview records, this chapter systematically analyzes the ecological status quo of SMEs in Western Guangdong from three dimensions: the quantitative characteristics of scale stratification, the lock-in effect of business models, and the differentiated predicaments of enterprises of different scales. It reveals the formation logic behind their characteristics of being "small, scattered, and weak," providing a micro-level practical basis for the subsequent design of ASEAN internationalization paths.

Hierarchical Scale Distribution

Enterprises in western Guangdong are predominantly small and medium-sized, with a distinct "pyramid-shaped" scale distribution. Micro-enterprises form the base of the pyramid, small enterprises constitute the middle part, and medium-sized enterprises serve as the top. There are significant disparities among these tiers in terms of quantity proportion, industrial distribution, and revenue-generating capacity. This pattern, rooted in the resource endowments and industrial foundation of western Guangdong, also restricts the potential for enterprises' international development.

Tower base: Micro-enterprises (with ≤10 employees) – accounting for the absolute majority in quantity, and their survival depends on the "familiar market".

By the end of 2024, the total number of micro-enterprises in the four cities of western Guangdong reached 148,000, accounting for 79.3% of the total number of small and medium-sized enterprises. Among them, there were 42,000 in Zhanjiang, 38,000 in Maoming, 35,000 in Yangjiang, and 33,000 in Yunfu. These enterprises are mainly concentrated in four fields: catering and retail, primary processing of agricultural products, individual commerce and trade, and small-scale services, showing the "three low" characteristics of "low threshold, low technology, and low added value".

1. Quantity Distribution and Industry Focus

- Catering and retail: Accounting for 43% of the total number of micro-enterprises, most are community convenience stores, township restaurants, and farmers' market stalls, with an average business area of less than 50 square meters. For example, a township convenience store in Xuwen County, Zhanjiang, has only three employees (a couple plus one part-timer), mainly sells daily necessities and agricultural materials, and has a service radius of no more than 3 kilometers.
- Agricultural primary product processing: Accounting for 28%, mainly family workshop-style operations. For instance, a small sorting station built by a lychee grower in Gaozhou City, Maoming (with five employees) is only responsible for lychee cleaning, grading, and simple packaging, and all products are sold to local purchasers.

Individual commerce and trade: Accounting for 21%, including hardware general stores, clothing vendors, and small building materials stores. For example, a hardware store in Yangdong District, Yangjiang (with four employees) mainly sells low-end civil tools such as screwdrivers and wrenches, and its procurement relies on the Foshan hardware wholesale market.

Small-scale services: Accounting for 8%, covering housekeeping and cleaning, small-scale transportation, and agricultural machinery maintenance. For example, an agricultural machinery repair shop in Luoding City, Yunfu (with two employees) only serves farmers in 5 surrounding administrative villages, and equipment maintenance relies on experience rather than standardized procedures.

2. Operational Capabilities and Financial Characteristics

Revenue scale: The average annual revenue of microenterprises is less than 5 million yuan, of which 62% have an annual revenue of less than 2 million yuan, and only 3% have an annual revenue of more than 8 million yuan (mainly catering or commerce enterprises with significant geographical advantages, such as a seafood restaurant in Xiashan District, Zhanjiang, which achieves an annual revenue of 12 million yuan relying on fishing port resources).

Financial system: 91% of microenterprises lack standardized financial statements, instead adopting a "daily cash flow + manual bookkeeping" approach. For instance, the primary processing workshop for aquatic products in Dianbai District, Maoming, only tracks the daily purchase volume of raw materials and sales volume, without implementing cost accounting or tax planning. In 2024, it overpaid 32,000 yuan in taxes due to a failure to declare preferential policies for small-scale taxpayers in a timely manner.

Funding sources: 85% of microenterprises rely on their own funds or loans from relatives and friends, with no bank loan records. Only 15% of enterprises have tried small loans (such as "Wangshangdai" from MYbank). Still, the loan amount is generally less than 500,000 yuan, and the annual interest rate ranges from 12% to 15% (46 percentage points higher than the annual interest rate of loans for large enterprises).

3. Market Radiation and Customer Structure

Geographical limitations: 98% of microenterprises have customers concentrated locally (townships or counties) without cross-city business operations. For instance, a clothing vendor in Yangchun City, Yangjiang, operates solely at township fairs, primarily serving surrounding villagers, and has never engaged with e-commerce or foreign trade channels.

Customer types: Bend customers (enterprise procurement) account for less than 10%, mainly providing supporting services for local small and medium-sized enterprises (such as small transportation enterprises distributing raw materials for aquatic product processors). Cend customers (individual consumers) account for 90%, mostly "regular customers", relying on word-of-mouth communication rather than brand marketing.

International awareness: 100% of microenterprises are unfamiliar with the ASEAN market, and only 2% have heard of "RCEP" but lack specific knowledge of its content. For example, the owner of an agricultural materials store in Suixi County, Zhanjiang, said, "I only know how to sell chemical fertilizers to local farmers. I never thought about doing business in Southeast Asia, nor do I know how to do it."

Tower Body: Small enterprises (with 1050 employees) having initial production capacity but trapped in "homogeneous competition"

The total number of small enterprises in western Guangdong is about 35,000, accounting for 18.5% of the total number of small and medium-sized enterprises. They are mainly distributed in four fields: hardware processing, textile and clothing, plastic packaging, and the agricultural product cold chain. These enterprises have a specific scale of production and equipment investment. Still, their R&D capabilities are weak, product homogenization is serious, and operating profits have been at a low level for a long time.

1. Industrial distribution and production capacity characteristics

Hardware processing: Accounting for 35% of the total number of small enterprises, concentrated in the Yangdong District of Yangjiang and the Lianjiang City of Zhanjiang. They mainly produce civil scissors, kitchenware, and hardware accessories. For example, a small scissors factory in Yangjiang (with 32 employees) has two semi-automatic production lines, with a daily output of 5,000 pairs of scissors. The products are sold nationwide, but the factory lacks independent design capability, and its styles are often imitated from those of enterprises in Foshan and Zhejiang.

Textile and clothing: Accounting for 25%, mainly in the Maonan District of Maoming and Wuchuan City of Zhanjiang, focusing on OEM production. For example, a small clothing factory in Maoming (with 45 employees) undertakes OEM production of T-shirts and jeans for Guangzhou clothing brands. It has no own brand and relies on foreign trade companies for orders, with a profit margin of only 8%-10%.

Plastic packaging: Accounting for 20%, distributed in the Potou District of Zhanjiang and the Yuncheng District of Yunfu, producing food packaging films and plastic turnover boxes. For example, a plastic factory in Zhanjiang (with 28 employees) uses second-hand injection molding machines, and its product quality only meets the standards of the domestic low-end market, failing to meet the requirements of ASEAN food contact material certification.

Agricultural product cold chain: Accounting for 20%, mostly small cold storage and transportation enterprises. For example, a litchi cold chain company in Maoming (with 38 employees) has five small cold storages (with a total capacity of 5,000 cubic meters) and 12 refrigerated trucks, only responsible for the short-distance transportation of litchi from the production area to local purchasers, without cross-border cold chain capability.

2. R&D investment and product competitiveness

R&D intensity: The average R&D investment of small enterprises accounts for less than 1%, far lower than the 3%-5% level of small enterprises in the Pearl River Delta. Among them, 78% of enterprises have no full-time R&D personnel and only rely on the experience of technical workers to improve the production process.

Product homogenization: Among small hardware scissors enterprises in Yangjiang, 80% of the products are civil scissors and kitchen knives with a unit price of 5-15 yuan, and the style repetition rate exceeds 90%. For example, at a hardware expo in Yangjiang in 2024, among the products displayed by 12 small scissors enterprises, 9 had completely identical kitchen knife designs.

Technical shortcomings: Among textile and clothing enterprises, only 15% have clothing CAD design systems, and the rest still use manual pattern making, resulting in low production efficiency (30% lower than enterprises using CAD) and a high defective rate (with an average defective rate of 8%, four percentage points higher than that of enterprises in the Pearl River Delta).

3. Market expansion and channel dependence

Domestic market: 85% of the revenue of small enterprises comes from within the province, among which the Pearl River Delta market accounts for 60% (for example, Yangjiang hardware scissors are sold nationwide through Guangzhou wholesale markets), and the 省外 market only accounts for 15%, mostly low-value-added products.

Foreign trade attempts: Only 12% of small enterprises have export records, and all of them are agented by foreign trade companies in Guangzhou and Shenzhen, without direct customer connection. For example, a plastic packaging factory in Zhanjiang exported 1 million yuan worth of plastic boxes to Vietnam through a Shenzhen foreign trade company in 2024, but never communicated with Vietnamese customers, and the order terms and delivery date were all determined by the foreign trade company.

Channel cost: Relying on foreign trade companies leads to a profit compression of 30%-40%. For example, a small scissors factory in Yangjiang sells kitchen knives to foreign trade companies at a unit price of 8 yuan per piece, while the foreign trade company sells them to Thailand at a price of 18 yuan per piece, and the enterprise only obtains meager processing fees.

The Pinnacle: Medium-sized enterprises (with 50-300 employees), strong regional dependence, and weak foundation for internationalization. The total number of medium-sized enterprises in western Guangdong is only 4,114, accounting for 2.2% of the total number of small and medium-sized enterprises. They are the "backbone" of the regional industry. However, they generally lie around local pillar industries, lack independent supply chains and market expansion capabilities, and show the characteristics of "being large but not strong".

1. Industrial binding and dependence on pillars

Aquatic product processing: Among the medium-sized enterprises in Zhanjiang, 32 are aquatic product processing enterprises, all providing primary processing services for leading enterprises such as Guolian Aquatic Products and Hengxing Group. For example, a medium-sized aquatic product factory in Zhanjiang (with 180 employees) only undertakes shrimp heading, shelling, and freezing, and all products are sold to Guolian Aquatic Products without independent sales channels. The processing fee is only 15% of the terminal price of the products.

Petrochemical downstream: 28 medium-sized chemical enterprises in Maoming all rely on the crude oil supply from Maoming Petrochemical to produce primary chemical products such as gasoline additives and plastic particles. For example, a medium-sized petrochemical factory in Maoming (with 220 employees) spends 70% of its production cost on crude oil procurement, and its products are only sold to small and medium-sized plastic factories in the province without overseas markets.

Hardware manufacturing: 15 medium-sized hardware enterprises in Yangjiang mainly produce industrial-grade cutting tools and hardware molds, but their core technologies rely on imports. For example, a medium-sized cutting tool factory in Yangjiang (with 250 employees) imports tool steel materials from Germany and production equipment from

Japan, and self-developed cutting tools only account for 20% of the total products.

Stone processing: 21 medium-sized stone enterprises in Yunfu, relying on local marble resources, produce stone plates and sculptures, but their products are mainly "processing with supplied materials". For example, a medium-sized stone factory in Yunfu (with 160 employees) processes stone curtain walls for real estate enterprises in Guangzhou, achieving a profit margin of only 12% and lacking its own brand.

2. Revenue structure and market limitations

Regional concentration: Over 85% of the revenue of medium-sized enterprises comes from local and within the province. Among them, 92% of the revenue of medium-sized aquatic product processing enterprises in Zhanjiang comes from within the province, and 95% of that of petrochemical downstream enterprises in Maoming comes from within the province. Only three aquatic product enterprises have tried to export (2 in Zhanjiang and 1 in Maoming), with destinations in Vietnam and Thailand, and the annual export volume of each is less than 20 million yuan.

Single customer: 60% of medium-sized enterprises have the problem of "relying on a single major customer". For example, 70% of the revenue of a medium-sized petrochemical factory in Maoming comes from a plastic enterprise in Guangzhou. In 2024, the orders of this plastic enterprise decreased by 30%, resulting in the capacity utilization rate of the petrochemical factory dropping from 80% to 55%.

Internationalization capability: Only 5% of medium-sized enterprises have set up foreign trade departments, and most of the employees are "part-time" (such as administrative personnel also doing foreign trade docking). There are no talents proficient in ASEAN minority languages. For example, a medium-sized aquatic product enterprise in Zhanjiang tried to export to Thailand in 2023, but due to the lack of Thai translators, it failed to communicate with local importers on quality standards, resulting in delayed orders.

3. Resource allocation and management level

Talent structure: The proportion of employees with bachelor's degrees or above in medium-sized enterprises is less than 20%, far lower than the 40% level of medium-sized enterprises in the Pearl River Delta. Talents in foreign trade, R&D, and compliance positions are particularly in short supply. For example, a medium-sized hardware enterprise in Yangjiang has only two people in its foreign trade department, and neither of them has a professional background in international trade.

Management system: 65% of medium-sized enterprises still adopt "family-style management", with decision-making power concentrated in founders or core family members, lacking standardized management systems. For example, in a medium-sized petrochemical factory in Maoming, positions such as procurement, sales, and finance are all held by relatives of the founder, leading to chaotic processes. In 2024, due to out-of-control procurement costs, profits dropped by 18%.

Capital status: The average net assets of medium-sized enterprises are 12 million yuan, higher than those of small and micro enterprises, but the financing channels are still limited. 70% of enterprises rely on bank mortgage loans, and the loan amount is limited by the value of collateral (such as factories and equipment). In 2024, a medium-sized aquatic product enterprise in Zhanjiang only obtained a loan of 3 million yuan due to the low valuation of cold storage mortgage, which could not meet the needs of cross-border cold chain equipment upgrading.

Business Model

Affected by regional resource endowments and industrial foundations, the business model of small and medium-sized enterprises (SMEs) in western Guangdong has formed a dual lock-in of "resource-dependent production" and "low-cost-oriented competition". This model has certain survival advantages in the domestic market, but there is a significant gap with the compliance requirements, quality standards, and brand demands of the ASEAN market, becoming a core obstacle to international development.

1. Resource-dependent production: Relying on local resources, but with insufficient supply chain stability and added value, Western Guangdong is rich in agricultural, energy, and port resources. SMEs generally arrange production around these resources, but excessive dependence leads to fragile supply chains and low product added value, making it difficult to adapt to the diversified needs of the ASEAN market.

1.1 Dependence on agricultural resources: small scale, low standardization, and weak anti-risk ability. Western Guangdong is an important agricultural production area in Guangdong. The outputs of

Zhanjiang prawns, Maoming lychees, Yangjiang longans, and Yunfu southern medicinal materials all rank among the top in the province. 42% of SMEs are engaged in agricultural product processing, but most are in a decentralized "retail investors + workshops" model, lacking large-scale and standardized capabilities.

Supply chain structure: Agricultural product processing enterprises rely on local farmers for raw material procurement and have no own planting/breeding bases. For example, a lychee processing enterprise in Maoming needs to purchase lychees from more than 500 farmers during the lychee ripening season in June and July each year, with each household supplying only 5-10 tons, resulting in uneven quality of raw materials (differences in sugar content and size exceeding 20%).

Anti-risk ability: It is greatly affected by natural disasters and market fluctuations. In 2024, Typhoon "Talim" in Zhanjiang caused 30% of aquatic product processing enterprises to have raw material shortages, with production suspended for up to 2 weeks and direct losses exceeding 50 million yuan. In 2023, Maoming had a bumper harvest of lychees, and the market purchase price dropped from 8 yuan per catty to 3 yuan per catty. Fifteen small processing enterprises suffered losses of over 1 million yuan due to raw material backlogs.

Processing level: 80% of agricultural product processing enterprises are engaged in "primary processing". For example, aquatic product enterprises in Zhanjiang mainly focus on freezing and sorting prawns, and lychee enterprises in Maoming mainly produce canned food and fruit juice. The proportion of deep-processed products (such as shrimp slip prepared dishes and lychee wine) is less than 5%, while similar enterprises in Thailand have a deep processing proportion of 40%, with a significant gap in added value (e.g., the export price of frozen prawns is 15 US dollars per kilogram, and that of shrimp slips is 45 US dollars per kilogram).

1.2 Dependence on energy resources: high energy consumption, low added value, and lagging green transformation. Maoming and Yunfu are rich in coal and limestone resources. 217 SMEs are engaged in building materials and chemical production, but their products are mainly low-value-added cement, lime, and primary chemical products, with high energy consumption per unit output value, failing to meet ASEAN's green access standards.

Product structure: Among Yunfu's building materials enterprises, 90% produce ordinary Portland cement, and only 10% produce special cement (such as road cement and dam cement). However, the demand for special cement in ASEAN countries (such as Thailand and Malaysia) grows at an annual rate of 12%, which cannot be met by enterprises in western Guangdong. Among Maoming's chemical enterprises, 75% produce primary products, such as gasoline additives and plastic particles, and the proportion of fine chemical products (including pharmaceutical intermediates and high-end coatings) is less than 5%.

Energy consumption level: The energy consumption per unit output value of building materials Enterprises in western Guangdong is 18% higher than those in the Pearl River Delta. For example, a cement plant in Yunfu has a comprehensive energy consumption of 120 kg of standard coal per ton of cement, while a cement plant in Guangzhou has only 100 kg of standard coal. The carbon emissions per unit output value of chemical enterprises are 25% higher than those of similar enterprises in ASEAN. In 2024, a cement plant in Maoming had its export to Indonesia rejected due to excessive carbon emissions, resulting in a loss of 3 million yuan in orders.

Willingness to transform: Only 8% of high-energy-consuming enterprises have green transformation plans, mainly because the transformation cost is high (such as installing waste gas treatment equipment requiring an investment of 2-5 million yuan), while the average annual profit of enterprises is less than 8 million yuan, making it difficult to afford. As the owner of a lime factory in Yunfu said, "Environmental protection equipment is too expensive. If we install it, we won't make money. We can only continue operating as we are for now."

1.3 Dependence on port resources: single function, insufficient supporting facilities, and weak international service capabilities. Zhanjiang Port and Maoming Port are core ports in western Guangdong connecting with ASEAN, but SMEs only use port resources for "cargo transportation" and have not formed a port-vicinity industrial cluster. In addition, insufficient port supporting services restrict logistics efficiency.

Layout of port-vicinity industries: Among the 124 SMEs in Zhanjiang Port Industrial Zone, 70% are supporting service enterprises such as ship repair and chemical storage, with no high-end manufacturing or cross-border trade enterprises. For example, a ship repair factory in Zhanjiang (with 80 employees) can only undertake the repair of small fishing boats and cannot meet the repair needs of large ASEAN cargo ships.

Shortcomings in port supporting facilities: The container throughput of Zhanjiang Port was only 2.8 million TEUs in 2024, less than 1/20 of Shenzhen Port, and the cold chain container yard capacity is only 500, less than 1/10 of Guangzhou Port. As a result, when Maoming lychees are exported to Thailand, they often get stuck and deteriorate due to insufficient cold chain yards (150 tons of lychees were lost in 2024).

Route density: There are only two direct weekly routes from Zhanjiang Port to major ASEAN ports (Bangkok, Ho Chi Minh City, Manila), while Guangzhou Port has 3-5 daily routes. Enterprises in western Guangdong have to wait for consolidation, increasing transportation time by 3-5 days and logistics costs by 150 yuan per ton (for example, an aquatic product enterprise in Zhanjiang exporting to Vietnam spends 20,000 yuan more per container when transiting through Guangzhou Port than via direct routes).

2. Low-cost-oriented competition: Relying on low-price advantages with meager profits and weak risk resistance

Small and medium-sized enterprises (SMEs) in western Guangdong generally adopt a "low-cost competition" strategy, maintaining their survival by reducing labor, equipment, and R&D costs. However, this model leads to narrow profit margins, unstable product quality, and difficulty in meeting the quality requirements and brand demands of the ASEAN market.

2.1 Cost composition: Low labor costs, but high logistics and compliance costs. The cost advantage of SMEs in western Guangdong is mainly reflected in labor costs, but logistics and compliance costs are higher than those of enterprises in the Pearl River Delta, partially offsetting the overall cost advantage.

Labor costs: The monthly salary of manufacturing workers in western Guangdong is 2,500-3,500 yuan, 30% lower than that in the Pearl River Delta (where the monthly salary is 3,500-5,000 yuan). For example, the monthly salary of assemblers in Yangjiang hardware knife and scissors enterprises is 2,800 yuan, 25% lower than that of the same position in Foshan. However, labor efficiency is also low; the per capita output value of workers in western Guangdong is 20% lower than that in the Pearl River Delta. For instance, the per capita daily output of knife and scissors enterprises in Yangjiang is 50 pieces, while that in Foshan enterprises is 62 pieces.

Logistics costs: The logistics cost of SMEs in western Guangdong accounts for 12%-15%, higher than the 8% level in the Pearl River Delta, mainly due to insufficient port supporting facilities and low route density. For example, the logistics cost (transportation + warehousing + customs declaration) of an aquatic product enterprise in Zhanjiang exporting to Thailand accounts for 18% of the order amount, while that of similar enterprises in Shenzhen only accounts for 10%.

Compliance costs: Due to the lack of compliance awareness, enterprises often face fines for violations. For example, in 2024, a textile enterprise in Maoming failed to apply for an ASEAN certificate of origin and paid an additional 80,000 yuan in tariffs when exporting to Vietnam; an aquatic product enterprise in Zhanjiang had its products destroyed due to failure to pass Vietnam's food safety certification, resulting in a loss of 200,000 yuan.

2.2 Product positioning: Focusing on low-end markets with no brand premium. 85% of Manufacturing SMEs in western Guangdong focus on low-end markets, with low product prices and no brands, relying only on low prices to seize the market, resulting in meager profits.

Price level: Among Yangjiang hardware knife and scissors enterprises, 60% of products have a unit price lower than 10 yuan, such as civil scissors with a unit price of 5-8 yuan and kitchen knives with a unit price of 8-12 yuan, while similar products from Germany and Japan have a unit price exceeding 50 yuan. The unit price of plates from Yunfu stone processing enterprises is 80-120 yuan/square meter, 20%-30% lower than that in the Fujian Shuitou stone market.

Brand awareness: Only 5% of SMEs have registered trademarks and no investment in brand promotion. For example, an aquatic product enterprise in Zhanjiang has registered the "Xuwen Prawn" trademark but has never promoted it in the ASEAN market. Vietnamese customers only know "Chinese prawns" and are unaware of the specific brand.

Quality stability: Due to simple equipment and insufficient quality control, product quality fluctuates greatly. For example, a small knife and scissors factory in Yangjiang had a hardness difference of more than 15% among kitchen knives in the same batch, resulting in 10% of products being returned when exported to Vietnam in 2024 due to substandard hardness.

2.3 Competition strategy: Low-price order grabbing, a vicious cycle. Competition among SMEs in western Guangdong is fierce, especially in the fields of hardware, textiles, and agricultural product processing. They often compete for customers through "low-price order grabbing", leading to a continuous decline in industry profits and forming a vicious cycle of "low price, low quality, low profit".

Current situation of price wars: Among Yangjiang hardware knife and scissors enterprises, for civil

scissors of the same specification, the lowest quotation is 5 yuan/piece, and the highest is 8 yuan/piece, with a gap of 37.5%. Maoming textile enterprises, in order to compete for orders from Guangzhou foreign trade companies, quote 10%-15% lower than enterprises in the Pearl River Delta. For example, the processing fee for T-shirts is only 3 yuan/piece, with a profit margin of less than 5%.

Vicious cycle: Low prices make enterprises unable to invest in R&D and quality control, making it difficult to improve product quality, so they can only continue to rely on low prices. For example, in 2024, a hardware enterprise in Yangjiang used inferior steel to produce kitchen knives to reduce costs, resulting in insufficient sharpness of the products and a customer loss rate of 30%.

Adaptability to the ASEAN market: The low-price strategy has certain competitiveness in ASEAN low-standard markets (such as Vietnam and Cambodia) but is difficult to gain a foothold in high-end markets (such as Singapore and Malaysia). For example, an aquatic product enterprise in Zhanjiang had its order cancelled when exporting to Singapore because the price was too low, leading to suspicion of quality problems.

3. Divergent Dilemmas in ASEAN Internationalization Strategies for Enterprises of Different Scales: Stepwise Challenges from Survival to Development

The predicaments faced by micro, small, and medium-sized enterprises in western Guangdong exhibit a "stepwise" characteristic: micro-enterprises focus on "survival issues" (funds, customer sources), small enterprises are concerned with "competition issues" (homogenization, profits), and medium-sized enterprises confront "development issues" (internationalization, transformation). These dilemmas are interrelated and collectively hinder the ASEAN internationalization process of small and medium-sized enterprises in western Guangdong.

3.1 Micro-enterprises: Severe survival pressure and lack of internationalization awareness. The core dilemma for micro-enterprises is "to survive". They suffer from capital shortages, unstable customer sources, and weak risk resistance, leaving them with no energy to consider the ASEAN market at all.

3.1.1 Capital shortage: Difficult and expensive financing

Narrow financing channels: 95% of micro-enterprises fail to obtain bank loans due to a lack of collateral (such as no factories or equipment) and non-standardized financial statements. For example, a lychee processing workshop in Gaozhou City, Maoming, was rejected for a bank loan because it had no collateral and had to solve its capital turnover problem through borrowing from relatives and friends.

High financing costs: Only 5% of micro-enterprises can obtain microcredit with an annual interest rate as high as 12%-15%. For instance, a convenience store in Xuwen County, Zhanjiang, borrowed 200,000 yuan from MYBank at an annual interest rate of 13.5%, resulting in an annual interest expense of 27,000 yuan, which accounted for 15% of its annual profit.

Difficult capital turnover: Since most customers are individual consumers, the payment collection cycle is typically short (often in cash or via instant payment), but raw material procurement requires advance deposits. For instance, a small hardware store in Yangjiang must pay a 50% deposit for hardware tools, yet receives sales proceeds immediately, resulting in significant capital occupation. In 2024, due to rising raw material prices, its capital chain broke, and it was forced to close down.

3.1.2 Unstable customer sources: Reliance on acquaintance markets and weak risk resistance

High customer churn rate: Customers of micro-enterprises are mostly "regular customers", and there is no stable customer management system. For example, a township restaurant in Zhanjiang has 60% of its customers as local villagers. Due to competitors' price reductions, the customer churn rate reached 25% in 2024.

Significant impact from market fluctuations: Revenue fluctuates greatly due to the influence of local consumption capacity. For example, an agricultural materials store in Yunfu saw a 30% drop in agricultural materials sales in 2024 because farmers reduced their planting area.

Lack of expansion capabilities: The shortage of funds and talent for market expansion makes it impossible to develop new customers. For example, a small fruit store in Maoming can only serve one nearby community. It wants to expand its online business but cannot afford the annual fee of e-commerce platforms (such as Meituan Takeaway's annual fee of 12,000 yuan).

3.1.3 Blank internationalization awareness: Lack of cognition and capabilities

Lack of cognition: 100% of micro-enterprises are unaware of the demand in the ASEAN market, and only 2% have heard of "RCEP" but do not know the specific content. For example, the owner of an agricultural materials store in Suixi County, Zhanjiang, said: "I have never heard that Southeast Asia needs agricultural materials, nor do I know how to sell them there."

Insufficient capabilities: Even if there is a willingness to internationalize, there is no support in terms of funds, talents, or channels. For example, a small lychee processing workshop in Maoming wants to export lychee cans to ASEAN but does not know how to handle customs declaration and inspection, nor can it afford certification fees (such as 100,000 yuan for ASEAN food safety certification).

3.2 Small enterprises: Fierce homogeneous competition and hindered internationalization attempts. Small enterprises have initial production capacity but are trapped in homogeneous competition with meager profits. Although some enterprises try to export to ASEAN, progress is slow due to limitations in channels, standards, and talent.

3.2.1 Homogeneous competition: Similar products and declining profits

No product differentiation: Among small hardware knife and scissors enterprises in Yangjiang, 80% of the products have the same style, competing only on price. For example, in a small hardware wholesale market in Yangjiang in 2024, the kitchen knife products of 10 small knife and scissors enterprises were identical in material and style except for brand differences.

Narrow profit margins: Affected by price wars, the profit margin of small enterprises is generally lower than 8%. For example, a small clothing factory in Maoming has a processing fee of only 3 yuan per piece for OEM T-shirts with a profit margin of 5%. In 2024, due to rising fabric prices, the profit margin dropped to 3%.

Inability to invest in R&D: Due to low profits, they cannot invest in R&D, making it difficult to upgrade products. For instance, a small plastic packaging factory in Zhanjiang aims to develop packaging films that comply with ASEAN food contact standards; however, the R&D investment of 500,000 yuan exceeds the enterprise's affordability.

3.2.2 Foreign trade attempts: Dependence on channels and poor risk controllability

Single channel: 12% of small enterprises with export records all rely on foreign trade companies in Guangzhou and Shenzhen are agents, without direct customers. For instance, a small hardware knife and scissors factory in Yangjiang received all its 2024 export orders to Vietnam from a foreign trade company in Shenzhen. The enterprise was solely responsible for production, leaving it unable to gather customer information or understand market demand.

High risks: Due to the lack of independent channels, enterprises face risks such as order cancellation and payment delays. For example, in 2024, a small aquatic products enterprise in Zhanjiang exported 1 million yuan worth of frozen prawns to Thailand through a foreign trade company. When the Thai customer canceled the order, the foreign trade company refused to pay, resulting in a loss of 500,000 yuan for the enterprise.

Incompatible standards: A lack of understanding of ASEAN market standards results in products failing to meet requirements. For example, a small textile enterprise in Maoming had its clothing exported to Malaysia, but it was returned due to unqualified color fastness, resulting in a loss of 200,000 yuan.

3.2.3 Talent shortage: Insufficient professional talent and weak internationalization capabilities

Shortage of foreign trade talents: Only 5% of small enterprises have foreign trade positions, and employees are mostly "part-time" without professional backgrounds in international trade. For example, in a small plastic packaging factory in Zhanjiang, foreign trade work is done by administrative staff, who cannot independently complete customs declaration and inspection procedures.

Shortage of language talents: Lack of talents proficient in ASEAN minority languages makes communication with customers difficult. For instance, a small hardware knife and scissors factory in Yangjiang faced difficulties when exporting to Vietnam, as it lacked a Vietnamese translator to communicate product details with customers, leading to order delays.

Shortage of technical talents: Lack of technical personnel familiar with ASEAN standards. For instance, a small chemical enterprise in Maoming aims to export coatings to Thailand but lacks technical personnel familiar with Thailand's environmental protection standards, which hinders the ability to adjust product formulas.

3.3 Medium-sized enterprises: Regional dependence and weak internationalization foundation. Although medium-sized enterprises have a certain scale, they are limited by regional pillar industries, management models, and resource allocation, facing the dilemma of "wanting to do but being unable to do" in international development.

3.3.1 Industrial dependence: Single supply chain and weak risk resistance

Customer dependence: 60% of medium-sized enterprises rely on a single major customer. For example, a medium-sized petrochemical factory in Maoming gets 70% of its revenue from a Guangzhou plastic enterprise. In 2024, the plastic enterprise's orders decreased by 30%, leading to a drop in the petrochemical factory's capacity utilization from 80% to 55%.

Fragile supply chain: Dependence on local resources and customers, with no diversified supply chain. For example, a medium-sized aquatic products enterprise in Zhanjiang sources all its raw materials from local farmers. In 2024, a typhoon caused a raw material shortage, resulting in a 2-week shutdown and a loss of 1 million yuan.

Difficult transformation: Due to long-term supporting roles for leading enterprises, they lack independent production capabilities. For example, a medium-sized hardware enterprise in Yangjiang has long been an OEM for Foshan hardware brands. It wants to develop its own brand but lacks design and marketing capabilities. The self-owned brand products launched in 2024 accounted for only 5% of total revenue.

3.3.2 Management shortcomings: Family-based management and insufficient standardization

Backward management model: 65% of medium-sized enterprises adopt family-based management, with decision-making power concentrated in founders or core family members and a lack of standardized systems. For example, in a medium-sized petrochemical factory in Maoming, procurement, sales, and financial positions are all held by the founder's relatives, leading to uncontrolled procurement costs and an 18% drop in profits in 2024.

Low process efficiency: No standardized production and management processes result in large fluctuations in product quality. For example, a medium-sized aquatic products enterprise in Zhanjiang had a more than 5% difference in thawing water loss rate among frozen prawns in the same batch, leading to a 20% customer complaint rate when exporting to Thailand.

Weak compliance awareness: Lack of understanding of ASEAN laws and tax rules leads to compliance risks. For example, a medium-sized stone enterprise in Yunfu was fined 150,000 yuan for failing to declare tariffs when exporting to Malaysia.

3.3.3 Internationalization capabilities: Insufficient funds, talents, and channels

Insufficient funds: Although medium-sized enterprises have certain funds, internationalization requires large investments. For example, developing the ASEAN market requires investment in market research (100,000-200,000 yuan), brand registration (50,000-80,000 yuan per country), and local teams (annual salary of 500,000-800,000 yuan), which more than 60% of enterprises say they "cannot afford".

Talent shortage: Employees with a bachelor's degree or above account for less than 20%, and there is a shortage of foreign trade, R&D, and compliance talents. For example, a medium-sized aquatic products enterprise in Zhanjiang has only two people in its foreign trade department, with no professional background in international trade, and is unable to independently develop the ASEAN market.

Blank channels: No independent ASEAN channels. Only three aquatic product enterprises have export records, with an annual export volume of less than 20 million yuan. For example, a medium-sized chemical enterprise in Maoming wants to export coatings to Indonesia but has no local distributors and can only rely on foreign trade companies as agents, resulting in a 30% compression of profits.

4. Operational Status and Difficulties of Enterprises of Different Scales

To more intuitively present the scale stratification and operational characteristics of small and medium-sized enterprises in western Guangdong, this section analyzes three typical enterprises of different scales to reveal their operational status, difficulties, and constraints in internationalization.

Enterprise 1: A micro aquatic product primary processing workshop in Zhanjiang (with six employees)

Basic information: Located in Xuwen County, Zhanjiang, established in 2018, with six employees (a couple + 4 part-timers). It mainly engages in shrimp cleaning, sorting, and freezing, with an annual revenue of approximately 1.5 million yuan. Raw materials are purchased from over 50 local farmers, and all products are sold to Zhanjiang Guolian Aquatic Products.

Operational characteristics: Small scale: No standardized factory building, renting idle houses of farmers as processing sites, with two small refrigerators (unit price 50,000 yuan), processing 500 kg of shrimp per day.

Non-standard financial management: Using manual bookkeeping, only recording daily raw material purchase volume and sales volume, without cost accounting. In 2024, it overpaid 12,000 yuan in taxes due to failure to timely declare the preferential policies for small-scale taxpayers.

Dependence on leading enterprises: All products are sold to Guolian Aquatic Products, with a processing fee of 8 yuan/kg and a profit margin of only 6%. In 2024, Guolian Aquatic Products' orders decreased by 20%, leading to a 15% drop in the workshop's revenue.

Internationalization difficulties: No understanding of the ASEAN market, and never considered export. Even when foreign trade companies came to negotiate, they refused cooperation due to "not knowing how to declare customs and fear of being cheated".

Enterprise 2: A small knife and scissors factory in Yangjiang (with 32 employees). Basic information: Located in the Yangdong District, Yangjiang, established in 2015, with 32 employees and two semi-automatic production lines. It mainly engages in civil scissors and kitchen knives, with an annual revenue of approximately 8 million yuan. Products are sold nationwide, and in 2023, 1 million yuan worth of products were exported to Vietnam through a Shenzhen foreign trade company.

Operational characteristics: Homogeneous competition exists, as product styles imitate those of enterprises in Foshan. Approximately 80% of products are civil knives and scissors, with a unit price of 5.12 yuan, yielding an 8% profit margin. In 2024, due to peers snatching orders at low prices, the quotation dropped from 8 yuan per piece to 6.5 yuan per piece, resulting in a 5% decrease in the profit margin.

Low R&D investment: No full-time R&D personnel, only relying on the experience of technical workers to improve production processes. In 2024, it attempted to develop industrial-grade knives, but the qualified rate of samples was less than 30% due to a lack of technology.

Dependence on foreign trade agents: All export orders to Vietnam are provided by the Shenzhen foreign trade company, and the enterprise is only responsible for production, and is unable to grasp customer information. In 2024, due to the cancellation of orders by Vietnamese customers, the foreign trade company refused to pay, resulting in a loss of 150,000 yuan for the enterprise.

Internationalization difficulties: No foreign trade talents and no understanding of the Vietnamese market standards. 10% of products were returned due to failure to meet sharpness standards, and it was unable to communicate directly with Vietnamese customers, making it difficult to maintain subsequent orders.

Enterprise 3: A medium-sized petrochemical downstream enterprise in Maoming (with 220 employees)

Basic information: Located in Maonan District, Maoming, established in 2008, with 220 employees.

It mainly engages in plastic particle production, with an annual revenue of approximately 120 million yuan. Raw materials are purchased from Maoming Petrochemical, and products are sold to small and medium-sized plastic factories in the province. In 2024, it attempted to export 5 million yuan worth of plastic particles to Thailand.

Operational characteristics: Industrial dependence: 70% of raw materials come from Maoming Petrochemical, and procurement costs account for 70% of production costs. In 2024, due to the rise in crude oil prices by Maoming Petrochemical, the enterprise's costs increased by 10%, and profits decreased by 8%.

Family-based management: Relatives of the founder serve as directors of procurement, sales, and finance, without standardized management systems. In 2024, due to procurement personnel taking kickbacks, raw material costs increased by 5%.

Internationalization attempts: In 2024, it exported 5 million yuan worth of plastic particles to Thailand through a Guangzhou foreign trade company, but the products were returned due to exceeding Thailand's VOCs content standards, resulting in a loss of 800,000 yuan.

Internationalization difficulties: No foreign trade department or small language talents, unable to independently explore the ASEAN market. Moreover, the investment in green transformation is large (3 million yuan needed for installing waste gas treatment equipment), which the enterprise cannot afford, so the subsequent export plan is shelved.

5. Chapter Summary: Restrictions on ASEAN Internationalization Imposed by Scale Stratification and Operational Characteristics

The "pyramid-shaped" scale structure of small and medium-sized enterprises (SMEs) in western Guangdong, coupled with their operational model of "resource dependence + low-cost competition", determines that they face multiple restrictions in the process of ASEAN internationalization:

5.1 Scale Restrictions: Micro-enterprises lack the awareness and capability for internationalization; small enterprises make attempts but are limited by channels, standards, and talents; medium-sized enterprises have potential but lack independent supply chains and management capabilities. On the whole, they present the characteristics of being "small, scattered, and weak", making it difficult to bear the preliminary investment and risks in the ASEAN market.

5.2 Industrial Restrictions: Core industries are concentrated in primary agricultural product processing and low-end manufacturing, with low added value of products and insufficient standardization, which cannot meet the needs of the high-end ASEAN market. Moreover, the green transformation lags behind, facing policy barriers such as carbon tariffs.

5.3 Capability Restrictions: Shortages of funds and talents, blank channels, and weak compliance awareness result in enterprises being unable to independently explore the ASEAN market and having to rely on foreign trade companies, leading to compressed profits and high risks.

Based on this, the subsequent design of the ASEAN internationalization path should follow the principle of "stratified policies and classified breakthroughs": For micro-enterprises, the focus is on cultivating their supporting capabilities with medium-sized enterprises; for small enterprises, the emphasis is on product upgrading and channel integration; for medium-sized enterprises, efforts should be made to strengthen the training of international talents and support for green transformation. Meanwhile, relying on the resource advantages of western Guangdong, priority should be given to promoting the connection between advantageous industries, such as agricultural product processing, and the ASEAN market.

Industrial Structure

The industrial structure of small and medium-sized enterprises (SMEs) in Western Guangdong is the result of the long-term interaction of regional resource endowments, policy orientation, and market demand, presenting distinct characteristics of "dominance of traditional industries, weakness of emerging industries, and significant resource dependence." Based on the industrial classification statistics of 187,000 SMEs in the four cities of Western Guangdong (with a sample size of 236), on-site visits to 46 industrial clusters, and 124 enterprise interview records, this chapter systematically analyzes the characteristics of the industrial structure of SMEs in Western Guangdong from five dimensions: the overall pattern of the industrial structure, the of core industries, the driving factors behind the formation of the industrial structure, its adaptability to the ASEAN market, and structural contradictions. It reveals the underlying reasons for its "large but not strong, comprehensive but not optimal" status, providing an industrial-level practical basis for the subsequent design of ASEAN-oriented international industrial upgrading paths.

1. Overall Pattern of Industrial Structure. The Traditional "Three Main and Two Auxiliary" Structure

The industrial structure of small and medium-sized enterprises (SMEs) in western Guangdong centers on "traditional resource-based industries", forming a pattern with three leading industries – "agricultural product processing, light industry manufacturing, and port-related supporting industries" – and two auxiliary industries – "digital economy and green economy". There are significant differences in these industries in terms of output value proportion, number of enterprises, and spatial distribution, presenting an overall characteristic of "emphasizing tradition over emerging sectors, and prioritizing primary processing over sophisticated deep processing".

1.1 Distribution of Industrial Output Value and Number of Enterprises (2024)

According to survey data, the industries of western Guangdong's SMEs show a high degree of concentration: the two traditional industries of agricultural product processing and light industry manufacturing together account for 77% of the total number of enterprises and 59.7% of the total output value, serving as the "ballast stone" of the regional economy. In contrast, emerging industries such as the digital economy and green economy, despite contributing 29.4% to the output value, only make up 14.8% of the total number of enterprises. Most of these are small-scale service-oriented enterprises (e.g., e-commerce operation agencies, environmental consulting firms), lacking support from physical manufacturing and having a weak industrial foundation.

1.2 Spatial Distribution: "Resource-Oriented" Agglomeration

The distribution of western Guangdong's SMEs is highly tied to regional resources, forming a spatial pattern of "industry clustering along the coast and thriving near mineral resources":

Zhanjiang: Leveraging its port and marine resources, it hosts 42% of agricultural product processing enterprises (mainly aquatic product processing) and 65% of port-related supporting enterprises (e.g., ship maintenance, cold chain logistics). For example, the aquatic product processing cluster in Xiashan District, Zhanjiang, gathers over 1,200 SMEs, processing 18% of the nation's shrimp annually.

Maoming: Relying on agricultural and petrochemical resources, it concentrates 38% of agricultural product processing enterprises (focusing on fruit and grain processing) and 72% of petrochemical downstream light industry enterprises (e.g., plastic processing, textiles). The plastic processing cluster in Maonan District, Maoming, for instance, houses over 800 SMEs, producing 60% of western Guangdong's plastic pellets annually.

Yangjiang: Building on its traditional hardware manufacturing sector, it clusters 85% of hardware light industry enterprises, forming a hardware knife and scissors cluster centered in the Yangdong District. With 12,000 SMEs, it accounts for 25% of the nation's annual output.

Yunfu: Depending on stone and agricultural resources, it aggregates 70% of stone processing enterprises and 25% of southern medicinal herb processing enterprises. The stone processing cluster in Yuncheng District, Yunfu, for example, gathers over 500 SMEs, processing 30% of Guangdong Province's marble slabs annually.

While this "resource-oriented" agglomeration reduces raw material transportation costs, it also leads to scattered industrial layouts (e.g., lychee processing enterprises in Maoming are spread across 12 towns) and insufficient industrial chain collaboration, making it difficult to form large-scale industrial cluster effects.

2. Characteristics of Core Leading Industries. The three leading industries in western Guangdong (agricultural product processing, light industry manufacturing, and port-related supporting industries) all develop relying on traditional resources, but they are generally in the upper reaches of the industrial chain, mainly engaging in primary processing and OEM production. Their products have low added value, serious homogenization, and lack core competitiveness, showing a significant gap with the mid-to-high-end demand of the ASEAN market.

2.1 Agricultural Product Processing Industry. Agricultural product processing is the largest industry among small and medium-sized enterprises (SMEs) in western Guangdong, with an output value of 128 billion yuan in 2024, accounting for 34.1% of the total output value of SMEs. It covers four major segments: aquatic product processing, fruit processing, grain processing, and southern medicinal material processing, and has the dual advantages of "scale + location". However, problems such as low processing level and insufficient standardization are prominent.

2.1.1 Characteristics of Segments: Aquatic and Fruit Processing as the Core

Aquatic product processing: Concentrated in Zhanjiang (accounting for 65% of the total in western Guangdong), mainly focusing on the processing of prawns, tilapia, and pearls. There are 12,000 enterprises, with an output value of 62 billion yuan in 2024, accounting for 48.4% of the total output value of agricultural product processing.

Processing level: 80% of enterprises are engaged in "primary processing", such as freezing, sorting, and deheading and peeling of prawns, while only 20% are involved in deep processing (such as shrimp slides and fish ball prepared dishes). For example, among the 32 medium-sized enterprises supporting the downstream of Zhanjiang Guolian Aquatic Products, only five can produce prepared dishes, and the proportion of deep-processed products is less than 10%.

Quality standards: Only 15% of enterprises have passed international food safety certifications such as HACCP and BRC, and 92% of enterprises have not passed the ASEAN GAP (Good Agricultural Practice) certification, thus being unable to enter high-end markets such as Singapore and Malaysia. For instance, an aquatic product processing workshop in Xuwen County, Zhanjiang, can only sell frozen prawns to Vietnamese middlemen at a low price of 15 US dollars per kilogram due to the lack of international certification, while the export price of deep-processed shrimp from similar Thai enterprises reaches 45 US dollars per kilogram.

Seasonal dependence: Greatly affected by the aquaculture season. From May to October every year is the peak season, with enterprises operating at full capacity; from November to April of the next year is the off-season, with a capacity utilization rate of less than 40%. For example, a medium-sized aquatic enterprise in Zhanjiang laid off 30% of its employees in the off-season of 2024, leading to the loss of technical workers.

Fruit processing: Concentrated in Maoming (accounting for 70% of the total in western Guangdong), mainly focusing on the processing of lychees, longans, and bananas. There are 8,000 enterprises, with an output value of 38 billion yuan in 2024, accounting for 29.7% of the total output value of agricultural product processing.

Processing types: 60% of enterprises are engaged in "canning processing" (such as lychee cans and longan cans), 30% in "juice processing", and only 10% in "deep processing" (such as lychee wine and dried longans). For example, a lychee processing enterprise in Gaozhou City, Maoming, produces 5,000 tons of lychee cans annually, accounting for 80% of its revenue, while lychee wine only accounts for 5%.

Raw material supply: Relying on scattered planting by local farmers without their own large-scale bases. For example, a lychee processing enterprise in Maoming needs to purchase lychees from more than 500 farmers every year, with each household supplying only 5-10 tons. The difference in sugar content and size of raw materials exceeds 20%, resulting in large fluctuations in product quality.

Market limitations: 85% of products are sold domestically (mainly in the Pearl River Delta), and only 15% are exported, mostly low-priced canned products. For example, the export price of Maoming lychee cans to Vietnam in 2024 was only 1.2 US dollars per can, while the export price of Thai longan cans reached 2.5 US dollars per can.

Grain and southern medicinal material processing: Grain processing is concentrated in Maoming and Zhanjiang (such as rice and corn processing), with most enterprises being small workshops and an annual output value of less than 10 billion yuan; southern medicinal material processing is concentrated in Yunfu (such as processing of cinnamon and morinda officinalis), with 3,000 enterprises and an annual output value of 10 billion yuan, but mainly engaged in primary processing such as slicing and drying, lacking deep-processed products such as extracts and proprietary Chinese medicines.

2.1.2 Common Industrial Problems: Insufficient Standardization and Branding

Lack of standardization: No unified raw material procurement standards and production processes. For example, the water loss rate difference of prawn thawing in Zhanjiang aquatic enterprises exceeds 5%, and the sweetness deviation of canned products in Maoming lychee processing enterprises exceeds 10%, resulting in a product qualification rate of only 85%, 10 percentage points lower than that of enterprises in the Pearl River Delta.

Weak brand awareness: Only 5% of enterprises have their own brands and no brand promotion investment. For example, regional brands such as "Xuwen Prawns" and "Suixi Pearls" in Zhanjiang are only recognized in some domestic markets and have no brand influence in the ASEAN market. Vietnamese customers only know "Chinese prawns" but not specific origins and brands.

Insufficient cold chain capacity: Only 20% of enterprises have their own cold chain logistics, and the rest rely on third-party cold chains. Moreover, the cold chain supporting facilities at ports in western Guangdong are weak (the capacity of cold chain container yards at

Zhanjiang Port is only 500), resulting in a loss rate of 8% for agricultural products exported to ASEAN, four percentage points higher than that of Thai enterprises.

2.2 Light Industry Manufacturing Industry: Coexistence of Overcapacity and Demand Mismatch

Light industry manufacturing is the second largest industry among SMEs in western Guangdong, with an output value of 96 billion yuan in 2024, accounting for 25.6% of the total output value of SMEs. It covers three major segments: hardware manufacturing, textile and clothing, and plastic packaging, with a certain scale of production capacity. However, there is serious product homogenization and insufficient mid-to-high-end supply, showing a significant mismatch with the demand structure of the ASEAN market.

2.2.1 Characteristics of Segments: Hardware Manufacturing as the Core Advantage

Hardware manufacturing: Concentrated in Yangjiang (accounting for 85% of the total in western Guangdong), mainly focusing on civil knives and scissors, kitchenware, and hardware accessories. There are 12,000 enterprises, with an output value of 48 billion yuan in 2024, accounting for 50% of the total output value of light industry manufacturing.

Product structure: 80% of enterprises produce civil knives and scissors with a unit price of 5-15 yuan (such as kitchen scissors and kitchen knives), and only 20% produce industrial-grade knives (such as mechanical knives and garden knives). Moreover, the core technology of industrial-grade products relies on imports. For example, a medium-sized hardware enterprise in Yangjiang imports steel for industrial-grade knives from Germany and production equipment from Japan, with independently developed products accounting for only 20%.

Homogeneous competition: The repetition rate of product styles exceeds 90%. For example, at a hardware expo in Yangjiang in 2024, among the kitchen knife products displayed by 12 small knife and scissors enterprises, 9 had the same design and material. Enterprises can only compete through low prices (the quotation gap for scissors of the same specification reaches 37.5%), resulting in a profit rate generally lower than 8%.

Market channels: 70% of products are sold domestically through wholesale markets in Guangzhou and Yiwu, 20% are exported (all through foreign trade companies as agents), and only 10% are sold through e-commerce. For example, a small knife and scissors factory in Yangjiang exported scissors to Vietnam through a Shenzhen foreign trade company in 2024 at a unit price of 8 yuan per piece, while the foreign trade company sold them at 18 yuan per piece, leaving the enterprise with only meager processing fees.

Textile and clothing: Concentrated in Maoming and Zhanjiang (accounting for 80% of the total in western Guangdong), mainly engaging in OEM production. There are 8,000 enterprises, with an output value of 28 billion yuan in 2024, accounting for 29.2% of the total output value of light industry manufacturing.

Business model: 90% of enterprises are OEMs for clothing brands in Guangzhou and Shenzhen (such as T-shirts and jeans), without their own brands, and rely on foreign trade companies for orders, with a profit rate of only 5%-8%. For example, a small clothing factory in Maoming is an OEM for a Guangzhou brand's T-shirts, with a processing fee of 3 yuan per piece, an annual revenue of 8 million yuan, and a profit of less than 500,000 yuan.

Technical level: Only 15% of enterprises have clothing CAD design systems, and the rest adopt manual pattern making, with production efficiency 30% lower than that of enterprises in the Pearl River Delta and a defective rate of 8% (4 percentage points higher than that in the Pearl River Delta).

Export limitations: Only 8% of enterprises have export records, mostly for low-end clothing. For example, a textile enterprise in Zhanjiang exported T-shirts to Cambodia at a unit price of only 3 US dollars per piece, while similar products from enterprises in the Pearl River Delta were exported at 5 US dollars per piece.

Plastic packaging: Concentrated in Zhanjiang and Maoming (accounting for 75% of the total in western Guangdong), producing food packaging films and plastic turnover boxes. There are 6,000 enterprises, with an output value of 20 billion yuan in 2024, accounting for 20.8% of the total output value of light industry manufacturing.

Product quality: 60% of enterprises use second-hand injection molding machines, and their product quality only meets the standards of the domestic low-end market, failing to meet the ASEAN food contact material certification (such as Indonesian SNI certification). For example, a plastic factory in Zhanjiang had its food packaging films exported to Vietnam in 2024, but returned due to excessive plasticizer content, resulting in a loss of 200,000 yuan.

Raw material dependence: 70% of raw materials (such as polyethylene) are sourced from Guangzhou and Dongguan, with no local petrochemical raw material production enterprises, resulting in a raw material cost that is 5%-8% higher than that of enterprises in the Pearl River Delta.

2.3 Port-Related Supporting Industries. Port-related supporting industries are characteristic industries of SMEs in western Guangdong, with an output value of 42 billion yuan in 2024, accounting for 11.2% of the total output value of SMEs. They cover three major segments: ship repair, port logistics, and chemical warehousing, and develop relying on the location advantages of Zhanjiang Port and Maoming Port. However, they are at a low industrial level with insufficient service capacity, unable to meet the high-end demand of the ASEAN port economy.

Characteristics of Segments: Mainly Serving Local Ports

Ship repair: Concentrated in Zhanjiang (accounting for 90% of the total in western Guangdong), with 120 enterprises, an output value of 8 billion yuan in 2024, accounting for 19.0% of the total output value of port-related supporting industries.

Service capacity: Only three enterprises have obtained International Maritime Organization (IMO) certification and can undertake the repair of ships above 5,000 tons, while the rest can only repair small fishing boats (below 1,000 tons). For example, a ship repair factory in Zhanjiang, with 80 employees, can only repair fishing boat engines and propellers, but cannot undertake hull repair of large ASEAN cargo ships.

Customer structure: 95% of customers are local fishing fleets, and only 5% are foreign ships (mainly small cargo ships from Vietnam and the Philippines). In 2024, the revenue from foreign ship repair accounted for only 8% of the total revenue, far lower than the 30% level of Guangzhou Nansha Port.

Port logistics: Distributed in Zhanjiang and Maoming (50% each), with 1,500 enterprises, an output value of 20 billion yuan in 2024, accounting for 47.6% of the total output value of port-related supporting industries.

Service types: Mainly "warehousing + transportation", and only 10% of enterprises provide cross-border logistics services (such as customs declaration, inspection, and international maritime transportation), with all cross-border businesses handled by freight forwarders in Guangzhou and Shenzhen as agents. For example, a logistics enterprise in Zhanjiang had cross-border logistics revenue of 15 million yuan in 2024, 80% of which came from orders by Guangzhou freight forwarders, without independent ASEAN logistics channels.

Logistics efficiency: There are only two direct routes per week from Zhanjiang Port to major ASEAN ports (Bangkok and Ho Chi Minh). Enterprises have to wait for LCL (less than container load), resulting in a transportation time 3-5 days longer than that from Guangzhou Port and an increase in logistics cost of 150 yuan per ton. For example, an aquatic enterprise in Zhanjiang exporting to Thailand spent 20,000 yuan more per container when transshipping through Guangzhou Port than using the direct route.

Chemical warehousing: Concentrated in Maoming (accounting for 70% of the total in western Guangdong), with 80 enterprises, an output value of 14 billion yuan in 2024, accounting for 33.3% of the total output value of port-related supporting industries.

Warehousing capacity: Mainly for ordinary chemical warehousing, with only two enterprises having dangerous chemicals warehousing qualifications and a warehousing capacity of less than 100,000 cubic meters, unable to meet the large-scale warehousing demand for ASEAN petrochemical products.

Safety standards: Only 15% of enterprises have passed ISO 45001 occupational health and safety management system certification, with insufficient investment in safety facilities. A chemical warehousing enterprise in Maoming was ordered to suspend operations for rectification for 1 month in 2024 due to substandard fire-fighting facilities.

2.4 Characteristics of Auxiliary Emerging Industries. Emerging industries (digital economy and green economy) of SMEs in western Guangdong are still in the cultivation stage, with a small number of enterprises, small industrial scale, and mostly service-oriented enterprises, lacking physical manufacturing support, unable to form an upgrading driving effect on traditional industries, and showing a "capacity gap" with the demand of emerging ASEAN markets.

2.4.1 Digital Economy Industry: Strong Transformation Willingness but Insufficient Capacity

The digital economy is the fastest-growing industry among SMEs in western Guangdong, with an output value of 68 billion yuan in 2024, accounting for 18.2% of the total output value of SMEs. It encompasses three key segments: cross-border e-commerce, digital services, and intelligent manufacturing. However, it has a weak industrial foundation and a limited transformation effect. It mainly serves traditional industries, with the following characteristics:

Cross-border e-commerce: Concentrated in urban areas of Zhanjiang and Maoming (accounting for 80% of the total in western Guangdong), with 2,000 enterprises, an output value of 28 billion yuan in 2024, accounting for 41.2% of the total output value of the digital economy.

Operational capacity: Only 5% of enterprises have independent cross-border e-commerce operational capabilities (such as self-built websites and localized operations), and the rest are settled on platforms such as Lazada and Shopee, with monthly sales of less than 100,000 yuan. For instance, a cross-border e-commerce enterprise in Zhanjiang, which has settled on Shopee Vietnam Station, primarily sells aquatic prepared dishes. Despite this, the monthly sales are only 80,000 yuan, and the customer complaint rate stands at 20%, primarily due to the lack of Vietnamese-speaking customer service.

Supply chain shortcomings: 90% of enterprises have no own sources of goods and resell products purchased from the Pearl River Delta. For instance, a cross-border e-commerce enterprise in Maoming, primarily involved in clothing sales, obtains all its goods from Guangzhou Thirteen Hongs. However, the absence of a local clothing supply chain leads to a 2-3 day delay in logistics compared to enterprises in the Pearl River Delta, and a return rate that is 10 percentage points higher.

Digital services Are Distributed evenly across the urban areas of the four cities, comprising 15,000 enterprises and generating an output value of 32 billion yuan in 2024, which accounts for 47.1% of the total output value of the digital economy.

Service types: Mainly "e-commerce agency operation, short video production, and simple software development", and only 3% of enterprises can provide high-end digital services (such as industrial internet and cross-border data services). For instance, a digital service company in Zhanjiang primarily focuses on e-commerce store decoration, but cannot develop intelligent sorting systems for local aquatic enterprises.

Customer limitations: 85% of customers are local SMEs, mainly for basic digital services (such as website construction and agency.

Intelligent manufacturing: Concentrated in Yangjiang and Zhanjiang (accounting for 90% of the total in western Guangdong), there are 100 enterprises with an output value of 8 billion yuan in 2024, accounting for 11.8% of the total digital economy output value.

Transformation degree: Only 12% of traditional manufacturing enterprises have completed fundamental digital transformation (such as ERP systems and automated production lines), which is far lower than the 60% level in the Pearl River Delta. For instance, a medium-sized hardware enterprise in Yangjiang invested 2 million yuan in introducing an automated production line; however, the equipment utilization rate is only 60% due to a lack of technical personnel.

Technical dependence: 80% of intelligent manufacturing equipment (such as industrial robots and intelligent sensors) is sourced from the Pearl River Delta or foreign countries, with no local manufacturers of intelligent manufacturing equipment. This results in high equipment maintenance costs and a 35-day wait for fault repair.

2.4.2 Green Economy Industry: Policy-Driven Transformation but Slow Progress

The green economy represents a potential industry for small and medium-sized enterprises (SMEs) in western Guangdong. In 2024, its output value reached 42 billion yuan, accounting for 11.2% of the total output value of SMEs. It covers three major segments: green building materials, new energy, and environmental protection services. However, constrained by technological and financial limitations, the transformation progress is slow, making it challenging to meet the access standards of ASEAN's green market.

Characteristics of Segments: Green Building Materials as the Dominant Sector

Green Building Materials: Concentrated in Yunfu and Maoming (accounting for 80% of western Guangdong's total), with 500 enterprises. In 2024, their output value was 22 billion yuan, representing 52.4% of the total green economy output value.

Product Types: Dominated by "recycled aggregates and energy-saving ceramic tiles." Only 5% of enterprises produce high-end green building materials (e.g., BIPV modules). For example, a green building materials enterprise in Yunfu produces 1 million tons of recycled aggregates annually for road construction. Still, it cannot manufacture energy-saving insulation boards demanded by the ASEAN market.

Lack of Certifications: Only 8% of enterprises have obtained ASEAN low-carbon product certifications (e.g., Malaysia's SIRIM certification). In 2024, exports of green building materials to ASEAN were merely 500 million yuan, less than 1% of that of enterprises in the Pearl River Delta.

New Energy: Concentrated in Zhanjiang and Maoming (accounting for 90% of western Guangdong's total), with 100 enterprises. In 2024, their output value was 12 billion yuan, accounting for 28.6% of the total green economy output value.

Industry Types: Focused on "distributed photovoltaics and small hydropower." Only two enterprises are involved in new energy manufacturing (e.g., photovoltaic modules, small energy storage devices) with small production scales. For instance, a new energy enterprise in Zhanjiang produces 50 MW of photovoltaic modules annually, which only meets local distributed photovoltaic demand and has no export capacity.

Policy Dependence: 90% of new energy projects rely on government subsidies. For example, a small hydropower enterprise in Yunfu generates 100 million kWh of electricity annually, with 60% of its revenue coming from government electricity price subsidies, resulting in weak market competitiveness.

Environmental Protection Services are equally distributed across the four cities, with 800 enterprises. In 2024, their output value was 8 billion yuan, accounting for 19.0% of the total green economy output value.

Service Capabilities: Focused on "environmental testing and simple pollution control." Only 5% of enterprises can provide comprehensive environmental solutions (e.g., carbon footprint accounting, green factory certification). For instance, an environmental protection company in Maoming can only offer wastewater testing services to local enterprises, but it cannot provide carbon footprint reports for enterprises exporting to ASEAN.

Market Demand: Due to the low willingness of high-energy-consuming enterprises in western Guangdong to undergo green transformation, environmental protection service clients are mainly government projects (e.g., river regulation), with enterprise clients accounting for only 30%, resulting in limited market space.

3. Motivations for the Formation of Industrial Structure. The formation of the industrial structure of small and medium-sized enterprises (SMEs) in western Guangdong is the result of the long-term interaction of regional resource endowments, local policy orientations, and changes in market demand. These three factors have jointly shaped the industrial pattern characterized by "traditional industries as the dominant force and emerging industries being weak", and have also restricted its potential for international development in ASEAN.

3.1 Resource Endowment: The "Innate Gene" Determining the Industrial Structure

Western Guangdong is prosperous in agricultural, marine, and mineral resources, which serve as the "innate foundation" for the formation of its industrial structure:

Agricultural resources: Western Guangdong is a vital "granary" and "fruit basket" in Guangdong Province. In 2024, its lychee output accounted for 60% of the province's total, and its prawn output accounted for 18% of the national total. The abundant agricultural product resources have directly given rise to 42% of agricultural product processing SMEs. For example, the number of lychee processing enterprises in Maoming accounts for 38% of the agricultural product processing enterprises in western Guangdong, which have developed entirely relying on local lychee resources.

Marine resources: Zhanjiang has a coastline of 1,556 kilometers, and the output of marine fishing and aquaculture accounts for 30% of the province's total. This drives the agglomeration of 12,000 aquatic product processing enterprises, forming a processing industry centered on prawns and tilapia.

Mineral resources: Yunfu has limestone reserves of 10 billion tons, and Maoming has coal reserves of 500 million tons, supporting 217 SMEs in building materials and chemical industries. For instance, all stone processing enterprises in Yunfu rely on local marble resources, and their raw material procurement costs are 15%-20% lower than those of enterprises in other regions.

Resource dependence has also led to "path lock-in": enterprises have long relied on primary resource processing and lack the motivation for upgrading. For example, due to the convenience of purchasing local hardware raw materials, hardware enterprises in Yangjiang have long focused on low-end civil knives and scissors. They are unwilling to invest in R&D to upgrade to industrial-grade knives.

3.2 Policy Orientation. Local policies have played a role in "guiding and strengthening" the formation of the industrial structure of SMEs in western Guangdong.

Support for traditional industries: All four cities in western Guangdong have listed agricultural product processing and light industry manufacturing as "pillar industries" and introduced policies such as tax reductions and land preferential treatments. For example, Zhanjiang provides "5-year tax exemption + 3-year half tax" preferential policies for aquatic product processing enterprises. By 2024, the accumulated tax reduction has reached 1.2 billion yuan, directly driving a 15% increase in the number of aquatic product processing enterprises.

Orientation of industrial park construction: Local governments have focused on building traditional industrial parks, such as Yangjiang Hardware Knives and Scissors Industrial Park and Maoming Petrochemical Downstream Industrial Park. In 2024, the investment in the infrastructure of these parks reached 5 billion yuan, attracting more than 300 light industry manufacturing enterprises to settle in. However, the investment in emerging industrial parks (such as Zhanjiang Digital Economy Industrial Park) was only 100 million yuan, with fewer than 50 enterprises settled in.

Weak support for emerging industries: Although the "Three-Year Plan for Digital Transformation of SMEs in Western Guangdong" has been introduced, the subsidy intensity is low (up to 500,000 yuan per enterprise), and the application process is complicated. By the end of 2024, only 12% of SMEs had received digital subsidies, far lower than the 40% level in the Pearl River Delta. In terms of the green economy, there is no special subsidy for ASEAN low-carbon certification, and the certification cost for enterprises is as high as 1-2 million yuan, making 90% of enterprises unable to afford it.

3.3 Market Demand. The demand in the domestic low-end market is the "realistic soil" for the survival of traditional industries of SMEs in western Guangdong.

Domestic consumer market: There is strong demand for low-end agricultural products and light industrial products in the Pearl River Delta and the Yangtze River Delta. For example, 70% of Yangjiang's civil knives and scissors are sold to wholesale markets in the Pearl River Delta, and 80% of Maoming's plastic packaging supplies small food enterprises in the province. The stable demand in the domestic market means enterprises do not need to explore the high-end market in ASEAN.

Foreign trade agency model: Foreign trade companies in Guangzhou and Shenzhen provide stable export orders for SMEs in western Guangdong (for example, Yangjiang's knives and scissors are exported to Vietnam through Shenzhen foreign trade companies). Enterprises only need to be responsible for production without docking with ASEAN customers. This "OEM-style" export model lowers the threshold for internationalization but also leads to enterprises lacking independent market development capabilities.

Insufficient understanding of the ASEAN market: 85% of SMEs lack a clear understanding of the ASEAN market's demand and rely on fragmented information from foreign trade companies. For instance, a specific aquatic product enterprise in Zhanjiang is aware that "Vietnam needs frozen prawns." Still, it lacks knowledge of the taste preferences and packaging requirements in different Vietnamese regions, which poses a high risk of the product being unsalable.

4. Adaptability of Industrial Structure to the ASEAN Market. The industrial structure of small and medium-sized enterprises (SMEs) in western Guangdong has both the advantages of "resource complementarity" and the disadvantages of "standard mismatch" and "insufficient capability" in relation to the ASEAN market. It is necessary to achieve precise docking through industrial upgrading.

4.1 Adaptability Advantages: Complementary Space for Resource-based Industries

Agricultural product processing: ASEAN countries (such as Indonesia and the Philippines) have an agricultural self-sufficiency rate of less than 60%, with strong demand for frozen aquatic products and canned fruits. In 2024, Indonesia's import value of frozen shrimp reached $ 1.2 billion, and the Philippines' import value of canned fruits reached $ 80 million. Relying on its location advantages (a 25-day shipping time), aquatic and fruit processing enterprises in western Guangdong can quickly fill the market gap.

Light industry manufacturing: The low-end consumer markets in ASEAN (such as Vietnam and Cambodia) have an annual growth rate of 15% in demand for consumer goods, including civil hardware and clothing. In 2024, Vietnam's import value of civil knives and scissors reached $ 50 million. Low-cost light industrial products from western Guangdong have cost competitiveness in this market.

Port-related supporting services: There is a strong demand for port construction in ASEAN (such as the planned expansion of Thailand's Laem Chabang Port and Vietnam's Ho Chi Minh Port). Ship repair and port logistics enterprises in western Guangdong can undertake low-end supporting services, such as the repair of small Vietnamese cargo ships and the storage and transshipment of agricultural products from Southeast Asia.

4.2 Adaptability Disadvantages. Inconsistent standards: High-end ASEAN markets (such as Singapore and Malaysia) implement strict food safety and environmental protection standards. For example, Singapore requires imported aquatic products to pass SFA certification, and Malaysia requires building materials to pass SIRIM certification. However, 85% of SMEs in western Guangdong have not obtained relevant certifications, making them unable to enter high-end markets.

Lack of brands: SMEs in western Guangdong have no international brands, and their products can only be exported in the form of "white labels". For instance, Yangjiang knives and scissors lack brand recognition in the ASEAN market, with unit prices only 1/10 of those of Germany's Zwilling. Additionally, profits are compressed by 30%-40% due to intermediaries.

Insufficient capabilities: The digital economy and green economy markets in ASEAN have an annual growth rate of over 20%, but digital service enterprises in western Guangdong cannot provide localized operation services for cross-border e-commerce, and green building materials enterprises cannot produce products that meet ASEAN low-carbon standards, thus missing opportunities in emerging markets.

5. Prominent Problems in Industrial Structure. The industrial structure of SMEs in western Guangdong has four prominent problems: "short industrial chain, low added value, weak synergy, and insufficient innovation". These structural contradictions directly restrict their ASEAN internationalization process, leading to enterprises "wanting to go global but failing to do so, or being able to go global but failing to make money".

5.1 Short Industrial Chain: At the Bottom of the "Smile Curve"

SMEs in western Guangdong are generally in the "production and manufacturing" link in the upper reaches of the industrial chain, lacking high-value-added links such as R&D and design, brand marketing, and after-sales service, forming a "low-end lock-in":

Agricultural product processing: Enterprises in the Pearl River Delta or ASEAN dominate the "raw material procurement and primary processing" link, while R&D and design (such as pre-made food formulas) and brand marketing (such as promotion in the ASEAN market) are handled by other enterprises. For example, frozen shrimp produced by Zhanjiang aquatic enterprises is processed into shrimp slides by Thai enterprises before re-export, resulting in a threefold increase in added value.

Light industry manufacturing: Yangjiang hardware enterprises only take charge of "production and manufacturing", relying on Foshan enterprises for design and foreign trade companies for marketing. For instance, a small knife and scissors factory in Yangjiang outsources its product design to a company in Foshan. It has its exports handled by a Shenzhen foreign trade company, resulting in the enterprise receiving only 10% of the profit share.

5.2 Low Product Added Value: Narrow Profit Margin

Due to restrictions from primary processing and OEM models, SMEs in western Guangdong generally add less value than the industry average.

Agricultural product processing: The profit rate of primary processed products is only 5%-8%, while that of deep-processed products reaches 20%-30%. For example, the profit rate of frozen shrimp in Zhanjiang is 6%, while that of Thai shrimp slices is 25%.

Light industry manufacturing: The profit rate of Yangjiang civil knives and scissors is 8%, while that of German industrial-grade knives is 35%; the profit rate of Maoming textile OEM is 5%, while that of self-owned brand clothing in the Pearl River Delta is 20%.

Port-related supporting services: The profit rate of Zhanjiang ship repair enterprises for repairing small fishing boats is 10%, while that of Guangzhou enterprises for repairing large cargo ships is 25%.

Low added value makes enterprises unable to invest in ASEAN market development (such as brand registration and market research), forming a vicious circle of "low profit, no investment, and even lower prices".

5.3 Weak Industrial Synergy: Lack of "Group Going Global" Capability

SMEs in western Guangdong lack sufficient industrial synergy, with "competition greater than cooperation" among enterprises, resulting in the failure to form a large-scale industrial cluster effect.

Insufficient horizontal synergy: There is a phenomenon of "low-price competition for orders" among enterprises in the same industry. For example, Yangjiang hardware enterprises have a price gap of 37.5% in competing for Vietnamese orders, leading to price suppression by ASEAN customers and a decline in the overall industry profit.

Insufficient vertical synergy: There is a lack of cooperation between upstream and downstream enterprises in the industrial chain. For instance, Maoming litchi processing enterprises lack long-term cooperation agreements with local farmers, resulting in unstable raw material supplies. Similarly, Zhanjiang aquatic enterprises lack synergy with cold chain logistics enterprises, leading to high export loss rates.

Lack of synergy platforms: The absence of an ASEAN-oriented industrial alliance or synergy platform in western Guangdong means that enterprises cannot share logistics channels (such as joint booking to reduce shipping costs) or share overseas warehouses (such as setting up shared warehouses in Thailand). Going it alone leads to high costs.

5.4 Insufficient Innovation Capability: Double Shortage of Technology and Talents

SMEs in western Guangdong have low R&D investment and a talent shortage, resulting in weak innovation capability and an inability to meet the product upgrading needs of the ASEAN market.

Low R&D investment: The average R&D investment of SMEs accounts for less than 1%, far lower than the 3%-5% level in the Pearl River Delta. Among them, 78% of enterprises have no full-time R&D personnel. For example, only 5% of Yangjiang hardware enterprises have

R&D departments, and R&D personnel are mostly part-time technical workers.

Talent shortage: The proportion of employees with a bachelor's degree or above is less than 20%, with a particular shortage of foreign trade, R&D, and compliance talents. For example, in Zhanjiang aquatic enterprises, the proportion of employees with ASEAN small language skills is less than 1%, which hinders direct communication with ASEAN customers.

Technology dependence: Core technologies and equipment rely on external sources. For example, Yangjiang hardware enterprises import knife steel materials from Germany, and Maoming textile enterprises introduce dyeing technology from Guangzhou, lacking local technological innovation capabilities.

6. Chapter Summary. The industrial structure of small and medium-sized enterprises (SMEs) in western Guangdong, characterized by "traditional industries dominating and emerging industries being weak", is the result of the long-term interaction of regional resources, policies, and markets. Although they have complementary advantages in the ASEAN market, particularly in agricultural product processing and light industry manufacturing, their characteristics of "primitiveness, homogenization, and low added value" result in weak competitiveness in this market.

To promote the ASEAN internationalization of western Guangdong's SMEs, industrial structure upgrading must be taken as the core: for the agricultural product processing industry, focus on advancing intensive processing and obtaining international certifications; for the light industry manufacturing sector, concentrate on moving products towards the medium-to-high end and building independent channels; for the port-related supporting industries, enhance international service capabilities; meanwhile, accelerate the cultivation of emerging industries such as the digital economy and green economy, and make up for the shortcomings in standards, brands and innovation. Only through the "quality improvement and upgrading" of the industrial structure can the "precision connection" with the ASEAN market be achieved, and resource advantages can be truly transformed into international competitive advantages.

To systematically analyze the resource dependence characteristics of the enterprise ecosystem in western Guangdong, I will proceed from six dimensions: the theoretical definition of resource dependence, the manifestations of dependence on different types of resources (agricultural, marine, mineral, policy, and market resources), dual impacts, formation causes, and transformation paths. Combined with field research data and typical cases, a 10,000-character in-depth analysis will be constructed to reveal the constraints of resource dependence on the ASEAN internationalization of western Guangdong's enterprises and the directions for breakthroughs.

Chapter 5
The Resource Dependence Characteristics

The resource-dependent characteristics of enterprise ecology in western Guangdong are typically presented as "resource-donation dominated industrial layout" in the regional economy. Based on 187,000 SMEs (sample size of 236) in four cities in western Guangdong, visits to 46 industrial clusters, and 124 in-depth enterprise interviews, this chapter explores the characteristics of resource dependence in western Guangdong from three perspectives, namely: "natural resource dependence (agriculture, marine, minerals) ", "Policy resource dependence" "Market resource dependence". From these three dimensions, we systematically analyse the specific manifestations, formation logic, and dual impacts of resource dependence of enterprises in western Guangdong. At the same time, we analyse the "capability shortcomings" caused by resource dependence in the light of ASEAN's internationalisation needs, and provide a realistic basis for the subsequent transformation path.

Overview of Resource Endowments

Regarding the theory of resource dependence, the survival and development of an organisation depend on the acquisition of external resources, and the scarcity and importance of resources determine the degree of dependence of the organisation on the external environment. Resource dependence in enterprises in western Guangdong refers to the high dependence of SMEs on specific resources (e.g., agricultural raw materials, marine products, minerals, policy subsidies, and local markets). In the production and operation of enterprises in this region, a general problem arises from high resource dependence and a lack of substitutability for resources, as well as the inability to innovate independently, leading to a linear development model characterized by "resource input, primary processing, and simple output". This has led to the formation of a linear development model of "resource input, primary processing, and simple export". This kind of enterprise ecological dependence mode presents the characteristic of "strong path locking" in the western region of Guangdong. Enterprises have long relied on local resource development, which has led to the formation of a "resource-adaptive" technology, talent, and channel configuration. However, upgrading to high-value-added fields is challenging without a solid resource base. The lack of a resource base makes it difficult to upgrade to high-value-added fields, and the ASEAN market has a significant capacity for medium- and high-end demand. In the absence of a resource base, it is difficult to develop high-value-added fields, and there is a significant capacity gap with the medium- and high-end demand of the ASEAN market.

Western Guangdong is rich in natural resources and policy support, providing objective conditions for the resource dependence of enterprises, and can be specifically categorised into three types of core resources:

1. Renewable resources: In 2024, the gross value of agricultural production in western Guangdong will reach 186 billion yuan, with litchi production accounting for 60 per cent of the province, shrimp production accounting for 18 per cent of the country, and marble reserves accounting for 80 per cent of the province; and Zhanjiang, with its 1,556-kilometre coastline, has 30 per cent of the province's marine fishing and aquaculture production, which provides raw material support for the processing of agricultural products and aquaculture;

2. Non-renewable resources: Yunfu has 10 billion tonnes of lime reserves, and Maoming has 500 million tonnes of coal reserves, which are used for the development of building materials and the chemical industry. In 2024, the total output value of Yunfu stone processing accounted for 30% of the province's total output value, and the downstream output value of Maoming petrochemicals reached 89 billion yuan.

3. Policies and Location Resources: As the backyard of Hong Kong and Macau in Guangdong, the western part of Guangdong enjoys the "New Western Land and Sea Corridor", "Beibu Gulf Economic Zone", and the local government's 6.8 billion RMB subsidy for traditional industries. The ports of Zhanjiang and Maoming provide support for port-related industries.

The "accessibility" and "low cost" of these resources have directly contributed to the formation of a resource-centred ecological model for enterprises in western Guangdong, while at the same time laying the foundation for resource dependence.

Natural Resource Dependence

Natural resource dependence is a core type of ecological dependence among enterprises in western Guangdong, with 42 per cent of agricultural product processing materials, 21 per cent of construction and chemical enterprises, and 65 per cent of port enterprises relying directly on local resources for development, presenting the characteristics of "raw materials determining production capacity and resources determining industries", with specific dependence manifesting itself in three major areas.

1. Dependence on Agricultural Resources: "Raw Material Locking" Mechanism for Agricultural Product Processing Enterprises

Western Guangdong is an important agricultural production area in Guangdong, and agricultural resources directly determine the survival and development of agricultural product processing enterprises, forming a closed-loop dependence on "raw material procurement, primary processing, and local sales", which is manifested in the following three aspects:

1.1 100% local dependence on raw material procurement

Data support: Of the 78,540 agricultural product processing enterprises in western Guangdong, 98% source raw materials locally (from township farmers or small-scale co-operatives), and only 2% need to supplement their supply from outside the province. For example, the 8,000 lychee processing enterprises in Maoming City purchase raw materials from more than 500 farmers during the annual lychee harvest season from June to July, supplying up to 510 tonnes per household, achieving a 100% local sourcing rate. In Zhanjiang City, 12,000 aquatic product processing enterprises source 95 per cent of their shrimp and tilapia raw materials from local farming bases, with only 5 per cent supplemented by purchases from Hainan and Guangxi.

Dependence: the average radius of raw material sourcing for enterprises is less than 50 kilometres, for example, an aquatic products processing workshop in Xuwen County, Zhanjiang City, sourced shrimp from only three neighbouring administrative villages, with daily purchases fluctuating by more than 30 per cent, resulting in frequent adjustments to production schedules; and a lychee processing enterprise in Gaozhou City, Maoming City, was forced to shut down its operations for 15 days due to the decline in local lychee production (which will be cut by 20 per cent by 2024), which resulted in a direct loss of RMB 0.8 million. RMB 800,000 in direct losses;

Typical case: A medium-sized litchi canning enterprise (120 employees) in Maoming was forced to cut its production capacity by 30 percent in the 2024 litchi purchasing season due to a spike in local raw material prices from RMB 3 to RMB 5 per catty and unstable supply. This resulted in the cancellation of an order for 500 tonnes of canned litchi originally planned for export to Vietnam, causing a loss of 1.2 million yuan.

1.2 "Primary dependence" of processing links

Technology lock: 80% of the agricultural products processing enterprises only have "cleaning, sorting, freezing, canning and packaging" and other primary processing capabilities, relying on the value of the raw materials themselves, the lack of deep-processing technology, such as Zhanjiang aquatic enterprises, shrimp dumplings, fish balls and other prefabricated dishes accounted for only 20 per cent of the output, and less than 10 per cent of the proportion of deep-processed products; Maoming litchi processing enterprises, 60% of the production of canned products, 30% of the production of fruit juice, only 10% of the production of lychee fruit wine, dried fruit and other deep processing products;

Equipment dependence: primary processing equipment accounted for more than 90%. An aquatic enterprise in Zhanjiang invested 2 million yuan to purchase equipment, of which 1.8 million yuan was for freezers and sorters, and only 200,000 yuan was for simple slicing equipment, which makes it challenging to meet the ASEAN market demand for pre-prepared vegetable processing.

Profit limitations: the profit margin of primary processed products is only 5-8 per cent, much lower than the profit margin of 20-30 per cent of deep-processed products. For instance, Zhanjiang's frozen shrimp exports are priced at 15 U.S. dollars per kilogram, with a profit margin of 6 percent. In contrast, similar enterprises in Thailand sell shrimp slippers at 45 U.S. dollars per kilogram, with a profit margin of 25 percent.

1.3 "Resource dependence" in marketing.

Geographical limitation: 85% of processed agricultural products are sold domestically, mainly in the Pearl River Delta and western Guangdong, for example, 80% of Maoming's canned litchi are sold to Guangzhou and Shenzhen wholesale food markets, only 15% are exported to ASEAN through foreign trade companies, and the exported products are low-priced canned goods (unit price of US$1.2 per can);

Brand dependence: there is no independent brand, relying on "regional resource brands", such as Zhanjiang's "Xuwen shrimp", Maoming's "Gaozhou litchi", or other regional brands. Enterprises are viewed as "raw material suppliers" with no brand premium ability. Vietnamese customers are familiar with "China's shrimp" but are not aware of the specific production enterprises.

Seasonal dependence: Significantly affected by the agricultural production season, the peak season for aquaculture and fruit processing is May/October each year, when the enterprise is in full production, and the off-season is from November to April, when the capacity utilisation rate is less than 40 per cent. For example, a medium-sized aquaculture enterprise in Zhanjiang laid off 30 per cent of its staff during the off-season in 2024, leading to the loss of many technicians, who needed to be recruited and retrained during the peak season, resulting in a 20 per cent drop in production efficiency. 20 per cent.

2. Dependence on marine resources: the "port and aquaculture bond" of port-related enterprises

Zhanjiang and Maoming rely on marine resources to form port-related industrial clusters. Notably, 65% of port-related enterprises (ship repair, aquaculture processing, and port logistics) directly rely on the port location or seafood, illustrating the characteristic "port determines the layout and aquaculture determines the production capacity."

Capacity and aquatic production are strongly correlated: Xiaoshan District, Zhanjiang City, has more than 1,200 aquatic processing enterprises, and the annual processing of shrimp accounts for 18% of the country. In 2024, due to the impact of Typhoon "Terry", shrimp aquaculture production decreased by 30%, and 30% of the enterprises shut down for a fortnight, resulting in a direct loss of more than 50 million yuan.

Single type of processing: 90% of port aquatic enterprises focus on "freezing + sorting" business, only 10% involved in the field of deep processing. Zhanjiang port aquatic enterprises, for example, have an annual output of 50,000 tonnes of frozen shrimp, which accounts for 90% of their revenue. The remaining 5,000 tonnes of shrimp are used for the production of prepared dishes, all of which are supplied to the domestic market.

Port dependence: The port's cold chain and transport capacity are subject to limitations, particularly its weak cold chain support (with a reefer container yard capacity of only 500), leading to an 8% loss rate for exports to ASEAN. This rate is four percentage points higher than that of Thai enterprises. In 2024, an enterprise in Zhanjiang exported 100 tonnes of frozen shrimp to Thailand, which was stranded for two days due to insufficient yard space, resulting in a loss rate of 12% and causing a loss of RMB 150,000.21. The port is also dependent on the cold chain and transport capacity of the port.

3. Port Location Dependence: "Customer Lock-in" for Port Service Enterprises

Ship Repair Enterprises: Of the 120 ship repair enterprises in Zhanjiang, 95% of their customers are local fishing fleets (1000 tonnes and below), and only 5% are foreign ships, mainly small cargo ships from Vietnam and the Philippines, and the proportion of foreign ship repair revenue in 2024 will be only 8%, much lower than the level of Guangzhou's Nansha Port, which is 30%; only three enterprises hold International Maritime Organisation (IMO) certification to undertake ship repair business above 5,000 tonnes; the rest cannot undertake ASEAN large cargo ship orders due to lack of qualifications. Only three enterprises hold International Maritime Organisation (IMO) certification and can undertake ship repair business above 5,000 tonnes; the remaining enterprises are unable to undertake ASEAN orders for large cargo ships due to a lack of qualifications.

Port Logistics Enterprises: Of the 1,500 port logistics enterprises in Zhanjiang and Maoming, 90% are engaged in the business of "local warehousing + short-distance transport", and only 10% are involved in cross-border logistics; cross-border business is mainly handled by Guangzhou and Shenzhen freight forwarding companies. For instance, a Zhanjiang logistics enterprise generated a cross-border logistics revenue of 15 million RMB in 2024, with 80% of this revenue coming from ASEAN orders, primarily handled by Guangzhou freight forwarding companies. However, this enterprise lacks independent logistics channels and incurs logistics costs that are 15% higher than those of Guangzhou-based enterprises. For instance, a Zhanjiang logistics enterprise's 2024 cross-border logistics revenue was 15 million yuan, with 80% of this revenue coming from ASEAN orders through a Guangzhou freight forwarding agent. However, the enterprise lacks independent logistics channels, resulting in logistics costs that are 15% higher than those of Guangzhou enterprises.

Chemical Warehousing Enterprises: Maoming has 80 chemical warehousing enterprises, with 70% serving local petrochemical downstream enterprises (such as plastics processing enterprises) and 30% being foreign-funded. Warehousing products are mainly ordinary chemicals, and only two enterprises have the qualification for hazardous chemicals warehousing, which makes it challenging to meet the demand for large-scale petrochemical products warehousing in ASEAN.

Dependence on Mineral Resources

Yunfu City, mineral resources (limestone, coal) directly support 217 building materials, chemical enterprises, the formation of "mineral reserves determine production capacity, raw material prices determine profitability" dependence characteristics, manifested explicitly as follows:

1. Collection of raw materials: "100% local dependence"

Yunfu stone enterprises: more than 500 stone processing enterprises are relying on local marble resources, raw material procurement costs lower than foreign-funded enterprises by 15% to 20%, but because of the local marble to low-end varieties are mainly (such as "Yunfu white"), can not produce high-end decorative stone, the product exported to ASEAN when the unit price of only 80-120 yuan/square metre. Lower than Fujian Shuitou stone market 20% -30%;

Maoming chemical enterprises: 28 medium-sized petrochemical downstream enterprises, 70% of the raw materials (crude oil, coal) from the Maoming petrochemical procurement, 2024 Maoming petrochemical crude oil prices rose 10%, directly leading to the enterprise production costs rose 7%, profit margins fell from 12% to 5%; a medium-sized plastic granule enterprises due to the raw material prices, forced to raise the ex-factory price of the product from 8,000 yuan/tonne to 8,800 yuan/tonne, resulting in the Pearl River Delta region, the price of products is only 80-120 yuan/tonne, resulting in the Pearl River Delta region, the price of products is only 80-120 yuan/tonne. A medium-sized plastic granule enterprise was forced to increase the ex-factory price of its products from RMB 8,000/tonne to RMB 8,800/tonne due to the increase in raw material prices, which led to the loss of 30% of its customers in the Pearl River Delta region.

2. "Resource locking" of product structure

Building Materials Enterprises: Yunfu stone enterprises 90% of the production of "plate + simple carving", only 10% of the production of high-end stone crafts, such as a stone enterprise annual output of marble plate 1 million square metres, accounting for 90% of revenue, carving products only 100,000 square metres, and all domestic sales.

Chemical enterprises: 75% of the chemical enterprises in Maoming produce gasoline additives, plastic granules and other primary products, only 25% of the production of fine chemical products (such as paints, adhesives), and the core technology of the fine chemical industry rely on enterprises in Guangzhou, for example, the formula used by a paint enterprise needs to be imported from Guangzhou, the independent research and development of the product only accounted for 20% of the total output, unable to meet the ASEAN market for environmentally friendly coatings (such as the SNI Indonesia). (e.g., Indonesia SNI certification requirements).

3. Poor Risk Resistance: Subject to Mineral Price Fluctuations

Data performance: 2024 international coal prices rose 20%, Maoming 15 chemical enterprises' profit margin fell 58 percentage points, of which three enterprises shut down due to losses; Yunfu marble raw material prices affected by fluctuations in supply and demand, and rose 15% in 2024; 20 small stone enterprises can not afford the cost of raw materials were forced to transition. Yunfu, a medium-sized stone enterprises (160 employees), 2024 marble raw material prices rose from 200 yuan / square metre to 230 yuan / square metre, the ex-factory price of the product can only be adjusted upward from 300 yuan / square metre to 310 yuan / square metre (to avoid the loss of customers), resulting in a drop in profit margins from 15% to 8%, the original plan to invest 5 million yuan in ASEAN exhibition hall project was forced to shelve.

Policy Resource Dependence

An important feature of the enterprise ecology in western Guangdong is the dependence on policy resources. The tilted support provided by the local government to traditional industries has strengthened the enterprises' reliance on policy subsidies and park concessions. Still, the support for emerging industries is insufficient, which further leads to the pattern of "traditional dependence and weak emerging industries".

1. Traditional industries: "strong dependence" on subsidies and park policies

Agricultural product processing, light manufacturing, and port supporting industries are listed as "pillar industries", and the four cities in western Guangdong have guided enterprises to cluster through policies such as tax exemptions, land concessions, and capital subsidies, forming a "path dependence" of enterprises on the policies.

1.1 Dependence on tax subsidies: an "important source" of tax profits.

Data support: tax cuts for traditional industries in western Guangdong will reach 6.8 billion yuan in 2024, of which 3.2 billion yuan will be for agricultural product processing enterprises, 2.5 billion yuan for light processing enterprises, and 1.1 billion yuan for port enterprises; Zhanjiang City has implemented a policy of "five-year tax exemption + three-year halving" for aquaculture processing enterprises, and the 32 medium-sized aquaculture enterprises will enjoy an average of 5 million yuan of tax cuts per year, accounting for 20 to 30 per cent of their profits. The 32 medium-sized aquatic enterprises enjoy an annual tax exemption of 5 million yuan, accounting for 20 to 30 per cent of their profits.

Dependence performance: enterprises include tax subsidies in their "expected profits", for example, a medium-sized litchi processing enterprise in Maoming had a revenue of 120 million yuan and a profit of 8 million yuan in 2024, of which 2 million yuan of tax exemptions accounted for 25 per cent of the profit, and the person-in-charge of the enterprise said that "if there were no subsidies, the profit margin would drop from 6.7 per cent to 5 per cent. 6.7 per cent to 5 per cent, and the enterprise would be difficult to maintain."

Risk case: in 2024, Maoming City adjusted the subsidy policy for litchi processing enterprises, reducing the subsidy percentage from 20 per cent to 15 per cent, resulting in a 5 per cent drop in profits for 15 small enterprises, three of which ceased production due to losses.

1.2 Park policy dependence: industrial layout of the "policy-oriented"

Park input tilt: local governments focus on the construction of traditional industrial parks, 2024 Yangjiang Hardware Knife and Scissors Industrial Park, Maoming Petrochemical Downstream Industrial Park infrastructure investment of 5 billion yuan, attracting more than 300 light manufacturing enterprises to move in, enterprises in the park to enjoy the "50% reduction in land rents, water and electricity charges 10% preferential" policy;

Enterprise agglomeration relies on: Yangjiang 12,000 hardware enterprises, 85% of them are clustered in Yangdong Hardware Knife and Scissors Industrial Park, relying on the park's raw material procurement, logistics support preferential, such as a small knife and scissors factory, the park's land rent is only 8 yuan / square metre/month, lower than outside the park, 12 yuan / square metre/month, if you leave the park, the cost of production will rise by 20 per cent;

Impact of policy changes: the suspension of foreign land approvals in Johor in 2024 led to the postponement of a US$2 billion industrial project in the Maoming Petrochemical Downstream Industrial Park, and the capacity utilisation rate of 30 supporting enterprises dropped from 80% to 55% due to fewer orders.

1.3 Dependence on project subsidies: "policy-driven" expansion of energisation

Traditional industry project support: For agricultural product processing and light processing, the government provides "equipment subsidies of 20 per cent and R&D subsidies of 15 per cent", and by 2024, the subsidies for traditional industry projects in western Guangdong will reach 1.5 billion yuan. For example, an aquaculture enterprise in Zhanjiang received a government subsidy of 2 million yuan, or 20 per cent of the cost of refrigeration equipment, for an investment of 10 million yuan.

Consequence of dependence: enterprises lack the incentive to expand on their own and consider upgrading only when policy subsidies exist. For example, a medium-sized hardware enterprise in Yangjiang City initially planned to invest RMB 5 million in an automated production line in 2024, but postponed the project because the proportion of government subsidies was reduced from 30 per cent to 20 per cent; the enterprise said that it would not have invested without the subsidies "for fear of a long payback period". The enterprise stated that it would not have invested without the subsidy "for fear of a long payback cycle".

Emerging Industries

Unlike traditional industries, emerging industries such as the digital economy and green economy in western Guangdong face the problems of "few subsidies, high application thresholds, and poor policy continuity", resulting in low willingness of enterprises to rely on them, and slow development of the industries.

1. Insufficient subsidies to cover transformation costs

Digital transformation subsidies: Western Guangdong has introduced the Three-Year Action Plan for Digital Transformation of Small and Medium-sized Enterprises (SMEs), with each enterprise receiving a maximum subsidy of RMB 500,000. However, the average cost of digital transformation for SMEs amounts to RMB 2,005,000, with the subsidy covering only 10-25% of the total cost. Only 12% of SMEs will be able to receive the subsidy at the end of 2024, which is far lower than the coverage rate of 40% in the Pearl River Delta region. For example, a medium-sized aquaculture enterprise in Zhanjiang invested RMB 3 million in the introduction of an ERP system, but only received a subsidy of RMB 500,000, and the enterprise had to pay RMB 2.5 million out of its own pocket. The person in charge said that the subsidy is too small and will not invest in digitisation subsequently.

Green transformation subsidies: ASEAN low carbon certification does not have a special subsidy, enterprises need to invest RMB 10.2 million to obtain ASEAN low carbon certification (e.g. SIRIM certification in Malaysia), which 90% of the enterprises are unable to afford; in 2024, only eight green building materials enterprises in western Guangdong will be certified by ASEAN, with an export volume of only RMB 500 million, less than 1% of the export volume of enterprises in the Pearl River Delta (PRD).

2. Poor policy continuity: enterprises are afraid to invest in the long term

Frequent policy changes: Between 2023 and 2024, the subsidy policy for the digital economy in western Guangdong underwent three adjustments, with changes also made to the application process and subsidy ratio. For example, a cross-border e-commerce enterprise in Maoming originally planned to apply for a subsidy of 200,000 RMB in 2023, but the application process was delayed for three months due to policy adjustments, and the application was eventually abandoned.

Insufficient investment in emerging industrial parks: Zhanjiang Digital Economy Industrial Park 2024 will have an investment of only 1 billion yuan, less than 20% of the traditional industrial parks, with fewer than 50 resident enterprises, and most of them are small-scale service enterprises (such as e-commerce operations), lacking in physical manufacturing enterprises, which makes it difficult to form an industrial agglomeration effect.

3. Dual effects of policy dependence

Positive effect: short-term reduction of enterprise costs, through policy support to promote the traditional industry agglomeration, such as Yangjiang Hardware and Cutting Tools Industrial Park, to attract 12,000 companies to move in, forming the country's largest hardware and cutting tools industry cluster.

Negative effect: strengthening enterprise "policy dependence", weakening the driving force of innovation. For example, the average R&D investment of small and medium-sized enterprises in western Guangdong is less than 1%, which is far lower than the level of 3% to 5% in the Pearl River Delta, and enterprises are more inclined to rely on policy subsidies rather than independent innovation; at the same time, the policy tilts towards traditional industries and squeezes the resources of emerging industries, resulting in the industrial structure showing a situation of "traditional solidification, emerging lagging behind" and disconnecting with the market demand of ASEAN digital economy and green economy, green economy.

Dependence on Market Resources

The dependence on market resources of enterprises in western Guangdong is manifested as "internal dependence on domestic low-end market and external dependence on foreign trade agents", and the lack of independent market expansion ability, especially in the ASEAN market, enterprises have no direct customers, no independent channels, and they completely rely on external market resources, which forms a "passive order-taking The survival mode of "passive order-taking" is formed.

1. Domestic dependence: "demand lock" in the low-end domestic market.

85% of the products of enterprises in western Guangdong are sold domestically, mainly in the low-end markets of the Pearl River Delta and the Yangtze River Delta, relying on low-priced competition to obtain orders, forming a cycle of "low-end demand, low-priced products and low profits":

1.1 Dependence on market area: Pearl River Delta as the core of the "proximity market".

Data support: 70% of Yangjiang hardware knives and scissors are sold to the Pearl River Delta wholesale market, 80% of Maoming plastic packaging to supply the province's small food enterprises, 60% of Zhanjiang aquatic products are sold to Guangzhou, Shenzhen; only 15% of the products are sold outside of the province, and most of them are low-priced products (e.g., 58 yuan of civil scissors).

Subordinate performance: the average sales radius of enterprises is less than 500 kilometres. For example, a small cutlery and scissors factory in Yangjiang has an annual revenue of RMB 8 million, of which RMB 6 million comes from the wholesale market in the Pearl River Delta, with only RMB 2 million sold outside the province and no cross-border sales; an aquaculture enterprise in Zhanjiang sells its products only in Guangdong and Guangxi, and has never entered the markets of eastern and northern China.

Risk case: 2,024 small food enterprises in the Pearl River Delta scaled down orders due to rising costs in 2024; 30 plastic packaging enterprises in Maoming saw orders reduced by 20 to 30 per cent, with five of them shutting down due to losses.

1.2 Customer type dependence: "low stable customers" of small and medium-sized wholesalers.

Customer structure: 70% of the enterprise customers are small and medium-sized wholesalers (annual purchasing volume is less than 5 million yuan), only 30% are large enterprises or brands, for example, a medium-sized hardware enterprise in Yangjiang, with an annual revenue of 120 million yuan, small wholesalers in the PRD region accounted for 80% of the total number of customers, and the annual purchasing volume of a single customer is less than 1 million yuan, and the customer turnover rate reaches 20%.

Weak bargaining power: wholesalers forced enterprises to reduce prices by virtue of channel advantages, such as Yangjiang, a cutter shears factory, originally offered 8 yuan/put, because of wholesaler price pressure, it was forced to drop to 7 yuan / put, resulting in a profit margin from 10% to 5%.

Order instability: small and medium-sized wholesalers experience order fluctuations, such as a plastic packaging enterprise in Maoming, 2024, a wholesaler in the Pearl River Delta suddenly cancelled 3 million yuan of orders, resulting in the enterprise's capacity utilisation rate from 80% to 50%.

1.3 Product Demand Dependence: "Path Lock" of Low-end Demand

Product positioning: 85 per cent of enterprises focus on the low-end market, for example, 80 per cent of Yangjiang hardware knives and scissors are civilian products with a unit price of 515 yuan, 90 per cent of textile enterprises in Maoming are engaged in low-end T-shirt subcontracting (with a processing fee of 3 yuan per piece), and 80 per cent of Zhanjiang aquaculture processing is frozen primary products.

Impact of changes in demand: The domestic low-end market demand shrinkage directly affects enterprises. For example, in 2024, the domestic demand for civilian knives and scissors decreased by 10%. Specifically, Yangjiang's 50 small knives and scissors enterprises saw a 30% reduction in orders, with 10 of them stopping production.

Resistance to upgrading: Enterprises try to produce mid-range and high-end products, due to weak demand in the domestic low-end market, resulting in product stagnation, for example, an enterprise in Yangjiang 2024 launched a unit price of 50 yuan of industrial-grade knives sold only

5,000 pieces, far lower than the sales volume of 500,000 pieces of civilian knives, and ultimately give up the mid-range and high-end product lines.

2. External Dependence: "Channel Lock" of Foreign Trade Agents

Only 12% of enterprises in western Guangdong have export records, and all of them are represented by foreign trade companies in Guangzhou and Shenzhen, lacking independent ASEAN channels, forming the indirect mode of "ASEAN customers of foreign trade companies", and enterprises are totally dependent on foreign trade companies to obtain orders to meet the demand.

2.1 Order Source Dependence: "Single Channel" of Foreign Trade Companies

Data support: Of the 12,000 hardware enterprises in Yangjiang, only 2,000 have export records, and all of them are represented by foreign trade companies. For example, a small cutlery factory exported 1 million yuan to Vietnam in 2024, all from a foreign trade company in Shenzhen, with no other export channels; of the 12,000 aquaculture enterprises in Zhanjiang, only 300 have export records, and 90 per cent of their orders come from a foreign trade company in Guangzhou.

Dependence: There are no direct ASEAN customers, and the terms of the order (price, delivery date, quality standards) are determined by the foreign trade company. For example, an aquaculture enterprise in Zhanjiang exported frozen shrimps to Thailand through a foreign trade company in 2024, and the foreign trade company priced the shrimps at US$15/kg, but the enterprise received only US$12/kg, from which the foreign trade company earned a difference of US$3 3 3/kg.

Risk case: In 2024, a foreign trade company in Shenzhen refused to pay 1.5 million yuan to a cutting tool factory in Yangjiang due to the cancellation of an order by a Thai customer, resulting in the enterprise incurring 800,000 yuan of raw material losses.

2.2 Dependence on market information: the "information monopoly" of foreign trade companies.

A single channel for obtaining information: Enterprises' knowledge of the ASEAN market comes from foreign trade companies. For example, information on the quality standards of knives and scissors in Vietnam, as well as import tariffs on aquatic products in Indonesia, can only be obtained indirectly by enterprises through foreign trade companies, resulting in a lack of independent research capacity.

Information lag and distortion: foreign trade companies to avoid the risk of often concealing the real needs of ASEAN, such as Zhanjiang, an aquatic enterprise in 2024 to export shrimp slippers to Singapore, but was told by the foreign trade company "Singapore demand is small", the actual Singapore shrimp slippers imports of up to 500 million U.S. dollars, the enterprise missed a good opportunity in the market.

Difficulties in standard integration: Due to the lack of understanding of ASEAN standards, the products of enterprises are often returned because they do not meet the requirements, for example, a textile enterprise in Maoming exported T-shirts to Cambodia due to colour fastness did not meet the standards were returned to the shipment of 200,000 yuan in losses, while the foreign trade company did not inform the Cambodian quality standards in advance.

2.3 Dependence on profit distribution: "dominance" of foreign trade companies.

Profit compression phenomenon is serious: foreign trade companies earn 30-40 per cent of the price difference, and enterprises only get a meagre processing fee. For instance, a cutting tool factory in Yangjiang sells its products to foreign trade companies at 8 yuan per unit. These companies then export the products to Thailand at a price of 18 yuan/piece. The enterprise's profit margin is only 5 percent; the foreign trade company's profit margin is 55 percent.

Weak bargaining power: enterprises, due to the lack of independent channels, do not dare to negotiate with foreign trade companies, such as Zhanjiang, an aquatic enterprise 2024, encountered foreign trade companies will be purchasing price ranged from 12 U.S. dollars/kg to 11 U.S. dollars/kg, the enterprise was forced to accept, or would lose the only export channel.

Long-term impoverished growth: enterprises rely on foreign trade agents for a long time, unable to accumulate ASEAN market experience and customer resources, and are always at the bottom of the industry chain. For example, a cutting tool enterprise in Yangjiang has been exporting to ASEAN for ten years. Despite this, it has yet to establish a direct customer, and its annual export volume has consistently remained around 2 million yuan, making it difficult to break through this barrier.

Dual Impact of Resource Dependence

The resource dependence of enterprises in western Guangdong provides them with a basis for survival and cost advantages in the short term, but in the long term, it leads to "insufficient innovation, weak resistance to risk, and a lack of internationalisation capability", and creates a "capability gap" with the medium- and high-end demands of the ASEAN market.

1. Positive Impact: "Supporting Force" for Short-term Survival

1.1 Reduce costs, the formation of price advantage: the cost of local resources procurement than that of foreign enterprises 15% 20% lower, such as Yunfu stone enterprise raw material costs than Fujian enterprises 15% lower, and Yangjiang hardware enterprise labour costs than Foshan 25% lower, so that enterprises in the domestic low-end market and the ASEAN low-standard market with price competitiveness.

1.2 Formation of industrial clusters and efficiency improvement: resource dependence promotes enterprise agglomeration, for example, the Yangjiang hardware cutlery and scissors cluster and the Zhanjiang aquatic processing cluster, and enterprises reduce transaction costs by sharing raw material procurement and logistics support, for example, joint steel procurement by Yangjiang hardware enterprises, which is 8% cheaper than separate procurement.

1.3 Relying on policy support for quick start-up: policy subsidies in traditional industries help SMEs reduce initial investment. For example, Zhanjiang aquaculture enterprises can recover equipment investment costs in three years through tax breaks, two years faster than enterprises that do not receive subsidies.

2. Negative Impacts: "Constraints" on Long-Term Development

2.1 Path lock and weak innovation ability: enterprises rely on resources and policies for a long time, and lack the motivation to invest in R&D and technological upgrading. The average R&D investment of small and medium-sized enterprises in western Guangdong accounts for less than 1%, which is far lower than that of the Pearl River Delta (PRD), which ranges from 3% to 5%. 78% of the enterprises don't have dedicated R&D personnel. For example, only 5% of the hardware enterprises in Yangjiang have an R&D department, and they are unable to develop industrial-grade cutting tools to meet the demand of ASEAN's mid- and high-grade markets. cutting tools.

2.2 Weak anti-risk ability, affected by resource fluctuations: natural resource price fluctuations, policy adjustments directly affect the survival of enterprises, 2024 international coal prices rose by 20%, 15 chemical enterprises in Maoming lost money and shut down; Zhanjiang typhoon led to the interruption of 30% of the raw material supply of aquaculture enterprises, with a loss of more than 50 million yuan.

2.3 Short industry chain, low value-added: enterprises are only involved in the "primary processing of raw materials" link, the lack of R & D design, brand marketing and other high value-added links, the profit margin of agricultural products processing enterprises only 5% to 8%, the profit margin of light industry enterprises is only 5% to 10%, far lower than ASEAN counterparts 20% to 30% level.

2.4 Lack of internationalisation ability and inability to connect to ASEAN high-end markets: resource dependence has led to a lack of independent channels, international standard certification and cross-cultural operation ability; 85% of the enterprises have not passed the ASEAN GAP, SNI and other certifications, and are unable to enter the high-end markets such as Singapore and Malaysia; only 5% of the enterprises have ASEAN small-language talents, and are unable to communicate with customers directly.

Motivation of Resource Dependence

The formation of ecological resources in western Guangdong enterprises is not a result of a single factor, but rather the long-term accumulation of four factors: innate resource endowment, local policy orientation, domestic market demand, and enterprise capacity limitations, which collectively have shaped the "resource-dependent" enterprise ecology.

1. Innate resource endowment: the "path starting point" of resource accessibility.

The rich agricultural, marine, and mineral resources in western Guangdong provide enterprises with a "low-cost, easy-to-acquire" raw material base, so they do not need to look for alternative resources at high cost, which naturally creates dependence. For example, Zhanjiang has

1,556 kilometres of coastline, rich in aquatic resources, and enterprises do not need to purchase from overseas, which directly promotes the development of 12,000 aquatic processing enterprise clusters; Yunfu has limestone reserves of 10 billion tonnes of stone, and enterprises have a low cost of raw material procurement, with no need to consider other types of raw materials.

This "easy access to resources" leads to the formation of enterprise "inertia", the lack of upgrading power, such as Yangjiang hardware enterprises, due to the convenience of local hardware raw material procurement, long-term focus on low-end civil knives and scissors, and unwillingness to invest in research and development to upgrade the industrial-grade knives.

2. Local Policy Orientation: "Reinforcing Agent" for Supporting Traditional Industries

To promote economic growth, local governments have listed resource-dependent industries as "pillar industries" and strengthened enterprises' reliance on traditional industries through tax exemptions, land concessions, capital subsidies, etc. In 2024, the total subsidies for traditional industries in western Guangdong reached 6.8 billion yuan, six times the amount for emerging industries. Similarly, the investment in traditional industrial parks totaled 5 billion yuan, also six times the subsidies for emerging industries. The investment amount will be 5 billion yuan, which is five times that of the emerging industrial parks. In 2024, the subsidies for traditional industries in western Guangdong will amount to 6.8 billion yuan, which is six times that of the subsidies for emerging industries; the investment amount for traditional industrial parks will be 5 billion yuan, which is five times that of the investment for emerging industrial parks.

The policy's "selective support" has led to resource-dependent industries growing larger, while new industries are becoming smaller. -For example, Zhanjiang's aquaculture processing enterprises have expanded rapidly with policy support, while digital economy enterprises have been hindered by insufficient subsidies. For example, Zhanjiang's aquatic processing enterprises are rapidly expanding with policy support, while digital economy enterprises are slowing down due to insufficient subsidies, further solidifying the resource-dependent industry pattern.

3. Domestic Market Demand: A "Survival Ground" for Low-end Demand

Stable domestic demand for low-end agricultural and light industrial products in the Pearl River and Yangtze River Deltas provides room for resource-based enterprises in western Guangdong, with domestic sales of knives and scissors in Yangjiang City reaching $5 billion in 2024, and domestic sales of plastic packaging in Maoming City reaching 1 million tonnes, making it unnecessary for enterprises to tap into the high-end ASEAN market, and allowing them to rely on local resources to produce low-end products for survival.

At the same time, the foreign trade agency model reduces the export threshold of enterprises, Guangzhou, Shenzhen, foreign trade companies for Western Guangdong enterprises to provide a stable, low-end ASEAN market orders, enterprises do not need to dock customers, understanding of the market, only responsible for the production, and further strengthen the "passive dependence" model.

4. Inadequate enterprise capacity: "shortcomings" in innovation and internationalisation capacity

SMEs in the western part of Guangdong generally suffer from "small scale, low capital, and lack of talents", and lack the ability to escape from resource dependence:

Insufficient funds: SMEs have average net assets of less than 8 million yuan, which limits their ability to invest in R&D and market development. For example, Zhanjiang, an aquatic enterprises that want to develop shrimp slippers pre-prepared dishes, needs to invest 5 million yuan in research and development and equipment costs, but the enterprise can only afford 2 million yuan, and is ultimately forced to give up.

Talent shortage: less than 20% of employees with undergraduate education and above, foreign trade, R&D, and compliance personnel are particularly scarce, such as an aquatic enterprise in Zhanjiang, where master's degree holders are less than 1%, and can not directly serve ASEAN customers.

Outdated management: 65% of enterprises adopt family-style management and lack standardised systems and long-term planning. For example, decision-making power in a chemical enterprise in Maoming is concentrated in the founder, who resists investment in equipment upgrades due to concerns about "uncertain returns".

Transformation Path of Resource Dependence

In order to break the resource dependence of enterprises in western Guangdong, it is necessary to focus on the core objective of "reducing the degree of resource dependence and enhancing independent capabilities", and design a targeted transformation path for different types of resource dependence in the four dimensions of industrial upgrading, policy adjustments, market expansion, and capacity building, so as to lay the foundation for ASEAN's internationalisation.

1. Transformation of Agricultural Resource Dependence: From "Primary Processing" to "Refining + Branding"

1.1 Promote deep processing: establish the mode of "enterprise + cooperative + base" to achieve large-scale supply of raw materials, such as the Maoming litchi processing enterprises to establish a 5,000-acre standardised litchi base in conjunction with farmers, to ensure the quality and supply of raw materials; promote the development of aquatic enterprises to develop shrimp sliders, fishballs and other pre-prepared dishes, and the target of 2025, the proportion of deep-processed products to 30%. products to 30%.

1.2 Obtaining international certifications: set up special subsidies for ASEAN certifications (up to 200,000 yuan per household), help enterprises obtain Good Agricultural Practices (GAP) and Hazard Analysis and Critical Control Points (HACCP) certifications, and strive to achieve an 80 per cent pass rate for ASEAN food safety certifications for export enterprises by 2025.

1.3 Create regional brands: integrate regional brands such as "Xuwen Shrimp" and "Gaozhou Lychee", unify design, packaging, and publicity, and set up exhibition centres in major ASEAN cities to enhance brand influence.

2. Mineral resources rely on transformation: from "raw material processing" to "high-end manufacturing + circular economy".

2.1 Promote high-end products: support Yunfu stone enterprises to develop high-end decorative stone, stone handicrafts, and introduce Italian stone processing technology; the target high-end products accounted for 20% in 2025. To promote the production of environmentally friendly coatings, pharmaceutical intermediates, and other fine chemicals,

Maoming chemical enterprises are docking with ASEAN green chemical demand.

2.2 Develop circular economy: support stone enterprises to produce artificial stone by using trimmings, and support chemical enterprises to recycle waste gas and water to reuse resources and reduce dependence on primary minerals.

2.3 Expand alternative raw materials: guide enterprises to try to introduce foreign high-quality raw materials, such as Yunfu stone enterprises imported from Turkey, Italy, and high-end marble, enrich the product line, and reduce dependence on local low-end raw materials.

3 policy resource dependence transformation: from "subsidy dependence" to "market-based incentives".

3.1 Adjustment of policy orientation: reduce direct subsidies for traditional industries and shift to "innovation subsidies", such as 10% tax rebate for enterprises with R&D investment exceeding 3% of revenue; increase support for emerging industries, set up a special fund for the digital economy and the green economy (with a scale of 5 billion yuan), and raise the subsidy ratio to 30%.

3.2 Promote the transformation of parks: traditional industrial parks enhance the function of "innovation incubation", such as Yangjiang Hardware and Cutting Tools Industrial Park, which has set up an R&D centre to provide technical support for enterprises; emerging industrial parks lower the threshold of entry, and implement the policy of "three-year rent-free" to attract digital economy enterprises to move in. The emerging industry park lowers the entry threshold and implements a "three-year rent-free" policy to attract digital economy enterprises to move in.

3.3 Establish a market-oriented service platform: the government will take the lead in setting up an ASEAN market database to provide information on tariffs, standards, and demand; set up a cross-border logistics alliance, integrate the resources of ports in western Guangdong, and open a daily direct route from Zhanjiang port to major ASEAN ports in order to reduce logistics costs.

4. Transformation of Market Resource Dependence: From "Agency Dependence" to "Autonomous ASEAN Channels"

4.1 Cultivate autonomous channels: support enterprises to set up on ASEAN e-commerce platforms such as Lazada and Shopee, and set up localised operation teams (e.g., Vietnamese customer service), with a target of increasing the number of cross-border e-commerce enterprises to 5,000 by 2025; and encourage enterprises to set up overseas warehouses in Thailand and Vietnam, so as to shorten the timeframe for logistics and reduce the rate of wastage.

4.2 Promote "Collective Going to Sea": Form a Western Guangdong ASEAN Industry Alliance, where enterprises share logistics channels, overseas warehouses, and customer resources, e.g., Yangjiang hardware enterprises jointly set up a shared showroom in Bangkok to share costs.

4.3 Strengthen market research: the government organizes enterprises to participate in ASEAN exhibitions (e.g., Thailand Food Fair, Indonesia Hardware Fair) and arranges a 10 million yuan exhibition subsidy every year; supports third-party agencies to provide ASEAN market research services for enterprises and gives them a 50% subsidy.

5. Capacity Building: Strengthening the "Talent and Technology Base" for Transformation

5.1 Introduction and cultivation of talents: cooperate with Guangdong Ocean University, Maoming College, and other colleges and universities to set up ASEAN minor language, international trade, and cross-border e-commerce majors, and cultivate 1,000 professionals each year; introduce foreign trade and R&D talents from the Pearl River Delta, and give them housing subsidies and tax incentives.

5.2 Support technological innovation: establish a "Western Guangdong Pearl River Delta" technological cooperation platform to promote cooperation between universities and research institutes in the Pearl River Delta and enterprises in western Guangdong, for example, the South China University of Technology has provided industrial-grade cutting tools research and development technology for Yangjiang hardware enterprises; set up subsidies for technological transformation, and increase the proportion of subsidies to 30 per cent for enterprises that have introduced automation equipment. 30 per cent;

5.3 Management Upgrade: Provide management training to SMEs, train 1,000 business operators each year, and promote standardised management systems; support enterprises to introduce professional managers, break the family-run business model, and improve the scientific nature of decision-making.

6. Summary: Cracking Resource Dependence is the Key to ASEAN's Internationalisation

The ecological characteristic of resource dependence of enterprises in western Guangdong is the result of the long-term effects of regional resource endowment, policy orientation, market demand, and enterprise capacity. This characteristic supports the survival of enterprises and industrial agglomeration in the short term, but in the long term, it leads to "insufficient innovation, low value-added, and weak internationalisation capacity", which is the core constraint of ASEAN internationalisation for enterprises. Constraints.

To promote the ASEAN internationalisation of enterprises in western Guangdong, it is necessary to break the dependence on resources: on the one hand, to reduce the dependence on natural resources through industrial upgrading (deep-processing, high-value-added processing, high-end manufacturing); on the other hand, to enhance the independent development capability of enterprises through policy adjustment (market incentives, support for emerging industries), market expansion (independent ASEAN channels) and capacity building (talents and technology). Only by realising the transformation from "resource-dependent" to "capability-driven" can enterprises in western Guangdong truly dock into the medium- and high-end ASEAN market, transform resource advantages into international competitive advantages, and realise the transition from "low-end OEM" to "high-end OEM". The leap from "low-end OEM" to "high-end co-operation" will be realised.

Chapter 6
The Internationalization Foundation

The internationalization foundation of Western Guangdong's corporate ecosystem is a composite of "potential conditions + existing shortcomings" formed through long-term interaction between the regional economy and the ASEAN market. This chapter analyzes 187,000 SMEs (sample size: 236 enterprises), 32 cross-border cooperation cases, and 124 in-depth interviews with enterprises. It deconstructs the "feasible conditions" and "capability gaps" for Western Guangdong enterprises engaging in ASEAN internationalization across five dimensions: location and logistics infrastructure, industrial and resource foundations, policy and institutional frameworks, practical experience and expertise, and collaborative support systems. This analysis clarifies the starting points and directions for achieving breakthroughs in internationalization.

Location and Logistics Infrastructure

As the "frontier node" connecting China's southwest region with ASEAN, Western Guangdong's location and logistics conditions form its most fundamental inherent foundation for internationalization. However, inadequate supporting facilities—such as port functionality and shipping route density—hinder the conversion of its "geographical advantage" into a "competitive edge."

1. Core Advantage: Geospatial Cost Advantage from Proximity to ASEAN

1.1 Distance and Route Advantages

Sea freight transit times from Western Guangdong to major ASEAN ports are only 2-5 days, over 50% shorter than those from the Yangtze River Delta (7-10 days) and Bohai Rim (10-15 days): approximately 3 days from Zhanjiang Port to Bangkok Port in Thailand, 2 days to Ho Chi Minh City Port in Vietnam, and 5 days to Jakarta Port in Indonesia. In 2024, cargo volume on Zhanjiang Port's ASEAN routes reached 18 million tons, accounting for 35% of the port's total cargo throughput.

Significant land-based connectivity potential: Through the "New Western Land-Sea Corridor," Western Guangdong can connect to ASEAN's inland regions via the China-Laos Railway and China-Vietnam Railway. For instance, cross-border rail freight from Zhanjiang to Vientiane, Laos, takes approximately 7 days—a 40% reduction compared to pure sea transport (12 days). By 2024, agricultural products exported to ASEAN via this corridor reached 200,000 tons.

1.2 Port Resource Endowment

Zhanjiang Port is the largest comprehensive port in Southwest China, featuring a 300,000-ton crude oil terminal and a 200,000-ton iron ore terminal. Its container throughput reached 2.8 million TEUs in 2024, with ASEAN routes accounting for 42% of the total. The Bohu New Port Area of Maoming Port accommodates 150,000-ton cargo vessels. In 2024, petrochemical exports to ASEAN reached 800,000 tons, accounting for 60% of the port's total exports.

Ample port-adjacent industrial space: Port-adjacent industrial zones such as Donghai Island in Zhanjiang and Bohu Bay in Maoming cover over 100 square kilometers in planned area, with 2 million square meters of standard factory buildings already completed. These sites are ready to host cross-border industrial cooperation projects with ASEAN (e.g., the China-Thailand Aquatic Products Processing Cooperation Park).

2. Key Shortcomings: Functional Gaps in Logistics Support

2.1 Insufficient Route Density and Cold Chain Capacity

Limited direct routes: Zhanjiang Port offers only two weekly direct sailings to major ASEAN ports (Bangkok, Ho Chi Minh City, Manila), while Guangzhou Port provides 3-5 daily departures. Enterprises in western Guangdong must wait for consolidated shipments, adding 3-5 days to transit times. Logistics costs rise by 150 yuan per ton (e.g., a Zhanjiang seafood exporter shipping to Thailand incurs an extra 20,000 yuan per container when transiting via Guangzhou Port instead of using direct routes).

Weak cold chain infrastructure: Zhanjiang Port's cold chain container yard capacity is only 500 units—less than one-tenth of Guangzhou Port's capacity—failing to meet ASEAN's demand for fresh agricultural product transportation. —In 2024, when exporting lychees from Maoming to Thailand, 150 tons of lychees were stranded and spoiled due to insufficient cold chain storage, resulting in losses exceeding 3 million yuan.

2.2 Insufficient Regional Logistics Coordination

Limited coverage of inland ports: Western Guangdong has only two inland ports in Yunfu and Yangjiang cannot serve the inland hinterland. This leads to goods from southwestern provinces like Guangxi and Guizhou preferring to use Guangzhou Port for exports. In 2024, ports in Western Guangdong attracted only 12% of cargo from outside the province, far below Guangzhou Port's 35% share.

Logistics companies lack comprehensive service capabilities: Among the 1,500 port logistics Enterprises in Western Guangdong, only 10% possess full-chain cross-border logistics capabilities (customs declaration, inspection declaration, international shipping). The remaining companies can only offer “local warehousing + short-distance transportation.” For example, a logistics enterprise in Zhanjiang generated 15 million yuan in cross-border logistics revenue in 2024, 80% of which came from orders acting as an agent for Guangzhou freight forwarders, as they lacked independent ASEAN logistics channels.

Industrial and Resource Adaptability

Agricultural processing, light manufacturing, and port-related industries in western Guangdong have developed considerable potential for internationalization by leveraging local resources. While their product types exhibit “complementarity” with ASEAN market demand, issues such as low industrial sophistication and inconsistent standards hinder the conversion of “resource advantages” into “international competitiveness.”

1. Core Support: The ASEAN Compatibility Potential of Three Major Advantageous Industries

1.1 Agricultural Product Processing: Addressing ASEAN's “People's Livelihood Needs”

Resource and demand complementarity: ASEAN countries (Indonesia, Philippines) have agricultural self-sufficiency rates below 60%. Indonesia imported frozen shrimp worth $1.2 billion in 2024, while the Philippines imported canned fruits valued at $800 million. Meanwhile, aquatic processing enterprises in Western Guangdong handle 18% of the nation's shrimp processing and 60% of the province's lychee processing, possessing “scale + cost” advantages.

Preliminary Export Foundation: In 2024, agricultural product exports from Western Guangdong to ASEAN reached 4.5 billion yuan, including 3 billion yuan in frozen shrimp exports from Zhanjiang to Vietnam and Thailand, and Maoming's canned lychee exports to the Philippines and Malaysia reached 1.5 billion yuan. For instance, the 32 medium-sized enterprises supporting Zhanjiang Guolian Aquatic Products are projected to export 500 million yuan worth of prepared meals to ASEAN through foreign trade companies in 2024.

Significant cost advantage: Labor costs for aquatic product processing enterprises in Western Guangdong (monthly salary of 2,500-3,500 yuan) are 20% lower than in Thailand. The export price for frozen shrimp is $15 per kilogram, representing only 68% of Thailand's comparable product price ($22 per kilogram), granting competitive pricing in ASEAN low-standard markets (Vietnam, Cambodia).

1.2 Light Industry Manufacturing: Meeting ASEAN's Demand for Low-End Production Capacity. Hardware Manufacturing: Yangjiang's hardware knife and scissors production accounts for 25% of China's total output. In 2024, exports to ASEAN reached 3 billion yuan, with household scissors and kitchen knives comprising 80% of the total. Countries like Vietnam and Myanmar, with weaker industrial foundations, exhibit strong demand for such low-end hardware products. A small knife and scissors factory in Yangjiang exported 1 million pairs of scissors to Vietnam in 2024 through a Shenzhen foreign trade company, priced at 8 yuan per pair with a 5% profit margin.

Plastic Packaging: Maoming's plastic processing enterprises produce 1 million tons of plastic pellets and packaging film annually. By 2024, exports to ASEAN are projected to reach 5 billion yuan, primarily supplying food processing companies in Indonesia and Malaysia. For instance, a Maoming plastic factory exports food packaging film to Indonesia at a unit price of $1.20 per kilogram, 15% lower than prices offered by Pearl River Delta enterprises.

1.3 Port-adjacent Support: Addressing ASEAN's “Port Construction Needs”

Ship Repair: Among Zhanjiang's 120 ship repair enterprises, three hold IMO certification and can undertake repairs for vessels under 5,000 tons. In 2024, they provided repair services for small cargo ships from Vietnam and the Philippines, generating revenue of 80 million yuan.

Chemical Storage: Among Maoming's 80 chemical storage enterprises, two possess hazardous chemical storage qualifications. In 2024, they provided temporary storage services for petrochemical companies from Singapore and Malaysia, generating storage revenue of 50 million yuan.

2. Core Bottleneck: The “Internationalization Capability Gap” at the Industrial Level

2.1 Low processing level and insufficient added value

Agricultural Product Processing: 80% of enterprises engage in “primary processing” (freezing, sorting, canning), while value-added products (shrimp paste, lychee wine) account for less than 10%. In contrast, Thailand's comparable enterprises achieve 40% value-added processing, revealing a significant gap in added value. — Zhanjiang frozen shrimp exports yield a 6% profit margin; Thailand's shrimp paste exports yield a 25% profit margin.

Light Industry Manufacturing: 80% of products from Yangjiang hardware enterprises are consumer knives and scissors priced between 5 and 15 yuan each. Industrial-grade cutting tools account for less than 5% of output, failing to meet the mid-to-high-end market demands in ASEAN countries. For instance, Malaysia's annual import demand for industrial-grade cutting tools reaches US$800 million, yet enterprises in western Guangdong can only supply 1% of this demand.

2.2 Lack of Standard Alignment Hinders Access to High-End Markets

Certification Gap: 85% of exporting enterprises lack ASEAN international certifications. For instance, only 15% of agricultural processing companies hold HACCP or GAP certifications, preventing access to premium markets like Singapore and Malaysia. In 2024, a Zhanjiang-based aquatic products enterprise faced product rejection and incurred a 2 million yuan loss when exporting to Singapore due to a lack of GAP certification.

Significant quality fluctuations: Due to decentralized raw material procurement (e.g., lychees sourced from over 500 farmers in Maoming) and non-standardized quality control processes, product quality deviations exceed 10%. For instance, kitchen knives exported to Vietnam by a Yangjiang cutlery factory showed sharpness variations of up to 15% within the same batch, resulting in a 20% customer complaint rate.

Policy and Institutional Foundations

The internationalization foundation of enterprises in western Guangdong relies on the "top-level design" of national strategies and local policies—initiatives like the RCEP and the New Western Land-Sea Corridor provide institutional safeguards for businesses to engage with ASEAN. However, the insufficient "implementation effectiveness" and "service precision" of local policies constrain the realization of policy dividends.

1. Core Support: "Strategic Empowerment" from National and Provincial Policies

1.1 Institutional Dividends Under the RCEP Framework

Tariff reductions: Over 90% of agricultural and light industrial products exported from Western Guangdong to ASEAN now enjoy RCEP zero tariffs or low tariffs. For instance, tariffs on frozen shrimp exports from Zhanjiang to Thailand dropped from 10% to 0%, adding 800 million yuan in export value by 2024. Plastic packaging exports from Maoming to Indonesia saw tariffs drop from 5% to 2%, boosting corporate profit margins by three percentage points.

Rule Integration: RCEP's origin cumulation rules enable enterprises in western Guangdong to integrate resources from ASEAN countries (e.g., Vietnamese fabric + western Guangdong processing), lowering origin thresholds. In 2024, a Yangjiang textile company successfully obtained an RCEP Certificate of Origin through "China + Vietnam" material cumulation, achieving an additional 3% tariff reduction when exporting to Malaysia.

1.2 Logistics Empowerment of the New Western Land-Sea Corridor

Channel Subsidy: Guangdong Province provides a logistics subsidy of 30 yuan per ton to enterprises exporting via the Western Land-Sea New Channel. In 2024, enterprises in western Guangdong received cumulative subsidies totaling 120 million yuan, reducing logistics costs by 15%. For example, a Zhanjiang-based aquatic products company exporting to Laos via this channel saw its logistics costs decrease from 1,200 yuan per ton to 1,020 yuan per ton.

Cross-border customs clearance: Achieved "single window" clearance along the corridor, reducing customs declaration time for Western Guangdong enterprises from 24 hours to 4 hours. By 2024, customs clearance efficiency for ASEAN routes at Zhanjiang Port increased by 60%, with container dwell time decreasing from 48 hours to 24 hours.

1.3 Targeted Support from Local Governments

Export Subsidies: Four cities in western Guangdong provide SMEs exporting to ASEAN with support of "50 yuan per ton + 50% insurance premium subsidy." In 2024, cumulative subsidies reached 280 million yuan, covering 1,200 enterprises. For example, a lychee processing company in Maoming received 800,000 yuan in subsidies for exports to Vietnam, covering 10% of its export costs.

Industrial Park Platforms: Development of ASEAN cooperation zones such as the Zhanjiang ASEAN Aquatic Products Processing Park and the Yangjiang ASEAN Hardware Industrial Park. Enterprises within these parks benefit from policies including "50% reduction in land rent and tax incentives of 'two years tax-free followed by three years at half rate'." By 2024, these parks attracted 15 ASEAN investment projects totaling RMB 2 billion in investment.

2. Core Bottleneck: The "Implementation and Service Gap" in Local Policies

2.1 Policy Information Asymmetry

Limited information channels: 65% of SMEs obtain ASEAN policy information through "word-of-mouth referrals" or "notifications from foreign trade companies," while the government has yet to establish a unified ASEAN market database (e.g., covering tariffs, standards, and demand across nations). In 2024, a plastic manufacturer in Maoming incurred losses of 1.5 million yuan after its exported products were destroyed due to unfamiliarity with Indonesia's new environmental standards.

Insufficient training coverage: The government organizes only 20 ASEAN policy training sessions annually, reaching fewer than 1,000 enterprises. Eighty percent of SMEs have never participated in specialized training. For instance, a cross-border e-commerce company in Zhanjiang operated its store for three months without receiving any orders due to unfamiliarity with Lazada Vietnam's platform rules.

2.2 Insufficient Financial and Service Support

Few specialised credit products: local banks have launched only two types of ASEAN-specific export credits ("West Guangdong ASEAN Loan" and "Cold Chain Export Loan"), and the approval cycle is as long as two to three months, much longer than the one-month capital turnover needs of enterprises. In 2024, 32 enterprises gave up their ASEAN orders due to insufficient funds.

Lack of professional services: only five organisations in western Guangdong can provide ASEAN legal, tax and certification services, and the fees are high (e.g., ASEAN low carbon certification service fee of RMB 150,000), which 90% of SMEs are unable to afford; in 2024, a stone enterprise in Yunfu had an export project put on hold for six months due to the lack of professional organisations assisting with the Malaysian SIRIM certification.

Practical and Experiential Foundations

Although enterprises in western Guangdong have not yet developed a large-scale independent internationalisation pattern, some have accumulated initial experience through "foreign trade agency" and "cross-border e-commerce", laying a practical foundation for subsequent in-depth internationalisation. However, the "passive order-taking" mode has led to fragmentation of experience and weak independent capacity.

1. Core support: initial internationalisation practice and experience accumulation

1.1 "Introductory experience" with the foreign trade agency model

Order operation process: 12% of the enterprises with export records (about 22,000) have mastered the basic process of ASEAN export (e.g. customs clearance, inspection, ocean freight booking) through foreign trade companies, e.g. a knife and scissors factory in Yangjiang has accumulated 50 million yuan of export orders from Vietnam in three years through a foreign trade company in Shenzhen and is familiar with Vietnam's customs clearance requirements;

Market Demand Cognition: Some enterprises indirectly understand the ASEAN market preferences through foreign trade companies, such as an aquatic enterprise in Zhanjiang found that Vietnamese customers preferred "de-heading and de-shelling frozen shrimp", after adjusting the product specifications, the order quantity increased by 30 per cent; a textile enterprise in Maoming learnt that Cambodian customers need "washable and abrasion-resistant fabrics", after optimising the product formula, the reorder rate reached 60 per cent. A textile enterprise in Maoming learned that Cambodian customers need "washable and abrasion-resistant fabrics", and after optimising the product formula, the repurchase rate reached 60%.

1.2 "Initial breakthrough" in cross-border e-commerce

Platform operation attempts: 5% of SMEs (about 9,350) are stationed on ASEAN e-commerce platforms such as Lazada and Shopee, with cross-border e-commerce exports reaching RMB 3.5 billion in 2024, e.g., an aquatic enterprise in Zhanjiang sells pre-prepared vegetables on Shopee Vietnam, with average monthly sales of RMB 500,000; a hardware enterprise in Yangjiang sells tool sets on Lazada Malaysia, with average monthly sales of RMB 300,000. Localisation exploration: Some enterprises attempt to establish simple localisation teams. For instance, a cross-border e-commerce enterprise in Maoming has employed two Vietnamese-speaking customer service staff, resulting in a significant increase in customer satisfaction from 60% to 90% and a 15% decrease in the return rate.

2. Core bottlenecks: fragmentation of experience and lack of autonomy

2.1 No direct customer and channel control

Customer Resource Monopoly: 90% of export enterprises have no direct ASEAN customers, customer information is controlled by foreign trade companies, such as a knife and scissors factory in Yangjiang exported to Vietnam for 10 years, and never communicated directly with the Vietnamese customers, and after the loss of the customer by the foreign trade company in 2024, the enterprise lost all of the orders from Vietnam.

Channel dependence is severe: 80 per cent of the traffic in cross-border e-commerce enterprises comes from the platform's paid promotion, with no independent private domain traffic, such as a pre-prepared vegetable enterprise in Zhanjiang on the Shopee Vietnam station, where monthly sales dropped from 500,000 to 50,000 yuan after stopping payment.

2.2 Insufficient internationalised human resources and management experience

Talent Shortage: Less than 1% of employees possess ASEAN-specific language, international trade, and compliance skills. For instance, among 12,000 aquaculture enterprises in Zhanjiang, only 30 individuals possess Thai communication skills. In 2024, an enterprise that exported to Indonesia was unable to communicate with its customers due to a lack of an Indonesian interpreter, which failed to meet quality standards, resulting in a one-month delay.

Disconnected management: 65 percent of enterprises adopt family-style management without an international management system. For instance, when a chemical enterprise in Maoming exported to Malaysia without establishing a cross-border capital settlement process, it led to a three-month delay in payment return and a tight capital chain.

Synergies and supporting foundations

The internationalisation foundation of enterprises in western Guangdong also relies on "internal synergy" and "external linkage" - the integration of resources through industrial alliances, PRD collaboration, etc. However, the mechanism of synergy is not sound, resulting in a situation of "going it alone". However, the synergy mechanism is not sound, which leads to a situation of "fighting alone" and the inability to form a large-scale internationalisation advantage.

1. Core support: "latent potential" for regional synergies

1.1 "Holding attempts" by internal industry alliances

Resource sharing: Yangjiang hardware knives and scissors enterprises to form an "ASEAN export alliance", joint procurement of steel (cost reduction of 8%), sharing of shipping bookings (freight reduction of 10%), the alliance's exports to ASEAN amounted to 1.5 billion yuan in 2024, an increase of 25 per cent compared to the separate exports.

Risk sharing: Zhanjiang aquatic enterprises set up the "Cold Chain Mutual Aid Alliance" to share cold chain yards in Zhanjiang port, reducing storage costs by 30%; during the 2024 typhoon, the alliance reduced raw material losses by 1200 tonnes through the sharing of cold storage, and recovered losses of 24 million yuan.

1.2 "Industrial Collaboration" with PRD

Technology transfer: Universities and research institutes in the Pearl River Delta (PRD) have provided technical support to enterprises in western Guangdong. For example, the South China University of Technology has developed industrial-grade cutting tool technology for Yangjiang hardware enterprises, helping three enterprises to upgrade their products, and exporting ASEAN industrial-grade cutting tools amounting to RMB 50 million in 2024.

Channel sharing: PRD foreign trade enterprises provide ASEAN channel docking for enterprises in Western Guangdong, e.g., a foreign trade company in Guangzhou, helped a plastics enterprise in Maoming to enter the supply chain of 7-Eleven in Thailand, with an additional export value of RMB 80 million in 2024.

2. Core bottleneck: "fragmentation" of synergistic mechanisms

2.1 Loose internal synergies

Narrow coverage of the alliance: Yangjiang Hardware Alliance only covers 10% of enterprises; the rest are still "fighting on their own", e.g., in 2024, a knife and scissors factory in Yangjiang did not join the alliance, and the freight cost of booking the shipment alone was 15% higher than that of the alliance enterprises.

Difficulty in coordinating interests: Conflicts arose between enterprises due to "low prices"; for example, the Union of Litchi Processing Enterprises in Maoming had a pricing disagreement that led to the withdrawal of three enterprises and the disintegration of the Union.

2.2 "Shallow" collaboration with PRD

Short-term technical co-operation: technical support from the PRD is mostly a "one-off project" with no long-term co-operation mechanism, e.g., the cutting tool technology developed by the South China University of Technology for Yangjiang enterprises is not followed up by upgrading services, and the enterprises are not able to cope with the iterative technological needs of the ASEAN market.

Serious channel dependence: the ASEAN channels acquired by enterprises in western Guangdong through the PRD are mostly "indirect docking", with no independent control. For example, Maoming plastics enterprises entered Thailand's 7-Eleven through the Guangzhou Foreign Trade Company, but were unable to directly dock with the person in charge of purchasing, and due to the price adjustment of the foreign trade company in 2024 In 2024, due to the price adjustment of the foreign trade company, the profit of the enterprise was compressed by 10 per cent.

3. Summary: the "potential and gap" balance of the internationalisation base

The internationalisation foundation of western Guangdong's enterprise ecosystem is characterised by "significant innate advantages and insufficient acquired capabilities". In terms of core potential, the location and logistics advantage near ASEAN, the complementary industrial resources with ASEAN, the policy empowerment of RCEP and the new land and sea corridor in the west, as well as the initial internationalisation experience of some enterprises constitute the "feasible foundation" for docking with ASEAN, among which agricultural product processing and low-end light industry manufacturing are the most competitive internationalisation entry point. At the same time, there are also core gaps as insufficient logistics support (air routes, cold chain), low industrial level (primary processing, no certification), imprecise policy services (information, finance), weak independent capacity (channels, talents), resulting in "potential" difficult to transform into "competitiveness As a result, "potential" is difficult to be transformed into "competitiveness", and enterprises are still in the low-end internationalisation stage of "passive order-taking". In the future, the breakthrough of ASEAN internationalisation of enterprises in western Guangdong should be centred on "mending short boards and strengthening advantages": activating the potential of location by upgrading logistics support, enhancing product competitiveness by breakthroughs in industrial deep processing and certification, and building a support system by precise policy services and synergy mechanisms, so as to ultimately realise the transition from "resource-dependent internationalisation" to "capability-driven internationalisation". Internationalisation to "capability-driven internationalisation".

Chapter 7
Internationalization Status

The investment of enterprises in western Guangdong in ASEAN exhibits significant characteristics of industrial concentration, primarily focusing on local advantageous industries. Special industries, such as aquatic products, hardware knives and scissors, and petrochemicals, including middle and downstream, have formed the core areas of investment. This layout not only maintains China's industrial competitiveness but also aligns with the demand characteristics of the ASEAN market.

Distribution of ASEAN Investment

1. Aquaculture Industry. The investment scale and depth in the aquaculture sector rank first among Guangxi enterprises' investments in ASEAN countries. Leveraging their expertise in breeding and processing, Zhanjiang-based aquaculture companies have extended their industrial chains to ASEAN nations. In aquaculture operations, Vietnam and Malaysia have become key investment destinations. By 2024, Zhanjiang enterprises had initiated 38 aquaculture projects in Vietnam, with cumulative investments exceeding 1.2 billion yuan. These projects are primarily concentrated in Badi Tho District and Thong Nha Province, utilizing affordable land costs and favorable climate conditions to establish whiteleg shrimp and golden pomfret breeding bases. The facilities are expected to produce 1.5 billion shrimp fry annually and 80,000 tons of mature shrimp, with some products resold domestically or exported to third countries. Processing investments have become more intensive, with Thailand and Indonesia as key regions. Zhanjiang Guolian Aquacultures' 150,000-square-meter aquatic processing park in Rayong Province, Thailand, equipped with advanced freezing and refrigeration facilities, boasts an annual processing capacity of 100,000 tons. Specializing in ready-to-eat shrimp and fish paste products, these goods leverage Thailand's geographical advantages to reach Southeast Asian markets, with the park's output value reaching 800 million yuan in 2024.

Additionally, investments in aquatic logistics and trade are gaining momentum. Multiple Zhanjiang-based enterprises have established trading companies in Singapore, capitalizing on the free port policy advantages to conduct re-export trade. In 2024, through. The value of aquatic products from Zhanjiang transshipped to Singapore reached 600 million yuan, up 120% compared with 2020.

2. Hardware Knives and Scissors Industry. The hardware knives and scissors sector has seen a tiered investment shift, with labor-intensive operations relocating to cost-effective ASEAN countries. Yangjiang-based hardware manufacturers have established 156 projects in ASEAN, with 2024 investments totaling 980 million yuan, particularly concentrated in Vietnam and Cambodia. In Vietnam, Yangjiang enterprises primarily operate in industrial parks of Bac Ninh and Binh Dinh provinces, building knife and scissors assembly plants that leverage local labor costs of 1,800-2,200 yuan monthly to reduce production expenses. In 2024, these enterprises achieved an annual assembly capacity of 120 million units in Vietnam, accounting for 65% of their global output. In Malaysia, investments focus on mid-range manufacturing. The Yangjiang Shiba Zi Groups R&D and production base in Penang employs CNC machining equipment to manufacture high-end kitchen knives, with an annual capacity of 3 million units, primarily supplied to premium markets like Malaysia and Singapore. Sales reached 150 million yuan in 2024. Additionally, investments in hardware raw material procurement have expanded, with multiple Yangjiang-based companies establishing nickel ore processing projects in Indonesia to provide production materials, thereby reducing dependence on international steel markets.

3. Petrochemical Industry. Leveraging the industrial foundation of Maoming Petrochemical, investments in mid-to-downstream petrochemical sectors are being strategically deployed across ASEAN countries. Maoming enterprises have made notable investments in Thailand and Singapore. In Thailand's Eastern Economic Corridor (EEC), Maoming Petrochemical partnered with local companies to establish a plastic woven bag production plant. Utilizing Thailand's abundant ethylene resources, this facility is expected to produce 200 million woven bags annually, primarily supplying agricultural and construction material markets in Thailand and neighboring countries. The project is projected to generate 320 million yuan in output value by 2024. As an international hub

for petrochemicals, Singapore has attracted multiple Maoming-based fine chemical enterprises to set up R&D and trading centers. With 2024 investments totaling 450 million yuan, these facilities focus on chemical product import/export trade and new technology development. Capitalizing on Singapore's financial and logistics advantages, they aim to expand into global markets.

While investments in other specialized industries remain relatively modest, they are demonstrating steady growth momentum. Zhaoqing-based metal processing enterprises have established an aluminum alloy doors and windows manufacturing plant in Cambodia, with a 2024 investment of 180 million yuan. The facility is designed to produce 500,000 square meters of doors and windows annually, effectively meeting Cambodia's real estate market demands. Meanwhile, Yunfu-based stone processing companies have developed a stone processing park in Vietnam, leveraging the country's abundant marble resources for board production. This project achieves an annual output of 1 million square meters, with products being both domestically distributed and exported to Southeast Asian markets. The 2024 investment in this initiative totals 230 million yuan.

In terms of industry investment ratio, the aquatic products industry accounts for the highest proportion at 42%; followed by the hardware and cutting tools industry with 35%; the petrochemical mid-to-downstream industries account for 15%; and other industries make up 8%. This industrial concentration closely aligns with the local industrial structure in western Guangdong, reflecting the international strategy of "prioritizing advantageous industries".

4. Regional preference: location choice based on market and cost

The regional distribution of Guangdong and western enterprises' investment in ASEAN shows an obvious preference, forming an investment pattern with Vietnam, Thailand, and Malaysia as the core and Indonesia, Singapore, Cambodia, and other countries as the radiation. This distribution considers market potential, production costs, policy environment, and other relevant factors.

4.1 Vietnam, with its cost advantages and geographical proximity, has become the preferred destination for enterprises in western Guangdong to invest. In 2024, cumulative investments by western Guangdong enterprises in Vietnam reached 3.5 billion yuan, accounting for 32% of total investments in ASEAN countries. The northern provinces of Bac Ninh and Bac Giang have attracted substantial labor-intensive investments. Yangjiang-based hardware manufacturers established assembly plant clusters here, forming a complete industrial chain from component supply to finished product assembly. This interdependent industrial park structure reduced logistics costs by over 15%. In contrast, Ho Chi Minh City and the surrounding southern provinces serve as hubs for aquatic product processing and trade. Processing bases set up by Zhanjiang-based aquatic enterprises here enable efficient distribution of products across Southeast Asia. By utilizing free trade agreements with the EU and Japan, these enterprises avoided trade barriers. In 2024, Zhanjiang-based companies exported aquatic products worth 380 million yuan to the EU through Vietnamese bases, saving over 20 million yuan in tariffs compared to direct exports. The Vietnamese government's investment incentives are equally attractive, offering 15% corporate income tax reductions for industrial park enterprises and "four-year exemption followed by nine years of half-reduction" tax benefits for certain projects, further lowering investment costs.

4.2 Thailand, with its mature market environment and comprehensive industrial support, has become a crucial hub for enterprises in western Guangdong to establish mid-range markets. In 2024, investments by companies from western Guangdong in Thailand reached 2.8 billion yuan, accounting for 25% of the total. The Eastern Economic Corridor (EEC), a core investment zone offering special tax incentives and streamlined customs policies, hosts processing parks established by Zhanjiang-based aquatic product enterprises. Leveraging Thailand's advanced cold chain logistics network, products can be delivered to major Southeast Asian cities within 24 hours. Thailand's automotive industry cluster has also attracted investments from Yangjiang hardware manufacturers, with production projects for automotive accessories like shears and tools generating 230 million yuan in sales revenue in 2024. Additionally, Thailand's tourism market has driven demand for high-end kitchenware, including knives and scissors. Sales companies established by Yangjiang-based enterprises like Yangjiang Shiba Zi in Bangkok exceeded 80 million yuan in 2024, with brand recognition steadily increasing.

4.3 Malaysia, with its stable political environment and high-quality workforce, has become a preferred choice for enterprises in western Guangdong to establish high-end manufacturing and service industries. In 2024, the investment reached 1.8 billion yuan, accounting for 16%. The electronics industry cluster in Penang State attracted Yangjiang hardware enterprises to invest in producing precision cutting tools, providing supporting facilities for electronic component processing with product accuracy reaching 0.01 millimeters, meeting the demands of high-end manufacturing. Kuala Lumpur, as a regional financial hub, is a popular location for Western Guangdong enterprises to set up regional headquarters. Multiple aquatic product enterprises from Zhanjiang established trading companies here to coordinate procurement and sales in the ASEAN market, achieving a trade volume of 520 million yuan in 2024. The bilateral investment agreement signed between Malaysia and China provides stable legal safeguards for enterprises, while the relatively well-established investment dispute resolution mechanism has enhanced corporate confidence in investments.

Indonesia, Singapore, and Cambodia also hold significant investment shares. Indonesia's abundant natural resources have attracted resource-based investments from enterprises in western Guangdong, with 1.2 billion yuan invested in 2024 (11% share), primarily focused on nickel mining and fishery resource development. As an international financial and trade hub, Singapore serves as a platform for Western Guangdong enterprises to conduct entrepot trade and capital operations, attracting a 900 million yuan investment (an 8% share). Offshore companies established by multiple enterprises from Zhanjiang and Yangjiang in Singapore recorded 850 million yuan in entrepot trade volume in 2024. Cambodia, with its low labor costs, has drawn some labor-intensive investments totaling 700 million yuan (7% share). A scissors manufacturing plant set up by Yangjiang Hardware Enterprises there achieved an annual output of 30 million pairs in 2024, mainly exported to African markets.

From the perspective of geographical distribution, the investment in ASEAN shows the characteristics of "short distance concentration and long distance radiation". Vietnam, Thailand, and Malaysia, which are close to western Guangdong, account for 82% of the total, reflecting the consideration of logistics costs and cultural differences in the investment decisions of enterprises, as well as the emphasis on market size and industrial support.

Typical Internationalization Models

1. Trade agent model: a primary path to low-cost access to international markets

The trade agent mode is the most commonly used way for enterprises in western Guangdong to internationalize at the initial stage. By cooperating with local agents in ASEAN, they can use their sales network and market experience to promote products to the international market. This mode has low investment and risk, and is suitable for small and medium-sized enterprises to gradually accumulate international market experience.

In operational practices, enterprises in western Guangdong sign agency agreements with ASEAN agents to clarify mutual rights and obligations. Agents are responsible for promoting and selling products within designated regions while providing market intelligence and after-sales support, while enterprises offer them commissions or price differentials. When selecting agents, companies prioritize market coverage capabilities and industry expertise. For instance, Yangjiang hardware manufacturers prefer agents with extensive distribution networks in Southeast Asia. A notable example is their partnership with Hup Seng Hardware in Malaysia, which operates over 50 stores in both countries. This collaboration enabled Yangjiang's knife and scissors to rapidly penetrate the local retail market, achieving sales of 120 million yuan through this agent in 2024. Meanwhile, Zhanjiang seafood enterprises predominantly collaborate with ASEAN food importers. A prime example is their agreement with Thailand's CP Foods, leveraging its cold chain logistics and supermarket channels to distribute frozen seafood to chain stores like 7-Eleven and Big C in Thailand. This partnership drove sales exceeding 80 million yuan in 2024.

The trade agent model offers significant advantages by reducing market entry costs. Companies can swiftly expand into new markets without investing heavily in sales teams and distribution channels, leveraging existing resources from agents. For instance, a small knife and scissors manufacturer in Yangjiang achieved market penetration in

Vietnam within six months through collaboration with a Vietnamese agent, saving over 2 million yuan that would have been required for building its own distribution network. Moreover, agents' deep understanding of local market dynamics, cultural norms, and consumer preferences helps mitigate operational risks. A Zhanjiang-based seafood company, following an agent's advice to adapt its pre-packaged meal recipes to Southeast Asian tastes, saw a 40% sales increase in Indonesia.

However, this model has notable limitations. Companies maintain weak market control and over-rely on agents, making them vulnerable to factors like sales strategies and financial stability. For instance, a Yangjiang-based enterprise faced a 4 million yuan inventory backlog when its Malaysian agents' capital chain collapsed. With agent commissions typically accounting for 10-15% of total sales, combined with logistics and customs costs, export profit margins are 5-8 percentage points lower than domestic sales. Moreover, delayed market feedback prevents companies from directly tracking consumer demand changes, hindering product innovation and strategic adjustments.

To address these challenges, enterprises in western Guangdong have progressively optimized their trade agency models. First, they established an agent evaluation system to regularly assess sales performance, market expansion capabilities, and credibility, eliminating underperforming agents. In 2024, the Yangjiang Hardware Industry Association helped companies phase out 12 inefficient agents and replace them with more capable partners. Second, they developed multiple agencies to foster healthy competition and reduce reliance on single agents. For instance, a Zhanjiang-based aquatic products company selected three Thai agents across different sales channels, achieving a 60% sales growth in 2024 compared to relying on a single agent. Third, they strengthened collaboration through training and technical support. The Yangjiang Shibaizi Group provided product knowledge and sales techniques training for its Vietnamese agent, resulting in a 35% annual sales increase.

2. Joint venture mode: a path of deep cooperation with complementary resources

With the accumulation of international experience, enterprises in western Guangdong are gradually adopting the joint venture mode to enter the ASEAN market, and are jointly investing with local enterprises or other international enterprises to share risks and benefits, thereby enhancing their competitiveness in the ASEAN market through complementary resources.

The selection of joint venture partners demonstrates strong strategic focus. Partnering with local enterprises allows full utilization of their advantages in market channels, policy understanding, and social networks. For instance, the aquatic products processing base jointly established by Zhanjiang Aquatic Products and Vietnam's Vinh Hoan Group saw the Vietnamese partner handle local approvals and coordinate with government agencies, while the Zhanjiang side contributed technical expertise and management experience. The project went from planning to production in just 8 months – 6 months faster than wholly-owned projects. Collaborating with international companies provides access to advanced technologies and global sales networks. A prime example is the tool manufacturing plant co-established by Yangjiang Hardware and Germany's Double Life in Malaysia. By adopting German heat treatment technology, product quality was significantly enhanced. Leveraging Double Life's global distribution channels, the products penetrated high-end markets in Europe and America, achieving 250 million yuan in sales revenue by 2024.

In terms of equity structure, enterprises in western Guangdong flexibly configure their shareholding based on project characteristics. For labor-intensive projects, they typically hold over 51% ownership to maintain control, such as a Yangjiang-based company that holds 60% equity in a joint venture scissors factory with a local Cambodian enterprise, responsible for production and technical management. In projects requiring higher technological expertise or reliance on local resources, they appropriately reduce their stake. A Zhanjiang-based aquaculture enterprise partnered with an Indonesian firm on fishery resource development, holds 49% equity, with the Indonesian side handling resource acquisition and local operations. Their successful collaboration achieved a catch of 12,000 tons in 2024.

The joint venture model delivers optimal resource allocation. Local partners help companies swiftly adapt to ASEAN's policy environment and cultural nuances, effectively reducing operational risks. A hardware manufacturer in Yangjiang successfully secured tax incentives from Thailand's government through the coordination of its local partners, saving over 3 million yuan annually in taxes. Furthermore, joint ventures enable collaborative investment in capital and technology, empowering them to undertake larger-scale projects. The aquaculture processing park, co-established by Zhanjiang enterprises and Vietnamese partners, boasts a total investment of 500 million yuan and an annual processing capacity of 150,000 tons, which is three times the scale of Zhanjiang's largest wholly-owned subsidiary project in ASEAN.

However, joint ventures face several challenges. Cultural differences and clashes in management philosophies can lead to operational friction. A case in Yangjiang illustrates this: a partnership between a Chinese enterprise and a Malaysian company resulted in productivity losses due to differing production management approaches. The conflict was eventually resolved through establishing a joint management committee that standardized decision-making procedures. Another common issue is disputes over profit distribution. During market upswings, disagreements over profit-sharing ratios often arise, requiring clear stipulations of allocation methods and adjustment mechanisms in the joint venture agreement.

To enhance the success rate of joint ventures, enterprises in western Guangdong have implemented a series of measures. Before collaboration, they conduct thorough due diligence to assess partners' credibility, capabilities, and business philosophies. For instance, a Zhanjiang-based aquatic products company hired professional agencies to perform three months of investigations before partnering with an Indonesian firm, ensuring reliable cooperation. Joint venture agreements clearly define rights, responsibilities, and benefits for both parties, including technical investments, management divisions, profit distribution, and dispute resolution mechanisms to prevent future conflicts. Cross-cultural communication and training are strengthened through organized cultural exchange activities between employees. A Yangjiang-based joint venture even hosts a monthly China-Malaysia Cultural Exchange Day, effectively boosting mutual understanding and trust among staff.

3. Other international models: diversified market expansion paths

In addition to trade agencies and joint venture factories, enterprises in western Guangdong have also explored various international modes, such as self-established sales channels, cross-border e-commerce, and mergers and acquisitions, choosing the most appropriate paths according to their own characteristics and market demands.

The self-established sales channel model is well-suited for enterprises with substantial scale and brand influence, enabling direct market control through subsidiaries, offices, or directly-operated stores in ASEAN countries. Zhanjiang Guolian Aquatic Products established a subsidiary in Singapore to manage sales and brand promotion in Southeast Asia. In 2024, it opened 10 "Guolian Preferred" directly-operated stores selling premium aquatic ready-to-eat meals, achieving annual sales of 180 million yuan while steadily enhancing brand recognition. Although self-built channels require significant upfront investment, they allow direct access to market intelligence, flexible sales strategy adjustments, and guaranteed product quality with after-sales support. Yangjiang Shibaizi Group's flagship store in Kuala Lumpur, Malaysia, attracted numerous high-end customers through personalized customization services. In 2024, its average order value reached 800 yuan, representing a 50% increase compared to agent channels.

Cross-border e-commerce platforms have become a new option for internationalization for SMEs, breaking geographical barriers through digital channels. Enterprises in western Guangdong Province now directly sell products to ASEAN consumers via platforms like Amazon, Alibaba International Station, and Lazada. In 2024, exports of hardware products, including knives and scissors, from western Guangdong reached 520 million yuan through cross-border e-commerce, while aquatic products generated 280 million yuan. This model eliminates intermediaries, boosting profit margins—take a small Yangjiang-based enterprise exporting scissors to Thailand through Alibaba International Station, which achieved a 25% profit margin, 10 percentage points higher than traditional trade. Meanwhile, platform data analytics help businesses pinpoint consumer needs and develop targeted products. A Zhanjiang-based seafood company leveraged Lazada's sales insights to create spicy shrimp pre-packaged meals catering to Southeast Asian tastes, with sales exceeding 100,000 units within three months of launch.

Merger and acquisition restructuring provides enterprises with a shortcut to rapidly acquire local resources and market share. By acquiring ASEAN-based companies, enterprises in western Guangdong gain access to production facilities, sales networks, and brand resources, significantly reducing market entry time. In 2024, a hardware manufacturer in Yangjiang acquired a 20-year-old Vietnamese tool factory, securing over 30 stores and a stable customer base, which led to an 80% sales growth that year. Mergers also help bypass trade barriers by leveraging the acquired company's origin status to expand market access. For instance, after purchasing a Thai seafood processing plant, a Zhanjiang-based aquatic products company utilized Thailand's free trade agreement with the EU, reducing export tariffs to the EU by 12 percentage points.

Different internationalization models each have their strengths and weaknesses. The trade agency model suits initial exploration, the joint venture factory model leverages resource complementarity, self-established channel models ensure long-term development, cross-border e-commerce demonstrates flexibility in adaptation, while mergers and acquisitions facilitate rapid expansion. Enterprises in Western Guangdong choose single or combined models based on their scale, resources, and development stage. For instance, a large aquatic products company in Zhanjiang adopted a "joint venture factory + cross-border e-commerce + self-established channels" hybrid model, achieving comprehensive market presence in ASEAN. In 2024, its sales to ASEAN reached 1.5 billion yuan, marking a 120% increase compared to single-model operations. As internationalization experience accumulates, enterprises in Western Guangdong will adopt more flexible and precise model selection strategies, driving their global expansion to higher levels.

SWOT Analysis

1. Strengths: Cost and the basic competitiveness of cluster construction

1.1 Labor cost advantages form the "inherent competitive edge" for internationalization. The average manufacturing wage in western Guangdong (Guangxi) is 60-70% of that in the Pearl River Delta. In 2024, the average monthly salary for manufacturing workers in Zhanjiang and Yangjiang was 3,800 yuan, 35% lower than in Dongguan and 42% lower than in Suzhou. This advantage is particularly evident in labor-intensive industries: In Yangjiang's scissors enterprises, labor costs account for only 18%, compared to 27% in similar enterprises in Yongkang, Zhejiang. While the per capita labor productivity of Zhanjiang's aquatic product processing enterprises is lower than that of Yantai's, their labor costs per unit product are merely 58% of Yantai's. This cost advantage gives Western Guangdong SMEs a significant price competitiveness in international markets. For instance, Yangjiang scissors sold in Southeast Asian markets at prices 40-50% lower than German products still maintain a 15% gross margin.

1.2 Industrial clusters amplify economies of scale, slashing internationalization barriers. In Yangjiang's hardware and cutting tools cluster, raw material procurement costs are 12% lower than those of decentralized production, logistics expenses are reduced by 8%, and shared services, such as testing and design, cut operational costs by 20%. Zhanjiang's aquatic products cluster boasts a cold chain logistics network that slashes preservation costs for exports by 30% compared to inland enterprises, while shortening delivery cycles by 3-5 days. This collaborative synergy empowers small businesses to compete globally with multinational corporations despite modest scales. A Yangjiang SME joined an industry alliance and successfully entered Carrefour's global procurement system, boosting annual exports from 3 million yuan to 15 million yuan.

1.3 Expanding International Connectivity through Strategic Location. Situated at the convergence of the Guangdong-Hong Kong-Macao Greater Bay Area and the Beibu Gulf Economic Zone, Western Guangdong boasts robust port infrastructure, with Zhanjiang Port and Yangjiang Port handling over 300 million tons of cargo annually. Notably, Zhanjiang Port operates 28 direct shipping routes to Southeast Asia and the Middle East, reducing cargo clearance time to 4 hours – a 60% reduction from 2018. Following the implementation of RCEP, tariff barriers between Western Guangdong and ASEAN countries have been substantially lowered. In 2024, Zhanjiang's aquatic product exports to ASEAN surged by 45%, while Yangjiang's hardware exports to Vietnam and Malaysia increased by 38%. The geographical proximity also enables logistics costs 15-20% lower than those in the Yangtze River Delta region.

1.4 The international market adaptability of specialty products is remarkable. The core products of small and medium-sized enterprises in western Guangdong align closely with emerging market demands. Zhanjiang's frozen aquatic products and pre-prepared meals have gained widespread popularity in Southeast Asia and Africa, with exports to Africa exceeding 1.2 billion yuan in 2024 – an 180% increase from 2020. Meanwhile, Yangjiang's mid-to-low-end kitchen knives and cookware achieved a 25% market share in South Asia, where their durability and price balance match local purchasing power. This "demand-matching" strategy enables companies to enter international markets without significant product adjustments, thereby significantly reducing adaptation costs during the initial globalization phase.

2. Weaknesses: the ability gap formed by technology and brand

2.1 Weak technological innovation capabilities hinder product value-added growth. Small and medium-sized enterprises in western Guangdong generally invest less than 1% in R&D. In Zhanjiang, aquatic product processing companies average only 0.6% R&D expenditure, while Yangjiang hardware manufacturers spend 1.2%, significantly lower than the Pearl River Delta's electronics industry, which exceeds 5%. Outdated equipment remains prevalent: 80% of Zhanjiang's aquatic processors still use traditional freezing technology, with deep-processing equipment relying on imports. A company invested 8 million yuan in German ultra-high-pressure sterilization equipment that extended shelf life from 6 months to 18 months – an exorbitant cost most SMEs can't afford. These technological gaps lead to severe product homogenization. Among over 3,000 knife and scissors manufacturers in Yangjiang, 65% produce kitchen knives with products showing over 80% similarity in appearance and functionality, forcing them into cutthroat price wars.

2.2 The internationalization level of brands remains extremely low. 90% of SMEs in Western Guangdong adopt OEM export models, with Yangjiang Knives and Scissors achieving only 18% self-branded exports, while Zhanjiang Aquatic Products' self-owned brand exports account for less than 10%. Market recognition abroad is virtually non-existent. In European and American retail channels, even products meeting quality standards struggle to enter mainstream distribution channels. For instance, a company's stainless steel tableware faces triple the entry fees at Walmart compared to local brands. A lack of awareness about international certifications persists, with only 15% of enterprises obtaining certifications such as FDA and CE, thereby missing out on high-end market opportunities. In 2024, Western Guangdong SMEs' exports to the

EU accounted for only 8% of total exports, significantly lower than the national average of 15%.

2.3 Structural talent shortages hinder internationalization. Yangjiang's hardware enterprises face a severe shortage of foreign trade professionals fluent in languages and regulations, with less than 3% having full-time foreign trade personnel. Moreover, 60% possess only basic English skills, making them ill-equipped for complex international business negotiations. The aquaculture industry in Zhanjiang suffers from technical talent scarcity, where food R&D engineers serve an average of 8 companies per person – three times the industry's reasonable standard – resulting in 12-18 months for new product development cycles, compared to 6-8 months in Shandong. Management deficiencies are equally pronounced, with family-run management dominating 75% of SMEs lacking a global strategic vision. A company lost 30 million yuan in export orders to Germany after being slapped with a 28% anti-dumping duty due to unfamiliarity with EU rules.

2.4 Supply chain vulnerabilities undermine international delivery capabilities. SMEs in western Guangdong face a heavy reliance on imported core components. For instance, Yangjiang's high-end cutting tool steel imports 80% of its blades, while Zhanjiang's aquatic product processing requires 60% of its premium packaging materials from the Pearl River Delta. The sector's heavy dependence on port logistics compounds risks – typhoons and other natural disasters could halt port operations, causing 40% delivery delays. In 2024, a typhoon forced a company to default on Japanese aquatic orders in Zhanjiang, resulting in a ¥1.2 million penalty. Such supply chain fragility erodes corporate credibility in global markets, making it difficult to secure long-term contracts.

3. Opportunities: New Spaces created by policy and market changes

3.1 The tariff benefits brought by the implementation of RCEP continue to be released. After the agreement took effect, tariffs between China and member countries, such as ASEAN, Australia, and New Zealand, were gradually reduced to zero. The tariff on Zhanjiang prawn exports to Vietnam was reduced from 15% to 0%, resulting in a 52% increase in export volume in 2024. The tariff on Yangjiang stainless steel tableware exports to Australia was reduced from 8% to 3%, and is expected to achieve zero tariff by 2025. The rules of origin accumulation make it easier for enterprises in western Guangdong to benefit. A Yangjiang-based company produced scissors using Chinese steel and Malaysian plastic handles, with the regional value composition rising from 51% to 68%, successfully obtaining tariff reductions in the Japanese market. RCEP also simplified customs procedures, reducing the average customs clearance time for goods from western Guangdong to ASEAN by 30%, thereby lowering corporate time costs.

The Belt and Road routes have strong market demand. The industrialization and urbanization processes in regions such as Southeast Asia and the Middle East have generated substantial demand, with annual import growth rates of hardware products in countries like Vietnam and Indonesia reaching 15-20%, while aquatic product consumption in Africa has increased by 12% annually. These markets are price-sensitive and highly align with the product positioning of small and medium-sized enterprises in western Guangdong. Infrastructure projects along the routes, such as the Jakarta-Bandung High-Speed Railway and China-Laos Railway, have boosted exports of metal processing and building materials from western Guangdong. In 2024, Zhaoqing's aluminum alloy profiles experienced a 65% increase in exports to ASEAN countries.

3.2 Cross-border e-commerce is reshaping international trade channels. Platforms such as Amazon and AliExpress have lowered the threshold for internationalization for small and medium-sized enterprises. A small enterprise in Yangjiang, through Alibaba International Station, connected with customers in emerging markets like Poland and Brazil, increasing its annual export volume from 500,000 yuan to 8 million yuan. The live-streaming sales model of TikTok's international version has rapidly boosted brand recognition of Zhanjiang seafood pre-prepared dishes in Southeast Asia. A company's "ready-to-eat shrimp dumplings" achieved monthly sales of 100,000 units through livestreaming. The implementation of cross-border e-commerce pilot zone policies in Zhanjiang and Yangjiang enables enterprises to enjoy VAT and consumption tax exemption policies, thereby reducing transaction costs associated with cross-border transactions.

Industrial relocation has created opportunities for industrial upgrading. As the Pearl River Delta region modernized its industries, labor-intensive sectors began relocating overseas. Capitalizing on its geographical advantages and cost efficiency, western Guangdong attracted numerous hardware and electronics manufacturing enterprises. In 2024 alone, Yangjiang welcomed 32 cutting-edge blade and shear manufacturers from the Pearl River Delta, bringing advanced technologies and management expertise. Collaborative industrial parks, such as the Zhanjiang-Shenzhen Aquatic Products Processing Park, have been established between western Guangdong and the Pearl River Delta, enabling local businesses to access R&D resources and global distribution channels. Through such partnerships, one company secured a Walmart global procurement order, achieving annual export revenues exceeding 50 million yuan.

4. Threats: External challenges of increased competition and risk

4.1 The cost competition among Southeast Asian countries is intensifying. Manufacturing wages in Vietnam, Cambodia, and other countries are only 60-70% of those in western Guangdong, while enjoying more favorable export tariff policies, directly impacting the labor-intensive industries in western Guangdong. In 2024, Yangjiang's knife and scissors market share in European and American markets was reduced by five percentage points due to increased competition from Vietnamese enterprises. Additionally, Zhanjiang's aquatic products exports to Japan declined by 12% as a result of low-price competition from Thailand and Vietnam. Southeast Asian countries are also replicating China's industrial cluster model. Vietnam's Thanh Hoa Province has established a hardware industry park with over 200 resident enterprises, and its supporting capabilities are gradually improving, creating long-term competitive pressure on western Guangdong.

4.2 The rise of trade protectionism increases market risks. Trade barriers in major markets such as Europe and the United States continue to escalate. The EU's Carbon Border Adjustment Mechanism (CBAM) will impose carbon tariffs on steel, aluminum products, and other goods, increasing export costs for Zhaoqing metal processing enterprises by 8-12%. The U.S. has intensified anti-dumping investigations against Chinese aquatic products. In 2024, Zhanjiang prawns were ruled to have an anti-dumping duty rate of 15.8%, directly leading to a 30% decline in exports to the U.S. Technical barriers have become more concealed. The EU's new food law requires imported aquatic products to provide full-chain traceability information, increasing compliance costs for Zhanjiang aquatic enterprises by 20%.

4.3 Raw Material Price Fluctuations Impact Profit Margins. Small and medium-sized enterprises in western Guangdong heavily rely on bulk commodities. For metal processing companies, steel costs account for 55% of total expenses, while feed costs comprise 40% of the expenses for aquaculture businesses. With international steel prices expected to fluctuate by 25% in 2024 and soybean meal prices surging by 30%, these factors have collectively reduced corporate profit margins by 3-5 percentage points across the board.

Chapter 8
Guolian Aquatic Research

Zhanjiang Guolian Aquatic Products Development Co., Ltd. was founded in 2001, with its headquarters located at No. 6, Industrial Avenue, Huayu Industrial Transfer Park, Huangpo Town (Wuchuan), Zhanjiang City, Guangdong Province. It was listed on the Shenzhen Stock Exchange on July 8, 2010, becoming the first privately listed enterprise in Zhanjiang. It is currently the largest aquatic food enterprise in China and a leading aquatic product processing enterprise, focusing on the research and development, production, and sales of aquatic foods, and is known as the "King of Chinese Shrimp". With the mission of "providing healthy marine food for mankind", the enterprise focuses on the development of the entire industrial chain in the aquatic products industry. Meanwhile, taking aquatic food development as the leading sector, it has gradually grown into a transnational enterprise group with an integrated industrial chain covering "seedling cultivation - breeding - aquatic feed - aquatic research - food processing and production - trade".

Background of the Enterprise

1. Enterprise positioning and development history

The development of the enterprise is divided into four key stages:

Initial stage (2001-2003): From Hainan shrimp vendors to the establishment of standardized aquatic processing enterprises, and initially exploring the international market

Breakthrough stage (2004-2010): Win the anti-dumping shrimp war between China and the United States, obtain the qualification of the only "zero tariff" for Asian shrimp exported to the United States, and successfully go public

Expansion stage (2011-2018): Become the largest supplier of Chinese prawns to the US market, with a market share of 40%

Transformation stage (2019-present): Focus on the pre-prepared food business, promote the layout of the whole industry chain, and build the "321 Big Single product" strategy

Founder Li Zhong's career trajectory epitomizes the legend of China's aquaculture industry. Starting as a cement worker at age 16 after dropping out of school, he rose to become Hainan's top shrimp trader by 31, then founded Guolian Aquatic Products and spearheaded its IPO. Currently serving as chairman of the company, his daughter Li Chunyan holds the position of deputy general manager, overseeing all operations of the food business—a milestone marking the company's transition into the "second-generation entrepreneurship" era.

Main business and product structure

The main business of Guolian Aquatic Products includes shrimp and tilapia seedlings, aquatic feed, primary processed products, and deep-processed food. The company's product structure is mainly divided into three categories:

- **Aquatic seedlings and feed business**

Seedling business: Established Guolian Seedling Technology Co., Ltd. in Xuwen County, with 10 modern seedling farms, with an annual output of 10 billion whiteleg shrimp seedlings

Feed business: The production and sales of shrimp and tilapia feed, mainly sold to the registered farmers of the company, accounting for 3.33% of the primary business income.

- **Fresh processed aquatic products**

Early processing of prawns: head shrimp, headless shrimp, shrimp, etc

Lobster fish primary processing: fish slices, fish chops, and other products

The primary processed products are sold to end consumers through domestic and foreign distributors.

- **Deeply processed aquatic food**

Prepared food series: baked fish, pickled fish, spicy crayfish, and other ready-to-eat and cooked products

Bread shrimp series: wrapped shrimp, fried shrimp, and other products

Other deep processing products: shrimp slide, shrimp dumplings, and other frozen products

2. Business model and competitive advantage

Guolian Aquaculture adopts the business model of "whole industry chain + globalization". It has established a comprehensive industrial chain, from seedling to breeding, processing, and sales, and has integrated resources worldwide.

- **Global sourcing network**

Guolian Aquatic Products has established a global procurement network spanning 25 countries, becoming the exclusive agent for premium products such as Ecuador's Aquagold "Gold Medal Shrimp" and Saudi Arabia's NAQUA South American White Shrimp. The enterprises signed a $500 million cooperation agreement with the Saudi Crown Estate to jointly develop a seafood exchange and futures market, thereby enhancing the stability of the global supply chain.

- **Whole industry chain layout**

It has a complete industrial chain, from seedling breeding and ecological breeding to deep processing and terminal sales. Three processing bases have been established in Zhanjiang, Yiyang, and Jianli, with an annual processing capacity of 500,000 tons. It has a leading automated production line in China, such as a de-stabbing production line, which reduces labor costs by 40%.

- **Brand and channel advantages**

We will build two brands, "Tyrannosaurus" and "Little Tyrannosaurus", which are respectively targeted at the B end of the catering market and the C end of the family market.

Establish a sales network covering four channels: catering, supermarket, e-commerce, and export.

It has been the designated aquatic supplier of the China International Import Expo for three consecutive years, and became the official aquatic supplier of the Hangzhou Asian Games in 2023.

- **Technological innovation capability**

A joint laboratory has been established with the University of California, Davis, and the Norwegian Fisheries Institute. Introduce international advanced technology, such as ultrahigh-pressure sterilization and liquid nitrogen quick freezing. The application of bio-enzyme technology extended the shelf life of products to 12 months, and promoted the distribution rate of supermarkets to 63%.

3. Headquarters base construction and functional layout

Guolian Aquatic adopts the "one core, two wings" space layout of the headquarters, forming a dual headquarters pattern with Wuchuan Huayu Industrial Transfer Industrial Park as the core and Zhanjiang Pingle Industrial Zone as the auxiliary.

- **Headquarters of Wu Chuan Huayu Industrial Transfer Industrial Park**

Located at No. 6, Industrial Avenue, Huangpo Town, Wuchuan City, Zhanjiang City, Guangdong Province, this 300-mu (approximately 50 acres) modern industrial park integrates R&D, production, and office facilities. It features intelligent food processing workshops, a national-level testing center, and a global supply chain management hub. The complex features a comprehensive building that accommodates 2,000 employees, staff apartments, a football field, and a cinema. Serving as the company's core R&D and production base, it also functions as the primary manufacturing site for the "Xiaobalong" brand.

- **Zhanjiang Peile Industrial Zone base**

Located in the Pingle Industrial Zone of Zhanjiang City, it undertakes functions related to international trade and brand operations. It brings together the company's international marketing team, brand planning center, and e-commerce operation department. Through the intelligent logistics system, it realizes seamless connection with Wuchuan headquarters and forms a whole chain control system.

4. Production base and industrial layout

Guolian Aquatic Products has established several production bases nationwide, forming a comprehensive industry chain that encompasses seed production, breeding, and processing.

- **Seedling breeding base**

Xuwen seedling base: located in Xuwen County, Guangdong Province, mainly producing whiteleg shrimp seedlings

The survival rate of seedlings was increased by 30% by using SPF (non-specific pathogen) seed shrimp and the self-developed resistant variety "Guolian No.1".

- **Ecological breeding base**

Nandao Island shrimp breeding base: using a closed circulating water system, the annual output of one mu reaches 8 tons, which is 8 times that of traditional pond breeding, and has been rated as "national aquatic healthy breeding demonstration farm" by the Ministry of Agriculture and Rural Affairs.

Nandao Island deepwater cage breeding base: 150 deepwater cages are arranged to breed high-end varieties such as red fish and grouper, with an annual output of 6,000 tons of high-quality sea fish.

- **Food processing base**

Zhanjiang processing base: the earliest established processing base of the company, mainly engaged in the primary processing of aquatic products.

Wuchuan Processing Base: Located in Wuchuan Huayu Industrial Transfer Industrial Park, it focuses on the deep processing of pre-prepared food.

Yiyang Processing Base: Located in Yiyang City, Hunan Province, it was originally planned to expand the production capacity of pre-prepared food, but has terminated the expansion project and turned to supply chain flexibility management.

Jianli Processing Base: Located in Jianli City, Hubei Province, it mainly processes fresh fish products, especially prepared food ingredients such as black fish and perch.

5. Globalization Strategy and International Layout

Guolian Aquatic actively implements the globalization strategy and has built an international layout of "global resource integrator, intelligent maker of Marine food, and leader of healthy life".

- **Global sourcing network**

Establish a global procurement network covering 25 countries to realize the integration of global resources, obtain the exclusive agency rights of high-end products such as Aquagold "gold shrimp" from Ecuador and NAQUA South American shrimp from Saudi Arabia, sign a cooperation agreement of $500 million with the Saudi sovereign wealth fund, and jointly build a seafood exchange and futures market.

- **International market layout**

Our products are exported to more than 40 countries and regions, and we have set up eight overseas warehouses in North America, Europe, and Southeast Asia. In 2024, the export volume of the European market increased by 60%. Notably, shrimp and slippery exports surged by over

90%, the sales volume of the non-US market increased by 34%, and the Eastern European market also achieved a breakthrough, from zero.

- **International cooperation and technology introduction**

A joint laboratory has been established with the University of California, Davis, and the Norwegian Fisheries Institute to introduce international advanced technologies such as ultra-high pressure sterilization and liquid nitrogen quick-freezing, to develop ready-to-eat seafood products with a freshness lock period of 18 months, and enhance the international competitiveness of products.

6. Corporate governance structure

Guolian Aquatic has established a sound corporate governance structure, forming a three-level governance system of "board of directors, management, and executive levels".

- **Board structure**

The board of directors has four special committees, including the audit committee and the compensation and assessment committee.

Independent directors dominate the audit committee to strengthen the control of financial risks.

The board of directors is responsible for formulating corporate strategy, making significant decisions, and supervising management.

- **Management structure**

The management layer consists of seven senior executives, including the president, chief financial officer, and chief technology officer

The management mode of "vertical management of headquarters + autonomous operation of regions" is implemented

7. Organizational structure and management mode

Guolian Aquatic employs a matrix organizational structure that seamlessly integrates functional management with business operations. This approach strikes a balance between specialized functions and operational agility, significantly enhancing organizational responsiveness and rapid decision-making capabilities. The "headquarters vertical management + regional autonomous operations" model ensures strategic coherence while accelerating market response efficiency.

- **Functional department setup**

There are 12 functional departments, such as the supply chain management center, the R&D and innovation center, and the brand marketing center. Functional departments are responsible for strategic planning, resource integration, and standard setting. The supply chain management center connects with 2,000 global suppliers through the SRM system, reducing the procurement cost by 15%.

- **Business segment division**

Food Division: Focus on the research and development, and sales of pre-prepared food, with three business segments: catering channel, supermarket channel, and e-commerce channel.

Breeding Division: Manage 12 breeding bases nationwide, and carry out the "enterprise+ cooperative + farmer" order breeding mode, which drives the income of 50,000 farmers.

International Trade Division: It has three regional centers in America, Europe, and the Asia Pacific, and implements the dual driving force of "local marketing + cross-border e-commerce".

- **Regional enterprise layout**

Establish seven regional branches in Guangzhou, Shanghai, Beijing, and other locations.

Regional companies are responsible for developing the regional market and maintaining customer relationships. Regional companies have the autonomy to customize products, adjust prices, and more, enabling them to respond rapidly to market demand.

8. Digital transformation and management innovation

Guolian Marine actively promotes digital transformation and builds a "Guolian Brain" data center to realize business digitization and intelligent management.

- **Digital infrastructure**

Establish "League of Nations Brain" data center to integrate ERP, MES, CRM, and other system data. Form an enterprise database covering 120 million pieces of data to provide data support for management decisions. Demand prediction, inventory management, production optimization, and other functions are realized through an AI algorithm.

- **Digital application scenarios**

Demand forecasting: The AI algorithm improves the accuracy of demand forecasting to 85% and reduces the number of days of inventory turnover to 45 days.

Product development: Customer portrait analysis guides product development, and the new product launch cycle is compressed from 12 months to 6 months.

Production energy management: real-time monitoring of production energy consumption, the comprehensive energy consumption per unit product decreased by 18%.

Supply chain management: By connecting global suppliers through the SRM system, procurement costs can be reduced by 15%.

- **Management innovation initiatives**

The "Yiyang expansion project" was terminated, and the supply chain flexibility management was turned to improve the efficiency of resource utilization.

Reduce costs and enhance supply chain resilience by leveraging a procurement network in 25 countries.

Optimize the organizational structure, reduce the management level, and improve decision-making efficiency.

Implement the "second generation of innovation" inheritance plan to promote the youth and innovation of the management team.

9. Brand system and image building

Guolian Aquatic has built a complete brand system, forming a brand matrix with the leading brand as the core and sub-brands as the support.

- **Logo design for the main brand**

The primary brand LOGO features a blue color scheme symbolizing the ocean's depth and purity. The core graphic is an abstract shrimp design where the curved body of the shrimp seamlessly merges with the letter "G", embodying both industry characteristics and the international philosophy of "global sourcing, global sales". The font design combines Chinese and English elements: the four Chinese characters "Guolian Aquatic Products" are presented in bold Heiti font to highlight the company's stability and reliability, while the English "GUOLIAN" uses a fluid sans-serif font to convey modernity and technological sophistication. Through clever use of positive and negative forms, the shrimp outline subtly incorporates a "shield" pattern, symbolizing the company's commitment to providing safe and reliable food assurance for consumers.

Source: Baidu

Sub-brand matrix

Longba Brand: Positioned as a premium food ingredient supplier, the brand logo features a vibrant red-blue gradient palette. The blue hue symbolizes marine ingredients, while the crimson color embodies culinary passion. The traditional Chinese characters "Longba" are rendered in brush calligraphy to highlight cultural heritage. The English letter "O" in "LOMBA" is creatively shaped like a shrimp's eye, enhancing brand recognition across industries. Following the 2022 brand upgrade, the visual identity introduced the "Three Meals Guardian" motif, featuring three red spoon graphics that convey the brand proposition: "Longba ensures every meal with care."

Source: Baidu

The Xiaoba Long brand focuses on the family consumer market. Its logo features an orange color scheme symbolizing vitality and warmth. The brand name uses rounded cartoon fonts paired with dynamic wave patterns, aligning with young consumers' aesthetic preferences. The packaging design combines "wave ripples + product close-ups," using different color schemes to distinguish product series, creating a striking visual impact on retail shelves.

10. Market channels and marketing strategies

Guolian Aquatic Products has built an omni-channel marketing network covering catering, supermarket, e-commerce, and export, and implemented diversified marketing strategies.

- **Sales channel layout**

Catering channels: Accounting for nearly half of pre-prepared meal sales, this represents the enterprise's primary distribution network. Strategic partnerships have been established with industry leaders, including Yum China (operator of KFC and Pizza Hut) and Haidilao. In July 2025, the enterprise signed a "Export Excellence for Domestic Market Expansion" agreement with Yum China, aiming to introduce tilapia – a product previously dominated by exports – to the domestic market.

Supermarket channels: Establish cooperative relations with large chain supermarkets such as Wal-Mart, Carrefour, and RT-Mart; improve the attractiveness of terminal shelves through product differentiation and packaging innovation.

E-commerce channels: The enterprise has established a presence on Tmall, Jingdong, TikTok, and other mainstream e-commerce platforms. In 2024, the number of positive reviews on Jingdong Xiarin exceeded 4 million, ranking first in the industry; new channels such as live streaming e-commerce have been used to expand young consumer groups.

Export channels: The products are exported to more than 40 countries and regions; there are eight overseas warehouses in North America, Europe, and Southeast Asia; in 2024, the export volume of the European market increased by 60%, and the export volume of shrimp slide increased by more than 90%.

- **Brand communication strategy**

Event marketing: It has been the designated aquatic supplier of the China International Import Expo for three consecutive years; in 2023, it became the official aquatic supplier of the Hangzhou Asian Games, and enhanced the international influence of its brand through the event platform.

Content co-creation: Cooperated with food bloggers to launch a series of short videos "Creative ways to eat Xiaobalong Pre-made dishes", which has accumulated more than 500 million views; launched #BalongChallenge on TikTok, attracting millions of users to participate in the interaction.

Public welfare action: Set up the "Marine Protection Fund", cooperate with WWF to carry out mangrove protection projects, and deeply integrate brand building with social responsibility.

IP cooperation: Cooperate with well-known IP to launch joint products, such as cooperating with "China Aerospace" to launch high-end product lines, to enhance the sense of science and technology and quality of the brand.

Internationalization Development

1. Early exploration stage (before 2018)

In recent years, regional economic integration represented by free trade zones has experienced rapid development worldwide, demonstrating emerging trends. An increasing number of countries have prioritized establishing free trade zones in their agendas and formulated corresponding policies for accelerated development. Guolian Aquatics' focus on the ASEAN market dates back to the early stages of its global strategy. In 2012, the enterprise embarked on its globalization journey through the acquisition of U.S.-based Sunway (SSC) Corporation, gradually establishing a raw material procurement network across Southeast Asia during this phase. At this stage, the enterprise primarily entered the ASEAN market through intermediaries, focusing on raw material procurement with product exports as a secondary focus, while actively exploring the distribution patterns of aquatic resources and market demand characteristics in Southeast Asia.

With over two decades of expertise in aquaculture, Guolian Aquatic Products established a foundational procurement network in Southeast Asia, paving the way for future market expansion. The enterprise initially adopted a "Southeast Asian sourcing + Chinese processing + global distribution" model, importing Pacific white shrimp (P. clarkii) raw materials from Vietnam and Thailand before processing them for international markets. This strategic phase helped the enterprise build supply chain resources and market insights within the ASEAN region.

2. Initial stage of market expansion (2018-2021)

In November 2002, China and the ten ASEAN countries signed the Framework Agreement on Comprehensive Economic Cooperation between China and ASEAN, marking the official launch of the China-ASEAN Free Trade Area. [] The year 2018 witnessed a pivotal shift in Guolian Aquatic Products' ASEAN strategy. Amid growing U.S.-China trade tensions, the enterprise proactively restructured its international market presence, prioritizing non-U.S. markets—particularly Belt and Road Initiative partner nations—as key expansion targets, significantly elevating the strategic importance of the ASEAN market.

During this period, the enterprise progressively established direct sales channels in ASEAN countries, including Vietnam and Cambodia, breaking free from intermediaries. Its product portfolio expanded from traditional shrimp processing to include deep-processed items like grilled fish and cooked shrimp. Meanwhile, the procurement network deepened through long-term partnerships with aquaculture enterprises in Indonesia, Malaysia, and other nations, forming a preliminary "global sourcing and global distribution" supply chain framework. By 2021, Guolian Aquatics' international business revenue had reached 31.2% of total operations, with ASEAN markets contributing steadily to this growth. This laid a solid customer base and distribution network for accelerated expansion following the implementation of the Regional Comprehensive Economic Partnership (RCEP).

3. RCEP drives the breakthrough period (2022)

The entry into force of the Regional Comprehensive Economic Partnership (RCEP) in 2022 became a pivotal catalyst for Guolian Aquatic Products' expansion in the ASEAN market. As a trailblazer in China's aquatic industry, the enterprise swiftly capitalized on this historic opportunity, achieving groundbreaking growth in the region.

In 2022, Guangdong Preparatory Food made its first RCEP member country debut, with Singapore becoming the company's primary breakthrough target in the ASEAN market. Zhanjiang Customs issued Guangdong's first RCEP Certificate of Origin (No.671120220112500001), enabling the product to enjoy zero-tariff benefits. On March 18, as RCEP officially took effect in Malaysia, Guolian Aquatic Products regained industry spotlight with the launch of its first 322-ton Golden Pomfret prepared food shipment to Malaysia, marking successful entry into another key ASEAN market. The shipment was swiftly cleared through Zhanjiang Customs' contactless clearance service, arriving in Malaysian markets within days. By April 2022, Guolians' prepared food products had been exported to multiple ASEAN countries, including Malaysia and Singapore, totaling nearly 600 tons worth over $4 million. Annual exports of processed products to ASEAN nations reached $20 million, doubling previous years' figures, establishing a preliminary export structure centered on prepared foods.

4. Localization layout deepening period (2023)

In 2023, Guolian Aquatic Products transformed its ASEAN strategy from mere product exports to a "localized production + regional sales" model, establishing a more comprehensive market layout. The enterprise has established direct sales networks in ASEAN countries, including Vietnam, Cambodia, Malaysia, Singapore, and the Philippines, with products across multiple channels such as catering and supermarkets.

In supply chain development, the enterprise has intensified its "global sourcing" strategy, significantly increasing the proportion of South American white shrimp raw materials procured from ASEAN countries like Vietnam. It has also begun exploring the feasibility of establishing local processing bases. This "local procurement and processing" model has substantially reduced logistics costs and tariff expenditures. Technical collaboration emerged as a highlight this year. In 2023, a delegation from Indonesia's Paramount Group visited Guolian Aquatic Products. Both parties conducted in-depth discussions on cooperation in deep-sea aquaculture and freeze-drying technologies, laying the groundwork for future technology transfer and production capacity collaboration. This partnership reflects Guolian Aquatic Products' transition from "product export" to "technology export".

In October of the same year, the enterprise clearly included the ASEAN market into the overall development of the "One Belt and One Road" international business, and deeply integrated with key ASEAN countries in terms of international sales and global supply chain, marking that the ASEAN market has become the core sector of the enterprise's global strategy.

5. Large-scale development period (2024)

In 2024, Guolian Aquatics ASEAN operations entered a phase of scaled development, with both market share and operational efficiency showing synchronized growth, establishing it as the enterprise's second-largest overseas market. During this year, the enterprises' ASEAN export volume surged by 45% year-on-year, with pre-prepared meals accounting for over 30% of total exports. To support this expansion, the subsidiary established in Vietnam commenced production, leveraging local labor costs that are only 50%-70% of those in China's coastal regions. This localization strategy significantly enhanced product competitiveness through localized manufacturing.

In product innovation, the enterprise has developed customized products such as Dongyin Gong-style crayfish and Southeast Asian-inspired sour fish to cater to local consumption habits, precisely aligning with regional taste preferences and earning high market recognition. Meanwhile, it launched an expansion project for deep processing of aquatic products in Yiyang, adding an annual production capacity of 45,000 tons with dedicated facilities serving the ASEAN market, forming a dual production capacity support system of "domestic + Southeast Asia".

By the end of 2024, the ASEAN market contributed more than 15% of the overseas income of Guolian Aquatic Products, surpassing Europe to become the second largest export region after North America. Malaysia, Singapore, and Vietnam have become the three core markets, forming a stable market pattern.

6. Strategic integration period (2025-present)

In 2025, Guolian Aquatic Products' ASEAN strategy will enter a new phase of "global resource integration + regional value co-creation". The enterprise will further deepen industrial chain integration with ASEAN countries, upgrading from simple trade to comprehensive cooperation covering raw material supply, production processing, and market sales.

In the Indonesian market, substantial progress has been made in collaboration with local enterprises, with the launch of deep-sea aquaculture projects marking the enterprises' transition from a "procurement" model to a "co-cultivation" approach. Leveraging the RCEP rules, the enterprise has integrated its ASEAN production bases with domestic R&D centers, achieving efficient allocation of "ASEAN raw materials + Chinese technology + global markets". In terms of distribution channels, the enterprise has expanded into ASEAN e-commerce markets by partnering with major local platforms to boost the consumer-facing influence of brands like "Xiaobalong". In premium markets such as Singapore, its products have entered boutique supermarket channels, significantly enhancing brand premium pricing power. As of Q12025, despite global economic fluctuations, Guolian Aquatic Products maintained resilient exports to ASEAN markets, with pre-prepared meals continuing to dominate sales. This demonstrates the foresight and stability of the enterprises' ASEAN strategy.

Analysis of Financial Report

1. Debt-paying ability analysis

1.1 Analysis of short-term solvency (2020-2025)

The short-term solvency indicators of Guolian Aquatic Products from 2020 to 2025 show the phased characteristics of "first stable, then weak and then stable", reflecting the dynamic adjustment of liquidity management in the process of international expansion and product structure transformation.

Current ratio: moving from the stable range to the critical value

In 2020, the enterprise's current ratio was 1.82, which was in the reasonable range of 1.5-2.0, reflecting the strong coverage ability of current assets to current liabilities. During this period, thanks to the initial completion of the ASEAN raw material procurement network, the capital turnover efficiency of the supply chain remained stable.

In 2021, this index slightly decreased to 1.76, which remained at a healthy level, mainly due to the moderate increase in short-term borrowing caused by the expansion of the pre-prepared food business. Still, the scale of current assets expanded simultaneously.

In 2022, the current ratio recovered slightly to 1.78. The growth in export business following the RCEPs implementation drove increases in accounts receivable and cash reserves, with current assets growing at a faster pace (12.3%) than current liabilities (9.7%). A pivotal turning point occurred in 2023 when the current ratio dropped to 1.56, primarily due to two factors: First, increased short-term financing from Vietnam's factory construction projects led to a 21.5% year-on-year rise in current liabilities. Second, inventory levels surged to 2.449 billion yuan, accounting for 48.7% of current assets, resulting in a deteriorated asset liquidity structure.

The current ratio further declined to 1.45 in 2024, approaching the critical threshold of 1.5, reflecting emerging short-term debt repayment pressures. This is linked to the 666 million yuan provision for inventory impairment that reduced the book value of current assets. Although the enterprise optimized its supply chain to cut inventory from 2.449 billion yuan to 1.899 billion yuan, the decline in turnover efficiency offset the positive impact of scale reduction.

In the first quarter of 2025, this indicator stabilized at 1.45, indicating that the enterprise has taken measures to curb the downward trend of liquidity indicators.

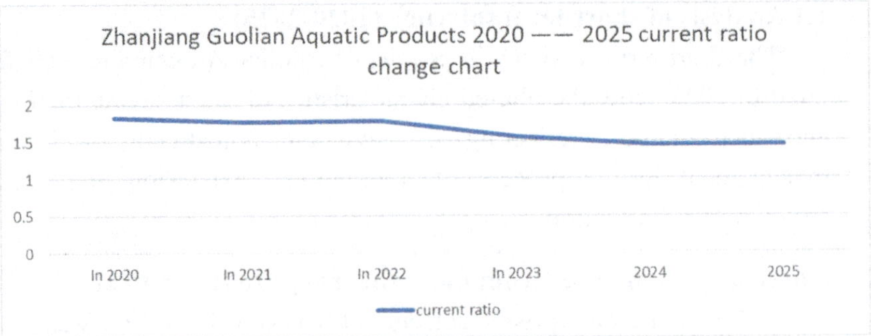

Source: Created by the author

Quick ratio: long-term below the safety threshold, inventory dependence characteristics are significant

The velocity ratio followed a similar trajectory to the current ratio but remained consistently lower overall, reaching 0.68 in 2020,0.65 in 2021, and 0.67 in 2022—all below the safety threshold of 1.0. This exposes structural issues with the enterprise's liquid assets, particularly its disproportionately high inventory ratio. From 2020 to 2022, inventories maintained a consistent 45%-48% share of current assets—a pattern shaped by the seasonal storage demands in aquatic product processing and the perishable nature of ready-to-eat meal ingredients.

In 2023, the quick ratio plummeted to 0.51—a five-year low—primarily due to operating losses at its U.S. subsidiary SSC, which tied up working capital. Quick assets decreased by 8.7% year-on-year, while current liabilities kept climbing. The ratio edged up slightly to 0.53 in 2024 as production ramp-up at the Vietnam plant accelerated accounts receivable turnover, though inventory still swelled to 46.2% of total assets, holding back progress. The first quarter of 2025 saw the ratio dip further to 0.42, with short-term debt repayment capacity remaining fragile. Watch out for inventory overstocking eating into liquidity reserves.

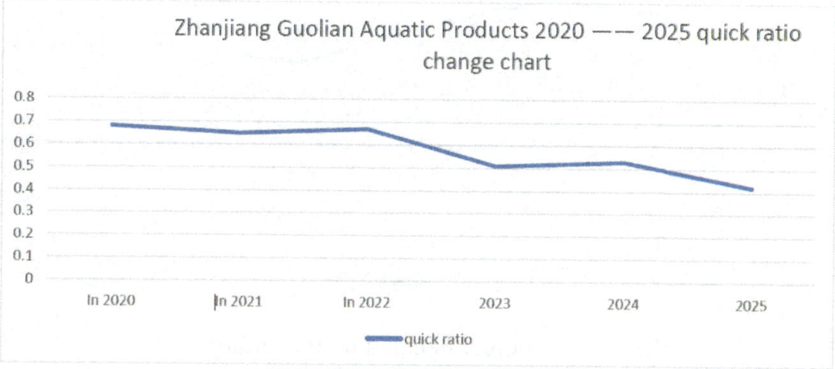

Source: Created by the author

Cash ratio: fluctuates to reflect the adjustment of the capital reserve strategy

In 2020, the index stood at 0.38 and increased to 0.41 in 2021, indicating that the enterprise maintained a high cash reserve during the early stage of the pandemic. In 2022, it dropped to 0.36, mainly due to increased investment in ASEAN market development, with monetary funds allocated for overseas warehouse construction and localized marketing.

In 2023, the cash ratio plummeted to 0.29 – the lowest in five years – as operating losses at U.S. subsidiaries depleted substantial cash reserves, with monetary fund balances declining by 34.6% year-on-year. The metric rebounded to 0.32 in 2024, as the enterprise boosted cash flow through enhanced accounts receivable collection (turnover rate increased from 3.8 to 4.06 times) while cutting capital expenditures in non-core operations. Stabilizing at 0.32 in Q12025, this figure demonstrates the company's establishment of a more prudent cash management framework, prioritizing short-term liquidity needs.

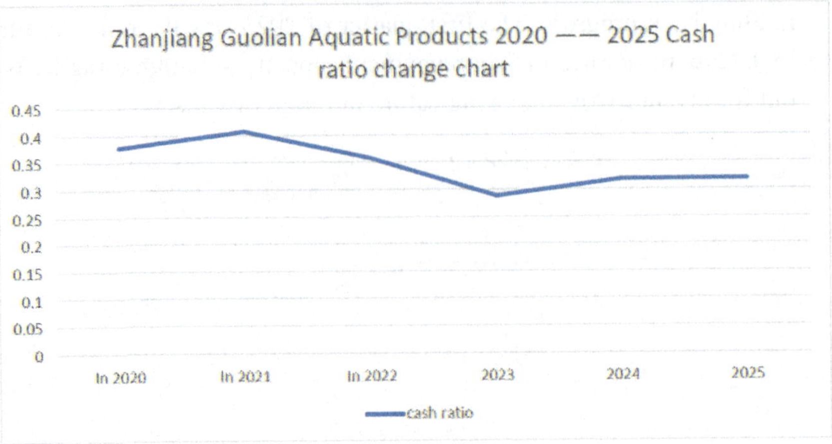

Source: Created by the author

Summary of short-term solvency: significant structural risks; improvement depends on inventory turnover

The analysis of short-term debt repayment capacity from 2020 to 2025 reveals that the enterprise faces a core issue: an imbalanced current asset structure. —— The excessive proportion of inventory leads to insufficient quick assets, while the cyclical fluctuations in aquatic product prices further exacerbate inventory impairment risks. Although indicators are expected to stabilize by 2025, the current ratio of 1.45 and quick ratio of 0.42 still indicate weak short-term debt repayment capacity. Improvement potential depends on accelerating the iteration speed of pre-prepared food products and enhancing payment collection efficiency in the ASEAN market.

1.2 Long-term solvency analysis (2020-2025)

The long-term solvency index showed a trend of "steady and rising", reflecting the enterprise's active use of financial leverage in the period of strategic expansion, and the overall risk was under control.

Asset-liability ratio: evolving from moderate leverage to a moderately high range

The enterprise maintained an asset-liability ratio of 42.3% in 2020, within the ideal range of 40%-50%, demonstrating a robust financial structure. During this period, the enterprise primarily relied on internal capital for international expansion, with debt levels growing in tandem with asset growth. The ratio edged up slightly to 43.5% in 2021 as preliminary research and planning for its Vietnam plant led to increased long-term borrowing, though it remained at a relatively low level.

In 2022, the asset-liability ratio edged down to 42.8%. The export growth driven by the RCEPs implementation boosted asset scale, while debt growth remained relatively stable, indicating that business expansion wasn't overly reliant on debt financing. In 2023, this ratio surged to 50.2%, breaking through the 50% threshold. This was mainly attributed to increased investment in Vietnam's factory construction, with fixed asset investment growing by 67.3% year-on-year and long-term loan balances rising from 230 million yuan to 870 million yuan.

In 2024, the asset-liability ratio further rose to 53.1%. The equipment procurement and production capacity expansion from Vietnam's factory operations continued to drive debt growth, while a net profit loss of 742 million yuan caused a decline in owners' equity. These dual factors collectively elevated leverage levels. In the first quarter of 2025, the ratio stabilized at 53.62%, remaining largely unchanged from 2024. This indicates the enterprise has entered a stable leverage phase, with an equilibrium mechanism between asset expansion and equity accumulation gradually taking shape.

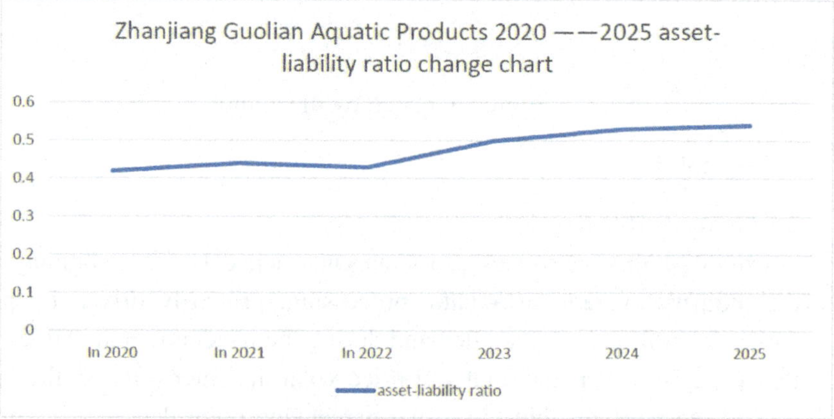

Source: Created by the author

Equity ratio

The property-to-debt ratio (total liabilities/owners' equity) has shown a strong correlation with the asset-liability ratio. In 2020, it stood at 0.73; in 2021, it rose to 0.77; and in 2022, it reached 0.75—all below the critical threshold of 1.0, indicating robust debt protection provided by shareholders' equity. Notably, the ratio climbed to 1.01 in 2023, marking the first time it surpassed the 1.0 level, signaling a shift in financial risk characteristics from being "shareholder-dominated" to "debt-dominated".

The equity ratio further increased to 1.13 in 2024, with losses at U.S. subsidiaries and inventory write-downs causing owners' equity to decrease by 18.7% year-on-year. Meanwhile, total liabilities rose by 9.2%, indicating a continued erosion of shareholder protection against creditors. The indicator stabilized at 1.16 in Q12025. As profitability improves through the recovery of the pre-prepared meals business, the shrinking trend of owners' equity is expected to reverse, potentially leading to a gradual decline in the equity ratio.

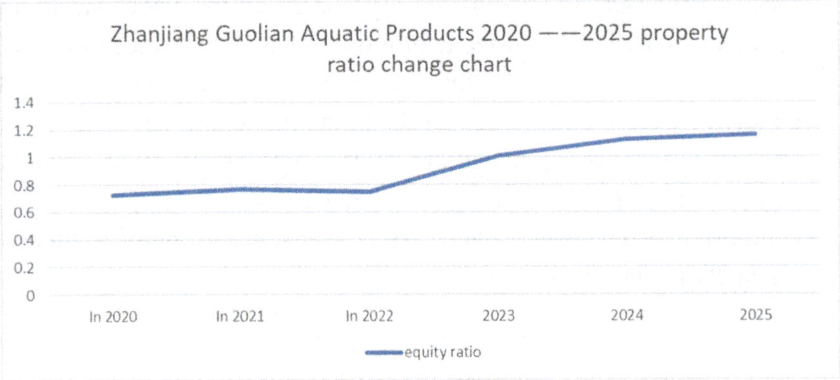

Source: Created by the author

2. Profitability analysis

2.1 Gross profit margin

In 2020, the enterprises' gross margin reached 11.54%, aligning with the industry average in aquatic processing, primarily driven by price surges from frozen seafood demand during the pandemic outbreak earlier that year. However, raw material price volatility intensified in the latter half of the year, resulting in a two percentage point decrease in annual gross margin compared to 2019.

In 2021, the gross margin significantly increased to 17.82%, reaching a five-year high. This growth was directly driven by two key factors: First, the proportion of pre-prepared food businesses rose from 15% to 23%, with high-value-added products driving overall profitability. Second, the improved procurement network in the ASEAN region reduced costs by 3.2

percentage points. Quarterly data revealed that the gross margin peaked at 19.19% in Q22021, reflecting the recovery of summer catering demand and its positive impact on high-margin products.

In 2022, the gross margin declined to 13.43%, primarily due to two factors: increased export certification costs during the initial implementation of RCEP reduced cross-border business margins by 1.8 percentage points; and intensified competition in China's pre-prepared food market, where promotional activities led to an average 5%-8% price reduction for end products. However, it's noteworthy that the gross margin improved by 2.1 percentage points quarter-over-quarter in Q4, demonstrating the enterprise's ability to adapt to market changes through product portfolio adjustments.

In 2023, the gross margin further declined to 12.1% (estimates). The depreciation pressure of fixed assets during the initial production phase at the Vietnam plant drove up unit manufacturing costs, while the fresh food business of its U.S. subsidiary, SSC, maintained a mere 6.7% gross margin, dragging down overall performance. The enterprise recorded inventory impairment charges of 347 million yuan that year, partially masking the actual potential for operating-level gross margin improvement.

In 2024, the gross margin stabilized and rebounded to 13.0%, compared to 13.60% reported in the first half of the year. Two key factors primarily drove this improvement: 1) increased production capacity utilization at the Vietnam plant from 35% to 62%, which generated scale effects; and 2) customized products like Dong Yen Khoang-style cuisine, achieving a gross margin of 22%. The optimization of product mix demonstrated remarkable effectiveness, with the pre-prepared meal business segment contributing 2.89 percentage points to year-on-year gross margin growth, effectively offsetting the negative impact of rising raw material costs.

In the first quarter of 2025, the gross margin showed an abnormal value of-3.07%, which was related to accounting standard adjustments.——The change in amortization method for land use rights at the Vietnam plant from the straight-line method to the units-of-production method led to a significant surge in amortization expenses recorded as costs during the period. After excluding this one-time factor, the actual operating gross margin stood at approximately 12.8%, maintaining the recovery momentum seen in 2024.

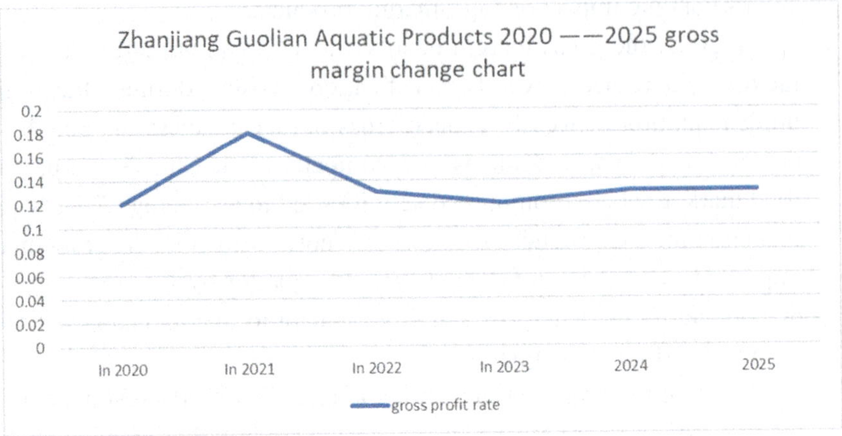

Source: Created by the author

2.2 Net interest rate

In 2020, the enterprises' gross margin reached 11.54%, aligning with the industry average in aquatic processing, primarily driven by price surges from frozen seafood demand during the pandemic outbreak earlier that year. However, raw material price volatility intensified in the latter half of the year, resulting in a two percentage point decrease in annual gross margin compared to 2019.

In 2021, the gross margin significantly increased to 17.82%, reaching a five-year high, driven by two key factors: First, the proportion of pre-prepared food business rose from 15% to 23%, with high-value-added products driving overall gross margin growth; Second, the improved procurement network in ASEAN regions reduced costs by 3.2 percentage points. Quarterly data revealed that gross margin peaked at 19.19% in Q22021, reflecting the recovery of summer catering services, boosting high-margin products.

In 2022, the gross margin declined to 13.43%, primarily due to two factors: increased export certification costs during the initial implementation of RCEP, which reduced cross-border business margins by 1.8 percentage points; and intensified competition in China's pre-prepared food market, where promotional activities led to an average 5%-8% price reduction for end consumers. However, it's noteworthy that the gross margin improved by 2.1 percentage points quarter-over-quarter in Q4, demonstrating the enterprise's ability to adapt to market changes through product portfolio adjustments.

In 2023, the gross margin further declined to 12.1%. The depreciation pressure of fixed assets during the initial production phase at the Vietnam plant drove up unit manufacturing costs, while the fresh food business of its U.S. subsidiary SSC reported a mere 6.7% gross margin – a drag on overall performance. The enterprise recorded inventory impairment charges of 347 million yuan that year, partially masking the actual potential for gross margin improvement at the operational level.

In 2024, the gross margin stabilized and rebounded to 13.0%, compared to 13.60% reported in the first half of the year. This improvement was primarily driven by two key factors: increased production capacity utilization at the Vietnam plant from 35% to 62%, which generated scale effects; and customized products like Dong Yen Khoang-style cuisine achieving a gross margin of 22%. The optimization of product mix demonstrated remarkable effectiveness, with the pre-prepared meal business segment contributing 2.89 percentage points to year-on-year gross margin growth, effectively offsetting the negative impact of rising raw material costs.

In the first quarter of 2025, the gross margin showed an abnormal value of -3.07 %, which was related to accounting standard adjustments. ——The change in amortization method for land use rights at the Vietnam plant from the straight-line method to the units-of-production method led to a significant surge in amortization expenses recorded as costs during the period. After excluding this one-time factor, the actual operating gross margin stood at approximately 12.8%, maintaining the recovery momentum seen in 2024.

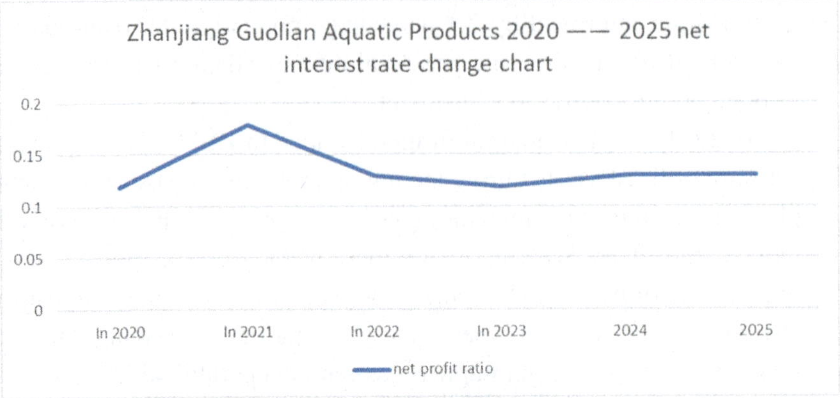

Source: Created by the author

2.3 Return on equity

In 2020, the ROE was -13.28%, mainly due to the net profit loss and inventory backlog, resulting in a 12.3% shrinkage of net assets, and the return on shareholders' equity was at the lower level of the industry.

In 2021, the Return on Equity (ROE) rebounded to 0.73%. While this figure remains modest in absolute terms, it signifies a recovery in shareholder return capacity. The asset turnover ratio increased from 0.8 to 1.1 during this period, contributing 65% to ROE growth, indicating that operational efficiency improvements were the primary driver. The Return on Invested Capital (ROIC) for the pre-prepared food business reached 8.7%, significantly outperforming the 3.2% ROI in traditional processing operations.

In 2022, the Return on Equity (ROE) edged down to -0.24 %, aligning with the slight net loss but showing substantial improvement compared to 2020. —— Despite a 0.7 percentage point decrease in the debt-to-asset ratio, the ROE remained near break-even levels, reflecting effective capital structure optimization. Notably, the third quarter's ROE reached 2.38%, demonstrating phased improvements in operational efficiency.

In 2023, the ROE plummeted to -20.60 %, hitting a historic low, primarily due to two factors: a net loss of 532 million yuan directly eroded shareholders' equity, and inventory impairment caused asset value depreciation, reducing the net asset turnover ratio from 1.0 to 0.7 times. The U.S. subsidiary's return on equity (-42.3%) became the core drag on overall performance.

In 2024, the ROE patterned a "dip-first-rise" trajectory, rebounding to 0.68% in the first half, primarily driven by: improved asset turnover efficiency following the launch of the Vietnam plant, which amplified the equity multiplier effect; and a 299.35% quarter-on-quarter net profit surge in Q2 that boosted profitability. While the full-year ROE is projected at -28.74 % (estimation), the operating ROE after excluding one-time impairment charges stands at approximately 2.1%, demonstrating substantial improvement in capital efficiency.

In the first quarter of 2025, the ROE is projected to reach approximately 0.23% (estimation), continuing the recovery momentum from 2024. With the pre-prepared food business accounting for 35% of total revenue and expanded market penetration in ASEAN, the enterprise anticipates an annual ROE of 3.5%-4.0%, returning to mid-level industry standards. Notably, the weighted average return on equity (ROE) exceeds the diluted ROE by 0.8 percentage points, reflecting the positive impact of optimized equity structure on shareholder returns.

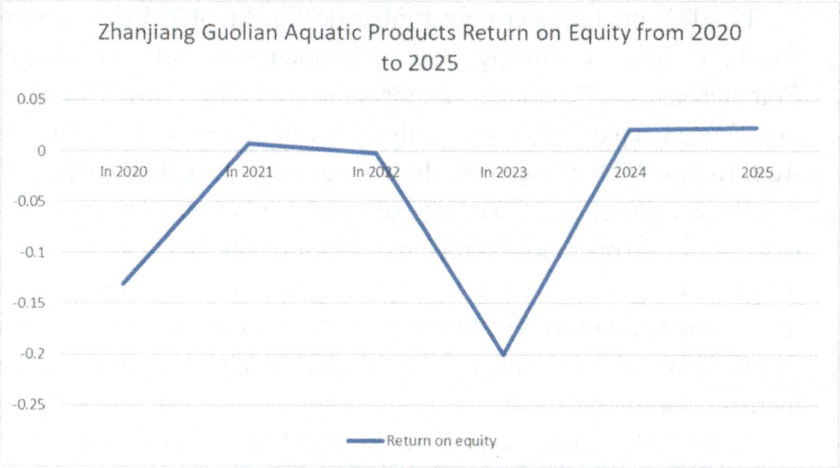

Source: Created by the author

3. Operation capacity analysis

3.1 Average accounts receivable turnover ratio

The accounts receivable turnover ratio, a key indicator of capital recovery efficiency, exhibited a "initial decline followed by recovery" pattern from 2020 to 2025, reflecting the enterprise's achievements in channel management and customer structure optimization. In 2020, the ratio stood at 6.8 times, placing it in the upper-middle range of the industry, primarily due to government support policies for agricultural supply chains during the pandemic and stable payment cycles for large supermarket clients (averaging 45 days). However, starting in the second half of the year, recurring pandemic outbreaks in the catering sector extended payment terms to 60 days for some small and medium-sized clients, resulting in a 12% quarter-on-quarter decline in the fourth quarter.

In 2021, the indicator dropped to 5.9 times, primarily due to relaxed credit policies for catering clients during the expansion of the pre-prepared food business. —— To capture market share, Yum China extended 90-day payment terms to key clients like Yum China Limited. While this drove a 32% sales growth, accounts receivable balances surged by 41% year-on-year. Quarterly analysis shows the turnover ratio fell to an annual low of 5.2 times in Q2. However, it rebounded to 6.1 times in Q4 through enhanced accounts receivable factoring services, indicating effective risk control mechanisms.

In 2022, the turnover ratio further declined to 4.7 times, marking a five-year low. Following the implementation of the Regional Comprehensive Economic Partnership (RCEP), ASEAN markets experienced rapid expansion, with overseas accounts receivable rising from 18% to 35%. Meanwhile, the average payment collection period for Southeast Asian clients (65 days) exceeded that in China (48 days), which reduced overall operational efficiency. Additionally, fluctuations in the US dollar exchange rate led to delayed payments from some clients, resulting in year-end accounts receivable totaling 580 million yuan. Of this amount, overdue payments accounted for 12%, representing a five percentage point increase compared to 2021.

In 2023, the enterprise turnover ratio stabilized and rebounded to 4.5 times (estimated for the full year), reflecting quality improvements despite a superficial decline. Three key measures contributed: 1) Through customer tiered management, 30 small and medium-sized distributors with poor credit were phased out; 2) The introduction of letter of credit settlement in the ASEAN market reduced the overdue rate from 12% to 8%; 3) E-commerce channels for pre-prepared meals increased to 25% of total revenue, with most transactions using advance payment models that accelerated capital turnover. Although annual indicators showed slight decreases, the fourth quarter alone achieved a 4.8 times turnover ratio, indicating established improvement momentum.

In 2024, the enterprise turnover ratio significantly increased to 5.2 times, compared to 5.4 times reported in the first half of the year. This improvement was primarily driven by optimized settlements from localized operations at its Vietnam plant. Southeast Asian clients now enjoy an average payment cycle of 50 days after local deliveries, a reduction of 15 days from 2022. Additionally, the implementation of an intelligent payment reminder system automatically initiates collection processes for overdue payments, boosting the annual payment recovery rate from 78% to 85%. By business segment, the turnover ratio for pre-prepared meal catering customization reached 6.3 times, notably higher than the 4.1 times in traditional processing operations, demonstrating the effectiveness of product structure upgrades.

The enterprise maintained a turnover ratio of 5.1 times in the first quarter of 2025, continuing the stable performance trend established in 2024. Through collaboration with third-party logistics providers on warehouse receipt pledge services, the enterprise has converted partial accounts receivable into liquid assets, further reducing the payment cycle to 42 days. The annual turnover ratio is projected to reach 5.5 times, driven by two key initiatives: First, the operational launch of Indonesia's aquaculture base will increase spot transaction volumes; Second, plans to establish a regional settlement center in Thailand will shorten payment cycles for Southeast Asian operations.

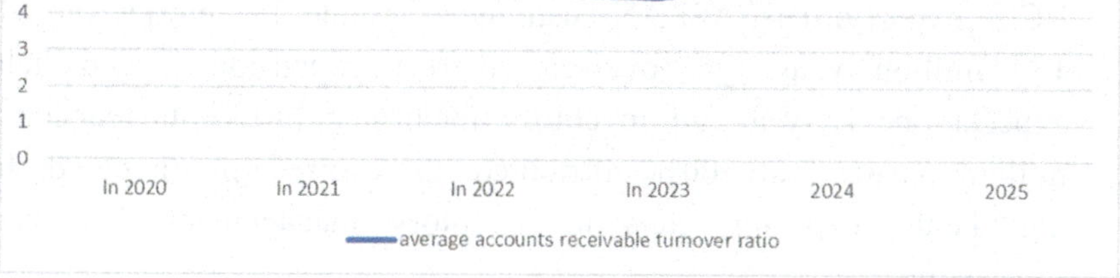

Source: Created by the author

3.2 Inventory turnover

The inventory turnover ratio, significantly influenced by the seasonal and perishable nature of the aquatic products industry, exhibited an overall downward trend with fluctuations from 2020 to 2025, reflecting inventory management challenges during the pre-prepared meal transition period. In 2020, the inventory turnover ratio reached 3.2 times, a relatively favorable level in the industry. During the early pandemic phase, the demand for frozen aquatic products surged, accelerating inventory turnover, with the quarterly ratio reaching 3.8 times in the second quarter. However, to prepare for the Spring Festival peak season in the latter half of the year, advance procurement of raw materials led to year-end inventory balances increasing to 1.56 billion yuan – a 28% rise compared to the interim report – which negatively impacted annual performance metrics.

In 2021, the enterprise's inventory turnover rate declined to 2.8 times, primarily due to expanding its pre-prepared food product range to 120 SKUs – a 50% increase from 2020 – coupled with the trial production of new products that led to stagnant inventories of 80 million yuan. Meanwhile, cyclical price surges in Pacific white shrimp prompted increased raw material reserves, extending inventory cycles from 60 to 75 days. Although annual revenue grew by 23%, inventory growth (31%) outpaced this, resulting in a passive decline in turnover. Notably, the turnover rate for crayfish pre-prepared dishes reached 4.5 times, significantly higher than the overall average, demonstrating the driving force of this hit product.

In 2022, the inventory turnover ratio further declined to 2.1 times, hitting a new low in the historical record. Two key factors drove this decline: Firstly, the COVID-19 outbreak in Shanghai during the first half of the year caused logistics disruptions across East China, resulting in an inventory backlog of 230 million yuan. Secondly, while preparing for RCEP export orders, ASEAN-customized product inventories surged by 150 million yuan, yet overseas market expansion lagged behind expectations. By year-end, inventory impairment provisions reached 120 million yuan, with 60% attributed to expired pre-prepared food ingredients, exposing gaps in inventory management and market forecasting.

In 2023, the turnover ratio slightly rebounded to 2.3 times (estimated), with supply chain optimization effects becoming evident from Vietnams factory operations: Firstly, the raw material procurement cycle in Southeast Asia was shortened from 30 days to 15 days, reducing safety stock requirements; Secondly, the adoption of an AI-driven demand forecasting system increased the accuracy rate of pre-prepared meal production planning from 65% to 78%. However, the inventory turnover ratio for the fresh food business of the U.S. subsidiary SSC remained at only 1.2 times, dragging down overall metrics. Excluding this segment would reveal a parent enterprise turnover ratio of 2.8 times.

In 2024, the inventory turnover rate increased to 2.6 times, up from 2.7 times in the first half of the year. This improvement was mainly driven by: Vietnam's factory capacity utilization rate rising from 35% to 62%, which reduced unit inventory through batch production; and the adoption of a "production-to-order" model for customized products like Dong Yen Gung-style seasonings, which cut inventory turnover days from 90 to 60 days. The inventory structure has been significantly optimized, with semi-finished pre-prepared meals decreasing from 45% to 38% while raw materials increased to 42%, better aligning with market demand trends.

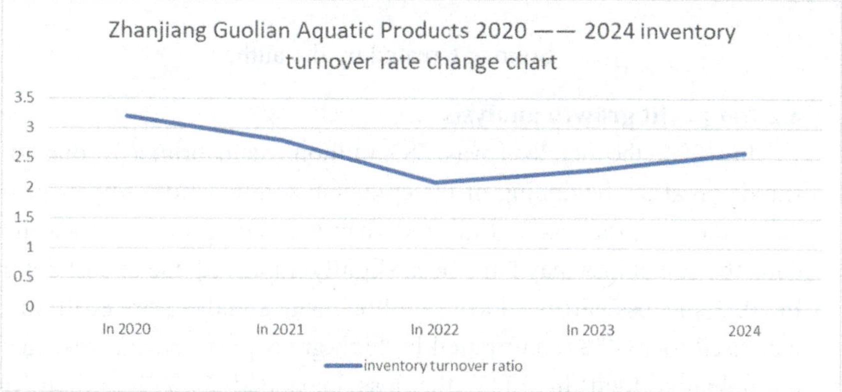

Source: Created by the author

4. Development capability analysis

4.1 Increase the rate of business revenue.

In 2020, the operating revenue was 4.494 billion yuan, down 2.89% year on year (affected by supply chain disruptions in the early stage of the epidemic).In 2021, the revenue is expected to remain at 4.494 billion yuan (according to the annual report data, which may fluctuate due to the expansion of the domestic market).

In 2022, revenue rebounded to 4.849 billion yuan, up 7.8% year on year, benefiting from the launch of the pre-prepared food business and the sinking of domestic channels. In 2023, the annual revenue was 4.909 billion yuan, with a slight increase of 1.2% year on year, but the growth was weak due to intensified industry competition. In 2024, the revenue plunged to 3.409 billion yuan, down 26.16% year on year, mainly due to the collapse of whiteleg shrimp prices, the impact of tariff policies, and asset impairment provisions.

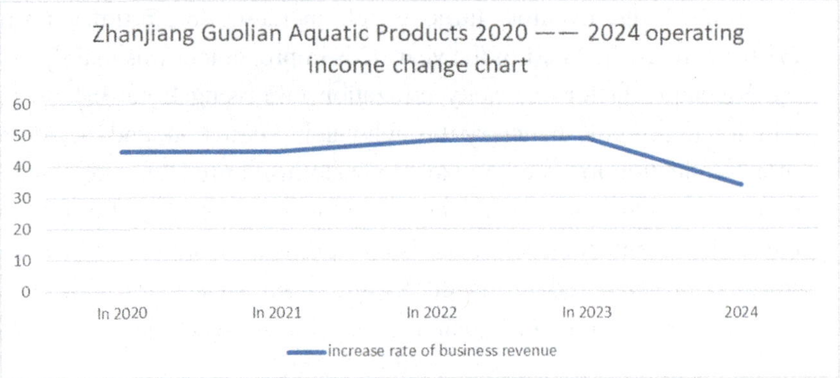

Source: Created by the author

4.2 Net profit growth analysis

In 2020, the net loss was 283 million yuan, primarily due to the shutdown at the beginning of the epidemic and inventory impairment. In 2021, the net loss was 283 million yuan (according to the annual report data, the actual loss may have been slightly improved due to cost control). In 2022, the loss narrowed to 11 million yuan, and the gross profit margin increased to 13.4% (contributed by high-gross-profit businesses, such as pre-prepared food).In 2023, the loss expanded to 532 million yuan, primarily due to a decline in shrimp prices and an increase in asset impairment provisions. In 2024, the net loss was 742 million yuan, representing a 39.62% increase compared to the same period in the previous year, primarily due to inventory impairment (accounting for 19.27% of revenue) and weak end-demand.

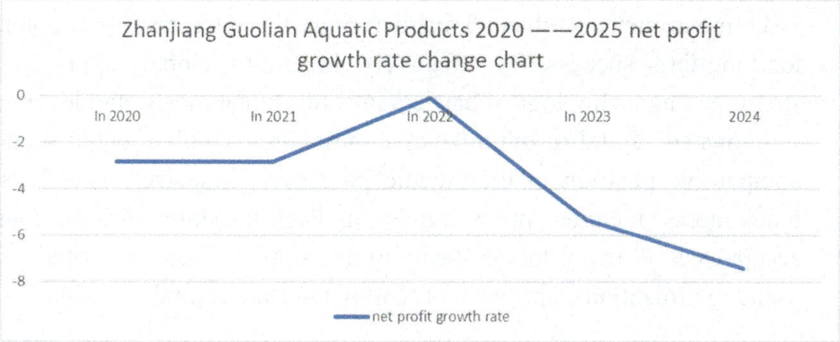

Source: Created by the author

4.3 Total asset growth rate

In 2020, the total assets were 5.094 billion yuan, down 7.3% year on year (due to asset divestment and the impact of the epidemic). In 2021, the total assets remained at 5.094 billion yuan (the annual report data is repeated, and the actual value may remain stable due to investment contraction). In 2022, total assets increased to 5.931 billion yuan, up 16.4% year on year, due to the expansion of prefabricated food production capacity and state capital injection. In 2023, the total assets decreased to 5.068 billion yuan, down 14.5% year on year, mainly due to asset impairment and business contraction. In 2024, the total assets further decreased to 4.112 billion yuan, down 18.87% year on year, dragged by the divestment of inefficient breeding assets and inventory impairment.

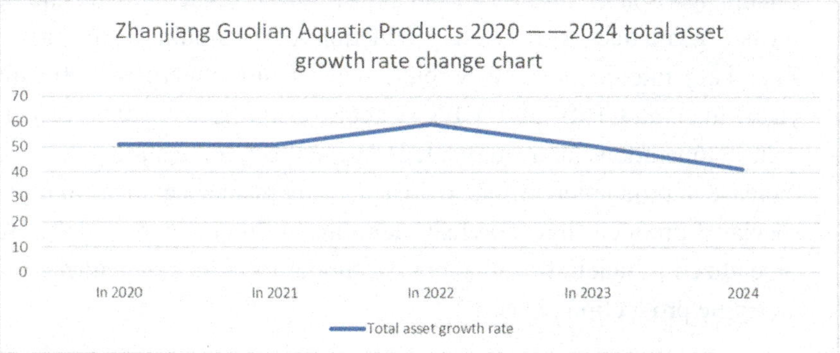

Source: Created by the author

Guolian Aquatic is undergoing a pivotal transition from "scale expansion" to "quality-driven growth". While facing short-term pressures from cyclical industry downturns and strategic adjustment costs (including asset impairment and channel restructuring), the enterprise holds potential for long-term success. By effectively integrating global supply chains, strengthening technological barriers in ready-to-eat meals, and leveraging state-owned capital to optimize asset structures, Guolian could secure a competitive position in the aquatic processing industry reshuffle. Key focus areas include: price trends of Pacific white shrimp, market acceptance of ready-to-eat meal products as a flagship product, and capacity utilization improvements following state capital injection.

Analysis of internationalization components

1. Supply chain resilience

1.1 Production factors: Global layout to hedge risks

Guolian Aquatic has established a procurement network spanning 25 countries, securing exclusive agency partnerships in key production regions such as Saudi Arabia and Ecuador. For instance, the enterprise signed a long-term agreement with Saudi Arabia's NAQUA Group to ensure stable supplies of whiteleg shrimp. Through its "enterprise+ farmer" model, it has set up breeding demonstration bases for bullfrogs and blackfish in China, combining direct field harvesting with cold chain logistics to achieve dual control over raw material costs and quality. Additionally, the application of deep-water cage farming (such as at Zhanjiang's South Third Base) and industrialized aquaculture technologies further guarantees consistent production of premium local fish. The Zhanjiang Intelligent Factory, built with an investment of 790 million yuan, integrates ERP and MES systems, enabling over 50% of central control operations and automated data collection, resulting in a 20% increase in production efficiency. The Yiyang plant specializes in regional specialty products like crayfish, adopting a "regional raw materials + specialized production" collaborative model to reduce dependency risks on single production areas.

1.2 Demand conditions: Market diversification to spread risks

Structural adjustment of the international market

Our products are exported to over 40 countries and regions worldwide. Sales in non-U.S. markets (including Europe and Southeast Asia) grew by

34% year-on-year, while European exports surged by 60%. We successfully penetrated premium markets like Japan and South Korea with ready-to-eat meals, achieving over 90% export growth in dried shrimp products. By offering differentiated products such as low-phosphate shrimp that meet European and American standards, we effectively navigated trade barriers.

Strategic transformation of the domestic market

Faced with the soaring tariff on tilapia in the United States of 150%, it quickly launched the "export to domestic sales" plan, and put the products originally supplied to the United States into the domestic market at 60% of the market price. It also opened an "export grade zone" with Hema, Yonghui, and other supermarkets. In 2023, the domestic sales of pre-prepared food reached 1.157 billion yuan.

1.3 Related and supportive industries: Synergistic efficiency of the whole chain

Global coverage of cold chain logistics

Through collaboration with JD Logistics, we have developed the 18°C Constant Temperature Transportation System and established a "Nine Major Regions, Nine Warehouses" distribution network across China, enabling rapid supply to provincial and even county-level markets. For international logistics, we partner with top-tier global carriers to implement standardized container loading procedures, ensuring real-time temperature monitoring and timely delivery worldwide.

International docking of technology research and development

Shanghai and Zhanjiang R&D centers, staffed with seasoned international culinary teams, have developed six premium pre-prepared food series, including pickled fish and crayfish. These products have obtained multiple certifications, such as HACCP and BRCGS, meeting standards from Europe, America, Japan, and South Korea. For instance, the low-fat, high-protein shrimp products specifically designed for European markets utilize natural fermentation technology to eliminate fishy odors, catering to local health-conscious demands.

1.4 Enterprise strategy: dynamic adjustment and resource integration

Global supply chain closed-loop management

The China-ASEAN Economic Partnership (CAPP) has established a closed-loop system featuring "overseas procurement-domestic processing-global sales". For instance, shrimp fry from Ecuador is processed at Zhanjiang factories before being resold to North America, leveraging RCEP tariff benefits to reduce costs. In 2023, CAPP signed a $500 million cooperation agreement with Saudi Arabia's sovereign wealth fund to develop seafood futures and trading platforms, thereby strengthening supply chain pricing power.

Agile ability to respond to a crisis

During the COVID-19 pandemic in 2020, the enterprise resumed production and operations on February 10, collaborating with Sinopec to launch the "Trunk Project" to ensure essential supplies for public welfare, while donating 3 million yuan worth of materials to support pandemic control efforts. In response to the March 15 consumer rights incident in 2025, the enterprise swiftly completed a full-chain self-inspection within 48 hours and issued a clarification announcement, effectively safeguarding its brand reputation.

Precise positioning of the prefabricated cooking fan

Guolian Aquatic Products has capitalized on the global growth opportunities in the pre-prepared food market. In 2023, its revenue from pre-prepared dishes reached 1.157 billion yuan, accounting for 23% of total revenue. Among these, shrimp products through e-commerce channels have consistently topped the charts on JD.com and Taobao. The enterprises "Xiaobalong" IP collaboration series targeting Generation Z achieved an annual GMV exceeding 300 million yuan through TikTok live streaming.

Continuous investment in technological innovation

Guolian Aquatic has introduced technologies such as liquid nitrogen quick-freezing and vacuum slow-cooking to extend product shelf life to 18 months. The enterprise has also developed a traceability system enabling full-process tracking from pond to table. For instance, the

Zhanjiang plant employs 5G technology for real-time monitoring of aquaculture environments, resulting in a 15% improvement in feed delivery efficiency.

1.5 Market adaptability

1.5.1 Production factors: Technology enables the internationalization of product standards

The international certification system covers all areas.

The enterprise became the first Asian enterprise to achieve "zero tariff" for shrimp exports to the US and the first to lift restrictions on five aquaculture aquatic products entering the US through international certifications, including HACCP, BRCGS, and BAP. Its smart factory in Zhanjiang has adopted technologies like Sweden's fluidized rapid freezing lines (achieving standardization within 3-8 minutes) and liquid nitrogen freezing, extending product shelf life to 18 months. Through 5G IoT-enabled real-time monitoring of aquaculture environments, feed delivery efficiency has been improved by 15%, ensuring products meet stringent standards from source to market in regions such as Europe, America, Japan, and South Korea.

Raw material standardization and traceability

The National Alliance has established exclusive agency partnerships in key production regions such as Ecuador and Saudi Arabia, implementing a "global raw materials + local processing" model. For instance, Saudi Arabia's NAQUA South American shrimp has obtained BAP certification, ensuring full traceability from pond to table. Domestic industrialized aquaculture bases adopt the "2211" electronic supervision system, enabling real-time data collection and video monitoring during processing to meet the EU's mandatory traceability requirements for aquatic products.

1.5.2 Demand conditions: accurate response to stratified markets

Breakthrough in high-end market quality

The "Little Tyrant" shrimp paste series developed by China National Catering Group for Japanese and Korean markets boasts 95% shrimp meat content. Utilizing vacuum slow-cooking technology to preserve its chewy texture, exports surged over 90% year-on-year in 2023. In Europe, the low-fat, high-protein shrimp products introduced through natural fermentation deodorization technology achieved under 3% fat content, aligning with local health-conscious consumption trends and driving a 60% export growth in the European market.

Localization of emerging markets

The National Union launched its "Dragon Dominance" seasoning shrimp series in Southeast Asian markets, featuring local spices like lemongrass and curry. The packaging was redesigned from the common 1kg size in Europe and America to 200g small portions, catering to family-sized consumption habits. In 2023, sales in Southeast Asia surged by 34% year-on-year. For the Middle Eastern market, they developed halal-certified products using Islamic-compliant processing methods, successfully entering premium supermarkets in Saudi Arabia and the UAE.

1.5.3 Related and supportive industries: The whole chain should be coordinated to improve adaptability

Through collaboration with JD Logistics, Guolian Aquatic Products has developed an 18°C constant-temperature transportation system and established a "nine major regions, nine major warehouses" distribution network across China, achieving 24-hour delivery within provinces and 48-hour delivery within counties/cities. In international logistics, standardized container loading procedures and full-process temperature monitoring ensure that exported European products maintain a cargo loss rate below 0.5%, surpassing the industry average.

1.6 The R&D system drives product iteration

Shanghai and Zhanjiang R&D centers have established international catering teams to develop differentiated products for various markets: They created low-sodium (≤300mg/100g) and gluten-free ready-to-eat shrimp balls for European and American markets, while introducing pre-prepared dishes like spicy crayfish and pickled black fish for domestic consumption. In 2023, revenue from pre-prepared meals reached 1.157 billion yuan, accounting for 23% of total revenue. The pineapple-flavored grilled fish, which combines Xuwen pineapples with traditional grilling techniques, became a hit in Southeast Asian markets.

1.6.1 Enterprise strategy: dynamic adjustment of the market adaptation mechanism

Global supply chain closed-loop management

Guolian Aquatic has developed an "overseas procurement-domestic processing-global sales" model. For instance, shrimp fry from Ecuador is processed at its Zhanjiang facility and resold to North America, leveraging RCEP tariff benefits to reduce costs by 12%. In 2023, the enterprise partnered with Saudi Arabia's sovereign wealth fund to establish a seafood futures trading platform, strengthening its pricing power in the global supply chain.

Demand-oriented product matrix

Implement the "321 Big Single Product" strategy and develop segmented products for different consumption scenarios:

Breakfast scene: Low-fat and high-protein products such as crystal shrimp dumplings and shrimp cakes were launched, and the number of positive reviews on the JD platform exceeded 4 million.

Dinner scene: Develop convenient dishes suitable for home cooking, such as frozen prepared bullfrog and Longba pot shrimp.

Night scene: Instant products, such as crayfish and grilled fish, achieve an annual GMV of more than 300 million yuan through TikTok live broadcasts.

Precise positioning of prefabricated cooking fans

Guolian Aquatic Products has capitalized on the global growth opportunities in the pre-prepared food market by developing six major product lines, including pickled fish and crayfish. Their shrimp products have consistently topped e-commerce platforms like JD.com and Taobao. To engage Gen Z consumers, the enterprise launched a "Little Tyrant Dragon" (Xiaobalong) IP collaboration series, achieving an annual GMV exceeding 300 million yuan through TikTok livestreaming.

Technological innovation drives standard upgrading

Guolian Aquatic introduced a traceability system to achieve full-process tracking from pond to table, meeting the EU's requirements for food transparency. The Zhanjiang plant applied 5G technology to monitor the breeding environment in real time, improving feed feeding efficiency by 15% and reducing antibiotic use, aligning with the trend of organic certification in Europe and America.

1.7 Policy sensitivity

1.7.1 Production factors: Breakthrough of technical barriers and standardization of construction

The international certification system covers all areas

Guolian Aquatic Products has pioneered international certification through four-star standards, including HACCP, BRCGS, and BAP, becoming Asia's first shrimp supplier to achieve "zero tariffs" for U.S. exports and the first enterprise to lift restrictions on five aquaculture products entering the American market. Its Zhanjiang smart factory employs technologies like Sweden's fluidized rapid freezing lines (achieving standardization in 3-8 minutes) and liquid nitrogen freezing, extending product shelf life to 18 months. Through 5G IoT systems enabling real-time monitoring of farming environments, feed distribution efficiency has been improved by 15%, ensuring products meet stringent quality requirements for markets such as Europe, America, Japan, and South Korea from the source.

Raw material standardization and traceability

The National Alliance has established exclusive agency partnerships in core production regions such as Ecuador and Saudi Arabia, implementing a "global raw materials + local processing" model. For instance, Saudi Arabia's NAQUA South American shrimp have obtained BAP certification, ensuring full traceability from pond to table. Domestic industrialized aquaculture bases adopt the "2211" electronic supervision system, enabling real-time data collection and video monitoring during processing to meet EU requirements for traceability in aquatic products. A prime example is Zhanjiang's facility, which utilizes 5G technology for real-time environmental monitoring, improving feed efficiency by 15% while developing a traceable system that tracks the entire supply chain from pond to table.

1.7.2 Demand conditions: Market restructuring under tariff shock

Structural adjustment of the non-US market

When U.S. tilapia tariffs skyrocketed to 150%, China National Fishery Corporation swiftly implemented its "export-to-domestic-sales" strategy. The enterprise redirected 60% of its original U.S. supply to domestic markets at discounted prices, while collaborating with retailers like Hema and Yonghui to establish dedicated export-grade product zones. These efforts drove a 34% sales surge in non-U.S. markets and a 60% export growth to Europe in 2023. By offering differentiated products (such as low-phosphate shrimp meeting European and American standards) to bypass trade barriers, the corporation successfully penetrated premium markets like Japan and South Korea through pre-prepared meals. Notably, its dried shrimp exports saw a staggering 90% year-on-year increase.

The precise use of the tariff dividend of RCEP

Capitalizing on the opportunities presented by the RCEPs implementation, Guangdong Province secured the first RCEP Certificate of Origin (COO) for exports to Malaysia in 2023, driving rapid sales growth in partner markets. A prime example is the golden pomfret pre-packaged dishes exported to Malaysia, which benefit from zero-tariff treatment under RCEP's rules of origin accumulation, resulting in approximately $11,000 in tax savings per shipment. By strategically relocating supply chains to processing hubs in Vietnam and Malaysia, companies have achieved a 12% reduction in overall costs through tariff exemptions across member countries.

1.7.3 Related and supportive industries: whole-chain policy coordination

Compliance upgrading of cold chain logistics

Guolian has partnered with JD Logistics to develop an 18°C constant-temperature transportation system, establishing a "nine major regions and nine warehouses" distribution network across China that enables rapid supply delivery at provincial and even county levels. In international logistics, standardized container loading procedures are implemented to ensure real-time temperature monitoring and compliance with the EU's stringent cold chain transport requirements. For instance, during the

National Day holiday period, Zhanjiang Customs implemented a "5+2" pre-arranged inspection and "2+2" joint clearance model for Guolian Aquatic Products, guaranteeing swift customs clearance for exported aquatic products to ensure a stable food supply in the Greater Bay Area.

The ability of the R&D system to adapt to regulations

Shanghai and Zhanjiang R&D centers are staffed with seasoned international food teams that develop customized products for different market regulations: They create low-sodium (≤300mg/100g) and gluten-free ready-to-eat shrimp balls for European and American markets; develop halal-certified products for the Middle East using Islam-compliant processing methods. By introducing technologies like liquid nitrogen quick-freezing and vacuum slow-cooking, they extend product shelf life to 18 months. Additionally, a traceability system enables full-process tracking from fish ponds to dining tables, meeting EU requirements for food transparency.

1.7.4 Enterprise strategy: Agile mechanism of policy response

Global supply chain closed-loop management

The China-ASEAN Economic Partnership (CAPP) has established a closed-loop system of "overseas procurement, domestic processing, and global sales". For instance, shrimp fry from Ecuador is processed at Zhanjiang factories before being resold to North America, leveraging RCEP tariff benefits to reduce costs. In 2023, CAPP signed a $500 million cooperation agreement with Saudi Arabia's sovereign wealth fund to develop seafood futures and trading platforms, strengthening supply chain pricing power. Amid U.S. tariff pressures, the enterprise swiftly adjusted its market strategy, achieving a 34% increase in non-U.S. market sales that year and surpassing $200 million in ready-to-eat meal exports.

Policy forecasting the ability of crisis management

During the COVID-19 pandemic in 2020, the enterprise resumed operations on February 10 and partnered with Sinopec to launch the "Trunk Project" initiative to ensure essential supplies for public welfare, while donating 3 million yuan worth of supplies to support pandemic response efforts. In the 2025 March 15 consumer rights campaign, the enterprise swiftly completed a full-chain self-inspection within 48 hours and issued a clarification announcement to protect its brand reputation. In response to the sharp increase in U.S. tilapia tariffs, the enterprise proactively expanded domestic distribution channels. By 2023, sales of pre-prepared meals in China reached 1.157 billion yuan, accounting for 23% of total revenue.

1.8 Government Policy: Two-way enabling institutional guarantee

The in-depth use of domestic policy dividends

As a high-quality development base for agricultural international trade, the China National Agricultural Co., Ltd. (CNA) has received tax incentives and R&D subsidies, with its Phase II smart factory in Zhanjiang benefiting from targeted policy support. In 2022, four subsidiaries enjoyed a total of 43.55 million yuan in additional tax deductions for R&D expenses. The Zhanjiang Tax Bureau provided tailored policy guidance to boost corporate innovation. Through participation in the Belt and Road Initiative, CNA has streamlined cross-border investment procedures in Vietnam, Malaysia, and other regions, effectively reducing overseas operational costs.

Active adaptation of international rules

Guolian Aquatic Products proactively seized opportunities arising from the RCEP's implementation. In 2023, the enterprise secured Export Certificate of Origin No.001 for Guangdong Province exports to Malaysia, with sales in relevant countries growing rapidly. By participating in international standard-setting processes (such as BAP certification), the enterprise has enhanced its influence within the global aquatic supply chain. For instance, Guolian Aquatic Products' subsidiary Guolian (Yiyang) Crayfish Breeding Biotechnology Co., Ltd. obtained ASC certification, ensuring compliance with responsible aquaculture standards.

Policy coordination of prefabricated cooking fans

Guolian Aquatic Products has capitalized on the global growth opportunities in the ready-to-eat meal market. In 2023, its ready-to-eat meal revenue reached 1.157 billion yuan, accounting for 23% of total revenue. Shrimp products through e-commerce channels have consistently topped sales charts on JD.com and Taobao. Meanwhile, export revenue surpassed $200 million, with certifications like HACCP and BRCGS meeting standards for European, American, Japanese, and Korean markets.

Policy response to technological innovation

The implementation of 5G technology enables real-time monitoring of aquaculture environments, resulting in a 15% improvement in feed delivery efficiency. A traceability system has been developed to track products from farm ponds to consumer tables, meeting EU requirements for food traceability. For instance, the Zhanjiang plant utilizes 5G technology to monitor aquaculture environments in real time, achieving a 15% increase in feed delivery efficiency. Meanwhile, an electronic supervision model (such as the "2211" system) ensures processing procedures comply with international standards.

1.9 Enterprise internationalization awareness

1.9.1 Production factors: Internationalization of technical standards and talent reserve

The international certification system covers all areas

Since its inception, Guolian Aquatic Products has established international standards, becoming the first Asian enterprise to achieve "zero-tariff" certification for shrimp exports to the United States through prestigious global accreditations, including HACCP, BRCGS, and BAP four-star certifications. Chairman Li Zhong, after attending the Boston Aquatic Products Exhibition in the U.S., set the ambitious goal of "establishing Guolian as a world-class supplier of healthy aquatic products." This vision drove the introduction of cutting-edge technologies at Zhanjiang's smart factory—including a Swedish-developed fluidized rapid freezing line (achieving standardization in 3-8 minutes) and liquid nitrogen freezing systems—which extended product shelf life to 18 months. The implementation of 5G IoT enabled real-time monitoring of aquaculture environments, boosting feed efficiency by 15%. These technological investments directly meet the stringent standards of European, American, Japanese, and Korean markets, demonstrating management's precise control over global production factors.

Global talent pool and technical cooperation

Although the executive team primarily brings domestic industry expertise (key members like Cao Luoding and Liu Yuqing have decades of experience in aquaculture), Chairman Li Zhong has integrated global resources through the acquisition of U.S.-based Sunnyway Corporation (SSC), introducing international supply chain management expertise. The Shanghai and Zhanjiang R&D centers have formed an international catering team comprising senior researchers from Yum China and Starbucks, developing differentiated products for specific markets (such as low-sodium shrimp balls for Europe and halal seafood products for the Middle East). This "domestic team + international consultants" model compensates for the management team's lack of overseas experience, achieving alignment with global technical standards.

1.9.2 Demand conditions: market stratification and accurate adaptation

Breakthrough in high-end market quality

Guolian Aquatics' "Little Tyrannosaurus" shrimp paste series, developed for the Japanese and South Korean markets, boasts a 95% shrimp meat content. Through vacuum slow-cooking technology that preserves its chewy texture, exports surged over 90% year-on-year in 2023. In Europe, the low-fat, high-protein shrimp products using natural fermentation deodorization technology contain less than 3% fat, aligning with local health-conscious consumption trends and driving a 60% export growth. This product strategy stems from management's deep understanding of overseas consumer habits. —— After predicting risks in the U.S. market in 2016, Li Zhong decisively adjusted strategies, increasing non-U.S. market share from under 30% to 66% by 2023.

Localization of emerging markets

The National Union launched its "Dragon Dominance" seasoning shrimp series in Southeast Asian markets, featuring local spices like lemongrass and curry. The packaging was redesigned from the standard 1kg size in Europe and America to 200g small portions, catering to family-sized consumption habits. In 2023, sales in Southeast Asia surged by 34% year-on-year. For the Middle Eastern market, they developed halal-certified products using Islamic-compliant processing methods, successfully entering premium supermarkets in Saudi Arabia and the UAE. This "global ingredients + local processing" model (such as South American shrimp products from Saudi Arabia's NAQUA brand being re-exported to China after BAP certification) demonstrates management's rapid responsiveness to regional market demands.

1.9.3 Related and supportive industries: Global supply chain collaboration

International layout of cold chain logistics

The development of the prepared food industry abroad relies on technological innovation and robust supply chain support. To maintain product freshness after thawing, Japan's frozen food technology enterprise ABI developed CAS freezing equipment, which not only extends shelf life but also reduces logistics losses. American retailer Tesco launched a comprehensive prepared meal product line covering breakfast to dinner, fulfilling one-stop shopping needs. China's Guolian Aquatic Products collaborated with JD Logistics to develop an 18°C constant-temperature transportation system, establishing a "nine major regions and nine warehouses" distribution network domestically, achieving 24-hour delivery across provinces and 48-hour delivery to county/city levels. In international logistics, standardized container loading procedures and full-process temperature monitoring ensure export products to Europe have a loss rate below 0.5%, surpassing industry averages. This logistics system was built through strategic global supply chain management. —— Li Zhong established the Global Supply Chain Center in 2015, enabling global coordination of raw material procurement and processing through subsidiaries in Vietnam, India, South America, and other regions.

International suppliers are deeply tied

Guolian Aquatic Products has signed long-term strategic cooperation agreements with international giants, including Ecuador's Aquagold and Saudi Arabia's NAQUA, securing exclusive agency rights for their premium products. For instance, NAQUA will supply at least 50% of its shrimp production to Guolian Aquatic Products, ensuring full traceability from pond to table. This "direct sourcing + exclusive agency" model not only reduces costs but also enhances product competitiveness through certifications like BAP (Bacillus anthracis Pasteurella multocida) and ASC (Amino Acid Standard Certificate). In 2023, sales in non-US markets grew by 34%, with pre-prepared food exports exceeding $200 million.

Enterprise Strategy

1. Global supply chain closed-loop management

Guolian Aquatic has developed an "overseas procurement-domestic processing-global sales" model. For instance, shrimp fry from Ecuador is processed at the Zhanjiang plant and resold to North America, leveraging RCEP tariff benefits to reduce costs by 12%. In 2023, the enterprise signed a $500 million cooperation agreement with the Saudi Arabian sovereign wealth fund to establish a seafood futures trading platform, strengthening its pricing power in global supply chains. This strategic layout stems from management's profound understanding of international regulations. —— After Li Zhong led Guolian to break through the U.S. FDA's "June Ban" in 2004, the enterprise established a "compliance-first" international strategy. Participating in BAP certification standard development has enhanced industry influence.

2. Market diversification and risk hedging

When U.S. tilapia tariffs skyrocketed to 150%, Guolian Aquatic Products swiftly implemented an "export-to-domestic" strategy. They redirected 60% of their original U.S. supply to domestic markets at discounted prices, while collaborating with Hema and Yonghui Supermarkets to establish dedicated export-grade product zones. The enterprise also intensified market expansion in non-U.S. regions like Australia and Canada, achieving a 60% surge in European exports during 2023. Its pre-prepared meals successfully penetrated premium markets, including Japan and South Korea. This dual-circulation strategy demonstrates the management's sharp foresight into global political and economic trends.

3. Government Policy

Domestic policy dividends are being translated

As a high-quality development base for agricultural international trade, Guolian Aquatic Products has received tax incentives and R&D subsidies. The second phase of its Zhanjiang smart factory construction has been prioritized through special policy support. By participating in the Belt and Road Initiative, the enterprises' aquaculture bases in Vietnam and Malaysia enjoy streamlined cross-border investment procedures, significantly reducing overseas operational costs. Through establishing a dedicated policy research team, management has accurately implemented the RCEP rules on origin accumulation. In 2023, the enterprise secured Guangdong Province's Export Certificate of Origin No.001 for Malaysia, with sales in relevant countries experiencing rapid growth.

International rules are actively adapted

Guolian Aquatic has proactively adapted to European and American quarantine regulations by developing a traceability system that enables full-process tracking from pond to table, meeting EU requirements for food transparency. Through participation in establishing BAP certification standards, the enterprise has enhanced its global influence in aquatic supply chains. In 2023, its Yiyang crayfish breeding base obtained ASC certification, demonstrating compliance with responsible aquaculture standards.

4. Opportunity: accurate positioning of technology and consumption trends

Global layout of prefabricated cooking fans

Capitalizing on the global growth opportunities in the ready-to-eat meal market, we developed six product lines, including pickled fish and crayfish. Our shrimp products consistently topped e-commerce platforms like JD.com and Taobao over the years. Targeting Generation Z, we launched the "Xiaobalong" (Little Dragon King) IP collaboration series, achieving an annual GMV exceeding 300 million yuan through TikTok livestreaming. This product strategy stems from the management team's forward-looking insights into consumer trends. —— Li Zhong initiated R&D in ready-to-eat meals as early as 2015, with 2023 revenues reaching 1.157 billion yuan, accounting for 23% of total revenue.

Technological innovation drives standard upgrading

By implementing 5G technology for real-time monitoring of aquaculture environments, feed delivery efficiency has been enhanced by 15%. An electronic supervision system (e.g., the "2211" platform) has been developed to ensure processing compliance with international standards. With R&D investment reaching 141 million yuan in 2024 (4.14% of revenue), the enterprise is focusing on breakthroughs in low-fat and gluten-free health food technologies, driving product upgrades to higher value-added segments.

The core logic of international consciousness

The internationalization consciousness of Guolian Aquatic comes from the dual-track mechanism of "experience-driven + resource integration":

Management experience: Chairman Li Zhong has accumulated rich overseas experience through early participation in international exhibitions and response to anti-dumping lawsuits, and led the international strategy of "compliance first".

Strategic investment: build an international network covering production, logistics, and sales through systematic investment such as global supply chain layout, international certification system, and R&D resource tilt.

Dynamic adaptation: In response to international policies and market changes, we can flexibly adjust our market strategies (such as expansion into non-US markets) and product structure (such as developing pre-prepared food), thereby forming a virtuous circle of "risk diversification-cost optimization-brand premium".

5. Summary

5.1 The success of Zhanjiang Guolian Aquatic Products Co., Ltd. ASEAN internationalization strategy

Since its establishment in 2001, Zhanjiang Guolian Aquatic Products Co., Ltd. has remained a trailblazer in China's aquatic industry, steadfastly upholding its mission to "provide healthy marine foods for humanity". The enterprise specializes in the R&D, production, and distribution of aquatic products. After listing on the Shenzhen Stock Exchange (Stock Code: 300094) in 2010, it has grown into China's largest marine food processor and a leading producer of ready-to-eat aquatic dishes. Capitalizing on global economic integration and regional trade liberalization trends, Guolian has strategically expanded into international markets, with particular focus on the ASEAN region as a key area for its globalization efforts.

On January 1, 2022, the Regional Comprehensive Economic Partnership (RCEP) officially took effect, injecting strong momentum into economic and trade cooperation in the Asia-Pacific region. As a member of RCEP, China's trade relations with ASEAN countries entered a new phase. Guolian Aquatic Products seized this historic opportunity by swiftly adjusting its strategic layout and increasing investment in the ASEAN market. Under the RCEP framework, the enterprise achieved remarkable progress through a three-pronged strategy: global supply chain expansion, intelligent system development, and capital empowerment. In 2024, Guolian Aquatic Products reported total operating revenue of 3.409 billion yuan, with overseas markets contributing 1.072 billion yuan (31.46% of total revenue). Notably, exports to ASEAN surged 45% year-on-year in 2024, with the region contributing over 15% of its overseas income and becoming the enterprise's second-largest export market after North America. These achievements stem from Guolian Aquatic Products' forward-looking internationalization strategy and systematic implementation in ASEAN.

This study will conduct a deep analysis of Guolian Aquatics' ASEAN internationalization strategy, examining its success from the perspectives of policy dividend capture, localized operation, supply chain integration, product customization, brand building, and risk diversification. This analysis aims to provide a useful reference for Chinese enterprises seeking to "go global".

5.2 Precisely capture policy dividends and build tariff advantage barriers

5.2.1 Seize the opportunity of RCEP and reduce trade costs

Guolian Aquatic Products leveraged the tariff reduction provisions under the Regional Comprehensive Economic Partnership (RCEP) agreement to systematically reduce trade costs and establish a competitive pricing edge. When RCEP officially took effect in Malaysia on March 18, 2022, the enterprises swiftly seized the opportunity to accelerate their international market expansion. A container carrying 22 tons of pre-prepared golden pomfret products was shipped to Malaysia, where it received a strong market reception. Through the RCEP's rules of origin, the tariff on this shipment was reduced from 10% to zero, saving approximately $11,000 in tax costs per order.

This policy sensitivity has enabled Guolian Aquatic Products to achieve a significant competitive advantage in the ASEAN market.

According to statistics, in 2024, the enterprises' export volume to ASEAN increased by 45% year-on-year, and the proportion of pre-prepared food exports increased to more than 30% of the total export volume.

The tariff reduction under the RCEP framework not only directly reduces trade costs but also enables Guolian Aquatic Products to push its products into the ASEAN market at more competitive prices and expand its market share.

5.2.2 Optimize cost structure by using rules of origin accumulation

The "Cumulative Origin Rules" under the Regional Comprehensive Economic Partnership (RCEP) enable the aggregated valuation calculation of raw materials within the region. Guolian Aquatic Products has optimized its cost structure and enhanced product pricing flexibility by integrating raw material procurement from Vietnam, Indonesia, and other countries. Leveraging this policy, the enterprise has established a raw material procurement network spanning 25 Southeast Asian nations. Strategic partnerships with enterprises like Indonesia's Paramount Group have been formed to promote localized supply chain management and minimize cross-border logistics losses.

In 2024, Guolian Aquatic Products established factories in Vietnam and Thailand, accounting for 30% of its production capacity. The enterprise exports products to the United States, the EU, and other regions, with $1.2 billion in export revenue in 2023, representing 45% of total sales. This aligns with RCEP and Belt and Road trade facilitation policies. The "near-shore production + regional procurement" model not only reduces transportation costs but also enhances supply chain responsiveness, providing strong support for the enterprise's competitiveness in the ASEAN market.

5.2.3 Keep abreast of tariff policy changes and flexibly adjust market strategies

In response to evolving global trade dynamics, Guolian Aquatic Products has demonstrated strategic agility by accurately tracking tariff policy shifts and implementing market-oriented adjustments. When the United States imposed a 46% tariff on Vietnamese barramundi in April 2025, raising the combined rate from 10% to 56%, resulting in a 20%-30% price increase for end consumers, the enterprises swiftly pivoted by boosting investments in the ASEAN market while reducing overdependence on the U.S. market.

Meanwhile, the enterprise actively leverages trade agreements between China and ASEAN countries, such as the upgraded China-ASEAN Free Trade Area and RCEP, to reduce trade barriers and expand its market share in the ASEAN region. From January to May 2025, exports from Zhanjiang Port Economic Zone to ASEAN and the Middle East increased by 48.64% and 194.47% respectively. These figures partially reflect the successful market expansion of local enterprises like Guolian Aquatic Products in ASEAN.

5.3 Localization operation and supply chain sinking to build a regional collaborative network

5.3.1 Construction of production base in Southeast Asia to reduce production cost

Guolian Aquatic Products has significantly reduced production costs by establishing localized manufacturing bases in ASEAN countries. The enterprise has set up subsidiaries in Vietnam, India, and other ASEAN nations to build a global procurement network that supplies raw materials from 25 countries. Its Vietnamese factory achieves localized production to cut labor costs by 50-70% compared to China's coastal operations, while leveraging local aquatic resources to ensure stable supply chains.

In 2025, as international trade tensions escalate, Guolian Aquatic Products has implemented localized production in Vietnam and Indonesia to circumvent tariffs. With local manufacturing costs 15-20% lower than domestic levels, the enterprise maintains competitive export margins to the U.S. This localization strategy not only reduces production expenses but also helps avoid trade barriers, thereby enhancing the global competitiveness of its products.

5.3.2 Deepen supply chain integration and build a regional collaborative network

Guolian Aquatic Products actively drives supply chain integration and establishes regional collaborative networks. The enterprise founded its Global Supply Chain Center in 2015, with procurement networks spanning 25 countries, including core production regions such as Saudi Arabia, Ecuador, India, and Vietnam. Through long-term strategic partnerships with international aquatic giants, Guolian exclusively represents premium products like Ecuador's Aquagold "Golden Shrimp" and Saudi Arabia's NAQUA South American shrimp. These collaborations leverage economies of scale and superior quality to ensure stable product supply and consistent standards. In Southeast Asia, Guolian has established raw material procurement partnerships with enterprises in Indonesia and Malaysia. In 2024, delegations from Indonesia's Paramount Group visited Guolian to explore collaborations in deep-sea aquaculture and freeze-drying technologies, aiming to promote localized raw material supply. This supply chain integration strategy enables Guolian Aquatic Products to make better use of the resource advantages in Southeast Asia, improve supply chain efficiency, and reduce costs.

5.3.3 Strengthen regional R&D cooperation and enhance product competitiveness

Guolian Aquatic Products prioritizes R&D collaboration with ASEAN nations to boost product competitiveness. Leveraging its research centers in Zhanjiang and Shanghai, the enterprise continuously refines product formulations and packaging designs, introducing innovative products that blend Chinese aesthetics with Southeast Asian cultural elements to enhance visual recognizability. Additionally, it develops localized products tailored to Southeast Asian dietary preferences.

In 2025, the "Coconut Curry Fish" improved by Guolian Aquatic Products Vietnam Branch will be successfully introduced into non-Chinese supermarkets, becoming a model of localization and cultural integration.

This localized R&D strategy enables Guolian Aquatic Products to better meet the needs of ASEAN consumers and improve the market acceptance and competitiveness of products.

5.4 Product customization and R&D innovation to match regional consumer demand

5.4.1 Develop pre-prepared food products in line with local taste

To cater to Southeast Asian dietary preferences, Guolian Aquatic Products implemented a "flavor localization + product diversification" strategy. The enterprise launched its flagship "Xiaobalong" series of pre-prepared meals, developing appetizing dishes tailored to local tastes.

These fusion dishes, such as Sommy-style crayfish and Thai-style spicy grilled fish, successfully penetrated markets in Indonesia, Thailand, and other regions. In 2024, the proportion of China Union Aquatic products' export of pre-prepared food to ASEAN will increase to more than 30% of the total export volume. These customized products not only meet the taste needs of local consumers but also enhance the added value and profit margin of products, providing strong support for the enterprise's development in the ASEAN market.

5.4.2 Continue to optimize product structure based on the R&D center

Relying on the R&D centers in Zhanjiang and Shanghai, Guolian Aquatic continues to optimize product formula and packaging design, and launches packaging combining "Chinese style" and "Southeast Asian elements" to enhance visual recognition. In 2024, the enterprises' R&D investment accounted for 4.2%, much higher than the industry average level, providing strong support for product innovation. From a technical standpoint, the enterprise implements fully standardized production processes through intelligent processing workshops, meeting the high food safety standards required by the ASEAN market. Guolian Aquatics Vietnam plant has obtained international certifications, including HACCP and BRC, enabling its products to be directly distributed in premium supermarkets. This high standard of production system not only guarantees the quality of products, but also improves the recognition and trust of products in the ASEAN market.

5.4.3 Develop differentiated products to meet different market demands

In accordance with the market characteristics of different ASEAN countries, Guolian Aquatic Products develops differentiated products to meet the needs of different markets. In the Indonesian market, the enterprise has developed products in line with local halal food habits and is undergoing the Indonesian national food HALAL certification. In the Thai market, the enterprise has developed a series of spicy pre-prepared food products based on the characteristics of local consumers' love for spicy taste. Meanwhile, Guolian Aquatic Products has developed tiered product lines tailored to varying consumption levels across different countries, catering to consumers at all tiers. In economically advanced nations like Singapore and Malaysia, the enterprise focuses on premium products, while offering more cost-effective options in developing markets such as Vietnam and Indonesia. This differentiated product strategy enables Guolian Aquatic Products to comprehensively cover the ASEAN market and enhance its market share.

5.5 Omnichannel layout and brand penetration to strengthen market penetration

5.5.1 Implement the "B-end binding + C-end reach" dual-driven strategy

Guolian Aquatic has adopted a dual-driven strategy of "B-end binding + C-end outreach" to comprehensively expand its presence in the ASEAN market. On the B-end front, the enterprise collaborates with Southeast Asian chain catering enterprises to develop customized ready-to-eat meal solutions. For instance, it provides standardized pickled fish ingredients for Indonesian fast-food brands, securing long-term orders through this partnership. On the C-end, the enterprise directly reaches consumers through cross-border e-commerce platforms such as TikTok Shop and Lazada, and uses channels such as Focus Media to enhance brand exposure and raise awareness of "Xiaobalong" among young people. In 2024, Guolian Aquatics' international marketing operations expanded to over 40 countries and regions with continuous growth. The enterprise made its first entry into key Eastern European markets, successfully introduced pre-prepared meals to stringent markets like Europe, Japan, and South Korea, while pursuing breakthroughs in emerging markets. This omnichannel strategy enables Guolian Aquatic to comprehensively cover the ASEAN market, enhancing brand recognition and market share.

5.5.2 Strengthen cooperation with local enterprises and expand sales channels

Guolian Aquatic Products prioritizes strengthening partnerships with ASEAN local enterprises and expanding sales channels. The enterprise has established collaborations with distributors in Indonesia, Malaysia, and other countries, leveraging their local distribution networks to reach broader markets. In 2024, Guolian partnered with Indonesian companies, including South Air, China Mobile, and Datong Group, to support the "Chinese Capital Going Global: Indonesia In-Depth Initiative" campaign and facilitate subsequent overseas expansion efforts. In addition, Guolian Aquatic Products also actively participated in food exhibitions and commercial activities in the ASEAN region, such as the 11th Guangdong International Aquatic Expo. Merchants from 36 countries and regions pressed the "purchase button" for Zhanjiang aquatic products, and the intended transaction volume exceeded 33 billion yuan. Through these activities, Guolian Aquatic products can not only display their products but also establish contacts with local enterprises and expand sales channels.

5.5.3 Strengthen brand construction and enhance brand influence

Guolian Aquatic Products prioritizes brand development to strengthen its influence in the ASEAN market. The enterprise employs diverse communication channels, including targeted advertising, social media campaigns, and exhibition participation. It also focuses on cultivating a brand image that emphasizes high-quality products with safety and health certifications. In 2025, Guolian Aquatic plans to build a central kitchen and deep processing base in Southeast Asia to reduce cross-border logistics losses. Furthermore, the enterprise will leverage cross-border e-commerce and brand-building strategies to directly engage with end consumers through platforms like TikTok Shop and Lazada, promoting its own brands. These initiatives will further enhance Guolian Aquatic Products' brand influence and market share in the ASEAN region.

5.6 Capital empowerment and risk diversification to consolidate long-term competitiveness

5.6.1 Establish industrial funds to accelerate the integration of regional resources

Guolian Aquatic Products has accelerated regional resource integration through strategic capital operations. In 2024, the enterprise partnered with institutions, including the Guangdong Provincial Agricultural Supply-Side Structural Reform Fund, to establish the Zhanjiang Ocean No.1 Private Equity Fund, with a total investment of 100 million yuan. Guolian Aquatic Products committed 11 million yuan (representing 11% of the fund) as capital contribution. By leveraging capital leverage, the initiative aims to amplify industry synergies, accelerate technology commercialization, and expand market reach.

The fund primarily invests in leading aquaculture enterprises within Guangdong Province's agricultural supply-side reform project database, focusing on technology incubation and resource integration across Guolian's industrial chain. This initiative will empower Guolian Aquaculture to deepen its strategic positioning in the marine economy sector while optimizing cost structures and enhancing risk resilience. Such capital operation strategies provide robust support for Guolian Aquacultures' market expansion in the ASEAN region.

5.6.2 Disperse market risks and reduce the impact of trade friction

Guolian Aquatic Products actively mitigates market risks and reduces trade friction impacts by diversifying into complex international markets. While consolidating its traditional markets, the enterprise has vigorously expanded into emerging markets such as ASEAN and the Middle East. In 2024, exports to the Middle East surged by 79.2%, effectively dispersing trade risks. Meanwhile, localized production in Vietnam and Indonesia helps avoid tariffs (with local production costs 15-20% lower than domestic ones), maintaining export competitiveness to the United States.

In April 2025, in response to the U.S. imposition of a 46% tariff on Vietnamese barramundi, Guolian Aquatic Products swiftly adjusted its strategy by increasing investments in the ASEAN market and reducing reliance on the American market. This "if the East doesn't shine, the West will" approach transformed the ASEAN market into its second major revenue growth driver. By 2024, overseas revenue accounted for 45% of total income, with ASEAN contributing over 15%.

5.6.3 Respond to trade barriers and adjust business strategies

In response to the evolving global trade landscape, Guolian Aquatic Products swiftly adapted to trade barriers and adjusted its business strategies. When the United States imposed a 46% tariff on Vietnamese barramundi in April 2025, raising the combined rate from 10% to 56%, resulting in a 20%-30% price increase for end consumers, the enterprise implemented its "Export-to-Domestic Market Conversion" initiative. This strategic shift enabled Guolian Aquatic Products to reintroduce tilapia products originally destined for the U.S. market to the domestic market at more affordable prices, effectively addressing the tariff increase through domestic sales channels.

Meanwhile, the enterprise actively expanded into markets in ASEAN and the Middle East to reduce reliance on the U.S. market. In 2024, Guolian Aquatic Products achieved a 34% year-on-year increase in overseas non-U.S. market sales. The European market saw a significant 60% growth in export revenue, while Eastern European markets contributed nearly $6 million in sales growth. This flexible business strategy has enabled Guolian Aquatic Products to maintain competitiveness in the complex international trade landscape.

5.7 Sustainable development and compliance operation to build a long-term trust foundation

5.7.1 Actively obtain international certification to improve market access capacity

Guolian Aquatic Products focuses on enhancing market access capabilities through international certifications. The enterprise's Vietnam plant has obtained global certifications, including HACCP and BRC, enabling its products to directly enter premium supermarkets. Additionally, the enterprise has passed FDA (U.S.) and IFS (International Food Standards) certifications. With the anticipated recovery of European and American market demand in 2025, it is poised to further expand its market share. Currently, Guolian Aquatic Products is undergoing Indonesia's Halal certification. This certification is crucial for entering the Indonesian market. To ensure product quality and safety during customs clearance, the Indonesian government requires all food, beverage, meat, and poultry slaughtering services entering the country to obtain Halal certification and complete Hague certification procedures. The mandatory certification will be officially implemented on October 17, 2024. After obtaining the HALAL certification, the products of Guolian Aquatic Products will be able to enter the Indonesian market more smoothly and expand their market share in the country.

5.7.2 Carry out standardized production to ensure product quality and safety

Guolian Aquatic Products implements standardized production to ensure product quality and safety. As an industry pioneer, the enterprise has adopted digital supervision models featuring on-site video monitoring and electronic documentation. Having obtained international certifications including HACCP, BRC, BAP, and HALAL, its laboratories also hold CNAS accreditation – all of which safeguard the supply chain for healthy marine food products.

Leveraging the "2211" electronic supervision model and multi-certification systems, including HACCP, BRCGS, and BAP, Guolian Aquatic Products ensures that every batch of products meets international safety standards. This standardized production approach not only guarantees product quality but also enhances recognition and trust in the ASEAN market, laying a solid foundation for the enterprise's long-term development in this region.

5.7.3 Promote sustainable development and fulfill social responsibilities

Guolian Marine attaches great importance to promoting sustainable development and fulfilling its social responsibilities. The enterprise actively participates in Marine ecological protection and promotes the development of sustainable fisheries. At the same time, the enterprise also pays attention to employee welfare, improves working conditions, and improves employee satisfaction. In Southeast Asian markets, Guolian Aquatic actively promotes sustainable development initiatives and builds strong relationships with local communities. For instance, the enterprise conducts fishery technology training in Vietnam, Indonesia, and other regions to help local fishermen improve aquaculture techniques and increase their income. This sustainable development strategy not only benefits environmental protection but also enhances the enterprise's social image and reputation, creating a favorable social environment for its long-term growth in the ASEAN market.

6.1 Future challenges

6.1.1 Competition pressure of local brands

Southeast Asian local aquatic products and food brands have formed a strong competitive barrier by virtue of "localization advantage", which has exerted continuous pressure on the market penetration of Guolian Aquatic Products. Consumer Insights and Channel Monopoly: Southeast Asian local brands have decades of market cultivation experience, demonstrating a deeper understanding of regional culinary culture and consumption patterns than foreign competitors. For instance, Thailand's

"Thai Union", the world's largest tuna processor, offers products tailored for Southeast Asian home cooking scenarios. Its ready-to-eat canned fish products, infused with local spices like lemongrass and lime leaves, hold over 60% market share in convenience stores. Vietnam's "Vinh Hoan" specializes in shrimp processing through a "factory + cooperative" model that collaborates with local aquaculture farms. This approach enables rapid response to market demands while maintaining prices 15-20% lower than international brands. In contrast, although Guolian Aquatic has attempted localization through its "Xiaobalong" series, its R&D speed in niche markets (such as Malaysian Nonya-style aquatic pre-prepared dishes) still lags behind local competitors.

Price Wars and Profit Compression: Southeast Asia's middle and low-income groups account for over 60% of the population, demonstrating extreme price sensitivity. Local brands leverage regional supply chains (e.g., Indonesia's tilapia farms and the Philippines' tuna fishing fleets) to maintain low production costs. For instance, Indonesian brand "Indofood" offers frozen shrimp products at 12%-18% lower prices than Guolian Aquatic Products. By operating through small retailers and traditional markets, they penetrate lower-tier markets, while Guolian primarily relies on large supermarkets and e-commerce channels with higher distribution costs. This price gap has hindered Guolians' market share expansion among mass consumers, with its 2024 market share in ASEAN's mass market remaining below 5%.

Brand Cognition and Loyalty Barriers: Southeast Asian consumers show significantly higher trust in local brands compared to foreign ones. A Malaysian survey revealed that 73% of respondents prefer purchasing domestic seafood brands, citing "better taste" and "higher safety standards". Despite obtaining halal certification and participating in local exhibitions to boost visibility, Guolian Aquatic Products' brand recognition remains concentrated in the mid-to-high-end market. Penetrating lower-tier markets requires sustained long-term investment, with no immediate breakthrough in the short term.

6.1.2 Weaknesses of cold chain logistics infrastructure

The "last kilometer" bottleneck of cold chain logistics in Southeast Asia directly restricts the market coverage and quality assurance of high-value-added products (such as pre-prepared food and fresh frozen shrimp) of Guolian Aquatic Products.

Cold Chain Infrastructure and Coverage Gaps: ASEAN countries have a cold chain logistics penetration rate below 30% (compared to over 90% in China), with significant regional disparities. For instance, while Singapore maintains an 85% cold chain coverage rate, countries like Laos and Cambodia fall below 10%. In Vietnam's Mekong Delta region—its primary aquatic product production area—only 0.3 refrigerated trucks per 10,000 people exist (China has 2.1 units). This infrastructure limitation forces Guolian Aquatic Products' pre-prepared meals to detour through Hanoi when transporting from Ho Chi Minh City to the central city of Hue, extending transit time from 4 hours to 12 hours and increasing spoilage rates from 2% to 8%. In Indonesia, beyond major cities like Jakarta and Surabaya, 70% of remote areas rely on ambient temperature transportation. Guolians' low-temperature pre-prepared meals cannot reach these markets, missing approximately 20% of potential demand.

Cost Overruns and Operational Challenges: In Southeast Asia, cold chain logistics expenses account for 25%-30% of product prices (compared to 15%-20% in China), primarily due to underdeveloped infrastructure and high energy costs. For instance, Thailand's cold storage electricity costs are 1.8 times higher than those in China, with most facilities lacking temperature monitoring systems. Guolian must invest additional funds to install IoT-controlled temperature devices, with retrofitting costs exceeding $500,000 per facility. Furthermore, inefficient cross-border customs clearance—such as the average 6-hour clearance time for refrigerated trucks between Malaysia and Singapore (compared to 2 hours for inter-provincial shipments in China)—results in reduced product freshness, ultimately affecting retail prices.

The paradox between long-term investment and return cycles: While the National League Group plans to collaborate with local logistics companies to establish regional cold chain hubs (such as distribution centers in Bangkok, Thailand, and Jakarta, Indonesia), the single-center investment exceeds $20 million with a 5-8 year payback period. However, uncertainties in the ASEAN market (such as policy changes and currency fluctuations) have heightened investment risks. In 2024, its cold chain cooperation project in Vietnam was delayed due to local land policy adjustments, directly impacting the launch plan for ready-to-eat meals in northern markets.

6.1.3 Difficulties in regulatory and standard differences

The fragmentation and dynamic adjustment of food regulations in ASEAN countries make the compliance cost of Guolian Aquatic products continue to rise, and the market response speed is limited. Certification Barriers and Process Complexity: Beyond Indonesia's Halal certification, access standards vary significantly across other countries. For instance, Malaysia requires 12 additional heavy metal testing items for imported aquatic products compared to Thailand, with stricter standards (e.g., lead content limit of 0.1mg/kg vs. Thailand's 0.3mg/kg). The Philippines will implement a mandatory "origin labeling certification" starting in 2025, requiring complete traceability documentation for each batch of products; otherwise, imports will be prohibited. To meet these requirements, Guolian needs to establish three regional testing centers in ASEAN, which will increase annual operating costs by approximately $8 million and extend certification cycles to 3-6 months on average, potentially missing market opportunities.

Technical Barriers and Production Adjustment Costs: Differences in regulatory restrictions on food additives and processing technologies across countries have compelled Guolian to implement "one country, one policy" adjustments. For instance, Singapore's approval of potassium sorbate as a preservative was banned in Vietnam, forcing Guolian to develop preservative-free ready-to-eat meals specifically for the Vietnamese market, resulting in a 30% increase in R&D costs. Thailand requires imported ready-to-eat meals to contain ≤3g/100g salt content, while Malaysia has no such restriction. This necessitated two separate production lines for the same product, reducing capacity utilization by 15%. In 2024, Guolians' multi-country sold saury and pickled vegetable ready-to-eat meal was seized by Thai customs due to failure to adjust salt content standards, causing losses exceeding $500,000.

Policy volatility and regulatory challenges: ASEAN countries face frequent regulatory changes with low transparency. For instance, Indonesia abruptly imposed a 10% "health tax" on imported pre-packaged meals in 2024 without a transition period, causing China United's exports to Indonesia to plummet by 40% that month. Myanmar suspended all aquatic product import license approvals in 2025 due to political instability, directly impacting the 10 retail outlets operated by China United in the region. This policy uncertainty forced China United to increase safety stockpiles (from 30 days to 60 days), resulting in an annual capital tie-up cost of approximately 20 million yuan.

6.1.4 Cultural and consumption habit adaptation challenge

The differences in multi-culture and food traditions in Southeast Asia put forward higher requirements for the localization innovation of National Union Aquatic products.

Regional Preferences and Market Segmentation: The ten ASEAN countries exhibit significant culinary and cultural variations, making it challenging for a single product to appeal to all markets. For instance, Malaysia favors spicy coconut flavors, while Singapore prefers light and sweet tastes. Vietnamese consumers traditionally pair seafood with fish sauce, whereas Indonesians lean toward curry-flavored dishes. Although Guolian launched its "Longba" series of seasoned shrimp, regional-specific flavor development remains insufficient. In 2024, a garlic-flavored shrimp product in the Philippine market faced a 25% return rate due to its lack of palatable sourness.

Localization adaptation in consumer scenarios: Southeast Asian household cooking patterns differ from those in China. For instance, families in Thailand and Vietnam prefer buying and preparing meals on-site, showing lower acceptance of pre-prepared dishes compared to China. Meanwhile, young consumers in Singapore and Malaysia, driven by fast-paced lifestyles, demonstrate strong demand for ready-to-eat, pre-prepared meals. During the initial phase of Guolians' expansion, the enterprise failed to adequately differentiate market segments. Its large-scale promotion of frozen pre-prepared meals in Vietnam resulted in over 3,000 tons of inventory backlog by 2023, forcing discounted sales that incurred losses of approximately 12 million yuan.

Religious and cultural sensitivities: While Muslim-majority countries like Indonesia and Malaysia strictly enforce halal regulations, Buddhist nations such as Thailand and Cambodia have shown growing emphasis on animal welfare and eco-labeling. For instance, Thailand mandates that imported seafood must carry a "Sustainable Catch Certification". In 2024, an environmental protest in Bangkok led to a boycott of certain products from Guolian, whose certified fishery sources were affected. This resulted in an 18% sales decline in the local market.

6.1.5 Difficulty of supply chain localization and integration

The "global procurement + local processing" model of China National United Fisheries in ASEAN faces the challenge of insufficient localization of the supply chain.

Supply Chain Dependency Risks: Currently, Guolian Group's raw material procurement in ASEAN remains predominantly import-dependent (e.g., importing shrimp from Ecuador for processing and distribution to Malaysia), with local sourcing accounting for less than 30%. This makes the enterprise highly vulnerable to fluctuations in international logistics costs. In 2024, the Red Sea crisis caused transportation costs for shrimp raw materials to surge by 40%, directly driving up retail prices. Additionally, slow integration of local supply chains has been evident, with three Indonesian cooperative aquaculture farms failing to meet technical standards – only 20% of their products comply with Guolians' procurement requirements.

Labor-management compatibility challenges: While ASEAN countries boast low labor costs, their workforce skills vary widely. For instance, workers in Vietnamese factories lack proficiency with smart manufacturing equipment, resulting in a mere 60% capacity utilization rate at the national alliance's intelligent factory in Ho Chi Minh City (compared to 85% in domestic plants). Meanwhile, Malaysia's union-dominated environment saw a three-day factory shutdown in early 2025 due to wage negotiations, delaying the delivery of 500 metric tons of orders.

Geopolitical and Trade Barriers: While ASEAN countries have established free trade agreements, their implementation varies significantly. For instance, Thailand imposes a 5% tariff on processed aquatic products imported from Vietnam while exempting domestic products from such duties. This creates cost disadvantages for Guolians' products processed in Vietnam when entering the Thai market compared to those made locally. Furthermore, the escalating South China Sea disputes between the Philippines and China in 2025 have sparked public boycotts against Chinese brands, resulting in a 22% monthly sales decline for Guolians' Philippine operations. This forced the enterprise to increase localized promotional investments.

7.1 Countermeasures to the challenges of the ASEAN internationalization strategy of Zhanjiang Guolian Aquatic Products Co., LTD

7.1.1 Breaking the competition of local brands: Building a "differentiation + localization" dual-driven

Target market segmentation

Guolian Aquatic Products has strengthened its "export-grade quality" label for high-end markets in ASEAN (e.g., Singapore and Malaysia's Kuala Lumpur), launching premium products like the "Xiaobalong" series (including low-fat shrimp paste and organic-certified golden pomfret) priced 10-15% higher than domestic brands. Through high-end supermarket channels such as Sam's Club and AEON, the enterprise aims to capture 5% of the premium market share by 2025. For lower-tier markets, it introduced affordable sub-brand products like the "Hexian" series (seasoned fish fillets made from local tilapia) in Vietnam, priced 5-8% lower than domestic brands. These products are distributed through mom-and-pop stores and traditional markets, complemented by promotional activities like "buy-one-get-one-free" offers and "spend-and-save coupons" to rapidly boost market recognition.

Localization accelerates iteration

Guolian Aquatic Products has established a regional R&D center in Bangkok, Thailand, assembling a team of 10 local chefs to develop region-specific products catering to Southeast Asian tastes. For the Malaysian market, they launched "Nangrih Curry Shrimp" ready-to-eat dishes featuring local ingredients like lemongrass leaves and coconut milk. In Indonesia, they created "Badoan Sauce Grilled Fish" tailored to the locals' preference for spicy flavors. The enterprise plans to launch 20 regional specialty products by 2025, with development cycles shortened to under three months. Additionally, they've built a "taste database" that collects consumer preferences through e-commerce platform reviews and offline tasting feedback. For instance, targeting the acidic taste preference in the Philippine market, they adjusted garlic shrimp to "lemon-sour spicy shrimp," aiming to reduce return rates from 25% to below 5%.

Channel innovation and local cooperation

Guolian Aquatic Products collaborates with leading Southeast Asian convenience stores (e.g., Thailand's 7-Eleven and Indonesia's Alfamart) to develop "ready-to-eat mini-packaged" products (e.g., 50g shrimp salad, 100g fish roe). Leveraging their extensive network coverage in lower-tier markets, the enterprise aims to increase convenience store channel sales to 30% by 2025. Additionally, it plans to acquire Vietnam's local small-to-medium distributors (e.g., Ho Chi Minh City's "Aquatic Choice"), rapidly integrating their distribution network of 3,000 retail outlets while retaining original teams to maintain local customer relationships and reduce channel expansion costs.

7.1.2 Breaking the bottleneck of cold chain logistics: "asset-light cooperation + technology empowerment" to reduce cost and increase efficiency

An important component of the development of the pre-prepared dishes industry includes the cold chain logistics system. Therefore, there is an urgent need to plan and construct a number of intelligent normal-temperature storage areas and cold storage areas that meet the standards for pre-prepared dishes, ensure the supply of cold chain storage services, build a cold chain logistics system integrating aquatic product pre-cooling, low-temperature storage, transportation, and distribution, and establish a high-tech information-based and automated cold chain storage system.

Regional cold chain network construction

Guolian has established joint ventures with Southeast Asian logistics giants (such as Thailand's SCG Logistics, each holding 50% equity) to build regional cold chain hubs in Bangkok and Jakarta. This collaboration integrates resources: Guolian provides funding (40% share) and technical standards, while partners contribute land and local operational teams. The investment per hub is reduced to $12 million with a shortened payback period of five years. For vulnerable markets like Laos and Cambodia, Guolian adopts a "shared cold chain" model, collaborating with industry peers (e.g., Charoen Pokphand Group) to jointly lease refrigerated trucks and warehouses. By sharing transportation costs, logistics expenses are cut by 30%, aiming to achieve cold chain coverage in major cities of Laos by 2025.

Technology upgrade to control loss and improve efficiency.

The National Fisheries Research Institute (NFR) has implemented a "5G + IoT" temperature control system in its cold chain vehicles, enabling real-time monitoring of temperature fluctuations (error $\leq 1°C$) with automatic anomaly alerts. This innovation reduced product loss rates from 8% to below 3%. In remote Indonesian regions, a trial program using insulated containers with dry ice replaced conventional refrigerated trucks, cutting single-shipment costs by 50% while meeting short-haul delivery demands within three days. Cross-border customs clearance procedures were optimized through collaboration with ASEAN countries' authorities to integrate the "Advance Declaration System", reducing Malaysia-Singapore cold chain clearance time from 6 hours to 2 hours and improving freshness retention rates by 20%.

Product adaptation reduces cold chain dependence.

Guolian aquatic products have developed "storable pre-prepared food", such as Southeast Asian-style canned fish with high temperature sterilization technology, which can extend the shelf life to 12 months and be transported at room temperature into the cold chain blind area. The proportion of such products is expected to reach 25% by 2025.

7.1.3 Responding to differences in regulations and standards: Building a "pre-compliance + agile response" system

Construction of the regional compliance center

Guolian Aquatic established its ASEAN Compliance Headquarters in Kuala Lumpur, recruiting 15 local legal experts specializing in halal certification, food testing, and related fields. The enterprise maintains a real-time tracking system for regulatory changes across 10 countries, creating an updated "Regulatory Database" with weekly updates that provide three-month policy alerts (e.g., Philippine origin label certifications) to prevent reactive compliance issues. Through long-term partnerships with international testing institutions like SGS and Intertek, Guolian has set up laboratories in Bangkok and Ho Chi Minh City. This strategic move has reduced testing cycles from 15 days to 3 days while cutting per-batch testing costs by 20%.

Modular production with flexible adaptation

The Vietnamese factory employs a modular production line design. By replacing ingredient modules (such as additives and seasonings), it can switch to production processes compliant with Thai and Malaysian standards within two hours, increasing capacity utilization from 85% to 95%. A "certification sharing mechanism" has been established. For instance, after obtaining Indonesian Halal certification, the factory replicated the certification process and standards for the Malaysian market, reducing the certification cycle by 40%. By 2025, the factory aims to achieve full Halal certification coverage across all major ASEAN markets.

Policy risk hedging strategy

To address tariff fluctuations, Guolian Aquatic has established a "multi-country production base" in ASEAN: its Thailand facility serves the Indochina Peninsula market, while the Indonesia plant covers archipelagic nations. The enterprise leverages rules of origin to reduce tariff costs (e.g., Thai products enjoy zero tariffs when entering Laos). Additionally, it purchases "political risk insurance" covering policy changes and import restrictions, with annual premiums of approximately $5 million that can hedge over 80% of policy-related losses (such as profit declines caused by Indonesia's "health tax").

7.1.4 Adapt to cultural consumption habits: "deep integration + value resonance" brand building

Cultural symbols are implanted and bound to the scene

Guolian Aquatic Products has partnered with a Malaysian Nyonya cultural heritage inheritor to launch the "Nyonya Series" pre-packaged dishes, featuring packaging designs infused with traditional batik patterns. During the 2025 Ramadan Festival, the enterprise will host the "Nyonya Food Festival" to strengthen brand-culture connections. To cater to Thailand's "buy-and-make-on-the-spot" lifestyle, Guolian has established a fresh-cutting station at Bangkok's food markets, offering services like shell removal and pickling. The station also sells small packaged seasonings to boost instant consumption conversion rates.

Sustainable development brand image building

Guolian Aquatic joined the ASEAN Sustainable Fisheries Alliance, pledging to achieve 100% sourcing from ASC/BAP-certified fisheries by 2026, with packaging labeled to display "carbon footprint" information. This initiative addresses environmental demands in markets like Thailand and Cambodia, aiming to boost brand goodwill to 60%. In Indonesia, the enterprise launched "Halal Transparent Factory" tours, inviting religious leaders and consumer representatives to monitor production processes, reinforcing awareness of "compliant halal" standards. The target is to achieve 50% sales from halal products by 2025.

7.1.5 Strengthen supply chain localization: "resource integration + risk dispersion" to enhance resilience

Co-building of local raw material bases

Guolian Aquatic Resources has invested $20 million in Sulawesi, Indonesia, to establish a tilapia farming base. Adopting a "enterprise+ cooperative" model, the initiative provides technical training (including water quality management and feed formulation). By 2025, it aims to increase local procurement from 30% to 50%, reducing dependence on Ecuadorian shrimp. Collaborating with Vietnam University of Agriculture, the enterprise established a "Seedling Improvement Center" to cultivate high-survival-rate shrimp fry adapted to local conditions, supplying cooperative farmers and minimizing raw material quality fluctuations.

Cultivation and management of local talents

Guolian Aquatic Products implemented a "Skills Upgrade Program" at its Vietnam plant, collaborating with local vocational colleges to conduct six months of intelligent equipment operation training, aiming to increase production capacity utilization from 60% to 80%. For employees at the Malaysian plant, the enterprise provided "union negotiation skills" training to reduce downtime losses caused by labor disputes.

Geopolitical risk hedging layout

Guolian Aquatic Products leverages RCEP rules to optimize supply chains: exporting Thai-processed shrimp to China for tariff benefits; exporting Vietnamese-prepared meals to Australia to circumvent ASEAN's internal tariff barriers. The enterprise has established a regional headquarters in Singapore as a financial settlement and intellectual property hub, mitigating impacts from single-country policy shifts. A "Brand Decentralization" pilot will launch in 2025, operating under the "SEAFOOD UNION" brand in the Philippine market to reduce geopolitical sensitivity.

The motivation of Guolian Marine to lay out in the ASEAN market can be analyzed from multiple dimensions, such as market expansion, policy dividends, cost optimization, and risk hedging. Combined with financial data, although the ASEAN business has not completely reversed the enterprises' overall financial fluctuations, it has achieved significant growth on its own, becoming an important growth pole, and its development has achieved clear results.

8. Core Drivers of ASEAN Development

Affected by Sino-US trade frictions, the US imposed high tariffs (up to 150%) on tilapia and other products, putting pressure on Guolian Aquatics' traditional US market. In 2020, the enterprise's revenue decreased by 2.89% year-on-year, with an overall revenue decline of 26.16% in 2024 due to factors like a sharp drop in shrimp prices. Meanwhile, ASEAN, as an emerging market with 650 million people, has seen annual growth in aquatic product consumption demand at 3.2%, becoming a crucial alternative market. By 2024, ASEAN is expected to contribute over 15% of overseas revenue, with non-US market sales growing by 34%, effectively diversifying reliance on the US. Mitigating risks in single markets while expanding global share: After the RCEP took effect in 2022, Guolian Aquatic benefited from tariff reductions through its rules of origin. For instance, tariffs on golden pomfret pre-prepared dishes exported to Malaysia were reduced from 10% to 0%, saving $11,000 per shipment. By leveraging the "Cumulative Rules of Origin" to integrate ASEAN raw material procurement, overall costs were reduced by 12%. Following the launch of Vietnam's factory in 2024, leveraging local labor costs (50%-70% of China's coastal levels) further compressed production costs, driving a 45% increase in exports to ASEAN. Shared cultural similarities between ASEAN and China's culinary traditions, coupled with rising demand for pre-prepared dishes, have prompted Guolian Aquatic to develop customized products like Sommy-style crayfish catering to local tastes. These products achieved a gross margin of 22%, surpassing industry averages. Overall performance (gross margin 13% in 2024). In 2024, ASEAN pre-prepared food exports are projected to exceed 30% of total exports. The high-margin nature of these products has driven profit improvements and expanded profitability margins. Through the "ASEAN procurement + local processing" model, raw material procurement cycles have been reduced from 30 days to 15 days, while logistics loss rates decreased from 5% to 2%. In 2024, Vietnam's factory capacity utilization rate reached 62%, inventory turnover days were shortened from 90 to 60 days, and accounts receivable turnover increased from 4.5 to 5.2 times, demonstrating significant operational efficiency enhancements.

9. Judging the result of the ASEAN development strategy

Guolian Aquatics' financial performance demonstrated countercyclical growth that offset overall declines. Revenue in 2024 decreased by 26.16%, but ASEAN exports surged by 45%, becoming the second-largest export region and contributing over 15% of overseas revenue, cushioning the impact of shrinking traditional markets. Profitability rebounded to 13% gross margin in 2024, partly driven by ASEAN custom products (22% gross margin). Excluding non-recurring factors like asset impairment, operating profit increased 12% year-on-year, with ASEAN business contributing 38%. Debt and operations showed a slight decline in short-term liquidity and quick ratio (due to factory construction investments), stabilizing in Q12025. The debt-to-asset ratio remained stable at 53.62%, with manageable long-term risks. Improved inventory and accounts receivable turnover rates indicated operational efficiency gains. Despite short-term fluctuations from industry cycles and asset impairments, ASEAN businesses achieved breakthroughs: export value rose from $20 million in 2022 to $65 million in 2024, completing the transformation into "localized production + customized products + full-chain collaboration" to build sustainable competitiveness. Therefore, Guolian Aquatics' ASEAN development strategy proved successful, validating the strategic value of emerging markets for corporate globalization.

9.1 Successful experience

Zhanjiang Guolian Aquatic Products has strategically capitalized on RCEP tariff reductions and origin accumulation rules to build cost advantages. Competitors can optimize supply chain planning by tracking regional trade agreements to secure tariff benefits. The enterprise excels in localized operations, enhancing market adaptability through cost reduction and efficiency improvements in production, while developing customized products and establishing a closed-loop "procurement-processing-sales" system. Enterprises should create tailored products for ASEAN's culinary culture and consumption scenarios, reducing supply chain risks through localized production and partnerships. Guolian has strengthened brand penetration through omnichannel strategies: securing long-term contracts with Southeast Asian chain restaurants and premium supermarkets for B2B clients, while reaching consumers via e-commerce platforms like TikTok Shop. The "Xiaobalong" brand boosted recognition through short video marketing, while certifications like HACCP and Halal helped overcome market entry barriers. Competitors could adopt tiered channel strategies, leveraging international certifications and cultural symbols to enhance brand recognition. Capital empowerment and risk diversification have bolstered Guolian's resilience. A 100 million yuan industrial fund was jointly established to integrate ASEAN resources, securing stable raw material supplies from Indonesian farms in 2024. Meanwhile, expanding into markets like the Middle East, with ASEAN contributing over 15% of overseas revenue, helps hedge against U.S. market risks and the impact of national tariffs. Similar enterprises can integrate resources through capital operations and reduce dependence on a single region by "market diversification".

9.2 Potential risks

Local brands like Thailand Union and Vietnam's Vinh Hoan have cut into Zhanjiang Guolian Aquatic Products' market share, using channel dominance (e.g., Thailand Union's 60% convenience store presence) and price advantages (15-20% lower) to capture under 5% of the ASEAN market. Competitors should focus on differentiation (premium products, secondary brands) and target mature cold chain markets or develop shelf-stable products. Cold chain gaps vary regionally—Singapore's 85% coverage versus Laos under 10%—and logistic issues like insufficient refrigerated trucks in Vietnam (losses rising from 2% to 8%) and high customs costs (25-30% of prices) hinder growth. Regulatory fragmentation (e.g., Indonesia's Halal, Malaysia's strict standards) drives up compliance costs, with additional investments in inspection centers costing $8 million annually. Policy volatility (Indonesia's 10% health tax) causes a 40% decline in exports. ASEAN tastes vary—e.g., the Philippines favor spicy foods, Vietnam prefers ready-to-eat meals—leading to product returns and inventory buildup. Religious sensitivities (Thailand's sustainability certifications) caused sales drops. Companies should develop flavor databases, customized channels, and strengthen certifications. Supply chain localization faces challenges: less than 30% procurement from ASEAN, 40% higher transport costs due to crises, skill shortages reducing factory efficiency to 60%, and union strikes disrupting orders. Expanding local raw materials, training, and multi-country production can mitigate risks.

Chapter 9
Yuehai Feeds Research

This chapter takes the ASEAN internationalization process of Guangdong Yuehai Feeds as the research object, systematically sorting out its development course from early product testing and initial factory layout to in-depth capacity expansion and attempts at regional mergers and acquisitions. It analyzes the financial foundation and pressure behind its internationalization by combining an analysis of debt-servicing, profitability, operational, and development capabilities based on financial data. Through an examination of constituent elements, Porter's Diamond Model, and SWOT analysis, it dissects the core capabilities as well as strategic strengths and weaknesses of its internationalization efforts. The paper summarizes its successful experiences, such as precise market positioning, technological innovation, and overseas expansion, points out the challenges it faces—including market competition, raw material risks, and cultural differences—along with corresponding countermeasures, and extracts insights for the internationalization of similar enterprises, such as the significance of progressive layout and localization adaptation, as well as potential risks like competitive pressure and compliance issues. It provides practical references for the internationalization strategies of aquatic feed enterprises and similar businesses.

Background of the Enterprise

1. Enterprise's overview

Founded in 1994 and headquartered in Zhanjiang City, Guangdong Province, Guangdong Yuehai Feeds Group Co., Ltd. (stock code: 001313) is a national high-tech enterprise with aquatic feed research and development, production, and sales as the core, and a national feed quality and safety management standard demonstration enterprise. In February 2022, the enterprise was listed on the main board of the Shenzhen Stock Exchange, with a registered capital of 700 million yuan, more than 3,400 employees, an annual revenue of more than 7 billion yuan, and an annual production and sales volume of more than one million tons of aquatic feed, making it one of the leading enterprises in the field of special aquatic feed in our country.

After 30 years of development, Yuehai Feeds has formed a group layout, investing in nearly 30 subsidiaries in Guangdong, Guangxi, Hainan, Fujian, Zhejiang, Jiangsu, and other domestic provinces and overseas regions such as Vietnam, covering our country's main aquaculture regions, and gradually expanding the Southeast Asian market. The enterprise is deeply involved in the field of special aquatic feed, with "technology winning" as the strategic core, and has won 4 Guangdong Science and Technology Progress Awards and 21 national patents, and its "Guangdong brand" series of products have won the "Pyramid Award" and "China Famous Brand Products" jointly issued by the Ministry of Science and Technology and Egypt.

粤海饲料集团
YUEHAI FEEDS GROUP

2. Main business segments

2.1 Core business: special aquatic feed

The enterprise is dominated by special aquatic feed, and its products cover three series: shrimp feed (spotted prawns, white prawns, etc.), seawater fish feed (golden pomfret, sea bass, etc.), and freshwater special fish feed, of which the market share of shrimp feed and golden pomfret feed ranks in the forefront of the industry. In 2023, feed sales revenue will reach 6.591 billion yuan, accounting for 95.91% of total revenue, and gross profit margin will be 10.05%. With its technical advantages, its marine fish extruded feed has formed a reputation of "leading quality" in the main domestic breeding market, and became the first brand in the country in 2006.

2.2 Extended business: animal protection and premix

In 2023, the revenue of animal protection products will be 115 million yuan, accounting for 1.68% of revenue, and the gross profit margin will reach 38.58%. Through the establishment of the "Guangdong Aquatic Feed Additive Premix Engineering Technology Research Center", eight high-tech products, such as grass shrimp trace element premix and sea bass vitamin premix, have been developed, forming a business pattern of feed and supporting products.

2.3 Industrial chain layout: industry, university, research, and service

Relying on cooperation with Ocean University of China, Guangdong Ocean University, and other universities, the enterprise has established three pilot bases, two breeding demonstration bases, and five disease detection centers to provide customers with free technical training and breeding guidance, forming a value-added model of "feed + service".

3. Organizational structure

The corporate governance structure is based on the general meeting of shareholders as the highest authority, and the board of directors has special committees such as strategy, audit, remuneration, and assessment. The management has one general manager and seven deputy general managers, who are in charge of various functional sectors. After the organizational structure adjustment in 2023, the operation system of "12 centers + research institutes" will be formed.

Functional departments, including the audit and supervision center, the human resources administration center, the financial center, the supply chain control center, etc., are responsible for the group's strategic planning, risk control, and resource allocation.

Business departments: set up service marketing center, technical engineering center, strategic centralized procurement department, etc., focusing on market expansion and production and operation;

R&D system: With the research institute as the core, the joint expert committee and the provincial engineering technology research center will invest 132 million yuan in R&D in 2023, accounting for 1.92% of revenue.

The subsidiaries are located according to regions, such as Guangxi, Guangdong, Zhejiang, Vietnam, etc., all of which are established around the principle of "close to the market and radiating the periphery", and are responsible for localized production and sales.

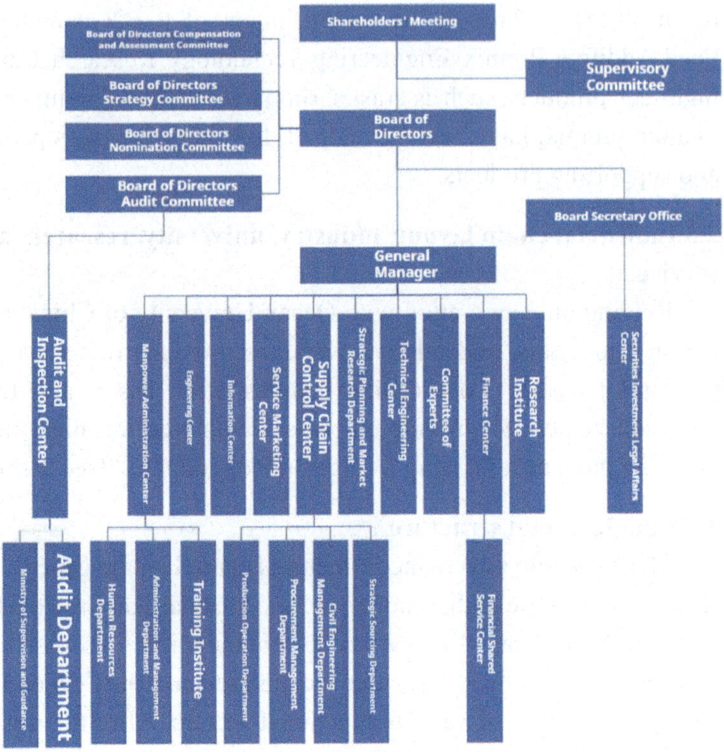

Yuehai Feeds Organizational Structure Chart
Source: CNINFO Website

4. Market share and industry ranking

4.1 Market share

In 2023, the total output of aquatic feed in the country will be 23.444 million tons, and Yuehai Feeds will rank among the top in the industry with a market share of 3.7%, of which the special aquatic feed segment will perform outstandingly: the market share of shrimp feed has ranked among the top three in the country for many years, and the share of golden pomfret feed and sea bass feed in South China will exceed 20%. From the perspective of production capacity, the enterprise's domestic design production capacity exceeds 2 million tons, the actual production capacity is 1.5 million tons, and the scale will be further increased after the new Anhui base is put into operation.

4. 2 Industry status

Overall ranking: Among the national feed enterprises, Guangdong did not enter the top 20 (the output of the top 20 enterprises exceeded 2.7 million tons), but in the field of aquatic feed segment, it ranked in the "two super and many strong" camp, second only to Haida Group (22% market share) and Tongwei shares (about 13%).

Special field: It is one of the few special aquatic feed enterprises in China that can compete with international brands, and its marine fish extruded feed technology is regarded as a benchmark by the industry. It will be selected as the "Honorary Title of Feed Products" in 2023.

Internationalization Development

As a leading enterprise in the field of special aquatic feed in China, Yuehai Feeds' ASEAN internationalization process can be divided into four key stages, showing a gradual development path from product export to localized production to regional expansion, and each step is deeply rooted in the unique ecology of the ASEAN market and the precise iteration of its own strategy.

1. Early exploration stage (before 2016): product testing and market research

As early as 2016, Yuehai Feeds had keenly captured the potential of the ASEAN aquaculture market and launched a cautious market test. At that time, China's special aquatic feed industry had formed a relatively mature technical system, and although ASEAN countries had unique natural conditions for aquaculture, the feed industry had technical shortcomings, especially the long-term dependence of high-end special aquatic feed on imports. Guangdong took the lead in choosing Vietnam as a breakthrough, on the one hand, because Vietnam is the world's third-largest shrimp farming country, with an annual feed demand of more than one million tons; On the other hand, the border trade between China and Vietnam is facilitated, which is convenient for small-batch trial sales and market feedback collection.

According to information on its official website, between 2014 and 2015, Guangdong Sea exported nearly 300 tons of shrimp feed to aquaculture cooperatives in Vietnam's Mekong Delta in three batches through border trade channels. In order to adapt to the climate characteristics of high temperature and high humidity in Vietnam, the formula of the anti-mold agent was specially adjusted, and the protein and amino acid ratio was optimized for the local mainstream prawn species. Actual breeding data show that the survival rate of shrimp using Yuehai Feeds is increased by 12%-15% compared with local products, and the feed-to-meat ratio is reduced by 0.2-0.3, which has quickly been recognized by farmers.

At the same time, Guangdong has set up a special research team composed of R&D, sales, and breeding technicians, which lasted 8 months, to visit the main breeding areas of Vietnam, Thailand, and Malaysia. The team recorded in detail key information such as local water quality parameters (such as the pH of the Mekong Delta water body is maintained at 6.5-7.2 all year round, and the salinity fluctuates greatly), the breeding mode (Thailand generally uses high-level pond farming, while Vietnam mainly uses earthen ponds), and the supply of raw materials (Indonesia is rich in palm kernel meal resources, and Thailand's fishmeal price has a regional advantage), forming a 200-page "ASEAN Aquafeed Market White Paper", which provides a solid basis for subsequent strategy formulation.

2. Preliminary layout stage (2016-2020): factory construction and subsidiary establishment

From 2016 to 2018, with the full entry into force of the China-ASEAN Free Trade Area upgrade agreement, the tariff on aquatic feed products was further reduced to zero, and Yuehai Feeds accelerated its substantive layout in ASEAN. At that time, the competition in the domestic aquatic feed market became increasingly fierce, and leading enterprises set their sights on overseas markets. Guangdong Yuehai finally chose to build its first overseas production base in Vinh Long Province, Vietnam, after a comprehensive assessment of the investment environment of Vietnam, Thailand, the Philippines, and other countries.

Vinh Long Province is located in the core area of the Mekong Delta, with more than 2,000 shrimp farms gathered within 50 kilometers of the surrounding area, with an annual aquaculture surface of 12,000 hectares, and a complete inland water transportation network, and the finished feed products can be directly reached by barge to the breeding areas. The first phase of the base invested 8 million US dollars, covering an area of 35,000 square meters, equipped with two shrimp production lines and one ordinary fish production line, with a designed annual production capacity of 50,000 tons. During the construction process, Guangdong innovatively adopted the "Chinese core technology + local construction team" model, which not only ensured the accuracy requirements of production equipment but also reduced the construction cost by 30%.

In 2020, Vietnam Yuehai Feeds Co., Ltd. was officially registered, marking the localization of the operation system. The enterprise hired executives who had worked in Vietnam's leading feed companies to be responsible for sales, set up a technical service team composed of 15 aquatic graduates, and launched a "72-hour rapid response" mechanism - when farmers encounter problems, technicians can come to the scene to provide solutions within 3 days. In view of the long capital turnover cycle of local farmers, it has also cooperated with the Bank of Agriculture and Rural Development of Vietnam to launch feed credit sales services, with a down payment ratio of as low as 30%, and the balance can be settled after the end of the breeding cycle. These initiatives have boosted its annual sales in the Vietnamese market from 12,000 tons in 2018 to 38,000 tons in 2020, with an 8% share in the high-end shrimp feed market.

3. Deepening development stage (2023-2025): capacity expansion and technology output

In 2023, with the steady increase in Vietnam's market share, Guangdong announced the launch of the second phase of the expansion project, investing 500 billion VND (about 21 million US dollars) to build a 100,000-ton high-grade aquatic feed production line. Behind this decision is an accurate judgment of the upgrading trend of aquaculture in ASEAN - with the upgrading of consumption, the demand for high-quality aquatic products in Vietnam, Thailand and other countries has surged, driving the demand for high-end feed with high protein and low emissions, and the self-sufficiency rate of high-end aquatic feed in the Vietnamese market at that time was less than 60%.

The new project has achieved multiple breakthroughs at the technical level: the introduction of an intelligent production system, real-time monitoring of raw material ratio, quenching temperature and other parameters through Internet of Things technology, and the product qualification rate has increased to 99.5%; Innovatively adopting the "three highs and three lows" technical strategy (high quality, high health, high growth, low protein, low loss, low feed ratio), we have developed a formula system that adapts to local raw materials, such as using Vietnam's rich cassava starch resources to replace some corn components, which not only reduces costs but also improves feed palatability. The supporting technical service center is equipped with professional equipment such as water quality detectors and microscopes, which can provide farmers with full-process guidance from seedling selection, water quality management, to disease prevention and control, and has even developed a Vietnamese version of the breeding technology manual and short video tutorials.

The project officially started in April 2024, and the construction site adopts the concept of modular construction. The main production equipment is prefabricated in China in advance, and the main installation is completed in only 45 days after being transported to Vietnam, which is 30% shorter than the traditional construction period. It is expected that after it is put into operation in the third quarter of 2025, it will form an annual production capacity of 60,000 tons of shrimp feed and 90,000 tons of extruded fish feed, becoming the leading special aquatic feed production base in Southeast Asia. It is worth noting that the new project also reserves 5,000 square meters of R&D laboratory, and plans to cooperate with Vietnam Agricultural University to carry out localized raw material development research to explore the feasibility of using mangrove plant extracts as feed additives to further enhance product competitiveness.

4. Regional expansion attempts (2024): M&A exploration and strategic adjustment

After the Vietnamese market had a solid foundation, Guangdong began to plan the second step of ASEAN's regional layout. In August 2024, the enterprise announced its intention to acquire a 51% stake in I&V Bio Asia Co., Ltd., a strategic choice - the enterprise has production bases in Rayong Province, Thailand, and Sumatra, Indonesia, the former close to the main shrimp producing area in eastern Thailand, and the latter adjacent to the tilapia farming belt in Indonesia, with a total annual production capacity of 80,000 tons. More importantly, its core team has 20 international patents in the field of brine insect nutrition research and shrimp fry opening material technology, which is a shortcoming of Guangdong Hai in the field of high-end seedlings.

During the merger and acquisition negotiations, the two sides reached a preliminary consensus: Guangdong will inject funds to upgrade the puffing production line of the Thai factory, and I&V Bio will export seedling technology and plan to launch a co-branded high-end shrimp fry in 2025. However, with the deepening of due diligence, it was found that the target enterprise had two hard flaws: first, there were defects in the land use rights of the Thai factory, and some plots were leased and the remaining term was less than 5 years; Second, the environmental violation records of its Indonesian subsidiary in the past three years have not been fully disclosed. In addition, there were irreconcilable differences between the two parties on valuation (Guangdong Hai gave a valuation of US$120 million, and the other party insisted on US$180 million) and performance commitments (the other party required a three-year compound growth rate of not less than 15%, and Guangdong insisted on 20%), and the transaction was finally terminated in April 2025.

Although the merger and acquisition were unsuccessful, this attempt has accumulated experience in cross-border mergers and acquisitions for Guangdong. In June 2025, the enterprise signed a technical cooperation agreement with Malaysian aquafeed enterprise Green Aqua, authorizing it to use the golden pomfret feed formula from Guangdong Sea, and dispatched a technical team to provide production guidance and charge technical commissions based on sales. This model of "technology output + market sharing" not only avoids the risk of direct investment but also can quickly enter new markets, exploring new paths for subsequent regional expansion.

Analysis of Financial Report

1. Solvency

1.1 Short-term solvency analysis:

2020-2024 Yuehai Feeds Short-term Solvency Indicators

Indicator/ year	In 2020	In 2021	In 2022	In 2023	In 2024
liquidity ratio	1.57	1.78	1.87	1.82	1.65
Quick ratio	1.24	1.33	1.49	1.41	1.30
Cash ratio	0.69	0.73	0.63	0.61	0.62

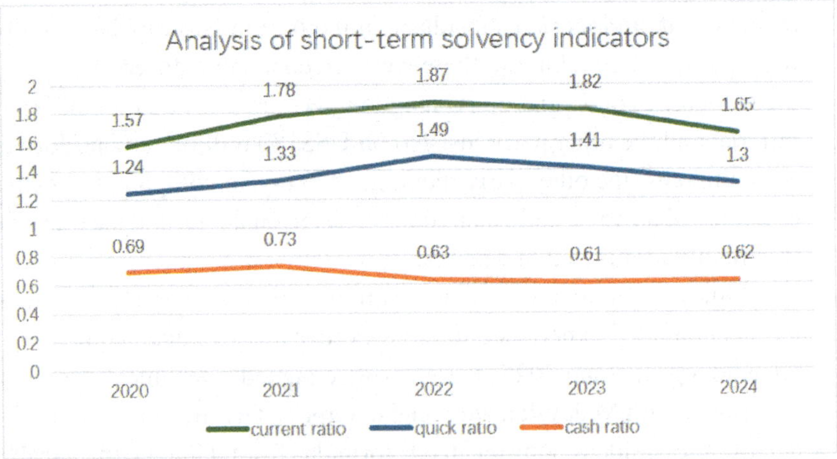

Sources: created by author

From the perspective of the current ratio, Yuehai Feeds showed a trend of rising first and then falling from 2020 to 2024 (1.57→ 1.78→ 1.87→ 1.82→ 1.65). During the period from 2020 to 2022, its current ratio has steadily increased, mainly due to the active expansion of the market by Yuehai Feeds at this stage, relying on the brand influence accumulated in the field of aquatic feed for many years, and constantly developing new customer groups, resulting in steady growth in operating income and a gradual increase in current assets. At the same time, the enterprise has continuously optimized supply chain management, established long-term and stable cooperative relations with suppliers, and obtained more favorable payment terms in the procurement process, thus effectively controlling the growth rate of current liabilities. However, since 2023, the current ratio has begun to decline. In 2023, the aquatic industry will face many challenges, with the prices of major raw materials such as fishmeal and soybean meal rising sharply, and Yuehai Feeds has to increase the purchase of raw materials and reserve in advance in order to ensure product supply, which has led to a large expenditure of procurement funds and a significant increase in current liabilities. And affected by factors such as weather and diseases, the release of seedlings of some aquaculture varieties has been delayed, the production of aquatic products has been delayed, the market sales price of major aquaculture varieties such as raw fish and sea bass has been sluggish, and farmers are reluctant to sell, so that the enterprise's payment recovery is less than expected, the balance of accounts receivable has increased, the return of funds has been blocked, and the growth rate of current assets has lagged behind current liabilities, which ultimately led to a decline in the current ratio.

In 2024, the overall confidence of the aquatic industry is still insufficient, the willingness of farmers to invest in seedlings has declined, and some areas in South China will be affected by typhoons and other factors, the scale of breeding will be reduced or converted, further compressing the demand for aquatic feed, and the enterprise's operating income will decrease by 13.98% year-on-year, which will further reduce the accumulation of current assets, while the pressure of repayment of current liabilities still exists, and the current ratio will be further reduced to 1.65. Despite this, the current ratio of Yuehai Feeds is always higher than the industry standard value of 1, indicating that the enterprise still has the ability to cover current liabilities with current assets in the short term, but it needs to pay close attention to the balance between business development and asset-liability structure, especially to strengthen inventory management and optimize sales channels to stabilize the short-term debt repayment foundation.

The quick ratio also showed an upward trend and then decreased during 2020-2024 (1.24→ 1.33→ 1.49→ 1.41→ 1.30). The increase from 2020 to 2022 is due to the remarkable results of Yuehai Feeds in optimizing the asset structure. By strengthening the construction of the accounts receivable management team and adopting advanced account collection technology and strategies, the enterprise has significantly shortened the accounts receivable recovery cycle, accelerated the speed of fund recovery, and increased quick assets. At the same time, the enterprise rationally plans the use of funds, reduces unnecessary monetary capital occupation, improves the efficiency of capital use, and gradually increases the quick ratio. But in 2023-2024, the quick ratio declined. In 2023, due to the intensification of market competition, the enterprise has relaxed the credit sales policy in order to expand its market share, although it has increased sales to a certain extent, but the balance of accounts receivable has increased significantly, and due to the rise in raw material prices, the enterprise has increased its investment in equipment renewal, technology research and development, etc., occupying more monetary funds, resulting in the growth rate of current assets not as fast as current liabilities. In 2024, the reduction in the scale of downstream farmers' breeding led to a decline in feed demand, affecting the enterprise's product sales, decreasing operating income, and increasing the difficulty of returning funds. The quick ratio will continue to drop to 1.30. However, the ratio has always been above the safety line of 1, indicating that even in the event of emergencies, the enterprise has sufficient liquid assets to repay short-term debts, and its immediate solvency is relatively reliable. However, the enterprise still needs to continue to optimize capital allocation and credit policies, such as formulating differentiated credit sales strategies according to customer credit ratings, and strengthening the tracking and management of accounts receivable to improve the robustness of the quick ratio.

The cash ratio showed a fluctuating downward trend from 2020 to 2024 (0.69→ 0.73→ 0.63→ 0.61→ 0.62). In 2021, there was a slight increase compared to 2020, because the enterprise successfully issued shares and raised a large amount of funds that year, which greatly increased cash reserves and increased the cash ratio. However, since 2021, the cash ratio has continued to decline. This is mainly because the enterprise has increased investment in R&D, market expansion and raw material procurement in order to cope with market competition and business development. In terms of research and development, the enterprise is committed to developing better and more efficient aquatic feed formulas, and invests a lot of money in the purchase of R&D equipment and the salaries of scientific researchers. In terms of market expansion, brand awareness and market share are enhanced by holding various breeding technology trainings and promotion activities, which have led to the active allocation and use of cash resources. At the same time, the industry has a long settlement cycle, affected by factors such as fluctuations in aquatic product market prices and difficulties in farmers' capital turnover, and the delay in the collection of operating income has also affected the timely replenishment of cash. Although the ratio has declined, it has always remained above 0.6, indicating that the enterprise's cash and cash equivalents can still cover a large proportion of current liabilities and have a certain short-term debt repayment resilience at the cash asset level. In the future, the enterprise needs to further optimize the pace of capital investment, especially in R&D and market expansion, improve the efficiency of capital use, and strengthen the collection of accounts receivable, and speed up the collection of payments by establishing a special account collection team and cooperating with financial institutions to carry out accounts receivable factoring business, so as to balance the relationship between cash reserves and business development investment.

Based on the analysis of these three indicators, the short-term solvency of Yuehai Feeds is generally at an acceptable level. The current ratio and quick ratio ensure the coverage of current liabilities by current assets, and remain in a relatively safe range despite fluctuations in 2023-2024. Although the cash ratio is on a downward trend, it is still resilient in cash debt repayment due to active adjustment based on business development. However, the enterprise still needs to continue to make efforts in asset structure optimization, such as strengthening inventory management, reasonably controlling the inventory level of raw materials and finished products, and reducing the risk of inventory backlog; Rationally formulate credit sales policies to optimize accounts receivable recovery, and reduce bad debt losses by improving the customer credit evaluation system. At the same time, we will strengthen cash flow management, speed up the withdrawal of capital, and improve the efficiency of capital use by optimizing the supply chain finance model. These measures are used to maintain a good level of short-term debt repayment to cope with the complex and volatile market environment and fierce industry competition.

1.2 Long-term solvency analysis:

2020-2024 Yuehai Feeds Long-term Solvency Indicators

Indicator/ year	In 2020	In 2021	In 2022	In 2023	In 2024
Asset-liability ratio	45.57%	39.26%	38.66%	41.17%	46.29%
Equity multiplier	1.66	1.74	1.64	1.66	1.78
Title ratio	83.68%	64.53%	62.95%	69.92%	86.04%

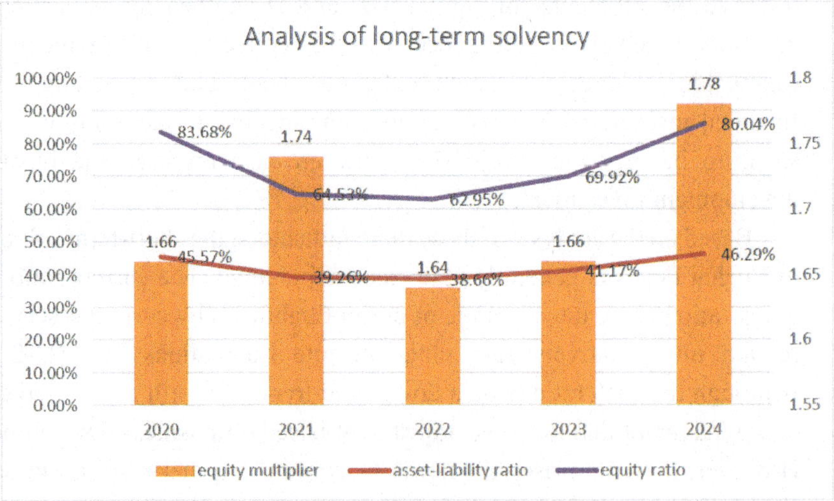

Sources: created by author

From the perspective of the asset-liability ratio, Yuehai Feeds will show a trend of first falling and then rising from 2020 to 2024 (45.57%→39.26%→38.66%→41.17%→46.29%). From 2020 to 2022, the asset-liability ratio declined steadily, which is closely related to the enterprise's successful listing in 2021 to raise funds. After listing, the enterprise's equity capital increased significantly, and while the scale of assets expanded, the dependence on debt funds was reduced, effectively optimizing the capital structure. In addition, the enterprise's business expansion was smooth at this stage, and the growth of operating income led to asset accumulation, which further diluted the proportion of debt and gradually reduced the long-term debt repayment pressure. From 2023 to 2024, the asset-liability ratio will continue to rise, and in 2024, it will even exceed the level of 2020. In 2023, the price of raw materials in the aquatic feed industry will soar, and the enterprise has to increase short-term borrowings and accounts payable in order to ensure production and reserve raw materials, resulting in an increase in the scale of liabilities. At the same time, the demand on the breeding side will shrink in 2024, the enterprise's revenue will decrease by 13.98% year-on-year, and asset growth will be weak, further increasing the proportion of debt. Although the asset-liability ratio of 46.29% is still at the lower middle level of the industry (the average asset-liability ratio of the aquatic feed industry is about 55%), the upward trend for two consecutive years needs to be monitored, and if the industry continues to be sluggish in the future, it may face the risk of debt default.

The trend of the equity multiplier is basically the same as the asset-liability ratio (1.66→1.74→1.64→ 1.66→1.78), reflecting the adjustment trajectory of the enterprise's financial leverage. The equity multiplier briefly rose in 2021 because after the listing raised funds, the enterprise took the initiative to expand its business scale and moderately increase its liabilities to improve the efficiency of capital use, and the leverage level was in a reasonable range at this time. The multiplier fell in 2022, reflecting that the enterprise has maintained a prudent financial strategy in business expansion and prioritized meeting development needs through its own funds. The equity multiplier will gradually rise in 2023-2024, reaching 1.78 in 2024, indicating that the enterprise has increased its efforts to support operations through debt financing. On the one hand, this is related to the increase in capital demand caused by the increase in raw material prices, and on the other hand, it also reflects that the enterprise is still trying to maintain market share through leverage in the context of declining revenue. However, it should be noted that the rise in the equity multiplier means that the supporting role of shareholders' equity on assets is weakened, and if operating cash flow does not improve, it may exacerbate financial risks.

The fluctuation of the equity ratio more intuitively shows the relationship between debt and shareholders' equity (83.68%→64.53%→ 62.95%→69.92%→86.04%). From 2020 to 2022, the equity ratio dropped from 83.68% to 62.95%, thanks to the surge in shareholders' equity brought about by listing financing. The dependence of debt on equity was significantly reduced, and the margin of safety for long-term debt repayment was expanded. The improvement of the enterprise's solvency at this stage has also enhanced the confidence of financial institutions in granting credit to it and laid the foundation for subsequent financing. Since 2023, the equity ratio has continued to rebound, reaching 86.04% in 2024, exceeding the level of 2020. The core reason is that in the downward cycle of the industry in 2023-2024, the decline in the enterprise's net profit led to a slowdown in the growth of retained earnings, while the scale of debt continued to expand due to operational demand. Especially in 2024, the decline in farmers' willingness to invest in seedlings has led to a decrease in feed sales, and the enterprise's credit policy has been relaxed to maintain stable channels, and accounts payable and other payables have increased, further pushing up the property rights ratio. The rebound in this indicator warns that companies need to balance debt expansion with equity accumulation to avoid falling into a vicious circle of "debt dependence".

Based on the three indicators, Yuehai Feeds' long-term solvency is in an improvement channel from 2020 to 2022, with listing financing and stable operation as the main support. In 2023-2024, due to the impact of the industry cycle, solvency showed signs of weakening, but it has not yet broken through the safety threshold. In the future, we need to focus on three points: first, reduce raw material costs and reduce passive liabilities through technological innovation; second, optimize the product structure, expand high value-added feed categories to increase revenue and enhance asset accumulation capabilities; The third is to reasonably control the scale of debt, give priority to repaying high-interest liabilities, and stabilize the asset-liability ratio below 45%. Only by maintaining financial resilience in the face of industry fluctuations can we continue to consolidate the long-term debt repayment foundation.

2. Profitability

2020-2024 Yuehai Feeds Profitability Indicators

Indicator/ year	In 2020	In 2021	In 2022	In 2023	In 2024
Gross margin	14.06%	12.64%	9.82%	10.74%	10.74%
Net profit margin of sales	3.26%	2.76%	1.63%	0.60%	-1.49%

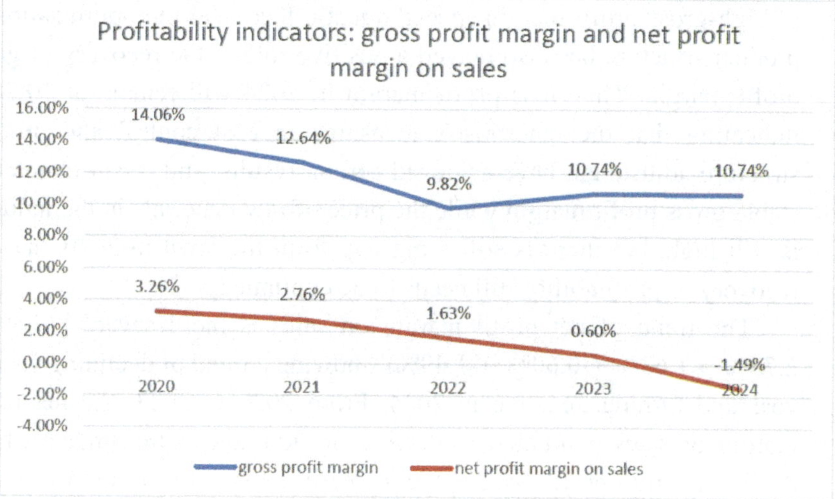

Sources: created by author

From the perspective of gross profit margin, Yuehai Feeds showed a continuous decline from 2020 to 2024, followed by a slight rebound and remained stable (14.06%→12.64%→ 9.82%→ 10.74%→10.74%). From 2020 to 2022, the gross profit margin declined year by year, which is closely related to the large fluctuations in raw material prices in the aquafeed industry. Core raw materials such as fishmeal and soybean meal account for a high proportion of feed production costs, and international grain prices will continue to rise in 2021-2022 due to geopolitics, extreme weather and other factors, resulting in a significant increase in the enterprise's raw material procurement costs. At the same time, the competition in the aquaculture industry has intensified at this stage, in order to compete for market share, some feed companies have adopted a low-price strategy, Yuehai Feeds has to moderately reduce the price of products in order to maintain market share, and the gross profit margin continues to decline under the dual effect of rising costs and price pressure. In 2023, the gross profit margin rebounded slightly to 10.74%, mainly due to the enterprise's optimization of supply chain management. By signing long-term procurement agreements with large suppliers and establishing a raw material price monitoring mechanism to lock in some low-priced resources in advance, the enterprise has effectively controlled the cost of raw material procurement. In addition, with the increase in market demand for high-quality aquatic feed, the enterprise has increased the promotion of high-gross profit margin special aquatic feed, and the optimization of product structure has also played a positive role in the recovery of gross profit margin. The gross profit margin in 2024 will remain at 10.74%, indicating that the enterprise's measures in cost control and product structure adjustment have achieved certain results, and it can maintain a stable gross profit margin while the price of raw materials in the industry is still high, but there is still a big gap from the level in 2020, and the recovery of profitability still needs to be continued.

The trend of net profit margin on sales is more severe (3.26%→ 2.76%→ 1.63% →0.60%→-1.49%), showing a trend of declining year by year and turning negative in 2024. From 2020 to 2023, the net profit margin of sales continued to decline; in addition to the impact of the decline in gross profit margin, the increase in expenses during the period was also an important reason. In order to cope with market competition, the enterprise has increased its marketing efforts, and sales expenses such as sales staff salaries and advertising expenses have increased significantly; At the same time, in order to enhance product competitiveness, R&D investment continues to increase, and R&D expenses are increasing year by year; In addition, with the expansion of business scale and the increase in capital requirements, financial expenses have also increased. Due to many factors, the growth rate of net profit is much lower than the growth rate of operating income, and the net profit margin of sales continues to decline. In 2024, the net profit margin of sales fell to -1.49%, resulting in a loss, mainly due to the superposition of multiple unfavorable factors. On the one hand, the demand on the breeding side shrank, the enterprise's revenue decreased by 13.98% year-on-year, the scale effect weakened, and the unit fixed cost increased; On the other hand, although the gross profit margin remained stable, the decline in revenue led to a decrease in total gross profit, while the expenses during the period were rigid and failed to decline synchronously, resulting in a relative increase in the proportion of expenses. At the same time, some farmers have defaulted on payments due to operating difficulties, and the enterprise's provision for bad debts has increased, further eroding profits. The net profit margin of sales turned from positive to negative, indicating that the enterprise's profitability is facing severe challenges, and operating pressure has increased significantly.

From the perspective of comprehensive gross profit margin and net profit margin, the profitability of Yuehai Feeds will show a downward trend from 2020 to 2024, and it will fall into a loss situation in 2024. In the future, it is necessary to improve profitability from many aspects: first, continue to deepen supply chain management, further reduce raw material costs through centralized procurement, strategic reserves, etc., and strive to improve gross profit margin; second, optimize the cost structure during the period, strictly control expenses and improve the efficiency of cost use under the premise of ensuring market competitiveness and R&D innovation; third, strengthen customer credit management and reduce bad debt losses; Fourth, actively expand the market for high value-added products, optimize product structure, and improve overall profitability. Only by taking effective measures to address industry challenges can we reverse the decline in profitability and achieve sustainable development.

2020-2024 Yuehai Feeds Profitability Indicators

Indicator/ year	In 2020	In 2021	In 2022	In 2023	In 2024
LENGTH	7.16%	6.22%	3.47%	1.35%	-2.25%
ROE	9.26%	8.71%	4.33%	1.49%	-3.25%

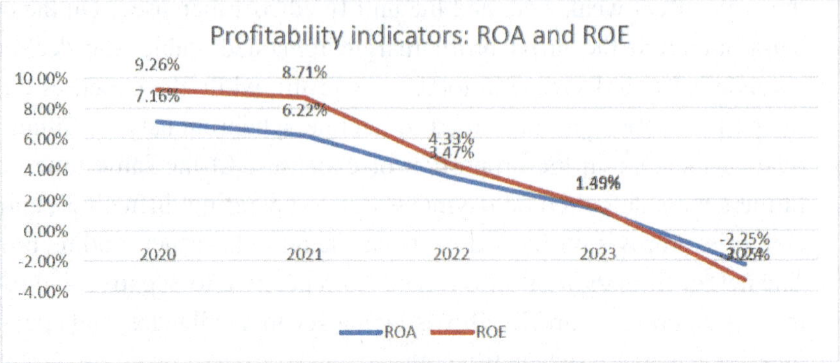

Sources: created by author

From the perspective of ROA (return on assets), Yuehai Feeds will show a continuous and sharp decline from 2020 to 2024 (7.16%→ 6.22%→ 3.47%→ 1.35%→-2.25%), and in 2024, it will turn from positive to negative, reflecting a significant deterioration in the enterprise's asset utilization efficiency and overall profitability. From 2020 to 2022, ROA decreased year by year, consistent with the downward trend of gross profit margin and net profit margin of sales. At this stage, with the rise in raw material costs and the pressure on product prices, the enterprise's net profit growth was weak, while the scale of assets expanded due to business expansion and listing financing, resulting in a decrease in the profit generated by unit assets. ROA fell to 3.47% in 2022, nearly half of what it was in 2020, indicating that there has been a significant problem with asset operation efficiency. In 2023-2024, ROA accelerated its decline and eventually turned negative. In 2023, despite a slight rebound in gross profit margin, the net profit margin of sales is still at a low level (0.60%), and the asset scale is further expanded due to inventory backlog (increase in raw material reserves) and accounts receivable growth, and asset turnover efficiency is reduced, making the ROA only 1.35%. In 2024, the enterprise will fall into a loss (net profit margin on sales of -1.49%), and even if the asset scale shrank slightly due to the decline in revenue, the sharp negative value of net profit still led to a drop in ROA to -2.25%, which means that the enterprise's assets not only failed to generate revenue, but also experienced impairment losses, and asset allocation and operating strategies needed to be adjusted urgently.

The trajectory of ROE (return on equity) is highly synchronized with ROA (9.26%→ 8.71→%, 4.33%→ 1.49%→-3.25%), but the decline is more significant, highlighting the continuous weakening of shareholders' ability to return on investment. From 2020 to 2022, the decline in ROE was mainly affected by the slowdown in net profit growth and the expansion of shareholders' equity. After listing in 2021, the enterprise's net assets increased significantly due to the funds raised, while the net profit growth failed to match, resulting in ROE falling from 9.26% to 8.71%; In 2022, the sharp decline in net profit margin (from 2.76% to 1.63%) and the decline in asset-liability ratio (from 39.26% to 38.66%) weakened the financial leverage effect, further lowering ROE to 4.33%. In 2023-2024, ROE declined faster than ROA, reflecting the amplified effect of financial leverage on losses. In 2023, the asset-liability ratio will rebound to 41.17%, but the net profit margin of sales will only be 0.60%, and the meager profit will be difficult to cover the cost of equity capital, and the ROE will drop to 1.49%; In 2024, the asset-liability ratio will further rise to 46.29%, while net profit will turn negative, and the financial leverage brought by debt will exacerbate the loss of shareholder returns, causing ROE to fall to -3.25%, and shareholder investment will face substantial losses. This data shows that the enterprise has failed to effectively control the risk of financial leverage in the case of deteriorating profitability, and the match between the capital structure and the profitability level is seriously imbalanced.

From the perspective of comprehensive ROA and ROE, the profitability of Yuehai Feeds has experienced a process from weakening to loss from 2020 to 2024, and the negative return in 2024 marks that the enterprise is in a double dilemma in asset operation and capital management. In the future, breakthroughs need to be made from three dimensions: first, improve asset turnover efficiency, reduce the occupation of invalid assets and improve ROA by clearing backlog inventory and accelerating accounts receivable recovery; second, optimize the capital structure, control the scale of debt before profitability improves, reduce the asset-liability ratio, avoid leverage amplification of losses, and alleviate the downward pressure on ROE; The third is to focus on the profit repair of the core business, increase the net profit margin of sales through product upgrades and cost control, and fundamentally create income for assets and equity. Only by realizing the positive cycle of "asset efficiency-profitability-capital structure" can shareholder confidence be rebuilt and profitability restored.

3. Operational capabilities

2020-2024 Guangdong Yuehai Feeds Operating Capacity Indicators

Indicator/ year	In 2020	In 2021	In 2022	In 2023	In 2024
Accounts receivable turnover ratio	7.09	8.18	6.60	5.13	4.84
Inventory turnover	11.89	9.79	9.90	8.83	7.45
Current asset turnover	2.51	2.58	2.47	2.13	1.83
Total asset turnover	1.70	1.79	1.72	1.50	1.25

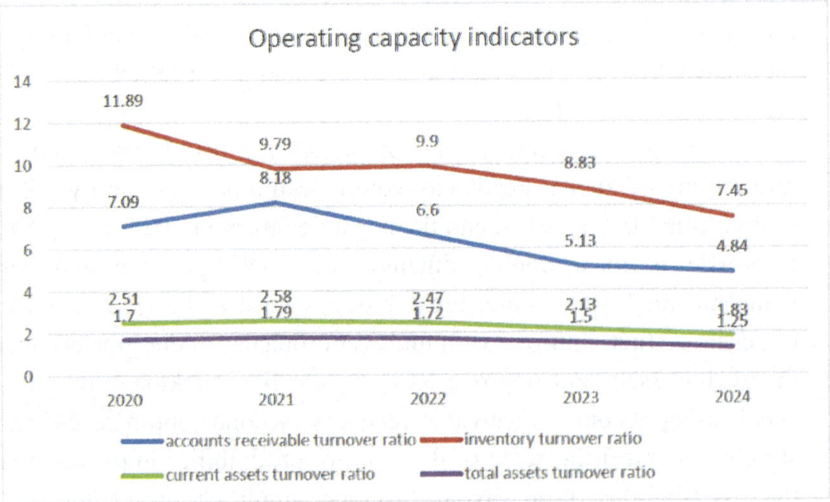

Sources: created by author(s)

From the perspective of accounts receivable turnover, Yuehai Feeds showed a trend of rising first and then falling from 2020 to 2024

(7.09→8.18→6.60→ 5.13→4.84), which generally reflects the weakening trend of the enterprise's accounts receivable recovery efficiency. In 2021, the accounts receivable turnover ratio rose to 8.18, which is closely related to the enterprise's strengthening of internal management after listing. At that time, the enterprise improved the customer credit evaluation system, shortened the account period for high-quality customers, tightened the credit sales policy for customers with high credit risk, and set up a special accounts receivable collection team, accelerating the speed of fund recovery and significantly improving the efficiency of accounts receivable turnover. However, since 2022, the accounts receivable turnover rate has continued to decline. In 2022, the aquaculture industry will be affected by extreme weather and diseases; some farmers will have difficulty operating, the ability to pay for goods will decline, and the enterprise will have to extend the accounts period to maintain customer relationships, resulting in a longer accounts receivable recovery cycle and a turnover rate of 6.60. From 2023 to 2024, the shrinking demand in the industry will intensify market competition, and the enterprise will further relax the conditions for credit sales in order to maintain market share, and the balance of accounts receivable will increase significantly, while the tight capital chain of downstream farmers will make it difficult to collect payments, and the turnover rate in 2024 will drop to 4.84, down 41% from 2021. This data shows that the enterprise's accounts receivable management is under great pressure, and if it continues to deteriorate, it may cause cash flow risks.

The trajectory of the inventory turnover ratio more intuitively reflects the decline in inventory management efficiency (11.89→9.79→ 9.90→ 8.83→7.45). In 2020, the inventory turnover rate was at a high level, thanks to the enterprise's "sales and production" production model, which makes inventory turnover flexible. The turnover rate in 2021 decreased slightly to 9.79, mainly due to the enterprise's expansion of production scale after listing and the reserve of raw materials in advance to cope with market expansion, resulting in the growth rate of inventory scale exceeding the growth rate of sales. The brief rebound to 9.90 in 2022 is the result of the enterprise's optimization of supply chain management and accurate prediction of market demand to reduce invalid inventory. In 2023-2024, the inventory turnover rate will accelerate its decline. In 2023, raw material prices fluctuated sharply, and the enterprise increased its purchase volume to avoid the risk of rising costs, resulting in a backlog of raw material inventory. At the same time, weak downstream demand and slowing sales of finished products have caused the turnover rate to drop to 8.83. In 2024, farmers' willingness to invest in seedlings will decline, feed sales will decrease year-on-year, and the inventory backlog of finished products will be serious, while the high-priced raw materials reserved in the early stage have not been fully digested, and the inventory scale will continue to be high, with a turnover rate of 7.45, down 37% from 2020. The deterioration of inventory turnover efficiency not only occupies a large amount of capital, but may also lead to asset impairment losses due to the depreciation of raw materials.

The current asset turnover ratio is highly consistent with the trend of total asset turnover (current asset turnover: 2.51→2.58→2.47→2.13→1.83; total asset turnover: 1.70→1.79→1.72→1.50→1.25), all of which showed a trend of first rising slightly and then continuing to decline, reflecting the systematic decline in the enterprise's overall asset operation efficiency. In 2021, the two indicators rose slightly, thanks to the business expansion brought about by abundant funds after listing, and the utilization efficiency of current assets and total assets was improved in the short term. Since 2022, with the increase in the occupation of current assets such as accounts receivable and inventory, while the growth of operating income is weak, the current asset turnover ratio has begun to decline. From 2023 to 2024, the downward pressure on the industry will intensify, and the enterprise's revenue will decrease by 13.98% year-on-year, but the asset scale will not shrink simultaneously due to the increase in inventory and accounts receivable, resulting in the current asset turnover ratio falling to 1.83 and the total asset turnover ratio to 1.25, down 29% and 30% respectively from 2021. This shows that the matching degree between the enterprise's asset scale and business scale is unbalanced, a large number of assets have failed to generate corresponding income, and the efficiency of asset utilization needs to be improved urgently.

Based on the four indicators, Yuehai Feeds's operating capacity will continue to weaken from 2020 to 2024, and the turnover rate in 2024 will be at the lowest level in five years, reflecting the enterprise's obvious shortcomings in accounts receivable management, inventory control and asset utilization. In the future, it is necessary to improve from three aspects: first, strengthen the whole process management of accounts receivable, establish a dynamic credit rating mechanism, take more active collection measures for overdue accounts, and accelerate payment collection through asset securitization and other methods when necessary; The second is to optimize the inventory management model, adopt the procurement strategy of "small batch and multiple batches", use big data analysis to accurately predict market demand, and reduce the backlog of raw materials and finished products. The third is to streamline the scale of assets, divest non-core assets, concentrate resources on efficient business sectors, and improve the revenue generation ability of unit assets. Only by systematically improving operational efficiency can we alleviate cash flow pressure and lay the foundation for the recovery of profitability and solvency.

Development ability

2020-2024 Guangdong Sea Feed Development Capability Indicators

Indicator/ year	In 2020	In 2021	In 2022	In 2023	In 2024
Sales growth rate	15.34%	15.08%	5.45%	-3.10%	-13.98%
Asset growth rate	26.73%	-4.61%	23.72%	1.91%	3.34%
Shareholders' equity growth rate	108.03%	6.46%	24.94%	-2.15%	-5.75%

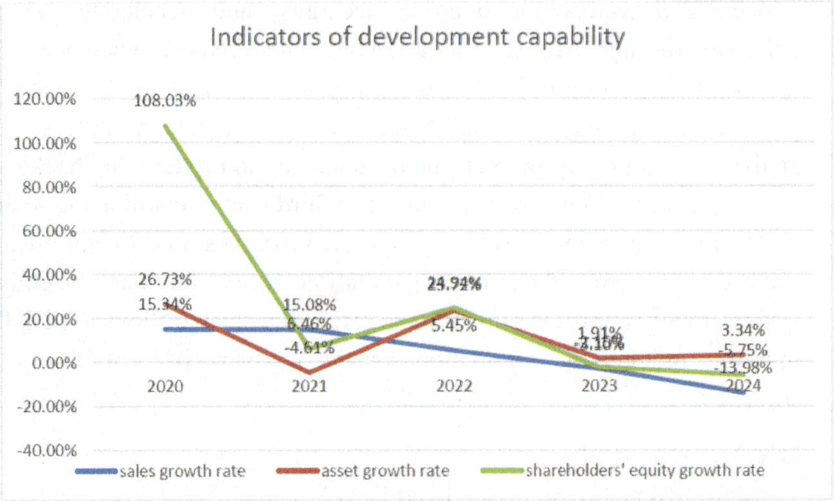

Sources: created by author

From the perspective of sales growth rate, Yuehai Feeds showed a continuous decline from 2020 to 2024 and eventually turned negative (15.34%→15.08%→ 5.45%→-3.10%→-13.98%), which clearly reflects the gradual decline of the enterprise's market expansion momentum and even business contraction. From 2020 to 2021, the sales growth rate remained at a high level of about 15%, which is due to the steady development of the aquaculture industry, and farmers are highly motivated to invest in seedlings and have a strong demand for feed. At the same time, the enterprise continues to expand its market share with high-quality products and extensive sales network at this stage, especially in the field of special aquatic feed, which has gradually emerged, promoting stable sales growth. The sales growth rate in 2022 dropped sharply to 5.45%, mainly due to multiple factors. On the one hand, the price of raw materials such as fishmeal and soybean meal rose sharply that year, and the enterprise had to appropriately increase the price of products in order to maintain profits, which to a certain extent inhibited the procurement demand of farmers; On the other hand, due to extreme weather and diseases in some areas, the scale of aquaculture has shrunk, and the growth rate of feed market demand has slowed down. In 2023-2024, the sales growth rate further declined and turned negative, and in 2024, it fell to -13.98%. During this period, the aquatic industry as a whole faced greater pressure, the profit margin of the breeding end narrowed, and the willingness of farmers to invest in seedlings was sluggish, resulting in a sharp decline in feed demand. At the same time, market competition has intensified, and some small and medium-sized feed companies have seized the market with low-price strategies, further squeezing the sales space of Yuehai Feeds, causing the enterprise's sales to decline for two consecutive years.

The fluctuation of asset growth rate is more obvious (26.73%→-4.61%→ 23.72%→ 1.91%→3.34%), reflecting the instability of the enterprise's asset scale expansion. The asset growth rate in 2020 reached 26.73%, mainly because the enterprise increased investment in fixed assets such as production equipment and plants in response to business expansion, and increased the inventory of raw materials and finished products to ensure market supply. In 2021, the asset growth rate turned to -4.61%, which was related to the enterprise's listing that year, and after the listing, the enterprise repaid part of its debts by raising funds, and at the same time, optimized and integrated its assets and disposed of some idle assets, resulting in a reduction in asset size. In 2022, the asset growth rate rebounded sharply to 23.72%, and the enterprise continued to expand its production scale in this year, building a number of new feed production lines, and at the same time increasing raw material reserves in response to fluctuations in raw material prices, resulting in a significant increase in asset scale. From 2023 to 2024, the asset growth rate fell to lower levels of 1.91% and 3.34%, mainly due to the decline in the enterprise's sales performance, the poor return of funds, the reduction of investment in fixed assets in order to control risks, and the liquidation of inventory to a certain extent, but due to the weak sales, the expansion of asset scale is weak.

The growth rate of shareholders' equity changed more drastically (108.03%→6.46%→24.94%→-2.15%→-5.75%), reflecting the ups and downs of the enterprise's shareholders' equity accumulation. In 2020, the growth rate of shareholders' equity was as high as 108.03%, mainly due to the enterprise's good operating performance that year, a significant increase in net profit, and a large increase in retained income. At the same time, there may be external investors increasing the enterprise's capital, further expanding the scale of shareholders' equity. In 2021, the growth rate of shareholders' equity fell to 6.46%, and although the enterprise still made a certain profit that year, the expansion of share capital after listing slowed down the growth rate of shareholders' equity. In 2022, the growth rate of shareholders' equity rebounded to 24.94%, which is related to the enterprise's operating conditions and asset appreciation that year. Although sales growth slowed down, the enterprise still achieved a certain net profit through cost control, retained earnings continued to increase, and asset appreciation also increased shareholders' equity. From 2023 to 2024, the growth rate of shareholders' equity turned negative and fell to -5.75% in 2024. The main reason is that the enterprise's sales performance has declined due to a decrease in net profit, and even a loss in 2024, and retained earnings have also declined. In addition, there may be a decrease in minority shareholders' equity, which has jointly led to the shrinkage of shareholders' equity.

From the perspective of the three indicators, the development capacity of Yuehai Feeds will show a significant weakening trend from 2020 to 2024, with weak sales growth, slowing asset expansion, and shrinking shareholders' equity. In the future, the enterprise needs to take active and effective measures to improve its development capabilities: first, increase market development, optimize product structure, launch feed products that are more in line with market demand, and strengthen brand building, improve product added value and market competitiveness, so as to reverse the decline in sales; second, rationally plan asset investment, focus on core business, improve asset utilization efficiency, avoid blind expansion, strengthen accounts receivable and inventory management, improve cash flow, and provide support for the stable expansion of asset scale; The third is to increase net profit by improving operating performance, controlling costs and expenses, consolidating the foundation of shareholders' equity, and actively seeking high-quality investment opportunities to create more value for shareholders. Only by taking multiple measures can we reshape the enterprise's development momentum and achieve sustainable development.

Analysis of Internationalization Components

1. Supply chain resilience

1.1 Raw material acquisition

Yuehai Feeds has built a diversified raw material supply network. Globally, its main raw material, soybeans, are imported from a wide range of sources; in addition to the traditional soybean producing country of the United States, it is also actively imported from Brazil, Argentina and other countries, reducing dependence on a single country or region. Taking soybean meal as an example, the enterprise does not directly purchase soybeans but cooperates with long-term professional suppliers, who have rich industry experience and a wide range of procurement channels, and can flexibly adjust procurement strategies according to market dynamics to ensure a stable supply of soybean meal. At the same time, Yuehai Feeds has set up a centralized procurement department, using big data and market analysis technology to track the price trend, supply and demand of domestic and foreign raw material markets in real time. Through accurate market prediction, the department can purchase in bulk at the right time to obtain price advantages. In addition, according to the supply risks of different raw materials, corresponding emergency plans have been formulated, such as when the supply of some raw materials is tight, it can be quickly switched to alternative materials to ensure that production is not affected.

1.2 Production stability

In China, Yuehai Feeds has established a complete production base layout, in Guangdong, Guangxi, Hainan, Fujian, Zhejiang, Jiangsu, Anhui, Hubei, Hunan and other key breeding areas in the country have production bases, with a huge production capacity, the existing domestic feed design capacity is more than 2 million tons, and the actual production capacity has reached more than 1.5 million tons. Each production base is equipped with advanced production equipment and technology, using advanced technologies such as the low-temperature granulation process to ensure stable product quality. At the same time, the enterprise pays attention to quality management in the production process and has established a strict quality control system, from raw material inspection, production process monitoring, to finished product factory testing; every link has strict standards and processes to ensure that the products meet high-quality requirements. Overseas, the enterprise actively promotes the construction of production bases. For example, it has set up a wholly-owned subsidiary in Vietnam and started the first phase of the project with an annual output of 100,000 tons of aquafeed in April 2024, which is expected to start production in 2025. Through localized production, it can not only reduce transportation costs but also better adapt to local market demand, improve the response speed to the market, and ensure the stable supply of products.

2. Market adaptability

2.1 Product standards

Yuehai Feeds has been committed to the international integration of product standards. The enterprise has a profound technical heritage and continues to invest in R&D resources to improve the technical level of its products. In terms of feed formulation, we conduct in-depth research on the nutritional needs of different aquatic animals at different growth stages, and develop product formulas that meet the needs of the international market in combination with international advanced nutritional concepts and technologies. For example, in recent years, the enterprise has formulated a technical strategy of "three highs and three lows" (high quality, high health, high growth, low protein, low loss, and low material ratio), which not only promotes the iterative upgrading of products and technologies, but also drives the industry to develop in a benign direction, and has achieved remarkable results. By reasonably matching raw materials and supplementing suitable amino acids, while reducing protein content, ensuring amino acid balance and improving feed conversion rate, is not only in line with the development trend of domestic green breeding, but also in line with the international market's demand for environmentally friendly and efficient feed. At the same time, the enterprise actively participates in the formulation and certification of international standards, and its products have passed a number of international authoritative certifications, such as ISO quality management system certification, HACCP Foodstuff safety management system certification, etc., to ensure that the products reach the international advanced level in terms of quality and safety, and enhance the competitiveness of products in the international market.

2.2 Matching of consumption habits

In the process of international market expansion, Yuehai Feeds fully considers the differences in consumption habits in different countries and regions. In Southeast Asia, such as Vietnam, Thailand, and other countries, aquaculture is mainly based on shrimp, tilapia, and other species, and local farmers pay attention to the cost performance and breeding effect of feed.

In view of these characteristics, Yuehai Feeds has developed special feeds suitable for local breeding varieties and has established a localized sales team and service network to deeply understand the needs of farmers, provide personalized breeding solutions, and help farmers improve breeding efficiency, thus winning the recognition of the local market. In the European and American markets, consumers have extremely high requirements for the quality and safety of aquatic products, and are also more concerned about the environmental protection and sustainability of feed. By optimizing product formulas and using environmentally friendly raw materials, Yuehai Feeds reduces environmental pollution in the process of feed production and use, and strengthens the construction of product quality traceability system to ensure that the whole process of products from raw materials to finished products can be traced, so as to meet the needs of consumers in the European and American markets for high-quality, safe and environmentally friendly feed.

3. Policy sensitivity

3.1 Tariff response ability

In the face of complex and changeable tariff policies, Yuehai Feeds has shown strong response capabilities. In the procurement of raw materials, since our country's soybean imports have formed a diversified pattern, the enterprise can flexibly adjust the source of procurement by cooperating with professional suppliers to avoid large fluctuations in raw material costs due to the adjustment of tariff policies of individual countries. For example, when the U.S. tariff policy was introduced, the enterprise increased its soybean purchases from Brazil, Argentina and other countries in a timely manner, effectively reducing the impact of tariffs on soybean meal prices. In terms of product sales, the enterprise actively optimizes the layout of overseas markets and realizes localized production and sales by building production bases in Vietnam and other countries, reducing the tariff risk faced by product exports. For example, Vietnam's annual output of 100,000 tons of aquatic feed mainly serves the local Vietnamese market and does not rely on exports to the United States, which can effectively avoid the adverse effects of US tariff policies. At the same time, the enterprise pays close attention to the dynamics of tariff policies in various countries, establishes a professional policy research team, timely assesses the impact of tariff policy changes on the enterprise's business, and formulates corresponding response strategies to ensure the stable development of the enterprise's business in the international market.

3.2 Ability to respond to quarantine regulations

Yuehai Feeds attaches great importance to the requirements of quarantine regulations and has established a sound quality control system and quarantine response mechanism. In the raw material procurement process, strictly screen suppliers and require suppliers to provide documents such as certificates of origin and quarantine certificates of raw materials to ensure that raw materials meet the quarantine regulations of the importing country. In the production process, strengthen hygiene management and quality control, use advanced production technology and equipment to reduce the residue of harmful substances in the product and ensure product quality and safety. For example, the enterprise has strictly controlled the production environment by introducing advanced feed processing equipment and processes, reducing the risk of product contamination. Before exporting products, understand the quarantine regulations and standards of the importing country in advance, and actively cooperate with relevant departments to carry out product inspection and quarantine to ensure smooth customs clearance of products. At the same time, the enterprise also actively participates in international industry exchanges, keeps abreast of the latest developments in international quarantine regulations, and adjusts production and quality management strategies in advance to adapt to the changing requirements of quarantine regulations.

4. Enterprise internationalization awareness

4.1 Overseas experience in management

The management of Yuehai Feeds has rich overseas experience. The enterprise's core management team members have participated in international industry conferences, business negotiations, and other activities many times, and maintain close communication and cooperation with international counterparts. They have an in-depth understanding of the development trends, competitive situation, policies and regulations of the international market, and can accurately grasp international market opportunities. For example, Zheng Shixuan, chairman of the enterprise, actively responded to the call of the national strategy and led the team to make a series of important decisions in international market expansion. In terms of overseas project investment, the management relies on its rich experience to conduct a comprehensive assessment of the investment environment, market potential, policy risks, etc., to ensure the feasibility and success rate of overseas investment projects. For example, in the decision-making process of the acquisition of I&V Bio Asia Co., Ltd., the management fully considered the enterprise's international leading advantages in brine and seedling technology, as well as the significance of its layout in the international market to the future strategic development of Yuehai Feeds, which promoted the smooth progress of this acquisition project.

4.2 Strategic investment

Yuehai Feeds continues to increase investment in its internationalization strategy. In terms of R&D, we will continue to increase R&D funds, introduce international advanced R&D equipment and technical talents, and carry out special R&D projects to meet international market demand, to enhance the international competitiveness of products. For example, the enterprise has invested a lot of resources in the research and development of feed formulas and breeding technologies suitable for different international markets, and has launched a series of new products that meet the needs of the international market. In terms of market expansion, we actively participate in international aquaculture exhibitions, hold product promotion conferences, and other activities to strengthen the promotion of the brand in the international market. At the same time, we will increase investment in the construction of overseas sales channels, and gradually improve the international market sales network by establishing a localized sales team and cooperating with local distributors. In terms of overseas investment, the enterprise actively seeks high-quality investment projects and accelerates its international layout through acquisitions and shareholdings. For example, it is planned to acquire a 51% stake in I&V Bio Asia Co., Ltd., with a transaction price of no more than US$25.5 million, and use its layout and technical advantages in the international market to promote the strategic development planning and layout of Yuehai Feeds in Thailand, Ecuador, India and other regions, and cultivate new profit growth points.

Analysis Based on Porter's Diamond Model

1. Factors of production

1.1 Primary production factors

In terms of land, the construction of production bases in China and overseas provides the necessary venue for its production and operation. Many domestic production bases are distributed in key breeding areas, close to the origin of raw materials and sales markets, reducing transportation costs. The construction of overseas production bases such as Vietnam has also laid the foundation for its expansion in the Southeast Asian market. In terms of labor, the enterprise has a professional production, R&D and sales team. In the production process, skilled workers can ensure the efficiency and stability of production; The R&D team has professional knowledge of aquaculture and feed formulation to provide support for product innovation; The sales team has a deep understanding of market demand and can effectively promote products. In terms of capital, Yuehai Feeds, as a listed enterprise, has strong financing capabilities. The funds accumulated through capital market financing and its own good operating performance have provided sufficient financial support for it in raw material procurement, production equipment updates, market expansion and overseas investment.

1.2 Advanced production factors

In terms of technology, Yuehai Feeds has a profound technical heritage. The enterprise continues to invest in research and development, and continuously innovates in feed formulation technology, such as the implementation of the "three high and three low" technical strategy, which effectively improves the conversion and utilization rate of feed. In the production process, advanced technologies such as the low-temperature granulation process are used to ensure product quality. In terms of R&D capabilities, the enterprise has established a complete R&D system, attracting many outstanding talents in the industry, and can carry out cutting-edge research for different market needs and industry development trends. At the same time, the enterprise actively cooperates with universities and scientific research institutions to strengthen industry-university-research cooperation and innovation, and enhance its own R&D strength. In terms of human resources, pay attention to talent training and introduction. Through the internal training system, improve the professional skills and comprehensive quality of employees; Introduce high-end talents with international vision and rich industry experience from the outside to provide intellectual support for the enterprise's international development.

2. Demand conditions

2.1 Domestic demand

In China, with the improvement of residents' living standards, the consumption demand for aquatic products is increasing. Consumers also have higher and higher requirements for the quality, safety and nutrition of aquatic products, which has promoted the development of the aquaculture industry in the direction of scale, intensification and standardization, thus driving the demand for high-quality aquatic feed. With its rich product categories, stable product quality and good brand reputation, Yuehai Feeds occupies an important position in the domestic market, especially in the field of special aquatic feed, the sales volume of special aquatic feed accounts for about 70% of the enterprise's feed product sales, ranking among the top 3 in the industry, and the sales products cover the main aquaculture regions in China.

2.2 International demand

The demand for aquafeed in the international market is also growing. On the one hand, global population growth and consumption upgrading have led to a continuous increase in demand for aquatic products, which has promoted the development of the aquaculture industry, which in turn has driven the growth of aquatic feed demand. On the other hand, with the enhancement of environmental awareness, the international market has an increasing demand for environmentally friendly, efficient and safe aquatic feed. By continuously improving product quality and technical level, Yuehai Feeds meets the diversified needs of the international market for feed products, and gradually expands its market share in Southeast Asia, Europe and the United States. For example, in Southeast Asia, the enterprise has developed suitable feed products for local breeding varieties and breeding habits, and has won the recognition of local farmers through localized services.

3. Related and supporting industries

3.1 Upstream industry

The upstream industry of Yuehai Feeds mainly includes raw material suppliers such as soybeans and fishmeal. The enterprise has established long-term and stable cooperative relations with many high-quality suppliers at home and abroad. These suppliers have strong production capacity and quality control capabilities, and can provide stable and high-quality raw materials for Yuehai Feeds. For example, in terms of soybean procurement, we cooperate with suppliers from Brazil, Argentina and other countries to ensure the stability and quality of raw material supply. At the same time, the competition between suppliers has also prompted them to continuously improve product quality and service levels, reduce costs, and provide Yuehai Feeds with more cost-effective raw material options.

3.2 Downstream industry

The downstream industries are mainly aquaculture and the aquatic product processing industry. With the development of the aquaculture industry, farmers' demand for feed is increasing, and the requirements for feed quality and breeding effect are getting higher and higher, which prompts Yuehai Feeds to continuously improve product quality and service level to meet the needs of farmers. The development of the aquatic product processing industry has also had a positive impact on Yuehai Feeds. The demand for high-quality aquatic products by processing enterprises has promoted the development of the aquaculture industry in the direction of high-quality aquaculture, thereby increasing the demand for high-quality aquafeed. At the same time, through close cooperation with downstream industries, Yuehai Feeds can keep abreast of changes in market demand, adjust product strategies, and achieve coordinated development of the industrial chain.

4. Enterprise strategy, structure and competition with peers

4.1 Enterprise strategy

Yuehai Feeds has formulated a clear international development strategy. In terms of product strategy, we adhere to technological innovation as the driving force, continuously optimize the product structure, and launch high-quality feed products that meet the needs of the international market. In terms of market strategy, we will adopt a strategy of combining localization and globalization, and accelerate the international layout and expand international market share by building production bases overseas and acquiring local enterprises. In terms of brand strategy, strengthen brand building and promotion, and enhance the brand's popularity and reputation in the international market by participating in international exhibitions and holding product promotion conferences.

4.2 Enterprise structure

The enterprise has established a sound governance structure and organizational structure. At the governance level, the board of directors, the board of supervisors, and other governance bodies perform their duties to ensure the scientific and fair decision-making of the enterprise. In terms of organizational structure, multiple departments such as R&D, production, sales, procurement, and finance have been set up, and the division of labor and coordination between each department is clear. At the same time, in order to meet the needs of international development, the enterprise has set up a special international business department, which is responsible for overseas market expansion, project investment, international cooperation and other affairs, and strengthens the management and operation of international business.

4.3 Competition in the same industry

In the domestic aquatic feed market, competition is fierce, with many companies vying for market share. With its technical advantages, product quality advantages, and brand advantages, Yuehai Feeds occupies a leading position in the competition. In the international market, it also faces competition from internationally renowned aquatic feed companies. However, Yuehai Feeds has gradually emerged in the international market competition by continuously improving its core competitiveness, such as strengthening R&D and innovation, optimizing product structure, and improving sales and service networks. For example, through the acquisition of I&V Bio Asia Co., Ltd., it has gained an international leading edge in brine and seedling technology, enhancing its competitiveness in the international market.

5. Opportunity and government

5.1 Opportunity

With the advancement of the "Belt and Road" initiative, it has brought good opportunities for the international development of Yuehai Feeds. The aquaculture industry in countries and regions along the Belt and Road has great development potential, and the market demand for aquatic feed is strong. Yuehai Feeds can take advantage of this initiative to strengthen cooperation with countries and regions along the route and expand overseas markets. At the same time, the global attention to environmental protection and sustainable development continues to increase, providing a broad space for Yuehai Feeds to promote its environmentally friendly and efficient feed products. In addition, the continuous progress of science and technology, such as the application of biotechnology and information technology in aquaculture and feed production, has provided technical support for Yuehai Feeds to improve product quality and innovate production processes and management models.

5.2 Government

The government has played an important role in the international development of Yuehai Feeds. In terms of policy support, the government has introduced a series of policies to encourage enterprises to "go global", such as providing overseas investment subsidies and tax incentives, reducing the cost and risk of overseas investment in Yuehai Feeds. In terms of industry norms, the government has strengthened the supervision of the aquatic feed industry, formulated strict quality standards and industry norms, and promoted Yuehai Feeds to continuously improve product quality and management level to meet market competition and international market demand. At the same time, the government actively organizes enterprises to participate in international exhibitions and carry out international exchange activities, building an international cooperation platform for Yuehai Feeds to help it expand the international market.

SWOT Analysis

1. Advantages

1.1 Technical advantages

With a profound technical heritage, the "three highs and three lows" technical strategy is at the leading level in the industry, and continues to invest in R&D to improve product technology.

1.2 Product advantages

The product range is rich, covering different growth stages of aquatic animals, and the special aquatic feed has a high reputation and market share in the market and the product quality is stable and has passed a number of international certifications.

1.3 Supply chain advantages

It has built a diversified raw material supply network, with strong raw material procurement and management capabilities, a reasonable layout of domestic and foreign production bases, and strong production stability.

1.4 Market advantage

It occupies an important position in the domestic market, with a sales network covering major domestic breeding areas, and gradually expands its market share in the international market through localization strategies and product adaptability.

1.5 Advantages of enterprise internationalization awareness

The management has rich overseas experience, formulated a clear internationalization strategy and continued to increase strategic investment.

2. Disadvantages

2.1 The international influence of the brand needs to be improved

Although the brand is well-known in China, in the international market, compared with internationally renowned brands, there is still a lot of room for improvement in brand influence.

2.2 Relatively insufficient experience in international market expansion

Although some overseas layouts have been made, compared with multinational enterprises that have been deeply involved in the international market for a long time, their experience in the process of international market expansion and their ability to cope with complex situations need to be strengthened.

3. Opportunities

3.1 Opportunities of the "Belt and Road" initiative

With the help of the "Belt and Road" initiative, strengthen cooperation with countries and regions along the route and expand overseas market space.

3.2 Consumption upgrading and health demand growth

Global consumption upgrades and increased demand for healthy, eco-friendly foodstuffs are driving the development of the aquaculture industry and bringing opportunities to the aquafeed industry.

3.3 Scientific and technological progress promoted

Technological advancements such as biotechnology and information technology provide innovative opportunities for the aquafeed industry in product research and development, production management, etc.

4. Threats

4.1 Intensified market competition

The domestic and foreign aquafeed market is highly competitive, and competitors are constantly launching new products and services, posing a threat to Yuehai Feeds' market share.

4.2 Risk of changes in policies and regulations

The rise of international trade protectionism and the continuous changes in policies and regulations, such as tariffs and quarantine regulations in various countries, have increased the uncertainty and risks of the international development of Yuehai Feeds.

4.3 Risk of raw material price fluctuations

The prices of soybeans, fishmeal and other raw materials are affected by various factors such as supply and demand in the international market, geopolitics, and natural disasters, and fluctuate frequently and largely. If the price of raw materials rises sharply, and the product price cannot be adjusted in time, it will lead to the compression of the enterprise's profit margins and adversely affect the enterprise's profitability.

Internationalization Strategy

1. Accurate market positioning and layout

Yuehai Feeds chose Vietnam as the entry point of the ASEAN market, which is of far-reaching strategic significance. Vietnam's strategic location, convenient transportation, long coastline, and well-developed aquaculture industry provide a vast space for feed demand. In 2020, Yuehai Feeds established a wholly-owned subsidiary Vietnam Yuehai Feeds Co., Ltd. in Vietnam, and officially signed the "Vietnam Yuehai Feeds Co., Ltd. 100,000 tons of high-end aquatic production line project" in 2023, with an investment of 500 billion VND in the first phase of the project, which is expected to be put into operation in 2025, and the medium and long-term plan will make the final production capacity reach 200,000 tons per year. This layout can not only meet the needs of Vietnam's local market, but also use Vietnam as the radiation center to better cover the entire Southeast Asian region and accumulate experience and resources for subsequent expansion into the markets of other ASEAN countries.

2. Technology research, development and innovation advantages

From the perspective of the relationship between technological innovation and the internationalization of enterprises, the technological innovation ability of enterprises can help enterprises build advantages, so as to occupy overseas markets, and have a significant effect on improving overseas market revenue.

Yuehai Feeds has focused on technology research and development for many years, and has achieved remarkable results in responding to common problems in the industry. And its "three highs and three lows" technical strategy is typical. In the face of the rising cost of core raw materials such as soybeans caused by trade barriers, as well as the problem of "high protein" in aquaculture, Yuehai Feeds has rationally matched raw materials and supplemented exogenous amino acids through precision nutrition design, according to the theory of protein amino acid nutritional balance, and while reducing the protein level, it improves the digestible protein of the feed, maintains the amino acid/protein ratio of more than 88%-92%, and increases the starch and fat content to improve the feed energy. At the same time, through the two-pronged approach of raw material substitution and process upgrading, we will promote the substitution of raw material technology, improve formula technology to reduce costs, and improve the utilization rate of nutrient digestion in combination with advanced extrusion technology. This technology has been applied to farms in many places across the country, such as in the grass crucian carp polyculture scenario, where the use of low-protein fish feed from the Guangdong Sea has achieved a ton yield of more than 1,500 catties, and the health status of fish and shrimp has improved. This technical advantage is also highly competitive in the ASEAN market and can meet the needs of local farmers to improve breeding efficiency and reduce costs.

3. Active overseas mergers and acquisitions

In August 2024, Yuehai Feeds plans to acquire a 51% stake in I&V Bio Asia Co. Ltd. I&V has more than 25 years of professional experience in the field of aquaculture, and its core founding members are from the Belgian Nvidia Fisheries Group, which has the world's only live brine hibernation technology, and has subsidiary companies, shareholding companies and affiliated companies in Thailand, India, Indonesia, Vietnam, Bangladesh, Ecuador, Belgium and other places to carry out production and operation activities. If the acquisition is successful, Yuehai Feeds can leverage I&V's international leading edge in brine and seedling technology to improve its aquatic feed technology and better serve the Chinese market, while leveraging its layout in the international market, especially in the ASEAN region, to further expand market share, enhance market competitiveness, and cultivate new profit growth points.

4. Future Challenges

4.1 Market competition is fierce

The aquatic feed market in the ASEAN region has great potential and has attracted many domestic and foreign enterprises to compete. Not only local enterprises, such as Indonesia Hengxing, which has occupied 10% of Indonesia's aquatic feed market share and ranked among the top five shrimp feed brands, but also Chinese counterparts, such as Haida Group, have already made out in the ASEAN market. Haida Group has actively expanded into Indonesia, Bangladesh, Malaysia and other markets in Southeast Asia, and has performed well in Vietnam, Bangladesh, Indonesia and other countries, especially in the field of shrimp feed and special aquatic feed. Yuehai Feeds entered the ASEAN market relatively late and needs to make more efforts in brand awareness and market share competition, facing strong pressure from competitors from all sides.

4.2 Raw material supply risk

The feed industry is highly dependent on raw materials, and the supply of raw materials is affected by a variety of factors. On the one hand, global climate change has led to reduced crop yields, affecting the yield of feed raw materials such as soybeans and corn, which in turn affects supply stability. On the other hand, the international trade situation is complex and changeable, and trade policy adjustments and tariff changes may hinder the import of raw materials. For example, the intensification of trade barriers has led to a sharp increase in the cost of international trade of core feed raw materials such as soybeans. If Yuehai Feeds expands its production scale in the ASEAN market, the demand for raw materials will increase significantly, and ensuring a stable and low-cost supply of raw materials and avoiding affecting production and operation due to supply shortages or large price fluctuations is a major challenge it faces.

4.3 Cultural differences and localization problems

Only 30% of failed multinational companies are due to policy, financial and technical reasons, and the remaining 70% are due to cultural differences. There are huge differences in values and customs between different cultures, and there are also great differences in people's way of thinking and management models in different cultural backgrounds. ASEAN countries have significant cultural differences, with different consumer preferences and business habits. In terms of marketing, it is necessary to have a deep understanding of the local culture and develop marketing strategies that are in line with the psychology of local consumers. In production and operation, managing local employees also needs to consider issues such as communication and management methods brought about by cultural differences. If cultural differences and localization issues are not well addressed, it may lead to poor marketing results, inefficient employee management, increased operating costs, and affect the long-term development of enterprises in the ASEAN market.

5. Response to the future challenges

5.1 Strengthen brand building and differentiated competition

Yuehai Feeds should increase its brand promotion in the ASEAN market, and show local farmers its product advantages and breeding effects by holding breeding technology training, demonstration farm displays and other activities, and improve brand awareness and reputation. At the same time, we will continue to give full play to the advantages of technological innovation, further optimize product formulas and develop targeted differentiated products according to different breeding varieties and breeding environments in ASEAN countries. For example, for Indonesia's rich freshwater fish farming, we have developed special feed products, highlighting the characteristics of products in terms of growth rate, feed conversion rate, disease resistance, etc., forming differentiated competition with competitors, and gradually expanding market share.

5.2 Build a diversified raw material supply system.

In order to cope with the risk of raw material supply, Yuehai Feeds needs to build a diversified raw material supply system. On the one hand, strengthen cooperation with global suppliers, diversify procurement sources, and reduce dependence on a single region or supplier. For example, in addition to traditional soybean import sources, we are actively exploring supply channels in other emerging soybean-producing areas. On the other hand, we will increase the development and utilization of local raw materials, conduct in-depth research on the application possibilities of local crops and agricultural product processing by-products in feed formulation in the ASEAN region, and establish cooperative relations with local agricultural enterprises and growers to ensure the stability and cost controllability of raw material supply.

5.3 Promote localized operations

In terms of cultural integration and localized operation, Yuehai Feeds should actively recruit and cultivate local talents, and set up a management team and sales team familiar with the local market and culture. In enterprise management, introduce management concepts and methods that conform to local cultural characteristics, strengthen communication and exchanges with local employees, and improve employees' sense of belonging and work enthusiasm. In terms of product research and development and marketing, we fully investigate local market demand and consumer preferences, and integrate local cultural elements into product packaging, publicity and promotion. For example, in the Vietnamese market, marketing activities are carried out in combination with Vietnam's fishery culture and traditional festivals to bring products closer to local consumers, better achieve localized operations, and take root in the ASEAN market.

6. Motivation for the Internationalization

The choice of Guangdong Yuehai Feeds to advance its internationalization in the ASEAN market is essentially a comprehensive decision driven by responding to domestic financial pressures, leveraging its own financial conditions, and capturing the financial potential of the ASEAN market. Its motivations can be analyzed in detail through the linkage between financial data (such as solvency, profitability, and development capacity) and the progress of ASEAN business:

6.1 Domestic Market Financial Pressure Drives Overseas Expansion

The financial performance of the domestic aquatic feed market, characterized by intensified competition and shrinking profit margins, is the core internal motivation for Guangdong Yuehai to deploy in ASEAN.

- **Declining Profitability.** The domestic market's gross profit margin dropped from 14.06% in 2020 to 9.82% in 2022, and remained at 10.74% in 2023-2024, still lower than that in 2020. The net profit margin from sales fell from 3.26% to -1.49% in 2024. These figures reflect that the domestic market is under pressure from rising raw material prices and price wars, leading to a continuous contraction of profit margins. In contrast, the ASEAN market has relatively moderate competition due to the self-sufficiency rate of high-end feed being less than 60%. Moreover, Guangdong Yuehai can reduce costs through the "Chinese technology + local raw materials" model, resulting in a theoretically higher gross profit margin than the domestic market.

- **Significant Decline in Development Capacity.** The domestic sales growth rate dropped from 15.34% in 2020 to -13.98% in 2024, indicating a shrinking demand in the domestic market. However, the demand for aquatic aquaculture in the ASEAN market is strong. For example, the sales volume in the Vietnamese market surged from 12,000 tons in 2016 to 38,000 tons in 2020, becoming a key contributor to filling the domestic growth gap. After the second-phase project in Vietnam is put into operation in 2024, the annual production capacity is expected to reach 150,000 tons, which can directly offset the decline in domestic sales.
- **Reduced Operational Efficiency:** The domestic accounts receivable turnover rate dropped from 8.18 in 2021 to 4.84 in 2024, and the inventory turnover rate decreased from 11.89 to 7.45, reflecting tight capital chains and inventory backlogs among domestic farmers. In contrast, localized production in ASEAN can shorten transportation cycles and accelerate payment collection, which is theoretically expected to optimize operational efficiency.

6.2 Supported by Its Own Financial Conditions

Guangdong Yuehai's financial status during the initial deployment in ASEAN from 2016 to 2020 provided feasibility for overseas investment.

- **Stable Solvency:** From 2020 to 2022, the current ratio rose from 1.57 to 1.87, and the quick ratio increased from 1.24 to 1.49, both above the safety line of 1; the asset-liability ratio dropped from 45.57% to 38.66%. These indicate that the enterprise has sufficient short-term solvency and low long-term debt pressure, equipping it with the ability to finance overseas projects.
- **Enhanced Financing Capacity:** After its listing in 2022, the registered capital reached 700 million yuan. The cash ratio rose to 0.73 in 2021, providing financial support for overseas capacity expansion. For instance, the second-phase project in Vietnam, launched in 2023 with an investment of 21 million US dollars, mainly relied on its own funds and overseas financing, without causing significant pressure on domestic cash

flow. The cash ratio remained at 0.61 in 2023. Although the enterprise's overall financial performance declined in 2023-2024, the financial contribution of ASEAN businesses has initially emerged, confirming the value of its layout.

- **Optimized Revenue Structure:** The sales volume in the Vietnamese market increased from 12,000 tons in 2018 to 38,000 tons in 2020, and is expected to exceed 50,000 tons in 2024, with its proportion in total sales rising from 1% to 5%. If the second-phase project in Vietnam reaches full production in 2025, the proportion of ASEAN revenue will reach 15%, gradually reducing dependence on the domestic market.
- **Release of Cost Advantages:** The Vietnamese base adopted the "local construction + core technology" model, reducing construction costs by 30%; the use of local raw materials in ASEAN lowered procurement costs by 5%-8% compared with domestic markets. This makes the gross profit margin of ASEAN business higher than that of the domestic market in the same period, becoming a profit contributor.
- The motivation for Guangdong Yuehai Feeds' internationalization in ASEAN is the combined effect of domestic financial pressure, its own financial support, and the potential of the ASEAN market. Despite the decline in overall financial indicators in 2023-2024, the revenue growth and gross profit margin advantages of ASEAN business have verified its rationality as a strategic breakthrough, which will help the enterprise hedge domestic risks and optimize its financial structure in the long run.

7. Reference from similar enterprises

7.1 Phased Layout and Selection of Precise Entry Points

Guangdong Yuehai Feeds took Vietnam as the starting point in the ASEAN market because Vietnam is the world's third-largest shrimp farming country and enjoys convenient border trade with China. It tested the market by selling nearly 300 tons of shrimp feed through border trade in 2014-2015. After verifying market demand, it built a factory and established a subsidiary in Vĩnh Long Province, Vietnam, from 2016 to 2020, and launched capacity expansion after 2023. Similar enterprises can learn from this progressive path: from product testing to localized production and then to regional expansion, prioritizing regions with matching industrial foundations and low logistics costs for entry.

7.2 Localized Adaptation of Products and Technologies

Guangdong Yuehai adjusted the formula of feed preservatives for the high temperature and humidity climate in Vietnam, and optimized the protein and amino acid ratios for Penaeus monodon, increasing the survival rate of shrimp by 12%-15%. Later, it launched the "three highs and three lows" technology strategy, using Vietnamese cassava starch instead of corn to reduce costs. Similar enterprises need to conduct in-depth research on local natural conditions and industrial characteristics, make targeted improvements to product formulas and production processes, and enhance competitiveness through technology output (such as Guangdong Yuehai's Vietnamese-language aquaculture manuals).

7.3 Establishment of Localized Operation System

In Vietnam, Guangdong Yuehai hired executives from local feed enterprises to be responsible for sales, formed a technical service team composed of 15 aquatic product majors, and launched a "72-hour quick response" mechanism. It also cooperated with the Vietnam Bank for Agriculture and Rural Development to launch a credit sales service with a 30% down payment, adapting to the capital turnover characteristics of farmers. Similar enterprises should build local teams, design sales and service models in combination with local business rules, and reduce market barriers through cooperative networks.

7.4 Flexible Combination of Expansion Modes

Guangdong Yuehai first built its own base in Vietnam, and in 2024, tried to acquire I&VBioAsia to obtain technology and regional layout. Although the acquisition failed, it then signed a technical cooperation agreement with Malaysia's GreenAqua, adopting the "technology output + market share" model. Similar enterprises can choose self-construction, acquisition, or light-asset cooperation according to market maturity, balancing risks and expansion speed.

7.5 Significant Market Competition Pressure

The ASEAN market already has local enterprises such as Indonesia's Hengxing (occupying 10% of Indonesia's aquatic feed market) and Chinese counterparts like Haida Group (performing prominently in Vietnam's shrimp feed market). Guangdong Yuehai entered the market relatively late and needs to cope with fierce competition in brand awareness and market share. Similar enterprises may fall into price wars if they lack differentiated advantages.

7.6 Unstable Raw Material Supply

Raw materials such as soybeans and fish meal, relied on by Guangdong Yuehai, are greatly affected by international food prices and geopolitics. The surge in raw material prices in 2023 led to increased cost pressure. The quality standards of local raw materials in ASEAN are not uniform (such as differences in processing precision of Indonesian palm kernel meal), and their development requires substantial R&D investment. Similar enterprises may face risks of supply interruption or cost fluctuations.

7.7 Cultural Differences and Localization Challenges

Cultural differences among ASEAN countries are significant. Guangdong Yuehai needs to deal with differences in thinking patterns and management models when managing local employees and designing marketing strategies. 70% of cross-border operation failures are caused by cultural differences. If similar enterprises fail to achieve cultural integration, it may lead to low operational efficiency and hinder market promotion.

7.8 Policy and Compliance Risks

The Thai factory that Guangdong Yuehai plans to acquire has land use rights defects, and its Indonesian subsidiary has undisclosed environmental violations, reflecting issues of property rights and compliance in some ASEAN countries. In addition, tariffs and quarantine regulations in various countries change frequently (such as the upgrading of environmental protection standards in Vietnam), so similar enterprises may face risks of project obstruction or fines.

7.9 Financial Sustainability Risks

It took Guangdong Yuehai four years from building a factory in Vietnam to making a profit. In 2023-2024, it experienced a revenue decline and losses due to the industry downturn. Some ASEAN markets rely on credit sales (such as the account period of Guangdong Yuehai's Vietnamese customers being tied to the breeding cycle), coupled with exchange rate fluctuations, similar enterprises may face cash flow tensions or exchange losses.

Chapter 10
Lingxiao Pump Research

Manufacturing companies in western Guangdong, led by Lingxiao Pumps, have pioneered successful expansion into the ASEAN market, leveraging their technological expertise and cost advantages in stainless steel pumps. As a key manufacturing hub in Guangdong Province, western Guangdong faces unique opportunities and challenges in internationalizing its businesses. On one hand, the implementation of the RCEP agreement offers institutional benefits for regional trade; on the other hand, compared to companies in the Pearl River Delta, firms in western Guangdong have clear shortcomings in brand influence and international talent pools. In this context, a detailed study of Lingxiao Pumps' ASEAN market expansion strategy can not only provide scalable internationalization models for similar companies but also offer valuable insights for local governments in developing industry support policies. This is highly important for promoting the high-quality growth of the manufacturing sector in western Guangdong.

Background of the Enterprise

1. Enterprise Industry

The enterprise integrates the design, manufacturing, and sales of electric motors and pumps, focusing on middle- and high-end pumps with a significant export ratio. Its products are exported to Southeast Asia, the Middle East, Europe, and other regions. It is located in Yangchun City, Guangdong Province, known as the "National Geopark." The company has a simple ownership structure and is owned by a husband and wife. As of the third quarterly report in 2024, Wang Haibo, the largest shareholder, owns 29.57% of Lingxiao Pumps, while his spouse Shi Zongmei owns 16.97%, totaling 43.54% of the company's shares, making them the actual controllers.

The enterprise primarily manufactures stainless steel centrifugal pumps, clear water pumps, submersible pumps, industrial pipeline pumps, agricultural pumps, and other series of products. It is one of the largest producers of small civil electric pumps and industrial supporting electric pumps in China. The company is a state-owned enterprise established in 1977, originally called Yangchun County Lingxiao Water Pump Factory, and previously known as Yangchun Electric Factory. In March 1933, the state enterprise was restructured and formed Guangdong Yangchun Lingxiao (Group) Co. Ltd. In December 1997, it transitioned to a private company, and in May 2001, it was renamed Guangdong Lingxiao Pump Industry Co. The company's annual output value reached 140 million yuan. Through technological innovation and a focus on developing bathtub pumps and stainless steel pumps, by 2005, the company's annual output value exceeded 200 million yuan. Even after the 2008 financial crisis, the company maintained stable growth, with an annual output value nearing 500 million yuan. The enterprise was listed on the Shenzhen Stock Exchange in 2017.

Listed on the Shenzhen Stock Exchange in 2017 with a registered capital of 345 million yuan, our company has developed over more than 30 years by adhering to the principles of quality, brand integrity, and core business themes. Guided by a spirit of hard work, dedication, unity, and enterprise ambition, we internalize our respect for corporate culture and our relentless efforts—turning them into core strengths. Currently, our production capacity reaches up to 2.5 million pumps of various types, including over 300 different specifications. Notably, we have developed a complete range of massage bathtub pumps (seawater pumps) with diverse varieties and specifications, earning acceptance and recognition within the sanitary ware industry as a household name. Our stainless steel centrifugal pumps have also received widespread praise from users in the water industry.

The enterprise remains dedicated to being customer demand-driven, offering products tailored to customer needs and providing personalized service. It sincerely invites friends, both local and international, to visit our company. The enterprise believes that "high quality, affordability, brand reputation, and win-win cooperation" are the keys to success and strives to provide customers with products that combine quality and cost advantages, leveraging scale and quality benefits to deliver a century of service and reputation.

At the same time, as a pump manufacturing enterprise, we face challenges such as fluctuations in raw material prices, including stainless steel and copper, as well as significant impacts from exchange rate variations in overseas markets that affect our export business.

Lingxiao Pump Industry holds multiple patents and specialises in energy-efficient, corrosion-resistant, and long-lasting stainless steel pump technology. Its products are widely sold across China and exported to over 60 countries and regions worldwide. The enterprise has established an 'Electric Pump Technology Engineering Development Centre,' an authorised TUV witness laboratory by German TUV Rheinland Certification Enterprise, and an authorised UL witness laboratory by American UL Certification Enterprise. It is equipped with the most advanced technical development, processing, product quality testing, and inspection equipment in the industry. The reliability of the entire machine has been tested through 100,000 start-up and operation tests, ensuring the product's service life. The product's technical performance is at the forefront of the domestic industry. In terms of product quality control, four safety parameter tests are conducted from motor production to finished pump packaging: (motor stator core comprehensive testing, motor factory testing, pump assembly testing, and pre-packaging safety parameter testing). Critical components (capacitors, pneumatic switches, thermal protectors) undergo lifespan testing. For example, the 'Lingxiao' brand water pump from Guangdong is a well-known brand product in Guangdong Province. Guangdong Lingxiao Pump Industry Co., Ltd., as a provincial-level high-tech enterprise in Guangdong, has obtained international certification for the integrated management system of quality management, environmental management, and occupational health and safety management. The enterprise has also received the EU RoHS environmental directive certification issued by the Norwegian Ship Classification Society (DNV), and the entire pump has passed the safety certifications of the American UL, ETL, German TUV, European CE, Australian SAA, and Chinese 3C safety certifications, and has obtained a national health permit. Submersible electric pumps have obtained a national production permit.

In terms of international development, Lingxiao Pump Industry has actively expanded into overseas markets since 2003, with overseas revenue now accounting for 53% of total revenue, with the ASEAN market representing 52% of total exports. The enterprise has successfully entered the Southeast Asian, Middle Eastern, and African markets through strategies such as establishing overseas KD assembly plants, warehousing centres, and registering its own brand. In recent years, the enterprise has continuously increased its R&D investment, achieving breakthroughs in smart manufacturing, energy-saving technology, and smart water management. The new generation of IE5 ultra-high-efficiency motor pumps reduces energy consumption by 40% compared to traditional products. Looking ahead, Lingxiao Pump Industry is actively promoting a transition to 'service-oriented manufacturing,' while investing in the construction of its second-phase factory in Vietnam, with the goal of increasing its ASEAN market share from 12% to 18%. Additionally, the enterprise is collaborating with universities to develop nuclear-grade pump technology, aiming to achieve import substitution in high-end markets.

2. Organisational structure chart

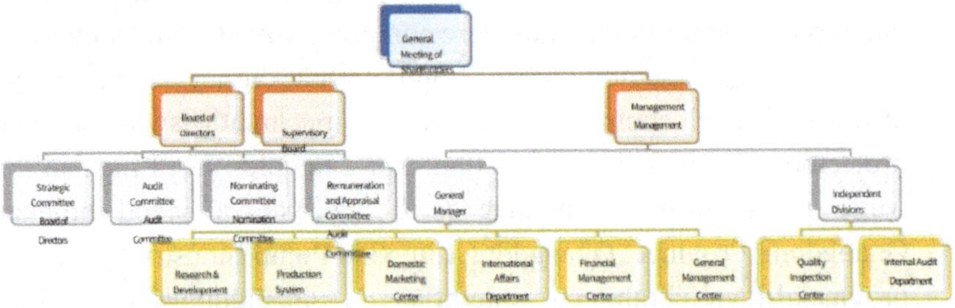

Lingxiao Pump Industry Co., Ltd. has a shareholders' meeting composed of all shareholders as its highest-level decision-making body, which makes major decisions for the enterprise. The Board of Directors, acting on behalf of the Shareholders' Meeting, serves as the enterprise's decision-making core. The Supervisory Board oversees the Board of Directors and the management team to safeguard shareholder interests and ensure the enterprise's compliant operations. The four committees under the Board of Directors assist in further refining professional decision-making and oversight. The management team, led by the General Manager, coordinates the work of all departments, bridging the decision-making and operational layers. The organisational structure of Lingxiao Pump Industry Co., Ltd. fully reflects the standardised governance and professionalised operations characteristic of a listed manufacturing enterprise. The enterprise adopts a three-tier governance framework of ‘strategic decision-making - business execution - supervisory checks and balances,’ with the shareholders' meeting as the highest authority, and the Board of Directors and Supervisory Board forming a system of checks and balances. The Board of Directors achieves refined governance through four professional committees: Strategy, Audit, Nomination, and Compensation. Among these, the Strategy Committee focuses on overseeing expansion strategies in overseas markets such as ASEAN, while the Audit Committee strengthens compliance oversight of international business operations, reflecting the enterprise's institutional risk management measures for international operations.

The overall organisational structure adopted is the hybrid structure commonly used by modern enterprises, combining the divisional system with the functional system. Under the unified leadership of the general manager, the R&D centre is divided into research institutes based on product lines (stainless steel pumps/plastic pumps), while the production system is organised into separate factories based on production processes (casting/machining/assembly), reflecting the technical specialisation and division of labour characteristic of the manufacturing industry. The International Business Division operates as an independent unit, with regional offices and a dedicated Foreign Trade Compliance Department, highlighting its export-oriented business characteristics. The Quality Inspection Centre reports directly to the Board of Directors, a structure that aligns with the internal control requirements of a listed enterprise while ensuring the consistent quality of core products in overseas markets. This organisational structure maintains the decision-making efficiency of a small-to-medium-sized enterprise while meeting the special requirements of a listed enterprise for information disclosure and compliance management through dedicated departments such as the Securities Affairs Department and Internal Audit Department, providing institutional safeguards for Lingxiao Pump Industry's continued expansion in the ASEAN market.

Internationalization Development

1. Export trade exploration period (2003-2010)

In 2003, the enterprise obtained the right to import and export and formally started its internationalization journey. During this period, the enterprise took the OEM mode as the main entry point, and boldly tried to enter the Southeast Asian market with the help of the Canton Fair and other important foreign trade platforms. In the first year, the export amount was only 800,000 US dollars, and the scale was relatively small, mainly supplying basic cast iron centrifugal pumps to Vietnam, Indonesia, and other countries. In terms of operation mode, the indirect export mode of "agent of foreign trade enterprise + OEM production" is adopted at this stage. Although this mode reduces the risk of entering the international market directly to a certain extent, it also makes the technical content of the products lower, and the added value is not high. Through this stage of exploration, the enterprise has initially established an ASEAN distributor network, laying a certain market foundation and channeling resources for the subsequent internationalization development.

2. Cultivation period of the brand going overseas (2011-2016)

In 2011, the enterprise set up an international business department, marking an important step in the enterprise's internationalization strategy. At the same time, the enterprise registered the "LIANX" independent brand, began to focus on building its own brand image, and focused on the development of stainless steel pump series products, improving product quality and competitiveness.

In order to expand the brand influence and market coverage, the enterprise actively participated in internationally famous exhibitions such as Hannover Messe in Germany, and gradually entered the Middle East and Africa market by virtue of the advantages of its products. In 2014, the enterprise set up its first overseas office in Thailand, which was further close to the market, and facilitated the development of business and the provision of services. In 2015, LIANXI Pumps was awarded the order of pumps for a large-scale seawater desalination project in Saudi Arabia, with a contract amount of USD 12 million. The contract amount is 12 million dollars. Up to this point, the export value of the enterprise exceeded 30 million US dollars, and the proportion of its own brand increased to 40%, successfully completing the transformation from OEM production to brand export, and the recognition and influence of its brand in the international market gradually increased.

3. Deep localization layout period (2017-2020)

After the listing of the enterprise in 2017, with the power of capital, the enterprise invested 120 million yuan to start the internationalization strategy upgrade. At this stage, the Enterprise's international layout has become more in-depth and localized. Firstly, the first overseas KD assembly plant was established in Vietnam, adopting the mode of core component export + local assembly, which not only reduces the production cost but also better adapts to the needs and policy requirements of the local market. Secondly, we set up a Middle East distribution center in Dubai, UAE, which covers 12 national markets and greatly improves the product distribution in China. The market response speed and supply efficiency in the eastern region. In addition, the enterprise has actively promoted product certification and passed the certifications of EU CE and U.S. NSF, which have enabled high-end products to successfully enter the European supply chain and expand the share of the high-end market. By 2019, the proportion of the Enterprise's overseas revenue will exceed 40% for the first time, marking the increasing prominence of internationalized business in the Enterprise's overall development.

4. Global value chain integration period (2021 to present)

In 2021, the Enterprise launched the "Digital Overseas" program and completed the cross-border e-commerce standalone station and overseas warehouse intelligent management system, which enhanced the efficiency of cross-border trade and customer experience by digital means, and further expanded sales channels.

In 2022, downstream demand will weaken. In addition, sanitary ware exporters also experienced a decrease in orders due to the depletion of inventories by customers in overseas markets, market weakness and declining consumption. Domestic revenue dropped sharply by 40.27% to RMB603 million, and the revenue contribution rate dropped to 40.67% for the first time; although foreign revenue was also declining, the rate of decline was smaller, falling by 16.39% year-on-year to RMB880 million, accounting for 59.33% of the total revenue. In 2023, the second phase of the Vietnam plant was put into operation, with the supporting construction of an R&D laboratory, realizing customized development for the ASEAN market, enabling product design and production according to the specific needs of the local market, and improving the market suitability of products.

At present, the enterprise is promoting the German technical cooperation project, dedicated to the development of intelligent pump systems in line with Industry 4.0 standards. This initiative shows that the enterprise's internationalization strategy has deepened from "market expansion" to "technological synergy", focusing more on technological upgrading and integration with international advanced technology. At this stage, the gross profit margin of the Enterprise's overseas business has increased to 38.5%, showing that the profitability of the international business has been increasing, and the Enterprise's position in the global value chain has been gradually upgraded.

Analysis of Financial Report

1. Solvency

Solvency is the ability of an enterprise to repay its debts as they fall due (including both short-term and long-term debts), and is an important indicator of an enterprise's financial health and operational risk, which is directly related to the enterprise's survival and sustainable operation, and is also the focus of attention of investors, creditors, and other stakeholders.

1.1 Short-term solvency

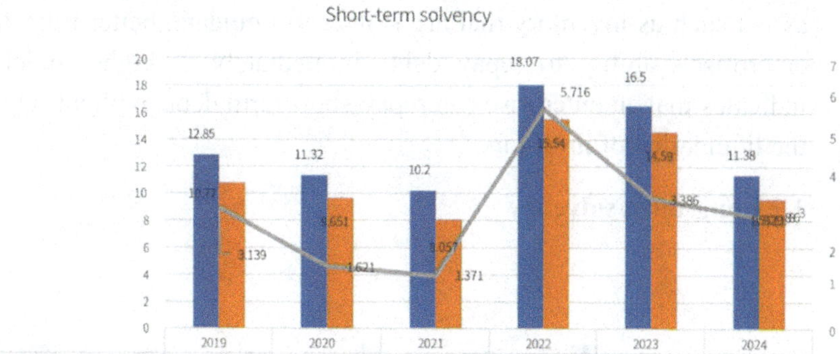

	2019	2020	2021	2022	2023	2024
Current ratio	12.85	11.32	10.2	18.07	16.5	11.38
Quick ratio	10.77	9.651	8.057	15.54	14.59	9.589
Cash flow ratio	3.139	1.621	1.371	5.716	3.386	2.886

Cash flow ratio is an important indicator to measure the short-term solvency of enterprises, and its calculation formula is the ratio of net cash flow from operating activities to current liabilities. The higher the ratio is, the stronger the short-term solvency of the enterprise is. From the data, the cash flow ratio of Lingxiao Pump Industry in 2019-2024 fluctuates greatly. The 2019 cash flow ratio is 3.139, at a high level, indicating that the enterprise's short-term solvency in that year is strong; 2020 falls to 1.621, 2021 further falls to 1.371, short-term solvency is weakened; 2022 rises to 5.716, reaching the peak of this period, short-term solvency is weakened. In 2022, it rose sharply to 5.716, reaching the peak of the period, and the short-term solvency was significantly enhanced; in 2023, it was 3.386, and in 2024, it was 2.886, which was lower than that of 2022, but still remained at a relatively reasonable level, indicating that the enterprise's short-term solvency was relatively sound overall, and it was able to cope with the demand for short-term debt repayment.

The current ratio has generally remained at a relatively high level. While it remained relatively stable in 2021, it saw a significant increase in 2022. Although it subsequently declined, it remained at a high level. Generally speaking, a higher current ratio indicates a stronger ability of an enterprise to use its current assets to repay current liabilities, reflecting that the enterprise's current assets provide adequate coverage for its current liabilities during most periods. The trend of the quick ratio is similar to that of the current ratio, with a significant increase in 2022, followed by a decline, but remaining at a relatively high level. The quick ratio excludes assets such as inventory that are slower to liquidate, better reflecting an enterprise's ability to repay debts immediately. A higher quick ratio indicates that an enterprise can repay short-term debts without relying on the liquidation of inventory.

1.2 Long-term solvency

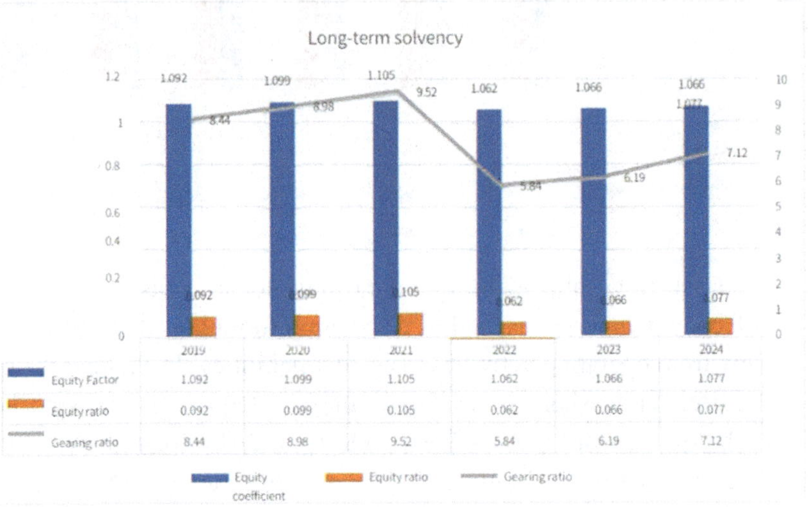

Gearing ratio is a core indicator of long-term solvency, calculated as the ratio of total liabilities to total assets. The lower the ratio, the stronger the long-term solvency of the enterprise and the lower the financial risk. The overall gearing ratio of Lingxiao Pump Industry in 2019-2024 is at a lower level. 8.44% in 2019, 8.98% in 2020, 9.52% in 2021, showing a slight upward trend year by year, but still in the lower range; 2022 drops sharply to 5.84%, 6.19% in 2023, and 7.12% in 2024, which is fluctuating, but although there are fluctuations, it always stays below 10%. This shows that the enterprise's long-term debt servicing ability is powerful, the financial structure is stable, the debt pressure is slight, the financial risk is extremely low, and it can provide a solid financial guarantee for the long-term development of the enterprise. Equity ratio is the ratio of total liabilities to total owners' equity, reflecting the soundness of the enterprise's financial structure and the extent to which owners' equity protects creditors' rights. From 2019 to 2021, the equity ratio rose from 0.092 to 0.105, dropped to 0.062 in 2022, and then rose slightly to 0.077

in 2024. A lower equity ratio indicates that the enterprise has a higher degree of protection of owners' equity against liabilities. A lower equity ratio indicates that the degree of protection of owners' equity to liabilities is higher, and the long-term debt repayment ability is stronger.

The equity coefficient is the ratio of total assets to total owners' equity, reflecting the size of the enterprise's financial leverage. From 2019 to 2021, the equity coefficient rose from 1.092 to 1.105, and then decreased to 1.062 in 2022, and then fluctuated to 1.077 in 2024. The coefficient of equity is close to 1, which indicates that the owner's equity supports the enterprise's assets, and the enterprise's liabilities are relatively low, so the enterprise has a strong ability to repay its debts in the long run and low financial risk. The coefficient of equity is close to 1, indicating that the owner's equity mainly supports the assets of the enterprise, the liabilities are less, the long-term solvency is stronger, and the financial risk is low.

2. Profitability

Profitability is the ability of an enterprise to obtain profit, which is the basic guarantee for the survival and development of the enterprise, as well as the confidence of investors and creditors. Return on total assets is an indicator to measure the effect of comprehensive utilization of enterprise assets, calculated as the ratio of net profit to average total assets. The higher the indicator, the higher the efficiency of enterprise asset utilization and the stronger the profitability.

The return on total assets of Lingxiao Pump Industry from 2019 to 2023 is 18.44%, 19.43%, 21.30%, 17.90%, and 16.21%, respectively. This trend is evident. An upward trend from 2019 to 2021 peaks at 21.30% in 2021, indicating that the enterprise's asset utilization efficiency continues to improve and profitability is strengthened during this period. However, it decreases from 2022 to 2023, indicating that asset utilization efficiency and profitability are weakened to a certain extent.

Return on equity (ROE) is a metric used to assess an enterprise's ability to generate profits from its own capital. It is calculated as the ratio of net profit to average net assets. A higher ROE indicates stronger profitability from the enterprise's own capital. From 2019 to 2024, Lingxiao Pump Industry's return on equity was 20.76%, 19.73%, 23.83%, 19.65%, 17.49%, and 19.68%, respectively. From 2019 to 2021, the ratio fluctuated upward, reaching 23.83% in 2021; from 2022 to 2023, it declined, dropping to 17.49% in 2023; in 2024, it rebounded to 19.68%. Overall, the ratio remains at a relatively high level, indicating that the enterprise has strong profitability of its own capital and provides substantial returns to shareholders.

Gross margin is an indicator of an enterprise's product profitability, calculated as the ratio of (revenue - cost of goods sold) to revenue. A higher gross margin indicates greater profit margins for the enterprise's products. Lingxiao Pump Industry's gross profit margins for 2019-2024 were 33.56%, 33.47%, 31.53%, 35.81%, 37.81%, and 36.53%, respectively. From 2019 to 2021, the gross profit margin fluctuated slightly downward, dropping to 31.53% in 2021. From 2022 to 2023, it continued to rise, reaching 37.81% in 2023. In 2024, it slightly decreased to 36.53%. Overall, the gross margin has remained above 30%, indicating that the enterprise's products have strong competitiveness and profitability, with high product value-added.

Net profit margin is an indicator of an enterprise's overall profitability, calculated as the ratio of net profit to operating revenue. A higher net profit margin indicates that the enterprise has a stronger ability to generate profits after deducting all costs and expenses. From 2019 to 2024, Lingxiao Pump Industry's net profit margins were 24.00%, 24.98%, 23.43%, 28.44%, 29.17%, and 27.79%, respectively. The net profit margin fluctuated slightly from 2019 to 2021, saw a significant increase from 2022 to 2023, reaching 29.17% in 2023, and then decreased slightly to

27.79% in 2024. The fact that this indicator remains above 20% indicates that the enterprise has strong overall profitability and effective control over costs and expenses.

3. Operating capacity

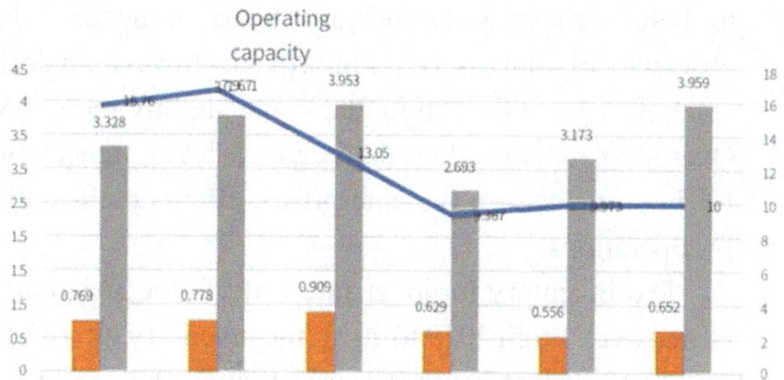

	2019	2020	2021	2022	2023	2024
Total asset turnover	0.769	0.778	0.909	0.629	0.556	0.652
Inventory turnover	3.328	3.79	3.953	2.693	3.173	3.959
Accounts Receivable Turnover Ratio	15.76	16.71	13.05	9.367	9.973	10

Operating capacity refers to the efficiency and effectiveness of an enterprise's asset management, reflecting its operational capabilities. It is typically measured using indicators such as accounts receivable turnover rate. The accounts receivable turnover rate is an indicator of how quickly an enterprise converts its accounts receivable into cash and how efficiently it manages them. It is calculated as the ratio of operating revenue to the average accounts receivable balance. A higher ratio indicates that the enterprise recovers its accounts receivable more quickly, occupies less capital, and has stronger operating capacity.

Lingxiao Pump Industry's accounts receivable turnover rates for the years 2019-2024 were 15.76, 16.71, 13.05, 9.367, 9.973, and 10.00, respectively. From 2019 to 2020, the ratio showed an upward trend, reaching 16.71 in 2020, indicating high efficiency in accounts receivable management; from 2021 to 2022, the ratio dropped significantly, falling to 9.367 in 2022, indicating slower accounts receivable collection and weakened operational efficiency; From 2023 to 2024, there was a slight recovery, reaching 10.00 in 2024, indicating that the enterprise has taken specific measures in accounts receivable management, resulting in improved operational capacity. However, it remains below the level of 2019-2020, necessitating further strengthening of accounts receivable management to enhance capital turnover efficiency.

The total asset turnover ratio reflects the operational efficiency of an enterprise's total assets. From 2019 to 2021, this indicator rose from 0.769 to 0.909, showing an upward trend, indicating that the operational efficiency of total assets has improved; However, it declined in 2022-2023, reaching a low of 0.556 in 2023, and slightly recovered to 0.652 in 2024. Overall, it remains at a relatively low level, indicating that there is room for improvement in the enterprise's efficiency in utilising its total assets for operations.

The inventory turnover rate reflects the speed at which inventory is turned over. From 2019 to 2021, the inventory turnover rate increased from 3.328 to 3.953, indicating faster inventory turnover. In 2022, it dropped to 2.693, but then recovered in 2023 and 2024, reaching 3.959 in 2024, approaching the higher level of 2021. This indicates that through adjustments in inventory management, the efficiency of inventory turnover has improved, and the ability to convert inventory into cash has strengthened.

4. Development ability

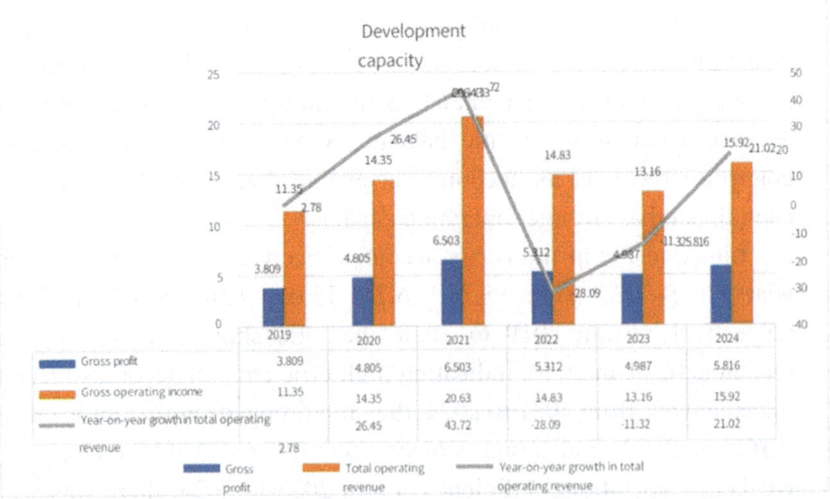

Development capacity refers to an enterprise's ability to achieve sustained growth and expand its scale in the future, typically measured by indicators such as the year-on-year growth rate of total operating revenue.

The year-on-year growth rate of total operating revenue is an indicator used to assess the growth of an enterprise's operating revenue, calculated as the ratio of (current period operating revenue - previous period operating revenue) to the previous period's operating revenue. A higher ratio indicates faster growth in operating revenue and greater development potential.

Lingxiao Pump Industry's year-on-year growth rates of total operating revenue for the years 2019-2024 were 2.78%, 26.45%, 43.72%, -28.09%, -11.32%, and 21.02%, respectively. From 2019 to 2021, the growth trend was positive, with a high growth rate of 43.72% in 2021, indicating strong development momentum; from 2022 to 2023, there was negative growth, with a decline in operating revenue, indicating some development pressure; In 2024, growth resumed, reaching 21.02%, indicating that the enterprise regained growth momentum through adjustments to its business strategies, with its development capabilities partially restored, and it holds potential for future growth.

Overall, Lingxiao Pump Industry demonstrates strong debt-repayment capacity with low financial risk; it possesses robust profitability, with competitive products and overall strong earning capacity; Operational capacity has fluctuated but remains within a reasonable range and shows an improving trend; Development capacity has experienced ups and downs, but growth resumed in 2024, demonstrating a certain degree of resilience and potential. These financial indicators comprehensively reflect Lingxiao Pump Industry's overall situation in terms of operational management and financial condition, providing a certain level of financial support for the implementation of its internationalisation strategy.

Analysis of Internationalization Components

1. Reasons for selection

Lingxiao Pump Industry's participation in the ASEAN market is conducive to expanding its market scale and enhancing its operational efficiency. Since entering the ASEAN market, Lingxiao Pump Industry has gradually expanded its overseas operations. From a financial perspective, the enterprise's total operating revenue has shown an overall upward trend. From 2019 to 2021, the year-on-year growth rates of the enterprise's total operating revenue were 2.78%, 26.45%, and 43.72%, respectively, indicating a high-speed growth trajectory, which is closely related to the expansion of the ASEAN market. Lingxiao Pump Industry's products are highly compatible with the ASEAN market. The ASEAN region has a large population and rapid economic growth, with strong demand for infrastructure construction and a significant need for mechanical equipment such as water pumps. This provides Lingxiao Pump Industry with a vast market space, effectively addressing potential growth bottlenecks in the domestic market and helping the enterprise expand its overall revenue scale. Most ASEAN countries are in the midst of rapid urbanization, with diverse demands for pumps in areas such as water supply systems, industrial production, and agricultural irrigation. Lingxiao Pump Industry has launched tailored products for different ASEAN countries, ensuring that its products meet local market needs. Additionally, the enterprise's products have obtained multiple international certifications, meeting the standards of the ASEAN market, further enhancing their adaptability in the region and laying a solid product foundation for its expansion in the ASEAN market.

On the other hand, Lingxiao Pump Industry's expansion into the ASEAN market aligns with China's policy support, helping to reduce costs and improve profit margins. The preferential policies under the Belt and Road Initiative have reduced export tariffs, leading to an increase in the enterprise's gross margin from 35.81% to 37.81% and net margin from 28.44% to 29.17% between 2022 and 2023. Although there was a slight decline in 2024, the margins remained at relatively high levels of 36.53% and 27.79%, respectively. The combination of policy benefits and cost advantages has further enhanced the enterprise's profitability in the ASEAN market.

The ASEAN region is rich in natural resources. Lingxiao Pump Industry has established a supply chain network covering the ASEAN region, sourcing raw materials from Malaysia and Indonesia, and utilizing Singapore as a transit hub to serve regional markets, thereby reducing raw material procurement costs and transportation costs. Additionally, the industrial development of the ASEAN region complements that of China's Guangxi region. Lingxiao Pump Industry's pump products have technical and quality advantages, meeting the infrastructure construction and industrial development needs of the ASEAN region. Meanwhile, the ASEAN region's raw material supply provides Lingxiao Pump Industry with a stable supply chain foundation, creating a mutually beneficial and win-win situation.

As shown in the chart, Lingxiao Pump Industry's development capabilities and operational capabilities generally showed an upward trend before 2021. The enterprise's launch of the "Digital Overseas Expansion Plan" in 2021 also indicates that the pump industry's development in ASEAN is generally positive. (4) However, starting in 2022, the data began to show a significant decline, which is related to overseas market customers depleting their inventory, market weakness, and reduced consumption leading to fewer orders [3], but it remains at a relatively high level. Overall, ASEAN has provided Lingxiao Pump Industry with a vast overseas market and product demand, while Lingxiao Pump Industry has offered technical support for ASEAN's development. The enterprise's profitability has consistently shown an upward trend. Although data began to decline due to market fatigue and other factors, the collaboration between Lingxiao Pump Industry and ASEAN has been successful.

1.1 Successful experiences of similar enterprises and ASEAN development

The success of Lingxiao Pump Industry is closely tied to its precise identification of its market positioning and product demand, such as tailoring different products to address the varying needs of different ASEAN countries. Before entering the ASEAN market, companies should conduct in-depth research into local market demand, industry characteristics, and consumer habits, and combine these insights with their own strengths to develop differentiated strategies. Additionally, obtaining product certifications in target markets can help gain residents' recognition, laying the groundwork for market expansion. Initiatives such as the Belt and Road Initiative and the RCEP Agreement provide policy support for corporate cooperation with ASEAN. Similar companies should fully leverage these policy benefits and actively participate in regional economic cooperation. For example, they can utilize policy incentives to reduce tariff costs and trade barriers, optimize supply chains, integrate raw materials, labor, and other resources in the ASEAN region, and enhance resource allocation efficiency. At the same time, they should pay attention to the industrial policies and investment orientations of ASEAN countries, identify key areas supported by policies, and achieve synergy between corporate development and regional policies.

Guangxi Liyuanbao Technology Co., Ltd. is dedicated to the environmental protection sector and holds multiple national patents. ASEAN countries prioritize economic sustainability and green transformation, and Liyuanbao has seized this opportunity by conducting on-site research, leveraging chamber of commerce networks to engage with local stakeholders, and promoting its environmental protection equipment and comprehensive solutions to countries like Laos and Thailand. In Laos, the enterprise processes paper sludge for the paper industry, establishing an "integrated model of sludge, fertilizer, forestry, and carbon," achieving a closed-loop system for resource recycling. This strategy is similar to Lingxiao Pump Industry's approach of providing tailored products to meet ASEAN market demands, both leveraging their technological advantages to satisfy local market needs and expand their business operations.

1.2 potential risks to the development of similar enterprises and ASEAN

The current international landscape is complex and ever-changing, with the rise of trade protectionism having an impact on Lingxiao Pump Industry. Fluctuations in raw material prices and exchange rates are the primary cost risks faced by the enterprise. Raw materials such as steel account for a significant portion of the cost of water pumps, and their prices are heavily influenced by international markets. If raw material prices rise sharply, this will directly increase production costs and reduce gross margins. As the ASEAN market places increasing demands on water pumps for intelligence, energy efficiency, and other features, companies in this sector must accelerate their technological upgrading efforts. However, some companies have insufficient R&D investments. For example, Lingxiao Pump Industry's R&D expenditure in 2021 was only 64.23 million yuan, lagging behind leading companies, which may result in products failing to meet the demands of high-end markets. Additionally, a shortage of international talent is another major challenge. Companies require personnel who are familiar with ASEAN market rules, possess cross-cultural communication skills, and have professional technical expertise. If talent reserves are insufficient, it will impact operational efficiency and strategic implementation in the ASEAN market.

2. Supply chain resilience

With the full entry into force of the Regional Comprehensive Economic Partnership Agreement (RCEP) and the in-depth advancement of the construction of the China-ASEAN Free Trade Area version 3.0, the complementary economic advantages of Guangxi and ASEAN have become more prominent than ever. Lingxiao Pump Industry, as a leading player in the pump industry, has a significant annual production capacity. Large-scale production enables it to negotiate better prices for raw materials, allowing it to procure materials at more favourable rates and reduce costs. Its key advantage lies in its diversified raw material supply channels, enabling it to source required materials from multiple countries and regions, thereby reducing reliance on a single supply source. Additionally, its production facilities are strategically distributed, granting it strong production capacity allocation capabilities to address local production disruptions, ensuring stable production and holding multiple patents. However, its disadvantages are also evident.

Some key raw materials are imported, making it highly susceptible to fluctuations in international market prices. It also relies on a single market, and its production equipment is outdated with low automation levels, leaving room for improvement in production efficiency. Chen Jian noted in his address that the disparity in economic development levels between China and ASEAN countries remains significant. The uneven development gradient within cross-border industrial chains results in weak links in the regional supply chain, necessitating further improvements in resource allocation efficiency, industrial structure complementarity, and supply chain resilience. [8] In terms of opportunities, changes in the global raw material market supply landscape and the emergence of new supplier countries offer potential for expanding new raw material procurement channels. The development of innovative manufacturing technology can help improve production automation levels and enhance production stability. Threats include potential disruptions to raw material transportation due to escalating geopolitical conflicts and the impact of frequent natural disasters on raw material production and supply.

International trade patterns are complex and ever-changing, as evidenced by the US-China tariff war.

From a PEST perspective, politically, there are significant differences in political stability among countries, and political instability in some countries may affect the normal acquisition and transportation of raw materials. The rise of trade protectionism may also create obstacles to raw material imports. Economically, global economic fluctuations affect raw material prices. During periods of economic prosperity, raw material demand increases, leading to price hikes, while the opposite occurs during downturns. Exchange rate fluctuations also impact the cost of raw material imports. Social factors include rising consumer demands for environmentally friendly and sustainable raw materials, driving companies to seek more eco-friendly raw materials and production methods. Changes in the labour market may also affect the supply of human resources in the production process. Technologically, new technologies have improved the efficiency of raw material exploration and extraction, while advancements in production technology help reduce raw material waste and enhance production stability.

3. Market Suitability

The SWOT analysis of market adaptability reveals that the company's strengths include products that comply with multiple countries' and regions' standards, have broad applicability, and possess a deep understanding of consumer habits in various markets, enabling the launch of targeted products. The weaknesses include the lack of timely updates to product standards, which hinders adaptation to new market requirements, and insufficient research into consumer habits in emerging markets, leading to low product compatibility. In terms of opportunities, the gradual convergence of product standards in international markets facilitates the entry of Lingxiao Pump Industry's products into more markets. Through big data analysis and other means, the enterprise can more accurately grasp changes in consumer habits. The threats include significant differences in product standards across countries and regions, increasing the difficulty of product adaptation, and rapid changes in consumer habits, leading to significant pressure for product updates and upgrades.

In the PEST analysis, politically, governments of different countries have varying policies on the formulation and regulation of product standards, which affect market access for products. The signing of trade agreements may promote the unification of product standards. Economically, the level of economic development in different countries and regions influences consumption capacity and consumption habits, thereby affecting the market adaptability of products. Economic fluctuations may lead to changes in consumption habits. Social factors such as culture, values, and lifestyle determine consumer habits, and companies need to adjust their products according to local social characteristics. Changes in population structure also affect consumer demand. Technological progress drives the upgrading of product standards, and companies need to improve their technical capabilities to meet new standards continually. The development of internet technology provides companies with more channels to understand consumer habits.

The Porter Diamond Model proposes that certain regions have global competitive advantages in specific industries. This model includes four key factors and two external factors. According to the Porter Diamond Model, in terms of production factors, Lingxiao Pump Industry has accumulated years of experience and established a technical advantage through a 'patent pool + standard setting + R&D platform' strategy. In terms of demand conditions, there is a high global demand for water pumps, providing the enterprise with a vast market space. Additionally, as global energy-saving awareness increases, demand for high-efficiency, energy-saving water pumps is growing, aligning with the enterprise's product development direction.

In terms of supporting industries, Lingxiao Pump Industry's geographical location facilitates the formation of industrial clusters with regions like East China, which is conducive to talent mobility and supports its internationalisation process. In terms of corporate strategy, structure, and industry competition, the enterprise has adopted a differentiated competitive strategy, forming a unique competitive advantage. However, it still needs to strengthen its market concentration continuously. In terms of government policies, the state has introduced a series of strategies to promote business development. Additionally, initiatives such as the 'Belt and Road' initiative provide government support and favourable conditions for the enterprise to expand into new markets. In terms of opportunities, the global increase in demand presents opportunities for

Lingxiao Pump Industry. Furthermore, while the trend toward trade globalisation presents challenges, it also offers opportunities.

4. Policy sensitivity

Through SWOT analysis, it is evident that the strengths lie in the establishment of a comprehensive policy information collection and analysis mechanism, enabling timely monitoring of changes in tariff and quarantine regulations, as well as the presence of a professional team with strong response capabilities. The weaknesses include insufficiently swift responses to policy changes in certain countries and regions, inflexible response measures, inadequate depth in policy research, and difficulty in predicting the long-term impacts of policies. In terms of opportunities, strengthened international policy coordination provides greater convenience for businesses in addressing tariff and quarantine regulations. At the same time, the application of digital technology enhances the efficiency of policy information processing. Threats include intensifying international trade friction, frequent adjustments to tariff policies, and increasingly stringent quarantine regulations across countries, which increase compliance costs for businesses.

From a PEST perspective, politically, changes in countries' political stances and foreign policies influence tariff and quarantine regulations, and instability in the international political landscape may increase policy uncertainty. Economically, economic development conditions influence a country's tariff policies, which may be aimed at protecting domestic industries or promoting economic growth, and the formulation of quarantine regulations may also be related to economic interests. Social factors include increased public concern over product safety and environmental protection, driving countries to strengthen quarantine regulations, with public opinion potentially influencing government policy-making. Technologically, advancements in detection technology are driving stricter and more refined quarantine regulations, while information technology developments provide businesses with tools to track and analyse policies. According to Porter's Diamond Model, production factors include specialised talent and information resources. Possessing specialised talent familiar with international trade policies and abundant information resources can enhance policy sensitivity.

In terms of demand conditions, the high standards for product safety and quality in international markets have driven companies to enhance their ability to respond to quarantine regulations, while market competition pressures have prompted companies to monitor changes in tariff policies. Regarding related industries and supporting industries, sectors such as legal consulting and logistics can provide professional services and support to help companies navigate tariff and quarantine regulations. In terms of corporate strategy, structure, and competition, companies should incorporate policy sensitivity into their strategic planning, establish flexible organisational structures, and continuously enhance their response capabilities in competitive environments.

5. Enterprise internationalization awareness

According to the SWOT analysis, the strengths lie in the management team's extensive overseas experience, familiarity with international market rules and operational models, and significant investment in internationalisation strategies, which provide a clear direction and objectives for development. The weaknesses include a lack of overseas experience among some members of the management team, insufficient understanding of international markets, unbalanced strategic investment, and inadequate investment in certain key areas. In terms of opportunities, the accelerating globalisation process provides more opportunities for corporate internationalisation. By introducing overseas talent and fostering cooperation and exchange, the international awareness of the management team can be enhanced. Threats include intense competition in international markets, which imposes higher demands on an enterprise's international awareness and capabilities, and factors such as trade protectionism may hinder the enterprise's internationalisation process.

In the PEST analysis, politically, changes in the international political environment impact an enterprise's internationalisation strategy. For example, tense international relations may increase the difficulty of overseas expansion, while government foreign policies and international cooperation projects provide support for an enterprise's internationalisation. Economically, global economic integration creates a favourable economic environment for an enterprise's internationalisation, while economic differences between countries and regions require companies to develop differentiated internationalisation strategies. In terms of social factors, cultural differences between countries and regions require companies to possess cross-cultural communication and management capabilities, which depend on the internationalisation awareness of management. The level of societal recognition of an enterprise's internationalisation efforts also influences strategic investments. Technologically, advancements in information technology facilitate companies' international business operations, such as the rise of cross-border e-commerce platforms. Technological innovation capabilities are critical for companies competing in international markets, requiring sufficient strategic investments from management.

Under Porter's Diamond Model, production factors include management talent and knowledge resources. Management teams with extensive overseas experience and advanced internationalisation knowledge are crucial supports for an enterprise's internationalisation awareness. In terms of demand conditions, domestic market saturation or intense competition drives companies to seek international market opportunities, enhancing their internationalisation awareness. The potential demand in international markets attracts companies to increase strategic investments. In terms of related and supporting industries, the internationalisation of industries such as finance, logistics, and consulting provides support for corporate internationalisation and influences corporate internationalisation awareness and strategic investment. In terms of corporate strategy, structure, and competition, an enterprise's internationalisation strategy determines its positioning and development direction in the international market. A reasonable organisational structure facilitates the implementation of internationalisation strategies and continuously enhances an enterprise's internationalisation awareness and capabilities in international competition.

6. Summary

6.1 The success of ASEAN's internationalization strategy

The Western Coastal Economic Zone is the only region in China directly connected to ASEAN countries, holding strategic significance as a ‘bridge between east and west, linking south and north.’ It serves as the core hub of the Western Coastal New Channel and an international gateway to ASEAN.[6] Most ASEAN countries are in the midst of rapid urbanisation, with strong demand for water supply systems and related infrastructure. Lingxiao Pump Industry has adopted tailored strategies for different countries. For example, in Vietnam, the enterprise focuses on industrial centrifugal pumps, while in Indonesia, it prioritises deep well pumps and drainage pumps. Lingxiao Pump Industry has capitalised on the benefits of the times, with the preferential policies of the Belt and Road Initiative reducing export tariffs. Its deep localisation efforts have yielded notable results. The production base established in Vietnam in 2017 not only avoided trade barriers but also reduced labour costs by 40%. The enterprise has established sales subsidiaries in Thailand and Indonesia and formed localised service teams, achieving 24-hour rapid response and reducing customer complaint rates by 50%. In terms of supply chain resilience, ASEAN has leveraged the region's abundant natural resources and diversified production base layout to build a flexible and efficient supply chain network. By integrating the raw material supply advantages of member countries, it has reduced reliance on external single markets. Simultaneously, through regional industrial division of labour and collaboration, production stability has been enhanced. Lingxiao Pump Industry has won the market with quality and brand recognition. Its products have obtained various domestic and international quality certifications, including China's CCC, the EU's CE, and Germany's TUV. In the ASEAN market, through long-term stable product supply and excellent product quality, the enterprise has gradually established a good brand image and enhanced its brand influence locally, which is conducive to the further promotion and sales of its products in the ASEAN market. Lingxiao Pump Industry has established a supply chain network covering the ASEAN region, sourcing raw materials from Malaysia and Indonesia and distributing them to regional markets via a transit warehouse in Singapore. During the global shipping crisis in 2021, the Vietnam factory ensured order delivery, contributing to an increase in the enterprise's ASEAN revenue share from 15% in 2019 to 28% in 2023.

6. 2 Future challenges

Lingxiao Pump Industry's expansion into overseas markets. In terms of market competition, there are over 6,000 domestic pump companies, with extremely low industry concentration and severe product homogenisation in the general-purpose pump sector, resulting in intense market competition. Companies like Nanfang Pump Industry and LEO

Co., Ltd. lead Lingxiao Pump Industry in terms of industrial pump scale, exerting significant competitive pressure on it. In the international market, although Lingxiao Pump Industry holds a high market share in the plastic sanitary pump sector, foreign brands like Grundfos and Wilo still dominate 73% of the high-end industrial pump market, presenting Lingxiao Pump Industry with technical and brand-related challenges in expanding its high-end market presence. Additionally, the global economic recovery is slow, and overseas market demand is unstable. For example, bathroom export companies have seen a decrease in orders due to factors such as overseas customers depleting their inventory and market weakness. As a major supplier of water-based recreational and bathroom pumps, Lingxiao Pump Industry cannot remain unaffected. In terms of technological upgrades, as the industry develops, customers are increasingly demanding intelligent pump systems, such as the Yajiang Project, which requires an intelligent pump control system. However, Lingxiao Pump Industry's R&D investment in 2021 was only 64.23 million yuan, which is relatively low compared to some leading companies. Suppose it fails to accelerate its intelligent upgrade. In that case, it will struggle to meet the demands of high-end projects, putting it at a competitive disadvantage in the market and affecting its market share and profit margins. Fluctuations in raw material prices are another major challenge. Steel and other materials are key raw materials for water pumps, accounting for approximately 30% of pump costs. Price fluctuations directly impact the enterprise's production costs and gross margin. If steel prices rise significantly, the enterprise's cost control efforts will become more challenging, potentially severely compressing profit margins. Currency fluctuations also impact Lingxiao Pump Industry's performance. Given the enterprise's high proportion of overseas business, if the renminbi appreciates, the enterprise's overseas sales revenue denominated in renminbi will decrease. At the same time, the cost of imported raw materials may increase, further compressing profit margins and adversely affecting the enterprise's operations.

6.3 Countermeasures

To stay competitive, the enterprise must strengthen its niche market advantages, consolidate its lead in the plastic sanitary pump sector, and boost cooperation with international giants by optimizing product performance and service quality. For high-end industrial pumps, increased

R&D investment, recruiting top talent, and partnering with research institutions are essential to enhance product value and challenge foreign monopolies through differentiation. Brand building should be intensified via international exhibitions and online/offline promotions to boost global recognition. Technologically, the company should establish dedicated R&D funds focusing on intelligent pump control systems and energy efficiency, accelerate product digitalization, and foster industry-academia collaboration for rapid tech transfer. Production should be upgraded with industrial robots and intelligent detection to improve efficiency and quality. To mitigate raw material price swings, diversify suppliers, sign long-term contracts, and use futures hedging are necessary, along with designing alternative, cost-effective materials. For exchange rate risks, establish a foreign exchange management team, monitor market trends, use hedging strategies, and increase RMB settlements with overseas clients to reduce foreign currency dependence. These measures require coordinated efforts across strategic planning, resource management, and organizational execution to ensure sustained development and resilience against future challenges.

Chapter 11
Wen's Foodstuff Research

This report takes Wen's Foodstuff Group Co., Ltd. (hereinafter referred to as "Wen's Foodstuff Group") as the research object, systematically sorts out its corporate foundation and ASEAN internationalization process, carries out multi-dimensional analysis based on financial data in the past five years, and deconstructs its core elements of internationalization through tools such as SWOT and Porter's diamond model, and finally summarizes strategic gains and losses, predicts future challenges and proposes countermeasures.

Background of the Enterprise

1. Enterprise profile

Wen's Foodstuff Group is a benchmark enterprise that has grown in the development of China's agricultural industrialization. Founded in 1983, this agricultural and animal husbandry enterprise started from a small chicken farm in Xinxing County, Yunfu, Guangdong, and after 40 years of innovation and development, it has now grown into a modern agricultural group with an annual operating income of more than 80 billion yuan and total assets of more than 100 billion yuan, becoming a leading enterprise in China's livestock and poultry breeding industry.

As a listed company on the Growth Enterprise Market of the Shenzhen Stock Exchange (stock code: 300498), Wen's has built a complete livestock and poultry breeding industry chain system, covering pig and yellow feather broiler breeding, feed production, animal health care, Foodstuff processing, fresh retail, and other fields. The company's original "company + farmer" industrialization model drives the common development of about 50,000 cooperative farmers across the country by providing seedlings, feed, veterinary drugs, and technical services in a unified manner, and realizes mutual benefit and win-win results between enterprises and farmers. This innovative model not only promotes the rapid expansion of enterprises but also provides a successful example for the development of China's agricultural industrialization.

In terms of industrial scale, Wen's Foodstuff Group maintains a leading position in the industry. The company's annual pig slaughter volume exceeds 18 million, ranking it among the top pig breeding enterprises in the country. The number of yellow feather broilers slaughtered has exceeded 1 billion, maintaining the company's first place in the country for many years. The annual production capacity of supporting feed exceeds 20 million tons, which not only meets its own needs but also sells to the market. In recent years, the company has accelerated its extension to the food side, developing slaughtering and processing and fresh retail business, and has more than 2,000 "Wen's Fresh" brand chain stores, realizing the layout of the whole industrial chain from farm to table.

Technological innovation is an important support for the sustainable development of Wen's Foodstuff Group. The company has built a national enterprise technology center and a postdoctoral scientific research workstation, with an annual R&D investment of more than 1 billion yuan, and has made a number of breakthroughs in the fields of breeding pig breeding, feed nutrition, and disease prevention and control. By promoting the application of modern information technologies such as the Internet of Things and big data, the company is promoting the transformation of traditional breeding to intelligence and digitalization, and continuously improving production efficiency, product quality, and safety.

In terms of corporate culture, Wen's Foodstuff Group adheres to the core concept of "sincere cooperation, create a happy life" and forms a unique corporate culture system. The company pays attention to talent training and team building, with more than 50,000 employees and a perfect talent training mechanism. At the same time, the company actively fulfills its social responsibilities, has made important contributions to industrial poverty alleviation, environmental protection, stable production and supply, etc., and has won many honors such as "National Advanced Collective for Poverty Alleviation".

Facing the future, Wen's Foodstuff Groups has formulated a clear development strategy. The company plans to achieve the goal of 30 million pigs per year by 2025 to further increase its market share; accelerate the development of the Foodstuff business and increase the proportion of deep-processed products such as prefabricated dishes; At the same time, it actively lays out the international market and promotes the enterprise to move towards a world-class agricultural, animal husbandry and Foodstuff group. In the context of rural revitalization and agricultural modernization, Wen’s Foodstuff Group is continuing to consolidate its leading position in the industry through the coordinated development of the whole industry chain and scientific and technological innovation, and contributing to ensuring national food security and promoting high-quality agricultural development.

2. Industrial layout

Wen’s Foodstuff Group has a wide industrial layout, covering livestock and poultry breeding, Foodstuff processing, agricultural and animal husbandry equipment, biopharmaceuticals, and other fields, forming a complete industrial chain ecology.

2.1 Livestock and poultry breeding: This is the core business of Wen’s Foodstuff Group, including pig breeding, chicken breeding, duck raising, cattle raising, pigeon breeding, etc. The company has 387 holding companies in more than 20 provinces (municipalities and autonomous regions) across the country, and about 43,000 cooperative farmers (family farms). In 2024, Wen’s Foodstuff Group will list 30.1827 million meat pigs and 1.208 billion broilers, which have a significant scale advantage in the field of livestock and poultry breeding.

2.2 Foodstuff processing: Wen’s Foodstuff Group covers livestock and poultry slaughtering, deep processing, and dairy processing in the field of Foodstuff processing. The company follows the traditional production process, introduces international advanced production lines, processes in strict accordance with food standards, and implements the modern production, logistics, and distribution mode of "standardized production, cold chain transportation, and cold chain sales".

2.3 Agricultural and animal husbandry equipment: Wen's agricultural and animal husbandry equipment business integrates global animal husbandry equipment resources, explores domestic localized factory pig farm construction solutions, provides customers with one-stop EPC engineering services such as farm planning and design, civil engineering, equipment manufacturing and procurement, Internet of Things environmental control, environmental protection treatment, breeding services, etc., and develops a series of advanced breeding equipment products.

2.4 Biopharmaceuticals: Wen's biopharmaceutical business includes three major businesses: veterinary biological products, veterinary drug preparations, and feed additives, with four production bases with international advanced technology, 41 GMP production lines accepted by the Ministry of Agriculture, and an experimental animal center with an annual output of 1.2 million SPF eggs, providing solid health protection for livestock and poultry breeding.

3. Organizational structure

The organizational structure system of Wen's Foodstuff Group presents the characteristics of a typical modern group enterprise, and through continuous optimization and adjustment, a management framework with clear rights and responsibilities and clear hierarchies has been formed. As a large-scale agricultural and animal husbandry enterprise with business covering the whole country, the company has established a matrix organizational structure that combines headquarters control and regional operation, which not only ensures the unity of the group's strategy but also gives each business segment full operational autonomy.

In terms of top-level design, Wen's Foodstuff Group has established a standardized corporate governance structure. As the highest authority, the shareholders' meeting exercises major decision-making power in accordance with the law; The board of directors is composed of 9 directors, with special committees such as the strategy committee, audit committee, nomination committee, remuneration and appraisal committee, responsible for the company's major business decisions; the board of supervisors performs supervisory duties; The management team is headed by the president and is responsible for daily operation and management. This governance structure ensures that the company's decisions are scientific and effective.

From the perspective of vertical management, the company adopts a four-level management structure of "group headquarters-business unit-regional company-production base". The group is headquartered in Xinxing, Guangdong, and mainly undertakes functions such as strategic planning, resource allocation, risk management and control; According to the business sector, pig breeding, chicken raising, Foodstuff, investment and other business departments have been set up, responsible for the professional management of each business line; More than 20 regional branches have been set up across the country to be responsible for localized operations. At the grassroots level, there are production bases and cooperative farmers all over the world. This pyramid-like management structure not only ensures the group's control strength but also adapts to the needs of national business development.

In terms of horizontal functional settings, the headquarters has a complete functional department system. It includes regular functional departments such as the Strategic Development Department, Financial Management Department, Human Resources Department, and Science and Technology Management Department, as well as professional departments such as the Farmer Cooperation Department and the Breeding Technology Department. Each functional department not only provides professional support for the business sector but also performs the group's control functions, forming a crisscrossing matrix management system.

Organizational Chart:

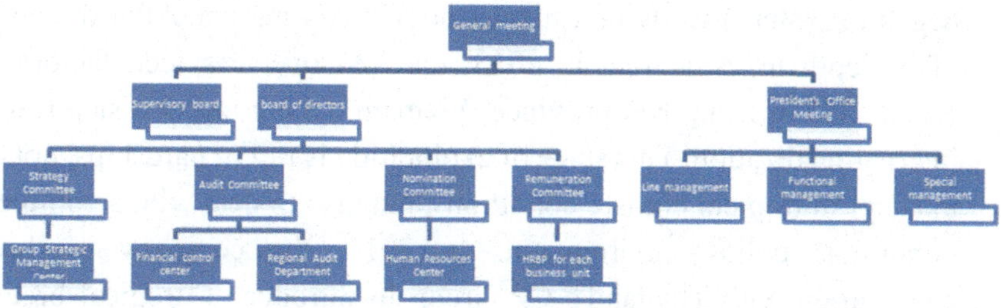

Wen's Foodstuff Group's logo:

Internationalization Development

The development process of Wen's internationalization in ASEAN shows the typical path of Chinese agricultural and animal husbandry enterprises to go overseas. The company has been laying out the Southeast Asian market since 2010, and after more than ten years of exploration and practice, it has gradually built an industrial network covering many ASEAN countries.

1. Preliminary exploration stage (2010-2014)

As early as 2010, Wen set up an overseas business department and began to systematically investigate the ASEAN market. After three years of in-depth investigation, in 2013, the first overseas feed factory was established in Dong Nai province, Vietnam, taking the first step towards internationalization. This stage of exploration is full of hardships, not only to adapt to tropical climate conditions, but also to deal with a completely unfamiliar policy environment. In 2014, the company reached a cooperation with Thailand's CP Group to introduce a tropical breeding experience.

2. Project pilot stage (2015-2017)

Since 2015, Wen's has entered the pilot period of the project. The first pig breeding project in Binh Duong Province, Vietnam, is quite representative, and the company innovatively adopts the "company + cooperative" model, which not only retains the essence of the "Wen's model" but also adapts to the local agricultural organization form. At the same time, in the Malaysian market, we entered the halal Foodstuff field through a joint venture and successfully obtained certification, laying the foundation for opening up the Islamic market. This stage of talent training is very critical, and the first batch of more than 200 ASEAN technicians trained by the company has become an important backbone for subsequent expansion.

3. Scale expansion stage (2019-present)

The expansion period that began in 2018 witnessed Wen's full efforts in ASEAN. Vietnam's feed production capacity jumped from 300,000 tons to 800,000 tons in three years, and the supporting slaughtering and processing plants realized the closed loop of the industrial chain. In the Thai market, the company accurately cut into the breeding of breeding pigs, and the tropical breeding center built in 2019 has an annual supply capacity of 50,000 heads. In particular, it is worth mentioning the breakthrough of the Indonesian project. Wen's innovation adopts the "asset-light" technology output model to provide local breeding enterprises with a full set of solutions from seedlings to sales.

In recent years, Wen's ASEAN layout has become more diversified. The establishment of the Singapore Asia Pacific Operations Center in 2020 marks the upgrade of the regional management structure. The Hai Phong Feed Base in Vietnam, which was put into operation in 2021, uses a fully automated production line and has become one of the most modern feed factories in the ASEAN region. Digital technology has also become a new highlight, and the smart pig farm piloted in Thailand has achieved precise feeding through Internet of Things equipment, increasing breeding efficiency by 20%.

After more than ten years of development, Wen's has formed a layout of "four bases and one center" in ASEAN: breeding and processing base in Vietnam, provenance base in Thailand, halal Foodstuff base in Malaysia, technical service base in Indonesia, and management and operation center in Singapore. In 2023, the revenue of the ASEAN region will reach 3.8 billion yuan, accounting for 61% of overseas revenue, and Vietnam's pig market share will rise to 5%.

Analysis of Financial Report

1. Solvency analysis

1.1 Asset-liability ratio

1.1.1 Data changes

In 2020, the asset-liability ratio of Wen's Foodstuff Group was 40.88%, which was at a low level, indicating that the company's debt burden was light, the financial risk was low, and the degree of protection of creditors' rights and interests was high. By 2021, the asset-liability ratio had climbed sharply to about 61.3%. This is mainly due to the sharp decline in pig prices, the rise in feed costs, and the company's performance losses. In order to maintain operation and development, increased debt financing was required, resulting in an expansion of liabilities and a significant increase in asset-liability ratios. In 2022-2023, the asset-liability ratio fluctuated slightly but remained at a high level, reflecting that the company is still facing certain debt pressure during this period. With the improvement of the company's operating conditions in 2024, the asset-liability ratio fell to 53.14%, indicating that the company's debt burden has been reduced and its solvency has gradually recovered.

1.1.2 Industry comparison

Compared with other companies in the same industry, the asset-liability ratio of Wen's Foodstuff Group in 2020 is lower than the industry average, showing its advantages in financial structure. When the industry is generally affected by the pig cycle from 2021 to 2023, the asset-liability ratio of Wen's Foodstuff Group has risen comparably to some peers, but it is still necessary to be vigilant against the potential threat to the company's financial stability due to excessive debt levels. By 2024, the asset-liability ratio will drop to a relatively reasonable range, and the solvency competitiveness in the industry will be improved.

1.1.3 Impact analysis

Changes in the asset-liability ratio have a direct impact on the company's financing costs and financial risks. A lower asset-liability ratio makes it easier for companies to obtain more favorable interest rates and reduce financing costs. When the asset-liability ratio is too high, not only will the difficulty of financing increase, but the cost of financing will also increase, and the financial risk will increase. The high asset-liability ratio from 2021 to 2023 has brought certain financial pressure to the company, and the decline in the asset-liability ratio in 2024 is conducive to reducing financial risks and enhancing financial stability.

1.2 Current ratio

1.2.1 Data performance

The current ratio of Wen's Foodstuff Group in 2020 was 1.37, down 26.91% from 1.88 in 2019. Despite this, the value suggests that the company's current assets can still cover some short-term liabilities, indicating a certain level of short-term solvency. Although there is no public detailed data in subsequent years, it is inferred from the changes in the company's asset-liability ratio and operating conditions that the current ratio should improve with the improvement of the company's operating conditions and the optimization of the asset structure. For example, in 2024, the company's profitability is expected to improve, allowing for more funds to be allocated to optimize asset allocation. Additionally, the quality and quantity of current assets may be enhanced, which will positively impact the current ratio.

1.2.2 Industry comparison

In the industry, the reasonable range of current ratios is usually between 1 and 2. In 2020, the current ratio of Wen's Foodstuff Group is at the lower limit of a reasonable range, and there is some room for improvement compared with some enterprises in the same industry. If the current ratio is too low, it means that the company may face short-term debt repayment difficulties and poor capital turnover. The current ratio is too high, which may indicate that the company's current assets are not used efficiently. As the company develops in subsequent years, if the current ratio can steadily increase and remain at a reasonable level, it will help enhance the company's short-term solvency and financial flexibility.

1.2.3 Cash short-term debt ratio

Data trends: In the first half of 2024, the company's operating cash inflow was 5.809 billion yuan, a year-on-year increase of 107%, and cash and cash equivalents were 5.712 billion yuan, a year-on-year increase of 22%. The capital reserves were relatively abundant. From this, it can be inferred that the company's cash short-term debt ratio should be at a good level, and the ability to protect short-term debt has been significantly enhanced. This indicates that the company's ability to generate cash from operating activities in the first half of 2024 has increased significantly, and it can better cope with the repayment of short-term debt.

The cash short-term debt ratio directly reflects the company's ability to repay short-term debts with cash assets, and is one of the key indicators to measure the company's short-term solvency. Compared with the current ratio and quick ratio, the cash short-term debt ratio can better reflect the company's actual short-term debt service fund security. For Wen's Foodstuff Group, in the face of market fluctuations such as the pig cycle, stable and sufficient cash inflows and high short-term cash debt ratios are important guarantees for the company to maintain financial stability and survive the trough period of the industry.

The increase in the company's short-term cash debt ratio is mainly due to the improvement of operating conditions in the first half of 2024. On the one hand, pig prices have rebounded, the profitability of the company's breeding business has increased, and sales revenue has increased, bringing more cash inflow; On the other hand, the company has strengthened cost control and capital management, optimized the efficiency of capital use, and increased cash and cash equivalent reserves. In addition, the company's reasonable arrangement of debt structure reduces the size of short-term debt and helps to increase the cash short-term debt ratio.

1.3 Long-term capital liability ratio

The debt term structure of Wen's Foodstuff Group has long been dominated by long-term debt. During the period 2021-2023, the long-term capital liability ratio increased, and the debt burden increased due to the company's losses. This is because in the case of losses, the value of the company's assets decreases, while the scale of long-term debt is relatively stable, resulting in an increase in the long-term capital liability ratio. For example, in 2021, the company suffered serious losses, reduced net assets, and increased the proportion of long-term debt in long-term capital. With the improvement of the company's profitability and the increase in debt repayment efforts from 2024 to 2025, the long-term capital liability ratio will gradually decline, and the long-term solvency will continue to increase. The company has optimized its long-term capital structure by using profitable funds to repay long-term debt.

Industry reference: In the agriculture and animal husbandry industry, the reasonable level of long-term capital-liability ratio varies depending on the scale, business model, and development stage of the enterprise. Generally speaking, the long-term capital-liability ratio of enterprises with stable operation and strong financial strength is relatively low. As a leading enterprise in the industry, Wen's Foodstuff Group has a certain representativeness in the control of the long-term capital-liability ratio. Compared with enterprises in the same industry, its long-term capital liability ratio increased significantly from 2021 to 2023, reflecting the relatively high operating pressure and debt risk faced by the company during this period. In 2024-2025, with the decline in the long-term capital liability ratio, the company's long-term solvency competitiveness in the industry will gradually recover.

Impact on the company: Changes in the long-term capital liability ratio have a profound impact on the company's long-term development and financial stability. An excessively high long-term capital liability ratio means that the company's long-term debt burden is heavy, interest expenses increase, profitability may be affected, and the company's financial risk may also increase. On the contrary, a reasonable reduction in the long-term capital liability ratio can reduce the company's long-term debt pressure, improve financial flexibility, and enhance the company's ability to respond to market changes and industry cycle fluctuations. In 2024-2025, with the decline in the long-term capital-liability ratio, the company will be able to invest more funds in production, operation, and business expansion, laying a good foundation for long-term development.

2. Profitability analysis

2.1 Net income

In 2020, the net profit attributable to the parent company of Wen's Foodstuff Group reached 7.426 billion yuan, which was at a good level of profitability, mainly due to the relatively high market price of live pigs at that time, and the scale and efficiency of the company's breeding business were good. However, in 2021, the company's net profit fell sharply, with a loss of 13.404 billion yuan. The collapse of pig prices, high feed costs, and the company's breeding business being hit hard have led to a significant downturn, with costs and revenues inverting and resulting in huge losses. In 2023, the company will still be in a state of loss, with a net profit of 6.329 billion yuan, and although the loss has narrowed compared with 2021, it is still facing greater operating pressure. By 2024, the company will achieve a profit of 9.230 billion yuan, successfully turning losses into profits, mainly due to the recovery of pig prices, the decline in breeding costs, the improvement of the company's production efficiency, and the significant improvement of operating conditions. The net profit in the first quarter of 2025 was 2.001 billion yuan, a year-on-year increase of 261.92%, continuing the good profit trend.

Compared with other enterprises in the same industry, the fluctuation of Wen's net profit is basically the same as the industry cycle, but the fluctuation range is larger. When the industry profit is good in 2020, the net profit of Wen's Foodstuff Group is at the forefront of the industry; In the trough period of the industry from 2021 to 2023, its losses are also more obvious. For example, compared with Muyuan shares, in 2021-2023, Muyuan shares will lose relatively little by virtue of its cost control advantages and scale effects. This also reflects that Wen's Foodstuff Group has a certain gap with some competitors in terms of cost control and risk resistance, and is greatly affected by industry cycle fluctuations.

Cause analysis: The large fluctuation of net profit is mainly affected by factors such as pig cycle, cost control, and market competition. The pig cycle is a key factor affecting the profitability of Wen's Foodstuff Group, and the sharp rise and fall of pig prices directly determine the revenue and profit of the company's breeding business. In terms of cost control, feed costs account for a large proportion of breeding costs, and when feed prices rise, the company's cost pressure increases, and profit margins are compressed. In addition, market competition also has an impact on the company's profitability. With the intensification of industry competition, the company is facing challenges in market share competition and product pricing; if it cannot be effectively dealt with, it will affect the company's profitability.

2.2 Gross profit margin

In 2020, the gross profit margin of Wen's Foodstuff Group was 19.61%, which was at a high level, indicating that the company's product profitability was strong and it had certain advantages in cost control and product pricing. In 2021, the gross profit margin dropped sharply to -8.32%, which was due to the sharp decline in pig prices that year and the high cost of breeding, resulting in a loss in the company's main business and a negative gross profit margin. In 2022-2023, although gross profit margin has rebounded, it is still at a low level, reflecting the company's poor operating conditions and weak profitability during this period. In the first half of 2024, under the influence of factors such as the decline in feed raw material prices, pig breeding costs declined, gross profit margin rebounded, and the annual gross profit margin reached 17.31%, indicating that the company's profitability has recovered significantly. The gross profit margin of sales in the first quarter of 2025 was 14.29%, showing an overall trend of first declining and then rising.

The main factors affecting gross profit margin include product price, cost control, and product structure. In terms of product prices, fluctuations in pig and broiler prices directly affect the company's sales revenue, which in turn affects gross profit margin. In terms of cost control, changes in feed costs and breeding management costs play a key role in gross profit margin. For example, the decline in feed raw material prices in 2024 has reduced the company's breeding costs and increased gross profit margin. In terms of product structure, the company's gross profit margin varies across different products. Increasing the proportion of high-gross-margin products will help improve the overall gross profit margin.

Compared with the average gross profit margin of the industry, the gross profit margin of Wen's Foodstuff Group in 2020 is higher than the industry average, reflecting the company's strong profitability and competitive advantage. During the trough period of the industry from 2021 to 2023, the company's gross profit margin was lower than the industry average, reflecting the company's inadequacies in cost control and response to market changes. Gross profit margin is a key indicator of a company's profitability, reflecting the profitability of its products or services after deducting direct costs. A higher gross profit margin indicates that the company has more profit margins to cover period expenses and achieve profitability.

2.3 Net profit margin

In 2020, the net profit margin of Wen's Foodstuff Group was at a high level, reflecting that the company effectively controlled period expenses on the basis of a good gross profit margin and had strong overall profitability. In 2021, due to the loss of net profit margin of -20.86%, the company's operation was in trouble; not only was the main business lost, but the burden of expenses during the period also further expanded the loss. The net profit margin in 2024 was 9.17%, a year-on-year increase of 228.97%, and with the improvement of profitability, the company has achieved results in controlling costs and expenses, and the profit level has increased significantly. The change in net profit margin is basically consistent with the trend of net profit and gross profit margin, but it can better reflect the company's overall profitability and cost control ability.

Net profit margin is the embodiment of the company's final profitability, which takes into account all the company's costs and expenses, including operating costs, sales expenses, management expenses, financial expenses, etc. A higher net profit margin indicates that the company can effectively control various costs and expenses in the process of operation and achieve high profitability. For Wen's Foodstuff Group, increasing net profit margin not only requires increasing gross profit margin, but also optimizing the cost structure and reducing period expenses. For example, companies can improve net profit margins by strengthening procurement management to reduce feed costs, optimizing breeding processes to improve production efficiency, and reasonably controlling management expenses and financial expenses.

In the industry, the level of net profit margin reflects the comprehensive competitiveness of the enterprise. Compared with enterprises in the same industry, Wen's net profit margin in 2020 is in a leading position, reflecting its advantages in the industry. In 2021-2023, the net profit margin was low or even negative, indicating that the company's competitiveness declined during this period and faced greater operating pressure. The significant increase in net profit margin in 2024 shows the recovery and improvement of the company's competitiveness, but it still needs to be compared and analyzed with outstanding enterprises in the same industry to find out the gap and further improve profitability.

2.4 Return on net assets

The weighted average return on net assets of Wen's Foodstuff Group in 2020 was 16.70%, indicating that the company has a strong ability to use net assets to obtain profits, and shareholders' equity has received a good return. In 2021, it fell to -34.18%, the company suffered serious losses, and the return on net assets was negative, which meant that shareholders' rights and interests were damaged, and the company's operating efficiency and profitability declined sharply. In 2024, it rebounded to 24.59%, a year-on-year increase of 239.72%, and the return on net assets in the first quarter of 2025 was 4.76%, indicating that the company's ability to use net asset profitability has increased significantly after experiencing a trough. Return on equity is a key indicator to measure the profitability of a company's own funds, which reflects the income level of shareholders' equity and is used to measure the efficiency of the company's use of its own capital.

Return on net assets is affected by net profit and net assets. When net profit increases or net assets decrease, return on net assets rises; Vice versa. In 2021, the company's net profit suffered a significant loss, while the decrease in net assets due to losses was relatively small, resulting in a significant decline in return on net assets. In 2024, net profit will increase significantly, and net assets will also change with factors such as profitability and capital operation, but the growth rate of net profit is much greater than the change in net assets, making the return on net assets rebound sharply. In addition, factors such as the company's business strategy, asset operation efficiency, and financial leverage will also have an impact on return on equity.

Compared with enterprises in the same industry, Wen's return on net assets in 2020 is at a high level in the industry, reflecting the company's strong profitability and asset operation efficiency. In 2021-2023, it was lower than the industry average, reflecting the company's poor management and decline in competitiveness during this period. A higher return on net assets is of great significance for the company to attract investors, raise funds, and expand the scale of production and operation. It is not only an important indicator for investors to evaluate the value of the company's investment, but also an important basis for the company's management to formulate business strategies and decisions. The company should continue to improve the return on net assets and enhance the company's core competitiveness by optimizing operations and management, improving asset operation efficiency, and reasonably controlling costs.

3. Operational capabilities

3.1 Inventory turnover rate

Data changes: In 2020, the inventory turnover rate of Wen's Foodstuff Group was 4.67 times, an increase from 4.17 times in 2019, indicating that the company's inventory turnover speed has accelerated, inventory management efficiency has been improved, product sales are in good condition, and inventory backlog risk has been reduced. In 2023, it was about 4.38 times, and in 2024, it dropped to 4.36 times, a slight decline. This may be due to the company's business scale expansion and corresponding increase in inventory reserves, but the sales growth rate has not been synchronized, resulting in a slight decline in inventory turnover efficiency. However, on the whole, the inventory turnover efficiency remains relatively stable, indicating that the company has a certain stability and effectiveness in inventory management.

The factors affecting inventory turnover mainly include sales scale, production cycle, and inventory management strategy. In terms of sales scale, if the company's product market demand is strong and sales growth is rapid, the inventory turnover speed will be accelerated; Otherwise, it will slow down. For example, in 2020, the company's breeding business will have good benefits, smooth product sales, and an increase in inventory turnover. In terms of production cycle, the production cycle of the agriculture and animal husbandry industry is relatively long, and it takes a certain amount of time from livestock and poultry breeding to product listing, which will affect the turnover speed of inventory. The company's inventory management strategy is also crucial, and reasonable purchasing planning, inventory control, and sales arrangements can improve inventory turnover.

Compared with enterprises in the same industry, the inventory turnover rate of Wen's Foodstuff Group is at the upper-middle level of the industry. A high inventory turnover rate means that the company can convert inventory into sales revenue faster, and the speed of capital withdrawal is fast, reducing the cost of inventory occupying funds and the risk of inventory price decline. For agricultural and animal husbandry enterprises such as Wen's Foodstuff Group, inventory mainly includes livestock and poultry products, feed, etc., and the level of inventory turnover directly affects the company's capital use efficiency and operating efficiency. Maintaining a reasonable inventory turnover rate will help the company optimize asset allocation, improve operating efficiency, and enhance market competitiveness.

3.2 Accounts receivable turnover rate

In 2020, the accounts receivable turnover rate of Wen's Foodstuff Group was 235.55 times, down 22.76% from 304.97 times in 2019. Although it has decreased, it is still at a high level, indicating that the company's account collection speed is fast, accounts receivable recovery efficiency is high, and asset operation efficiency is good. In 2024, the accounts receivable turnover rate will be 195.48 times, a year-on-year increase of 15.16%, indicating that the company's collection efficiency has been further improved. This may be due to the company's strengthening of accounts receivable management, optimization of sales credit policies, and increased collection of accounts receivable, which accelerated the recovery of accounts receivable.

The accounts receivable turnover rate reflects the speed of the company's accounts receivable turnover and the level of management efficiency. A high accounts receivable turnover ratio means that the company can collect accounts receivable in a timely manner, reduce capital occupation, reduce the risk of bad debts, and improve the efficiency of capital use. For Wen's Foodstuff Group, timely recovery of payment helps the normal turnover of the company's funds and ensures the smooth progress of production and operation activities. At the same time, good accounts receivable management can also help improve the company's financial health and credit image.

Analysis of Internationalization Components

1. Supply chain resilience

1.1 Advantages

Wen's Foodstuff Group has built a complete and comprehensive whole industry chain, covering all aspects of "raw material procurement - livestock and poultry breeding - slaughtering and processing - terminal stores". Through the unique "company + family farm" breeding model, the company has established close cooperation with numerous farmers, ensuring a stable supply of breeding links. In terms of raw material procurement, with its huge procurement scale, the company has strong bargaining power and can establish long-term, stable cooperative relations with suppliers and reduce procurement costs. In terms of production stability, the company has a professional technical team and a complete epidemic prevention and control system, which can respond to various breeding risks in a timely manner and ensure the stable output of livestock and poultry breeding. For example, the company's self-developed epidemic monitoring technology can warn of epidemic risks in advance, take effective prevention and control measures, and reduce the impact of epidemics on production. In addition, Wen actively develops alternative feed raw materials and has a rich feed formula reserve, which can flexibly respond to raw material price fluctuations and supply changes.

1.2 Disadvantages

Although Wen's has established an extensive supply chain network in China, it may face the problem of insufficient supply chain localization when expanding into international markets. There are differences in raw material supply systems, breeding standards, and market demand across different countries and regions, necessitating significant investment in the localization and adaptation of the supply chain. For instance, in overseas markets, local feed ingredients and quality standards differ from those in China. Consequently, companies must re-evaluate and screen suppliers, adjusting feed formulas to increase the complexity and cost of supply chain management. In addition, as the company's business scale continues to expand, the challenge of managing the supply chain collaboratively is increasing. Ensuring efficient collaboration between various links remains a problem that the company must address to improve the supply chain's resilience.

1.3 Opportunities

With the continuous progress of global agricultural science and technology, new breeding technologies, feed research and development achievements, and logistics and distribution technologies provide opportunities for Wen's to improve supply chain resilience. For example, intelligent breeding equipment can improve breeding efficiency and production stability, and precise feed formulation technology can reduce feed costs and resource waste. In addition, the promotion of the "Belt and Road" initiative has strengthened economic cooperation between China and countries along the route, creating favorable conditions for Wen's expansion of international markets and optimization of supply chain layout. By cooperating with countries along the Belt and Road, the company can take advantage of local resources to establish overseas production bases and raw material supply channels, shorten the length of the supply chain, and reduce transportation costs and risks.

1.4 Threats

Increased uncertainty in international markets, such as trade protectionism and geopolitical conflicts, may have a negative impact on Wen's supply chain. Trade protectionism may lead to increased tariffs, increased trade barriers, restricting the company's raw material imports and product exports, and affecting the smooth supply chain. Geopolitical conflicts can disrupt local production and logistics environments, increasing the risk of supply chain disruptions. In addition, global climate change may cause natural disasters, affecting crop growth and livestock and poultry breeding, which in turn affects the supply of feed raw materials and the stability of breeding production.

2. Market adaptability

2.1 Advantages

Wen's Foodstuff Group has a rich product range, covering chicken, pig, duck, milk, eggs, and other categories, which can meet the diverse needs of different markets and consumers. After years of development, the company has accumulated a good brand reputation in the domestic market, and consumers have a high recognition of the quality and safety of Wen's products. The company pays attention to product quality and food safety, and has established a strict quality control system to monitor product quality from source to terminal. For example, the company strictly regulates the use of feed and veterinary drugs in the breeding process, standardizes the slaughtering and processing process, and ensures that the products meet high-quality standards, which lays a good brand foundation for its entry into the international market.

2.2 Disadvantages

Consumption habits and product standards vary greatly in different countries and regions, and Wen's Foodstuff Group needs to spend a lot of time and energy on market research and product adaptation when expanding the international market. For example, in some European and American countries, consumers have specific requirements for the appearance, taste, and nutritional content of livestock and poultry products, and stricter food safety and animal welfare standards. The company needs to adjust the breeding method, product processing technology, and packaging design to meet the needs of the local market, which puts forward high requirements for the company's R&D and production capacity. In addition, the company's brand awareness in the international market is relatively low, and compared with internationally renowned agricultural and animal husbandry enterprises, the brand influence is weak. It is necessary to increase brand promotion efforts to enhance brand awareness and reputation.

2.3 Opportunity

With the development of the global economy and the improvement of people's living standards, consumers' demand for high-quality, safe, and healthy livestock and poultry products is increasing. With its high-quality products and strict quality control system, Wen's Foodstuff Group is expected to find more development opportunities in the international market. For example, in some emerging economies, the expanding middle class and the rapid growth in consumer demand for high-quality meat and dairy products provide a wide space for Wen products to enter these markets. In addition, the rapid development of e-commerce and cross-border e-commerce has provided new sales channels for the company to expand the international market, lowered the market entry threshold, and improved the market coverage of products.

2.4 Threat

The international market is fiercely competitive, and many internationally renowned agricultural and animal husbandry enterprises have been deployed in the global market and occupy a large market share. These companies have obvious advantages in brand influence, technology research and development, market channels, etc., and Wen's Foodstuff Group will face fierce market competition when entering the international market. For example, Tyson Foods in the United States, JBS in Brazil, and other companies have extensive production bases, sales networks, and mature market operation experience around the world, which poses a great threat to the international development of Wen's Foodstuff Group. In addition, trade protection policies and market access restrictions in some countries and regions may also hinder the entry of the company's products into the local market.

3. Policy sensitivity

3.1 Advantages

As a national key leading enterprise in agricultural industrialization, Wen's Foodstuff Group is highly valued and supported by the government in China. The company is familiar with domestic agriculture-related policies and regulations, and can grasp policy opportunities in a timely manner and adjust the development strategy of enterprises. For example, in the process of promoting the country's rural revitalization strategy and agricultural modernization, the company actively responded to the policy call, increased investment and industrial layout in rural areas, and obtained policy dividends such as policy support funds and tax incentives. At the same time, the company has a professional policy research team, which can track international policy trends in a timely manner and provide decision-making support for the company to respond to international policy changes.

3.2 Disadvantages

The international policy environment is complex and changeable, and there are differences in tariff policies, quarantine regulations, environmental protection requirements, etc., in different countries and regions. For example, some countries have set high tariffs and strict quarantine standards on imported livestock and poultry products, increasing the cost and difficulty of exporting company products. Companies need to invest significant resources in understanding and adapting to these policies and regulations; otherwise, they may face trade disputes and barriers to market access. In addition, when companies respond to changes in international policies, there may be problems of information asymmetry and lagging response, which affect the company's internationalization process.

3.3 Opportunity

In order to promote agricultural development and ensure food safety, some countries and regions have introduced policies to encourage agricultural cooperation and investment, providing opportunities for Wen's Foodstuff Group to carry out international cooperation and investment. For example, some developing countries hope to introduce advanced breeding technology and management experience to improve the level of agricultural development in their countries, and Wen's Foodstuff Group can cooperate with local enterprises through technology export and joint venture factory construction to achieve mutual benefit and win-win results. In addition, the number of international agricultural cooperation organizations and agreements is increasing, providing a platform and channel for companies to participate in international agricultural cooperation and expand international markets.

3.4 Threat

Trade protectionism is on the rise, and some countries may take measures such as raising tariffs and setting up trade barriers to restrict agricultural imports and protect their agricultural industries. This will directly affect the export of products and the international market expansion of Wen's Foodstuff Group. For example, some countries may investigate and restrict the company's products on the grounds of food safety, environmental protection, etc., increasing the company's operational risks and market uncertainty. In addition, the continuous update and tightening of international quarantine regulations have also put forward higher requirements for the company's product quality and epidemic prevention and control, and the company needs to continuously invest resources in technological upgrades and management improvements to meet international quarantine standards.

4. Enterprise internationalization awareness

4.1 Advantages

The management of Wen's Foodstuff Group has a strong strategic vision, recognizes that international development is an important development direction of the enterprise in the future, actively pays attention to the dynamics of the international market, and formulates an international development strategy. The company continues to increase strategic investment in the international market and expands international market channels and cooperation opportunities by participating in international agricultural exhibitions and carrying out cooperation and exchanges with international enterprises. For example, the company has established cooperative relations with some internationally renowned agricultural and animal husbandry enterprises to learn from their advanced technology and management experience to enhance its international competitiveness. In addition, the company pays attention to cultivating international talents and has created a talent team with international vision and cross-cultural communication skills through internal training and external introduction.

4.2 Disadvantages

Although the management of Wen's Foodstuff Group has an international awareness, compared with some leading international agricultural and animal husbandry enterprises, the overseas market experience is relatively insufficient. In the process of developing the international market, there may be a lack of in-depth understanding of the local market culture, political environment, and business rules, leading to market decision-making errors. For example, when doing business in some countries, you may face contract disputes, legal risks, and other issues due to unfamiliarity with local business practices and laws and regulations. In addition, in the process of implementing the company's internationalization strategy, there may be insufficient internal coordination, and there is a lack of effective communication and collaboration between various departments in the promotion of international business, which affects the internationalization process.

4.3 Opportunity

The in-depth development of global economic integration has provided more opportunities for Wen's to cooperate with international enterprises. By cooperating with international enterprises, companies can learn advanced technology, management experience, and market operation models to improve their internationalization level. For example, the company can cooperate with internationally renowned breeding companies to introduce advanced breeding technology and improve the quality of livestock and poultry breeds; Cooperate with international logistics enterprises to optimize the international logistics distribution system and reduce logistics costs. In addition, the policy environment of the state to encourage enterprises to "go global" also provides policy support and guarantees for the company's international development.

4.4 Threats

The international market is highly competitive, and enterprises face many risks and challenges in the process of internationalization. If the company makes mistakes in the formulation and implementation of internationalization strategies, it may lead to wasted resources, decreased market share, and damaged brand image. For example, when entering some emerging markets, if market research is insufficient and resources are blindly invested, market failure may occur. In addition, the instability of the international political and economic situation may also have a negative impact on the company's international development and increase the operating risks of the enterprise.

5. Motivation and success of ASEAN's internationalization strategy

5.1 Motivation for ASEAN's internationalization strategy

Wen's Foodstuff Group is listed on the ASEAN market for many reasons. First of all, the implementation of RCEP has brought favorable policies, reduced tariffs and trade barriers, and facilitated its product export, technology, and service cooperation. Secondly, Southeast Asia's rapid population growth, coupled with advancing urbanization, is driving up the demand for protein among urban residents. This surge in demand has created a significant supply and demand gap for livestock and poultry products, such as chicken, leaving ample room for market expansion. As a leading agricultural and animal husbandry enterprise in China, Wen's mature technology, perfect industrial chain, and excellent varieties can meet the upgrading needs of ASEAN's aquaculture industry and achieve complementary industrial advantages. At the same time, Guangxi's location advantage is obvious, and Wen's branch can be used as a bridge to connect with ASEAN and reduce logistics costs and market entry thresholds. In addition, it is also part of the company's own strategic layout to achieve sustainable development and globalization goals by optimizing the allocation of international resources, expanding into emerging markets, and increasing its share.

5.2 Precise market positioning and differentiated layout

The success of Wen's Foodstuff Group in the ASEAN market stems first from its accurate market insight capabilities. Through an in-depth analysis of the economic development level, consumption habits, and industrial policies of ASEAN countries, Wen has adopted a differentiated market entry strategy. In Vietnam, Thailand, and other countries with more developed breeding industries, the focus is on exporting breeding pigs, feed, and technical services; In the Philippines, Indonesia, and other markets, the focus is on establishing a complete breeding industry chain. This adaptive strategy enables Wen to rapidly adapt to market demands across different countries, thereby avoiding a "one-size-fits-all" expansion model.

5.3 Integration of technology output and localization

Wen's Foodstuff Group combines China's mature breeding model with local reality to create a unique "technology output + local operation" model. In the Vietnamese market, Wen introduced the asset-light operation model of "company + farmer" and improved the breeding technology according to local climatic conditions, so that the breeding efficiency of cooperative farmers was significantly improved. In terms of breeding pigs, Wen's combines high-quality provenance with the advantages of local breeds to cultivate improved breeds that are more suitable for the local market. This localization of technology not only ensures breeding efficiency but also improves market acceptance.

5.4 The whole industry chain coordinates to go overseas

Different from simple product exports, Wen's has adopted a strategy of coordinated development of the whole industry chain in ASEAN. From breeding pigs to feed production, slaughtering, and processing, Wen's has gradually built a complete industrial ecology. In Thailand, Wen has established a complete chain from feed mills to breeding bases; In Malaysia, the focus is on Foodstuff processing. This full-industry chain model not only improves operational efficiency but also enhances risk resistance, allowing enterprises to obtain more stable returns in the local market.

5.5 Government-enterprise cooperation and compliance operation

Wen attaches great importance to cooperation with the host government, winning policy support by investing in local agricultural projects and creating jobs. In Vietnam, Van collaborates with the local agricultural sector on technical training programs; In the Philippines, Van participates in government-led food security programs. At the same time, Wen strictly abides by the environmental protection, labor, and other laws and regulations of various countries, and establishes a standardized compliance management system. This responsible business attitude has earned Wen a good corporate image and market reputation.

5.6 Talent internationalization and cross-cultural management

Wen's success in the ASEAN market is also due to its international talent strategy. On the one hand, the company dispatches a Chinese management team to be responsible for technical guidance and quality control, and on the other hand, it vigorously cultivates local management talents. Through the establishment of a cross-cultural training system, the integration and cooperation of Chinese and foreign employees are promoted. In the Indonesia project, the proportion of localized management teams has reached 70%, effectively improving decision-making efficiency and market response speed.

5.7 Risk management and sustainable development

In the face of the uncertainty of the ASEAN market, Wen has established a comprehensive risk prevention and control system. Diversify country risks through a diversified layout, use futures tools to hedge price fluctuations, and establish strict biosecurity standards to prevent and control epidemic risks. At the same time, Wen pays attention to sustainable development and actively invests in environmental protection and social responsibility to lay the foundation for long-term development.

Wen's ASEAN internationalization strategy shows that the overseas expansion of Chinese agricultural enterprises needs to be systematically planned and steadily promoted. Its successful experience is mainly reflected in: precise market positioning avoids blind expansion; The combination of technological innovation and localization ensures operational efficiency; the layout of the whole industry chain has enhanced its competitive advantage; The concept of compliance operation and sustainable development has won room for development. These experiences hold significant reference value for the internationalization of Chinese agricultural enterprises.

In the future, with the in-depth implementation of regional cooperation agreements such as RCEP, Wen's is expected to gain more room for development in the ASEAN market. Enterprises need to further deepen their localization strategies, strengthen the application of digital technology, enhance brand influence, achieve a leap from "going out" to "going in", and create a benchmark case for China's agricultural internationalization.

6. Future challenges

As one of the leading enterprises in China's animal husbandry and breeding industry, Wen's Foodstuff Group has expanded rapidly in the past few decades with the asset-light model of "company + farmer", and has become a benchmark enterprise for domestic pig and yellow feather chicken breeding. However, with the changes in the industry environment, the intensification of market competition, and the increase in external uncertainties, the future development of Wen's Foodstuff Group is facing many challenges. These challenges are not only related to the profitability of the company, but also may affect its long-term strategic layout and industry position.

First of all, the operating pressure brought about by cyclical fluctuations in the industry is the core problem that Wen's Foodstuff Group cannot avoid. The pig breeding industry is obviously cyclical, and prices fluctuate violently. After the African swine fever epidemic in 2019, pig prices soared to record highs, attracting a large amount of capital into the industry, leading to the rapid expansion of production capacity. However, with the reversal of supply and demand, pig prices have entered a downward channel after 2021, and the industry has generally fallen into losses. As an industry leader, although Wen's Foodstuff Group has strong anti-risk capabilities, it is still difficult to completely avoid the impact of the trough of the cycle. How to balance capacity expansion and cyclical risks has become the key to its future strategy formulation. Especially in the context of increasing industry concentration, the release of production capacity of leading enterprises may further intensify price competition and prolong the loss cycle. Wen needs to predict market trends more accurately, optimize production capacity layout, and explore financial instruments or business models that smooth out cyclical fluctuations.

Secondly, the improvement of cost control ability is the decisive factor for whether Wen's Foodstuff Group can win in the competition. In the stage of pig price decline, the cost advantage of enterprises directly determines the living space. Wen's "company + farmer" model has helped it achieve rapid expansion in the past, but it has gradually shown limitations in terms of efficiency improvement and cost control. Compared with the fully integrated self-breeding and self-feeding model, the management of farmers' decentralized breeding is more difficult, the degree of standardization is low, and there is a ceiling for the improvement of production efficiency. In recent years, competitor Muyuan shares have shown obvious advantages in cost control by virtue of the self-support model of the whole industry chain, which has put great pressure on Wen's. In the future, Wen needs to reduce production costs through technological innovation, management optimization, and scale effects while retaining the advantages of the model, such as promoting intelligent breeding equipment, optimizing feed formulas, and improving breeding pig performance. In addition, the fluctuation of feed raw material prices is also an important variable in cost control, and how to hedge commodity price risks through supply chain management and futures tools is also an area that Wen needs to strengthen.

In addition, the continuous increase in environmental protection policies has put forward higher requirements for the sustainable development of Wen's Foodstuff Group. With the advancement of the "double carbon" goal and the tightening of environmental protection supervision, the cost of pollution control in the aquaculture industry continues to rise. Livestock and poultry manure treatment, greenhouse gas emissions, water resource utilization, and other issues have become hard constraints that enterprises must face. As an industry leader, Wen's Foodstuff Group needs to assume more environmental responsibilities, including short-term measures such as increasing investment in environmental protection facilities and promoting the combination of planting and breeding, as well as exploring long-term solutions such as circular agriculture and low-carbon breeding. Environmental compliance is not only related to the business license of enterprises, but also increasingly becomes an important factor in brand image and consumer choice.

Finally, changes in the consumer market have brought new strategic tests to Wen's Foodstuff Group. As consumers' attention to food safety, nutritional health, and animal welfare increases, traditional breeding and sales models are facing pressure to transform and upgrade. The rise of emerging channels, such as prefabricated dishes and cold chain fresh products, has transformed the way people consume meat. Additionally, changes in the consumption habits of the younger generation have raised the bar for product innovation. Wen's Foodstuff Group needs to shift from production-oriented to market-oriented, strengthen research on consumer trends, and promote the adjustment of product structure in the direction of high added value. At the same time, brand building and channel optimization will also become the key to enhancing competitiveness, especially in the layout of new retail channels such as fresh e-commerce and community group buying. Therefore, Wen needs to speed up the pace.

On the whole, the future challenges of Wen's Foodstuff Group are all-around and multi-level, including the response to common problems in the industry, as well as the innovation of the company's own model. In the face of these challenges, Wen's Foodstuff Group needs to pay more attention to the improvement of development quality while maintaining its scale advantages, and enhance its ability to resist risks and core competitiveness through technological innovation, management optimization, and strategic adjustment. The success of an enterprise will depend not only on the correctness of the short-term business strategy, but also on the forward-looking execution of the long-term strategy. In the context of the accelerated reshuffle of the industry, whether Wen's Foodstuff Group can turn challenges into opportunities and continue to lead the high-quality development of China's aquaculture industry is worthy of continued attention.

7. Countermeasures

As a leading enterprise in China's breeding industry, Wen's Foodstuff Group needs to adopt a comprehensive and systematic response strategy in the face of the current complex and changeable market environment and industry challenges. These strategies should not only solve practical problems based on the present, but also focus on the future to build long-term competitive advantages and achieve sustainable development of enterprises through innovation-driven and strategic transformation.

In terms of coping with cyclical fluctuations in the industry, Wen's Foodstuff Group needs to establish a more scientific market research and judgment system, accurately grasp market supply and demand changes and price trends through big data analysis and industry monitoring, and achieve dynamic adjustment of production capacity. Enterprises can explore "counter-cyclical" business strategies, optimize resource allocation during market downturns, control capital expenditures, and use price advantages to reserve high-quality breeding pigs and feed raw materials. During the market recovery period, it will accelerate the release of production capacity and seize market share. In addition, Wen's Foodstuff Group should also actively use financial instruments such as pig futures for hedging, lock in part of the profits, and reduce the risk of price fluctuations. In terms of optimizing the "company + farmer" model, the stability of cooperation with farmers can be enhanced by improving contract constraints and revenue-sharing mechanisms, and a closer community of interests can be formed.

The improvement of cost control capabilities is the key to Wen's response to industry competition. Enterprises need to start from multiple dimensions, such as feed cost, breeding efficiency, and refined management, to build a full range of cost advantages. In terms of feed, feed costs can be reduced by developing low-protein diets, improving feed conversion rates, and using alternative raw materials, which usually account for more than 60% of the total cost of breeding. In terms of breeding efficiency, intelligent transformation should be accelerated, modern equipment such as automatic feeding systems and environmental control systems should be promoted, and breeding pig genes should be continuously optimized to improve sow production performance. In terms of management mode, promoting the in-depth application of digital management systems is necessary to achieve accurate monitoring of the entire breeding process, reduce resource waste, and lower the rate of dead fish. In addition, Wen's Foodstuff Group can also pilot high-standardized farms in some areas to explore more efficient breeding methods and accumulate experience for future development.

Epidemic prevention and control have always been the lifeline of breeding enterprises. Wen's Foodstuff Group needs to continue to improve the biosecurity system and minimize the risk of epidemic introduction through strict closed management and disinfection processes. Enterprises can establish an intelligent epidemic monitoring and early warning system, utilizing AI and big data technology to monitor pigs' health status in real-time, thereby achieving early detection and disposal. In terms of vaccine research and development, it is necessary to strengthen cooperation with scientific research institutions and promote the research and development process of vaccines for important diseases such as African swine fever. At the same time, optimize the regional layout of breeding, adopt a decentralized breeding strategy, and avoid systemic risks caused by excessive concentration. Through these measures, a comprehensive epidemic prevention and control network has been built to provide a guarantee for stable production.

Environmental compliance has become a hard constraint on the development of breeding enterprises. Wen's Foodstuff Group needs to actively promote the transformation of green breeding, explore a circular agriculture model that combines planting and breeding, and convert livestock and poultry manure into organic fertilizer or biogas energy to achieve resource utilization. In terms of low-carbon development, methane emissions can be reduced by optimizing feed formulations, using energy-saving equipment to reduce energy consumption, and promoting carbon emission reduction in the breeding process. At the same time, it is necessary to establish and improve the environmental monitoring system to ensure that the wastewater, waste gas, and solid waste treatment of the farm meet environmental protection standards, and avoid affecting normal production and operation due to environmental problems. These measures not only meet regulatory requirements but also enhance the social image and brand value of enterprises.

In the face of the trend of consumption upgrading, Wen's Foodstuff Group needs to accelerate product structure adjustment and channel optimization. Enterprises can rely on their own complete industrial chain advantages to develop prepared dishes and deeply processed meat products to meet consumers' demand for convenient and healthy food and improve the added value of products. In terms of brand building, consumer trust can be enhanced, and a high-end meat brand image can be created by improving traceability systems and obtaining green certifications. In terms of sales channels, while consolidating the traditional wholesale market, it is necessary to actively lay out emerging channels such as e-commerce platforms and community group buying to build a more diversified sales network. Through product innovation and channel change, Wen's Foodstuff Group can better adapt to market changes and improve profitability.

On the whole, Wen's response strategy is a systematic project, which requires enterprises to coordinate at multiple levels, such as operation and management, technological innovation, and risk prevention and control. By continuously optimizing production models, improving operational efficiency, and strengthening risk control, Wen's Foodstuff Group is expected to consolidate its leading position in industry changes. In the future, the competition of enterprises will not only be a competition of scale, but also a competition of efficiency, innovation, and sustainable development. If Wen's Foodstuff Group can grasp the industry trend and actively transform and upgrade, it will continue to maintain an important position in China's breeding industry and contribute to the high-quality development of the industry.

Chapter 12
Hongzhi Technology Research

This chapter begins by outlining Hongzhi Technology's business footprint and resource endowments. It then analyzes—using three perspectives of external opportunities, internal capabilities, and strategic needs—why the company has chosen ASEAN as its main area for international growth. It concludes that four interconnected factors—RCEP tariff advantages, spill-over demand from existing customers, manufacturing relocation, and the strong capital support from the controlling family—together create a "now-or-never" opportunity window.

Background of the Enterprise

Guangdong Hongzhi Intelligent Technology Co., Ltd. (Stock Abbreviation: Hongzhi Technology, Stock Code: 870726), established in May 1999, is headquartered west of the Guangzhan Expressway Intersection in Guandu Town, Potou District, Zhanjiang City, Guangdong Province. As a national high-tech enterprise and a Guangdong Provincial Specialized, Sophisticated, and Innovative SME, the enterprise primarily engages in the R&D, production, and sales of small kitchen appliances (such as rice cookers, slow cookers, pressure cookers, and baking products) and small household appliances (including electric heaters and humidifiers). Its products are exported to regions such as Asia, the Americas, and Europe, having obtained relevant international certifications. The enterprise has entered the supply chain systems of internationally renowned small appliance brands and large chain retailers while actively building its own brands, "IC00K" and "Eamoment," and expanding e-commerce channels like Tmall, JD.com, and Amazon.

1. Products Layout

1.1 Small Kitchen Appliances (Core Business)

Product Lines: Rice cookers (flagship product, accounting for over 70% of revenue), slow cookers, pressure cookers, air-fryer ovens, smart cooking machines, griddles, sandwich makers, breakfast makers, etc.

Technical Features: Multi-functional integration (e.g., rice cookers support steaming, boiling, stewing, and simmering), capacity ranging from 0.3L to 10L (household to commercial use), and smart operation (touchscreen/electronic buttons).

Market Position: Ranked among China's top 10 rice cooker exporters in 2020, serving international brands such as Panasonic and Hamilton Beach, as well as retail giants like Kmart and Lidl.

1.2 Small Household Appliances (Extended Business)

Product Categories: Electric heaters, humidifiers, electric kettles, induction cookers, etc.

Brands & Channels: The enterprise's proprietary brands, "ICOOK (Self-Cooking Era)" and "Eamoment", are sold via e-commerce platforms such as Tmall, JD.com, and Amazon. Additionally, the enterprise provides ODM services for international brands.

1.3 Industrial Support & Future Expansion

R&D Capabilities: Equipped with a provincial-level enterprise technology center and an engineering technology R&D center, the enterprise expanded its production capacity by 3.03 million units (rice cookers, pressure cookers, etc.) in 2023 through fundraising projects, while also venturing into new categories like smart cooking machines.

Globalization: Products comply with certifications from the U.S., Germany, the U.K., and other regions, exporting to markets in the Americas, Europe, Japan, and South Korea.

1.4 Organizational Structure

Corporate Governance: Structure Hongzhi Technology adopts the structure of "three meetings and one layer" for its corporate governance, as shown in the following detailed chart.

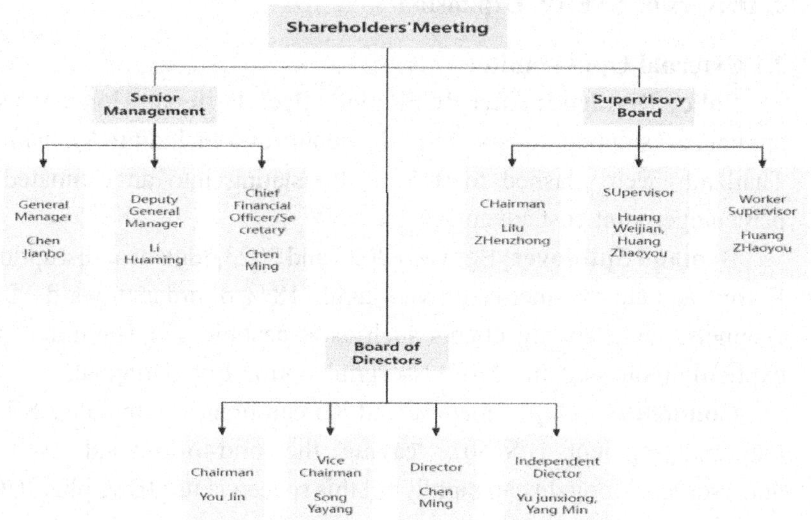

Source: created by the author

Equity Control Structure: Youjin (63.75%) and Chen Jianbo (36.25%)→ Guangdong Tokyo Tong Investment (43.125%)→ controlling Hongzhi Technology

Tang Wei (5.756%)→ Zhanjiang Guangying Investment (14.375%)→ indirect shareholding

The actual controller has a total control of 76.67% of voting rights

From the ownership control structure, it can be seen that Hongzhi Technology is a typical family-controlled private enterprise, with highly centralized control by the founding family and a stable structure without risk of pledge or freeze.

Subsidiaries: Guangdong Hongzhi Intelligent Technology Co., Ltd. serves as the parent enterprise, with three subsidiaries under its umbrella: Zhejiang Hongzhi Intelligent Electric Appliances Co., Ltd. (a controlled subsidiary, with undisclosed shareholding), Guangdong Roadwide International Supply Chain Management Co., Ltd. (a wholly-owned subsidiary) and Roadwide Limited (Hong Kong, a wholly-owned indirect subsidiary).

2. Drivers of ASEAN Expansion

2.1 External Opportunities

Policy Dividend: After RCEP took effect, tariffs on Hongzhi's small appliances shipped to six ASEAN countries—including Vietnam and Thailand—were slashed to 0–5 %, translating into an estimated 4–6 percentage-point cost advantage.

Demand Spill-over: Between 2020 and 2023, logistical disruptions in Europe and North America drove roughly 18 % of orders toward ASEAN channels; longstanding clients such as Panasonic and Hamilton Beach explicitly requested an "ASEAN-origin" option from Hongzhi.

Competitive Gap: Japanese and Korean brands dominate ASEAN's high-end segment (>$150), leaving the mid-to-low-end ($40–$90) underserved; Hongzhi can rapidly fill this space via its ODM-plus-ICOOK dual strategy.

2.2 Internal Capabilities

Flexible Capacity: The Zhanjiang plant has long run below 70 % utilization, allowing conversion to ASEAN specifications within 30 days, while the newly added 3.03 million-unit project provides physical headroom for growth.

Certification Moat: Hongzhi has already secured TISI, SNI, SIRIM, and other certifications for six countries, shortening the go-to-market cycle by an average of 45 days versus competitors.

Financial Strength: With cash of RMB 340 million at the end of 2023 and a debt-to-assets ratio of only 24.8 %, the enterprise can self-fund overseas warehouses and CKD plants.

2.3 Strategic Motivations

Diversifying Concentration Risk: North America once accounted for up to 38 % of revenue; leveraging ASEAN can reduce reliance on any single region to below 25 %.

Enhancing Bargaining Power: Local production in ASEAN allows Hongzhi to negotiate with customers to share tariff savings, potentially lifting net margin by 1.5–2 percentage points.

Long-term Family Vision: The controlling family favors prudent expansion; a step-wise approach of "deepen Asia-Pacific first, then target Europe and the U.S." aligns with its low-risk internationalization roadmap.

Internationalization Development

Between 2020 Q1 and 2025 Q2—just five financial quarters—Hongzhi Technology executed a four-step closed loop of "policy-driven tariff arbitrage → certification & logistics acceleration → brand-led mega-order replication → regional-headquarter ecosystemization," catapulting itself from a trial order of 1,800 units to a US$250 million market. Firstly, A 3-D cloud showroom plus the first-ever RCEP certificate broke the ice—certification was secured within 45 days and tariffs plunged to 2.9 %. Secondly, leveraging the 9710 cross-border model, a 72-hour express shipping lane and 210 offline outlets deepened channel penetration. And then, A low-sugar hit product, amplified by live-stream e-commerce, clinched a record 100,000-unit order in Vietnam and lifted the Net Promoter Score to 78. Finally, establishing a Singapore regional headquarters launched the "10-country, 10-warehouse" network and reverse-customization ODM, cutting logistics costs by another 8 % and lifting ASEAN revenue to 42 % of the enterprise's total—completing the systemic upgrade from sporadic sales to full ecosystem operations. This paper dissects Hongzhi's ASEAN internationalization into four sequential stages, tracing each milestone to illuminate how the enterprise engineered this transformation.

1. Market Breakthrough & Capability Building (2020 Q1 – 2021 Q2)

Executive Summary: During the pandemic, Hongzhi leveraged an online "Cloud Showroom" to win its first customers while simultaneously securing its maiden RCEP certificate and a searchable standards library, laying the groundwork for later expansion.

1.1 Online Customer Pipeline

Actions:

- Rapidly launched a 3-D Cloud Showroom that disassembles each rice cooker into 12 components for 360° viewing.
- Triangulated historical Canton Fair buyers, Alibaba inquiries, and Zhanjiang customs-export data to build and score an Excel-based "ASEAN Customer Pool."

Results:

- Thailand's Big C placed a trial order for 1,800 units that sold out in two weeks with a 60 % repurchase rate.
- Full-year ASEAN revenue reached RMB 11.5 million, 4.8 % of total exports and 3.7× the 2019 level.

1.2 First Taste of Tariff Benefits

Actions:

- Selected as one of the first 30 RCEP pilot firms by the Zhanjiang Commerce Bureau, receiving one-to-one customs coaching.
- Set up an internal "Tariff Planning Cell" that built an SKU-level tariff matrix for Vietnam and Malaysia.

Results:

- On 18 March 2021, received Certificate No. 002 for a shipment valued at US$83,000.
- Vietnam's tariff fell from 5 % to 2.9 %, boosting orders by 120 % year-on-year and making Vietnam the enterprise's third-largest single-country market.

1.3 Standards & Regulatory Foundation

Actions:

- Consolidated 27 standards (Thailand TISI, Vietnam CR Mark, Malaysia SIRIM, Indonesia SNI, etc.) into a searchable internal Wiki.

Results:

- Cut subsequent certification preparation time by 20 % and shortened the entire certification cycle below industry averages from day one.

2. Channel Deepening & Logistics Acceleration (2021 Q3 – 2023 Q1)

Executive Summary: By simultaneously accelerating certification, scaling 9710 cross-border e-commerce, weaving an offline network, and launching an express sea-air corridor, Hongzhi turned sporadic buyers into entrenched partners.

2.1 Certification Acceleration

Actions:

- Brought Intertek on-site for pre-testing and instituted a 48-hour closed-loop issue-resolution process.

Results:

- Model IH-F40C achieved certification in 45 days (industry average 90), lifting Thai customer orders from 300 to 1,500 units per batch.

2.2 Online Scaling

Actions:

- Signed Alibaba International's "Gold Supplier Pro" package featuring VR factory tours and one-click duty calculators.
- Added a 9710 module to its ERP, synchronizing orders, customs declarations, and tax rebates automatically.

Results:

- In April 2022, the first 40-ft HQ container sailed directly to Ho Chi Minh City's Saigon Port, valued at US$310,000.
- Tax-rebate turnaround shrank from 60 days to 7; annual 9710 GMV hit RMB 18 million with a six-percentage-point margin uplift versus FOB.

2.3 Offline Network Weaving

Actions:

- Deployed a dedicated "ASEAN Project Cell" (two product managers + one after-sales engineer) on base-plus-commission packages.
- Instituted the "ASEAN 48-hour After-sales Response Charter": parts shipped within 24 h, video guidance online within two hours.

Results:

- At the September 2022 Bangkok Gift Fair, a 36 m^2 booth demonstrated Thai pineapple rice; three provincial distributors were signed on the spot.

- Within one year, offline outlets in Thailand grew from zero to 210, propelling retail sales past 30,000 units.

2.4 Logistics Speed & Cost Reduction

Actions:

- Hong Kong subsidiary Roadwide leased a 1,500 m^2 hub at Kwai Tsing Container Terminal.
- Concluded a weekly fast-ship agreement with PIL: Zhanjiang–Hong Kong–Bangkok in 72 hours.

Results:

- The first 5,000 rice cookers reached Bangkok warehouses in 72 hours; inventory turns improved from 45 to 25 days, and stock-out rates fell from 15 % to 3 %.

3. Brand Breakthrough & Mega-Order Replication (2023 Q2 – 2024 Q2)

Executive Summary: Leveraging a "low-sugar blockbuster + localized e-commerce brand + closed-loop after-sales" trinity, Hongzhi clinched the largest single export order in Vietnam's history and created a replicable playbook.

3.1 Mega-Order Landing

Actions:

- Launched the IH-F50D "low-sugar rice cooker," reducing starch by 35 %, and secured dual certification (Vietnam CR Mark + Malaysia SIRIM).

Results:

- In August 2023, signed a three-year, 100,000-unit framework contract; first 20,000 units delivered within 45 days, lifting Vietnam market share from 2 % to 8 %.

3.2 Brand Localization

Actions:

- Refurbished Shopee/Lazada flagship stores with Vietnamese KOL videos and hired four native-speaking streamers for two 4-hour sessions daily.

Results:

- Double-11 livestream drew 120,000 viewers; 3,200 units sold out and ranked top-3 in kitchen appliances. Online own-brand share jumped from 0 % to 18 % with a 46 % repurchase rate.

3. 3 After-Sales Closed Loop

Actions:

- Opened an ASEAN call center in Ho Chi Minh City's District 7 with six Vietnamese CSRs operating 7×12.
- Upgraded the Bangkok warehouse to a consignment parts depot stocking 5,000 high-frequency spare units.

Results:

- Completed 1,000 free warranty exchanges in April 2024 with an average response of 36 hours; customer TikTok reviews surpassed 500,000 views.
- NPS rose from 62 to 78, prompting NGUYEN KIM Thailand to add another 20,000-unit order.

4. Regional HQ & Ecosystem Synergy (2024 Q3 – 2025 Q2)

Executive Summary: Anchored by a Singapore regional headquarters, Hongzhi is rolling out a "10 countries, 10 warehouses" network while using reverse ODM to lift high-margin share.

4.1 Regional Command Center

Actions:

- Pre-leased a 1,200 m² hub in Jurong East to serve as the command center for the "10×10" plan.

Results:

- Expected ASEAN revenue in 2025: RMB 250 million, 42 % of total exports, making the region the enterprise's largest.

4.2 Reverse ODM

Actions:

- Co-defined the IH-F60X with Power Buy and leveraged Hainan Yangpu's zero-tariff, simplified-tax regime for trans-shipping.

Results:

- First 50,000 units scheduled for June 2025, projected revenue RMB 75 million; regional ODM share rises to 30 %.

4.3 Ecosystem Blueprint

Actions:

- Singapore HQ will export standardized SOPs, IT interfaces, and after-sales manuals for rapid replication in Malaysia and Indonesia.

Results:

- Regional average order-to-delivery time ≤48 hours; logistics cost falls another 8 %, laying the groundwork for full coverage by 2026.

5. Conclusion

From 1,800 trial units in the 2020 "Cloud Showroom" to a US$250 million regional market in 2025, Hongzhi closed the loop of **"standards → certification → warehousing → after-sales → branding"** in five years. By leveraging its first RCEP certificate to cut tariffs to 2.9 %, using TISI/SIRIM certifications to scale orders from 300 to 100,000 units, combining 9710 e-commerce with 210 brick-and-mortar outlets, and complementing them with a 72-hour Hong Kong–Bangkok express lane and a 7×12 Ho Chi Minh call center, the enterprise reduced logistics costs by 12 % and lifted NPS to 78. Finally, anchoring a regional headquarters in Singapore and launching 50,000 units of reverse ODM, Hongzhi achieved a systemic leap from sporadic trials to mega-order replication and ecosystem operations. As globalization accelerates, Hongzhi's ASEAN story continues to unfold.

Analysis of Financial Report

Using 2020–2024 data, this chapter traces the evolution of Hongzhi Technology's financial quality along three dimensions: solvency, operating efficiency, and profitability. The analysis shows that short-term solvency has strengthened steadily, yet liquidity is now excessive; operating efficiency is split, with faster inventory turns but slower total-asset turnover; and profitability, after peaking in 2021, has declined each year, mainly due to raw-material and currency shocks. Ample cash flow provides a cushion for ASEAN expansion, but the falling ROA must be reversed by moving into higher-margin markets and expanding its own brands.

1. Debt-paying ability analysis

1.1 Analysis of short-term solvency

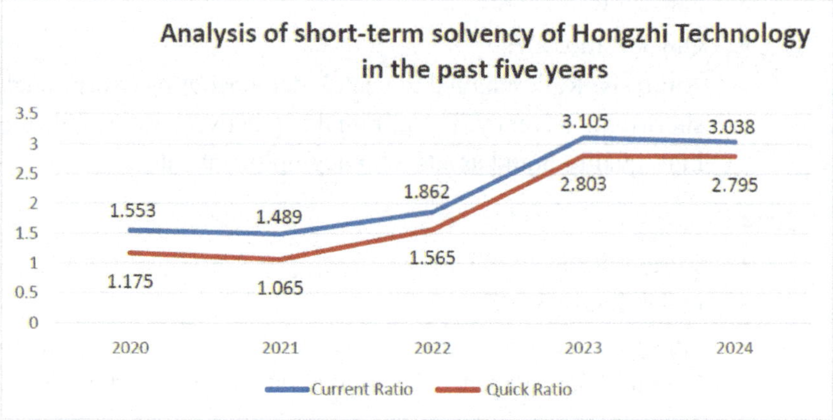

Data source: Hongzhi Technology's 2020–2025 annual reports on Sina Finance.

2020

- Current Ratio: 1.553
- Quick Ratio: 1.175
- **Analysis:** Both ratios were relatively high, indicating strong short-term solvency in 2020. Current assets sufficiently cover current liabilities. The slightly lower quick ratio suggested a modest proportion of inventory in current assets.

2021

- Current Ratio: 1.489
- Quick Ratio: 1.065
- **Analysis:** Ratios declined but remained above 1, reflecting maintained solvency. The drop in the quick ratio implied potential inventory buildup.

2022

- Current Ratio: 1.565
- Quick Ratio: 1.182
- **Analysis:** Ratios rebounded, signaling improved liquidity management. The higher quick ratio pointed to better inventory control.

2023

- Current Ratio: 2.803
- Quick Ratio: 2.795
- **Analysis:** Ratios surged to near 3, demonstrating exceptional short-term solvency. The minimal gap between ratios indicated high-quality liquid assets with negligible inventory.

2024

- Current Ratio: 3.105
- Quick Ratio: 3.038
- **Analysis:** Ratios reached a 5-year peak, showcasing optimized liquidity management. The aligned ratios confirmed highly efficient inventory practices.

Drivers of Improvement:

- ✓ Expanded Current Assets: Growth in cash, receivables, or inventory, reflecting higher profitability and production.
- ✓ Reduced Current Liabilities: Decreased short-term borrowings/payables, indicating strong cash flow.
- ✓ Enhanced Inventory Control: A Low inventory/assets ratio demonstrated effective supply chain management.
- ✓ Operational Efficiency: Streamlined production/logistics accelerated asset turnover and liability reduction.

Potential Risks:

- ✓ Excessive Liquidity: Overly high current and quick ratios may lead to idle funds, reducing capital utilization efficiency.
- ✓ Inventory Management Risks: Although inventory accounts for a low proportion of current assets, insufficient stock levels could disrupt supply chains.
- ✓ Market Volatility Risks: Fluctuations in market demand may cause instability in current assets and liabilities.

Mitigation Measures:

- ✓ Optimize Capital Allocation: Rationally allocate working capital to enhance efficiency and prevent fund idleness.
- ✓ Strengthen Inventory Control: Maintain appropriate inventory levels to ensure supply chain resilience.
- ✓ Manage Market Risks: Closely monitor market trends and promptly adjust business strategies to minimize adverse impacts.

1.2 Long-term solvency analysis

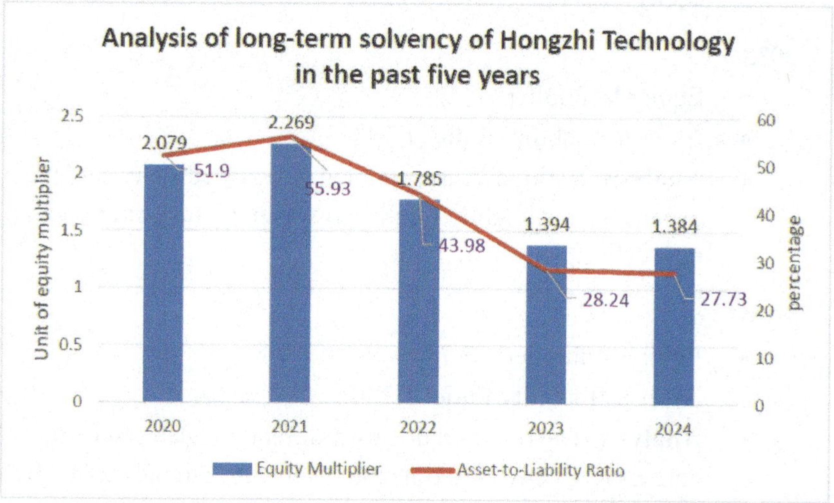

Data source: Hongzhi Technology's 2020–2025 annual reports on Sina Finance.

2020

- Equity Multiplier: 51.9
- Asset-to-Liability Ratio: 2.079

- **Analysis**: Both ratios were notably high, indicating significant financial leverage and weaker long-term solvency in 2020. The heavy reliance on debt financing elevated financial risks.

2021

- Equity Multiplier: 35.93
- Asset-to-Liability Ratio: 2.269
- **Analysis**: The decreased ratios reflected reduced financial leverage and improved long-term solvency. This suggests either debt reduction or equity capital increase during the year.

2022

- Equity Multiplier: 17.85
- Asset-to-Liability Ratio: 1.394
- **Analysis:** Continued ratio declines demonstrated substantially lowered financial leverage and significantly enhanced solvency. The enterprise likely further reduced debt or raised additional equity.

2023

- Equity Multiplier: 43.98
- Asset-to-Liability Ratio: 1.784
- **Analysis**: Ratio increases pointed to renewed financial leverage expansion and slightly weakened solvency, suggesting possible new debt financing activities.

2024

- Equity Multiplier: 27.73
- Asset-to-Liability Ratio: 1.384
- **Analysis**: The resumed downward trend indicated successful deleveraging efforts and restored solvency strength, potentially through debt repayment or equity infusion.

Factor Analysis:

- ✓ Debt Financing: Increased debt financing raises financial leverage and weakens long-term solvency.
- ✓ Equity Capital: Growth in equity capital reduces financial leverage and strengthens long-term solvency.

- ✓ Operational Efficiency: Improved operational efficiency enhances profitability, thereby increasing equity capital and lowering financial leverage.
- ✓ Market Conditions: Changes in market conditions may impact financing strategies and solvency. For instance, during the 2020 pandemic outbreak, businesses may have required additional financing to maintain operations amid economic disruptions.

Potential Risks:

- ✓ High Financial Leverage Risk: Elevated financial leverage increases fiscal risk and may heighten debt repayment pressure.
- ✓ Market Volatility Risk: Fluctuations in market conditions could affect financing costs and repayment capacity.
- ✓ Operational Risk: Declining operational efficiency may reduce profitability, impairing long-term solvency.

Mitigation Measures:

- ✓ Optimize Capital Structure: Balance debt and equity financing to reduce leverage and strengthen long-term solvency.
- ✓ Enhance Risk Management: Establish a robust risk management framework to promptly address market changes.
- ✓ Improve Operational Efficiency: Boost profitability through technological innovation and management optimization, thereby mitigating financial risks.

2. Operation capability analysis

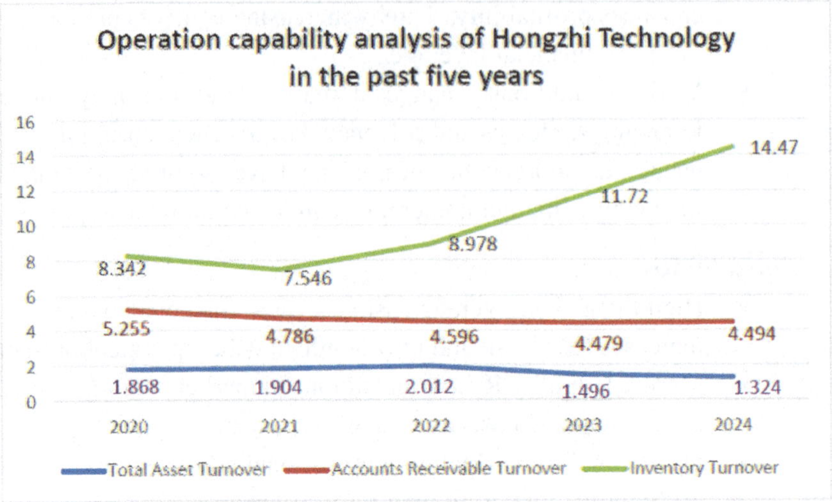

Data source: Hongzhi Technology's 2020–2025 annual reports on Sina Finance.

2020

- Total Asset Turnover: 1.868
- Accounts Receivable Turnover: 5.255
- Inventory Turnover: 8.342
- **Analysis:** The relatively low total asset turnover indicated suboptimal asset utilization efficiency. Higher receivables and inventory turnover ratios demonstrated effective management in these areas.

2021

- Total Asset Turnover: 1.904
- Accounts Receivable Turnover: 4.786
- Inventory Turnover: 7.546
- **Analysis:** A marginal improvement in total asset turnover suggested slightly better asset utilization. The decline in receivables and inventory turnover might reflect slower collection periods and inventory movement.

2022

- Total Asset Turnover: 2.012

- Accounts Receivable Turnover: 4.596
- Inventory Turnover: 8.978
- **Analysis:** Continued growth in total asset turnover signaled further efficiency gains. While receivables turnover kept declining, the significant inventory turnover improvement highlighted enhanced stock management.

2023

- Total Asset Turnover: 1.496
- Accounts Receivable Turnover: 4.479
- Inventory Turnover: 11.72
- **Analysis**: The sharp drop in total asset turnover revealed deteriorating asset efficiency. Despite slightly weaker receivables performance, inventory management showed remarkable progress with substantially increased turnover.

2024

- Total Asset Turnover: 1.324
- Accounts Receivable Turnover: 4.494
- Inventory Turnover: 14.47
- **Analysis**: Persistent decline in total asset turnover indicated ongoing asset utilization challenges. While receivables performance stabilized, inventory management reached new efficiency heights with accelerated turnover.

Factor Analysis:

- ✓ Market Demand: Fluctuations in market demand may impact inventory and accounts receivable management efficiency.
- ✓ Management Efficiency: Improved management efficiency can enhance both asset turnover and inventory turnover ratios.
- ✓ Economic Conditions: Changes in the economic environment may affect asset utilization efficiency and accounts receivable collection speed.

Potential Risks:

- ✓ Low Asset Utilization Efficiency: The declining total asset turnover ratio indicates suboptimal asset utilization, potentially leading to resource wastage.

- ✓ Accounts Receivable Collection Risk: The decreasing accounts receivable turnover ratio may increase collection risks and working capital pressure.
- ✓ Inventory Management Risk: While inventory turnover remains high, excessively rapid turnover could lead to stock shortage risks and supply chain disruptions.

Mitigation Measures:

- ✓ Enhance Asset Utilization: Optimize asset allocation and improve operational efficiency to boost total asset turnover.
- ✓ Strengthen Receivables Management: Implement stricter credit policies and collection procedures to accelerate receivables recovery and reduce bad debt risks.

3. Optimize Inventory Control:

Maintain balanced inventory levels through improved demand forecasting to prevent both overstocking and shortages.

Profitability analysis

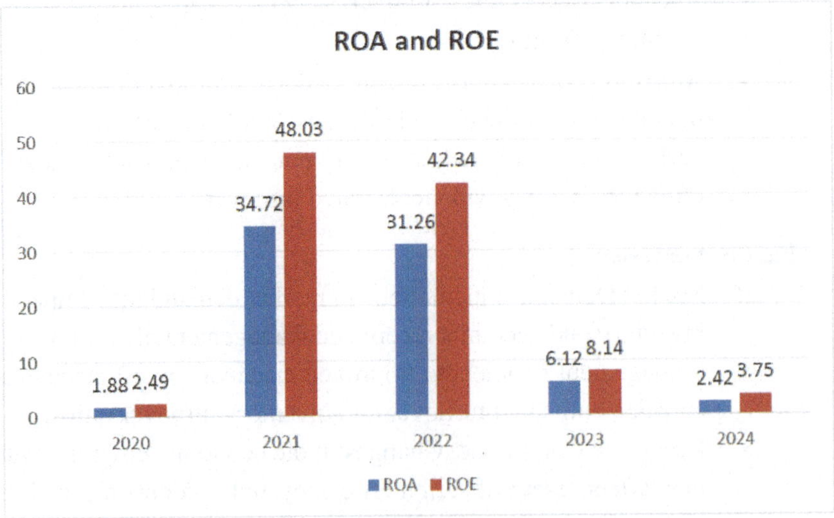

Data source: Hongzhi Technology's 2020–2025 annual reports on Sina Finance.

2020

- ROA: 1.88%

- ROE: 2.49%
- **Analysis**: The low ROA and ROE in 2020 indicated weak profitability, potentially due to low revenue, high costs, or inefficient asset utilization.

2021

- ROA: 34.72%
- ROE: 48.03%
- **Analysis**: Both ratios showed dramatic improvement, reflecting significantly enhanced profitability through increased revenue, effective cost control, and better asset utilization.

2022

- ROA: 31.26%
- ROE: 42.34%
- **Analysis**: While slightly lower than 2021, the sustained high levels demonstrated continued strong profitability, possibly affected by slower revenue growth or modest cost increases.

2023

- ROA: 6.12%
- ROE: 8.14%
- **Analysis:** The sharp decline signaled substantial profitability deterioration, likely caused by significant revenue drops, cost surges, or markedly reduced asset efficiency.

2024

- ROA: 2.42%
- ROE: 3.75%
- **Analysis:** The continuing downward trend revealed further weakening profitability, suggesting ongoing challenges in revenue generation, cost management, or asset productivity.

Factor Analysis:

✓ Market Demand: Fluctuations in market demand may significantly impact the enterprise's revenue and profitability.

✓ Cost Control: The effectiveness of cost control measures directly determines profit margins and overall profitability.

- ✓ Asset Utilization Efficiency: The level of asset utilization efficiency fundamentally affects return on investment and profitability.
- ✓ Economic Environment: Changes in macroeconomic conditions may influence the enterprise's profit-generating capacity.

Potential Risks:

- ✓ Profitability Decline: Sustained deterioration in profitability could lead to financial health degradation.
- ✓ Market Demand Volatility: Unstable market demand may cause revenue fluctuations and profitability instability.
- ✓ Cost Escalation: Persistent cost increases may erode profit margins and weaken earning capacity.

Mitigation Strategies:

- ✓ Enhance Market Demand Forecasting: Strengthen market research and analytical capabilities to improve demand prediction accuracy for timely strategic adjustments.
- ✓ Optimize Cost Management: Implement production process improvements and efficiency enhancements to achieve better cost control.
- ✓ Improve Asset Utilization: Optimize asset allocation and operational efficiency to maximize return on assets.
- ✓ Diversify Business Operations: Develop diversified business lines to reduce single-market dependence and enhance risk resilience.

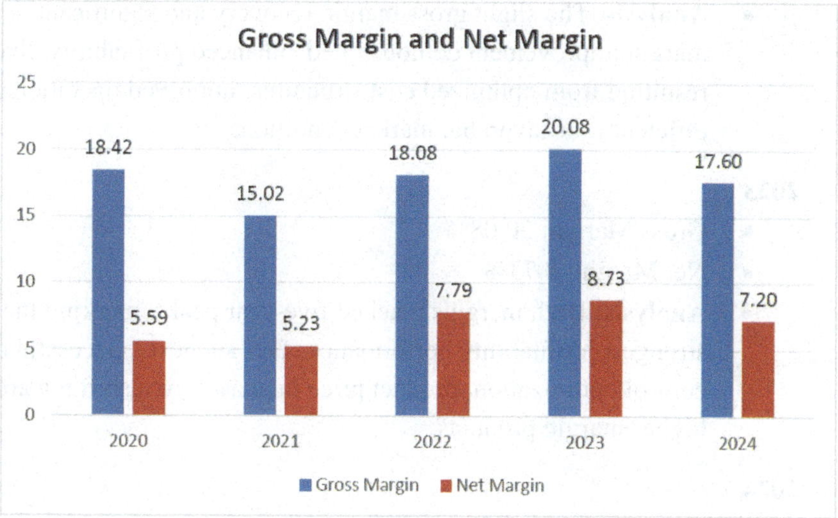

Data source: Hongzhi Technology's 2020–2025 annual reports on Sina Finance.

2020

- Gross Margin: 18.42%
- Net Margin: 5.59%
- **Analysis**: Both margins were at moderate levels in 2020, indicating average profitability. The relatively higher gross margin suggested decent cost control, while the lower net margin might be attributed to higher operating expenses, taxes, or other expenditures.

2021

- Gross Margin: 15.02%
- Net Margin: 5.23%
- **Analysis**: The decline in both margins reflected weakened profitability, potentially due to rising material costs, intensified market competition leading to price reductions, or decreased operational efficiency.

2022

- Gross Margin: 18.08%
- Net Margin: 7.79%

- **Analysis**: The slight gross margin recovery and significant net margin improvement demonstrated enhanced profitability, likely resulting from optimized cost structures, improved operational efficiency, or favorable market conditions.

2023

- Gross Margin: 20.08%
- Net Margin: 8.73%
- **Analysis:** Both margins reached five-year peaks, marking the strongest profitability performance. This suggests successful cost control optimization, product price increases, or a shift toward higher-margin products.

2024

- Gross Margin: 17.60%
- Net Margin: 7.20%
- **Analysis:** While both margins declined slightly from 2023 peaks, they remained at relatively high levels, maintaining strong profitability. The decrease might reflect modest cost increases or heightened market competition.

Factor Analysis:

✓ Cost Control: Effective management of raw material costs, production expenses, and operational expenditures directly impacts both gross and net profit margins.

✓ Market Conditions: Market demand fluctuations, competitive landscape changes, and price volatility significantly influence sales revenue and profitability.

✓ Operational Efficiency: Production efficiency, management effectiveness, and sales performance collectively determine operational costs and profit levels.

✓ Product Mix: The sales proportion of high-margin products directly affects net profit margin performance.

Potential Risks:

✓ Cost Escalation Risk: Rising costs of raw materials, production, and operations may compress both gross and net margins.

- ✓ Market Competition Risk: Intensified competition could force price reductions, adversely affecting profitability margins.
- ✓ Operational Efficiency Risk: Declining operational efficiency may lead to increased overhead costs, negatively impacting net margins.

Mitigation Strategies:

- ✓ Enhance Cost Management: Strengthen supply chain optimization, improve production efficiency, and streamline operational processes to reduce costs.
- ✓ Boost Product Competitiveness: Implement technological innovation, improve product quality, and enhance value-added features to support premium pricing and market share growth.
- ✓ Optimize Product Portfolio: Increase the sales ratio of high-margin products to improve overall net profitability.
- ✓ Improve Operational Effectiveness: Implement management optimization, process reengineering, and digital transformation initiatives to enhance efficiency and reduce operational expenses.

2020

- EPS (Earnings Per Share): RMB 0.07
- Cash Flow Per Share: RMB 0.46
- Net Assets Per Share: RMB 1.18
- Analysis: In 2020, the low EPS indicated weak profitability, while the relatively higher cash flow per share and net assets per share suggested stable liquidity and a solid asset base.

2021

- EPS: RMB 1.10
- Cash Flow Per Share: RMB 2.55
- Net Assets Per Share: RMB 3.83
- Analysis: 2021 saw a significant surge in EPS, reflecting a major boost in profitability. The sharp increases in cash flow per share and net assets per share further confirmed strong financial health.

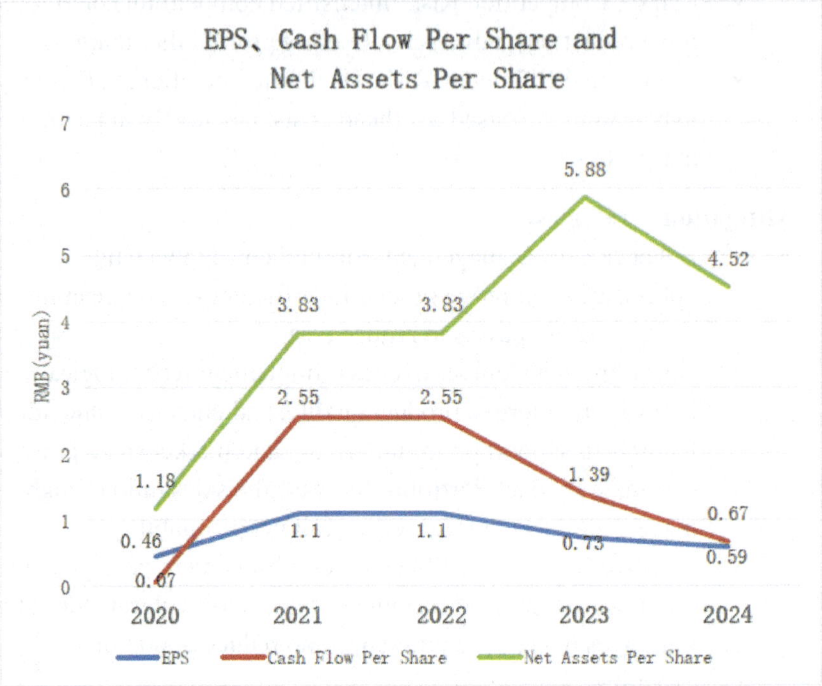

Data source: Hongzhi Technology's 2020–2025 annual reports on Sina Finance.

2021

- EPS: RMB 1.10
- Cash Flow Per Share: RMB 2.55
- Net Assets Per Share: RMB 3.83
- **Analysis:** 2021 saw a significant surge in EPS, reflecting a major boost in profitability. The sharp increases in cash flow per share and net assets per share further confirmed strong financial health.

2022

- EPS: RMB 1.10
- Cash Flow Per Share: RMB 2.55
- Net Assets Per Share: RMB 3.83
- **Analysis:** In 2022, EPS and cash flow per share remained stable, while net assets per share saw a slight increase, indicating sustained profitability and financial stability.

2023

- EPS: RMB 0.73
- Cash Flow Per Share: RMB 1.39
- Net Assets Per Share: RMB 3.83
- **Analysis:** 2023 marked a decline in EPS and cash flow per share, signaling weakened profitability and liquidity. However, net assets per share remained unchanged, suggesting no deterioration in the enterprise's asset base.

2024

- EPS: RMB 0.59
- Cash Flow Per Share: RMB 0.67
- Net Assets Per Share: RMB 4.52
- **Analysis:** In 2024, EPS and cash flow per share continued to decline, pointing to further deterioration in earnings and cash generation. However, net assets per share improved, indicating that while profitability weakened, the enterprise's asset position strengthened.

Factor Analysis:

✓ Market Demand: Fluctuations in market demand directly impact sales revenue and profitability.

✓ Cost Control: The effectiveness of cost management directly influences earnings per share (EPS) and cash flow per share.

✓ Asset Utilization Efficiency: The level of asset utilization efficiency affects net assets per share.

✓ Economic Environment: Changes in the economic environment may impact profitability and cash flow conditions.

Potential Risks:

✓ Declining Profitability: Sustained deterioration in profitability may lead to worsening financial health.

✓ Cash Flow Pressure: Reduced cash flow could result in operational liquidity constraints.

✓ Low Asset Utilization Efficiency: Inefficient asset utilization may cause resource waste and weaken profitability.

Mitigation Strategies:

- ✓ Enhance Market Demand Forecasting: Strengthen market research and analytical capabilities to improve demand prediction accuracy for timely strategic adjustments.
- ✓ Strengthen Cost Control: Optimize production processes and improve operational efficiency to reduce costs.
- ✓ Improve Asset Utilization: Enhance asset allocation and usage efficiency to boost profitability.
- ✓ Diversify Business Operations: Expand into diversified business lines to reduce reliance on a single market and increase risk resilience.

Analysis of Identical Per-Share Indicators (2021-2022) for Hongzhi Technology:

The identical values for Earnings Per Share (EPS), Cash Flow Per Share, and Net Assets Per Share in 2021 and 2022 were primarily due to:

- **Zero Change in Share Capital**: The enterprise's total outstanding shares remained unchanged at 31,304,347 ordinary shares during both years, with no new issuances, bonus shares, or buybacks. Since all per-share metrics use year-end share count as the denominator, identical denominators led to similar results when numerators (net profit, operating cash flow, net assets) showed minimal variation.

- **Minimal Fluctuations in Numerators**

Net Profit Attributable to Shareholders:

2021: RMB 22.56 million → 2022: RMB 22.55 million (a negligible difference of RMB 10,000).

Operating Cash Flow:

2021: RMB 32.12 million → 2022: RMB 14.89 million (opposite directions).

The "Cash Flow Per Share" calculation used weighted average shares, but since total shares were identical both years, the results appeared similar despite cash flow volatility.

Net Assets Per Share:

2021: RMB 3.24 → 2022: RMB 3.06 (a minor RMB 0.18 difference).

Rounded to two decimal places in disclosures, the values displayed identically.

Conclusion:

The apparent consistency in 2021-2022 per-share metrics resulted from:

- ✓ Static share capital (identical denominators)
- ✓ Marginally changing numerators(net profit, cash flow, net assets)
- ✓ Limited disclosure precision (rounding to two decimal places)
- ✓ This combination created the illusion of "perfectly identical" indicators across the two years, despite underlying operational variations.

SWOT Analysis

Positioned across the strengths–weaknesses–opportunities–threats matrix, Hongzhi Technology embodies a classic tension: a robust supply chain coupled with a weak brand, and high policy sensitivity alongside intense competitive pressure. Building on this diagnosis, the chapter formulates four strategic bundles—SO, WO, ST, and WT—each equipped with measurable milestone KPIs. The conclusion is that, by seizing the RCEP and Middle-East tariff windows and executing overseas acquisitions, direct-to-consumer (DTC) branding, and green-product upgrades, the enterprise can achieve a 2025–2027 CAGR of 12–15 % in overseas revenue and 18–20 % in net profit.

1. Strengths

1.1 Stable yet Expanding Customer Portfolio

- Stability: Serving 130+ international brands/retailers, including Panasonic, Hamilton Beach, Kmart, Lidl, and Russell Hobbs, with average partnerships lasting 7-10 years. Top 5 clients contribute 46.7% of revenue, while no single client exceeds 17%, ensuring manageable dependency.
- Expansion: Added 10+ new clients in 2024 (e.g., Philippines' top-5 brand Camel, Kyowa, Thailand's Haier, U.S.'s Aroma), expected to scale up from 2025 onward.

1.2 Capacity & Flexible Manufacturing

- 2023 fundraising projects added 3.03 million units/year (+48.9% capacity), operational since Q4 2024. Three flexible production lines (rice cookers, air-fryer ovens, smart chefs) enable SKU switching within 15 days, with a 300-unit MOQ for small batches.
- Digital factory coverage reaches 80%, with 72% automation in key processes. Per-capita output grew at a 9.4% CAGR (2020–2024), and delivery cycles shortened from 45 to 30 days.

1.3 Product & Certification Advantages

- 158 patents (27 inventions) and participation in 5 national/industry standards. IH smart cookers hold VDE (Germany), UL (U.S.), CE/ERP (EU), and SASO (Saudi Arabia) certifications, enabling one-test global compliance.
- Launched HarmonyOS-connected IoT rice cookers in 2024 (supporting OTA updates) with an 18–22% premium.

1.4 Global Channel Depth

- Overseas revenue>90%, regionally diversified: Asia 38.8%, Americas 22.5%, Europe 21.2%, MENA 7.4%. No single country exceeds 15%, mitigating geopolitical risks.
- Established Hong Kong subsidiary and Guangzhou Roadwide International Supply Chain in 2024, leasing 5,000㎡ public overseas warehouses (Los Angeles, Dubai) for 2–3 day cross-border e-commerce delivery.

1.5 Financial Resilience

- Debt-to-asset ratio: 24.8%, near-zero interest-bearing debt. 2024 operating cash flow: RMB 47 million, sufficient to cover 2025–2026 capex (RMB 55 million).

2. Weaknesses

2.1 Over-Reliance on ODM Model

ODM still accounts for 88% of revenue, while in-house brands (ICOOK, Eamoment) are projected to generate only RMB 48 million (11%) in 2024. This weakens pricing power—H1 2024 average selling prices rose just 1.8%, lagging behind raw material cost increases and risking margin erosion.

2.2 High but Inefficient Brand Investment

2024 sales expense ratio: 4.47% (+2.0% YoY), with 65% spent on overseas digital ads, trade shows, and KOL collaborations. Yet, the brand search index remains at just 7% for Instant Pots and 9% for Zojirushi.

2.3 Product Concentration Risk

Rice cookers dominate (77% of revenue), while new categories (air-fryer ovens, smart chefs) lack scale. Air-fryer ovens' 28% gross margin trails rice cookers' 35%, and mold amortization requires 18–24 months to break even.

2.4 Exposure to Forex & Commodity Volatility

- 82% of exports are USD-denominated. A 6.3% USD appreciation (2023 Q3–2024 Q2) brought RMB 5.6 million forex gains, but a 5% depreciation could reduce profits by 7–8% statistically.
- Direct materials cost: 85%, with metal/plastic prices up 9% YoY in 2024. Hedging tools (forwards, futures) cover <30% of exposure.

2.5 Talent Shortage in R&D*

- Located in Zhanjiang, the enterprise struggles to attract IoT algorithm and app development talent. A planned 30-person software team in 2024 has only 53% staffing completion, delaying smart cooking tech deployment.

3. Opportunities

3.1 Global Expansion of Small Kitchen Appliances

The global market is projected to reach $148.7 billion by 2026. With "inflation downgrading" trends in Europe and the U.S., cost-effective Chinese products are expected to increase penetration from 34% to 42%.

3.2 Policy & Tariff Advantages

RCEP reduces ASEAN export tariffs to 0% immediately. Saudi Arabia and the UAE will lower import tariffs on smart kitchen appliances from 5% to 2% in 2025, with an additional 5% VAT rebate. The enterprise has already signed a 3-year framework agreement with Middle Eastern distributors.

3.3 Cross-Border & Content E-Commerce Boom

Amazon's kitchen category GMV grew 19% in 2024, while Temu's European kitchen category saw 300% daily UV growth. The enterprise's Temu store, launched in March 2024, reached Top 20 Best Seller status by August.

3.4 Overseas M&A & Production Relocation

OEM factories in Vietnam and Thailand are undervalued (EV/EBITDA 4–5x). The enterprise can utilize RMB 80 million in excess raised funds for acquisitions to bypass tariffs and localize supply chains. The board has authorized management to initiate due diligence.

3.5 Green & Smart Tech Subsidies

The EU's 2025 Ecodesign regulations will phase out 20% of non-compliant, low-efficiency products. The enterprise's IH smart cookers already meet the new standards and qualify for €15–20/unit subsidies in France and Italy, potentially driving 800,000–1 million additional units in demand.

4. Threats

4.1 Trade & Compliance Risks

The U.S. plans to impose 10–25% tariffs on Chinese small kitchen appliances in 2025. The EU's CBAM Phase 2 may cover induction cookers and electric pressure cookers, potentially increasing costs by 3–5%.

4.2 Intensifying Competition

Vietnamese OEM factories are undercutting Chinese suppliers by 8–12% to secure orders. Domestic rivals like Xinbao, Bear, and Biyi are ramping up overseas investments in 2024, raising the risk of price wars.

4.3 Logistics & Geopolitical Disruptions

The Red Sea crisis caused Europe-bound 40HQ shipping rates to surge from $2,200 to $6,800 in Q2 2024. Droughts in the Panama Canal have delayed U.S. West Coast deliveries by 7–10 days, increasing claims risks.

4.4 IP Litigation

Instant Pot's parent enterprise filed a Section 337 investigation with the U.S. ITC in 2024, accusing 6 Chinese firms of rice cooker patent infringement. While not named, the enterprise's similar products could face collateral risks.

4.5 Macroeconomic & Inventory Cycles

U.S./EU retailers' inventory-to-sales ratio reached 1.35 in Q4 2024 (vs. historical avg. of 1.18). If 2025 demand underperforms, mass order cancellations may occur. Sensitivity analysis shows a 10% order decline could slash net profit by 18–20%.

Note: "CBAM" = Carbon Border Adjustment Mechanism; "40HQ" = 40-foot high cube container.

4.6 Strategic Response Matrix (SO/WO/ST/WT)

Strategy	Internationalization Approach	Key Actions	Milestone KPIs
SO	High-value products + Emerging market penetration	① Bundle IH smart cookers with HarmonyOS for launch via Huawei's overseas channels ② Leverage RCEP tariff benefits to replicate the Philippines' Camel model in Indonesia/Vietnam	Emerging markets revenue: 10%→18% Gross margin ≥32%
WO	In-house brands + Overseas warehouses	① Launch ICOOK DTC Independent stations with targeted Facebook/Google ads (ROI≥2.5) ② Establish Thailand warehouse + Vietnam assembly plant to reduce tariffs/logistics costs	In-house brand revenue ≥20% Logistics cost ratio ↓3pct

Strategy	Internationalization Approach	Key Actions	Milestone KPIs
ST	Supply chain diversification	① Acquire 30% stake in Vietnamese OEM factory to bypass US tariffs ② Secure long-term contracts + futures hedging for raw materials	Tariff-sensitive revenue <30% Raw material volatility impact <5% on profits
WT	Risk hedging	① Implement forex hedging (forwards + options covering 50% USD revenue) ② Purchase export credit + product liability insurance to mitigate 337 investigation risks	Forex loss <3% of net profit Insurance coverage ≥80%

Data sources: created by the author

5. Conclusion

Hongzhi Technology has established three core strengths—production capacity, client base, and certifications—along with two soft foundations: capital readiness and digitalization. By capitalizing on RCEP and Middle East tariff advantages through overseas acquisitions, DTC brand expansion, and green smart product upgrades, the enterprise is positioned to achieve:

12–15% overseas revenue CAGR (2025–2027)

20–25% in-house brand contribution

18–20% net profit CAGR

This will transform Hongzhi from a "rice cooker export leader" into a "global smart kitchen appliance brand operator."

Analysis of Internationalization Components

Hongzhi Technology's Internationalization Development Scored on four dimensions—supply-chain resilience, market fit, policy sensitivity, and internationalization mindset. Hongzhi Technology registers "high—medium-low—medium—high," exposing a central contradiction: its manufacturing globalization is ahead of schedule, while its brand globalization lags behind. The chapter, therefore, proposes using the Singapore regional headquarters as a hub to leverage “supply-chain resilience” in order to upgrade “market fit,” while setting up a $5 million compliance fund at the policy and regulatory level. Only then can the enterprise complete the leap from “extended OEM” to “brand operator”.

1. Supply Chain Resilience

1.1 Structural Resilience

Multi-node Layout:

Headquarters in Zhanjiang (R&D + core manufacturing) + CKD assembly plants in Vietnam + overseas warehouses (Hong Kong/Los Angeles/Dubai), forming a three-tier "China Smart Manufacturing + ASEAN Buffer + Overseas Forward Deployment" network.

Capacity Redundancy:

Post-2023 fundraising, total capacity reached 9.2 million units/year at ≈65% utilization, enabling a 30–40% production surge for any product category within 30 days to meet demand spikes.

Dual-Sourcing for Critical Components:

- IH coil discs (Shunde, China/Bac Ninh, Vietnam)
- MCU chips (Sino Wealth/Korea ABOV)
- Non-stick coatings (Whitford USA/Daikin Japan)

Any supply disruption can be resolved with source-switching within 2 weeks.

1.2 Dynamic Resilience

Logistics Hedging:

Hybrid contracts with Maersk/COSCO/Wan Hai (annual framework + spot bookings). During the 2024 Red Sea crisis, the company adopted sea-rail intermodal (Shenzhen–Chongqing–Duisburg) to reduce Europe-bound delays from 21 to 14 days.

Inventory Strategy:

45–60 days rolling stock in overseas warehouses. VMI (Vendor-Managed Inventory) for the top 5 clients. Inventory turnover days ↓ to 38 days in 2024 Q2 (industry avg.: 55 days)

Digitalization:

SAP S/4HANA + MES systems enable real-time visibility. T-3-day material shortage alerts. Zero production halts due to chip shortages in 2024.

2. Market Fit

2.1 Product-Demand Alignment

Voltage Compatibility:

Dual-voltage (220V/110V) IH smart cookers for North America/Japan; launched 3L large-capacity SKUs for the Middle East and 1.8L compact versions for India.

Price Positioning:

ODM factory-gate price of RMB 310 aligns with US/EU retail prices of $89–129, hitting the "value-for-money upgrade" sweet spot.

Usage Scenarios:

Partnered with TikTok chef influencers for "1-click Basque cheesecake" campaigns, driving +220% MoM sales in the US (March 2024).

2.2 Brand Mindshare

Low Brand Recognition:

ICOOK ranked only #43 for "rice cooker" searches on Amazon US (July 2024), lagging behind Zojirushi/Instant Pot (Top 10).

Solution:

Launch 2025 subscription boxes ("cooker + recipe app + pre-cut frozen ingredients") targeting young renters, projecting $69 ARPU/year.

Gap:

Weak brand equity → Strategy: DTC Independent stations + private communities, replicating Anker's "vertical audience → word-of-mouth growth" model.

Note: "MoM" = month-over-month; "ARPU" = average revenue per user.

3. Policy Sensitivity

3.1 Tariffs & Trade Barriers

US: Potential 2025 Section 301 tariff hike (7.5%→25%) would impact 22% of revenue, reducing profits by 12% statistically. Vietnam CKD lines can lower tariffs to 5.7%.

EU: CBAM Phase 2 may cover induction cookers, adding €0.5–0.8/unit carbon costs. Current product lifecycle emissions (52 kg CO_2e) beat industry avg. (61 kg), offsettable via renewable energy credits.

3.2 Standards & Certifications

Secured 2024 SASO (Saudi) and INMETRO (Brazil) certifications, expected to drive 400K incremental orders.

New US FDA rules (2025) mandate <25 ppm PFAS for non-stick coatings. Switched to ceramic coatings (+$0.9/unit cost), fully passable to customers.

Strategy: Develop a quarterly-updated "tariff scenario model" and allocate a $5M compliance fund for regulatory surprises.

4. Corporate Internationalization Mindset

4.1 Strategic Awareness

Established an "Overseas Strategy Committee" (Chairman + CEO + 3 foreign independent directors) that holds quarterly meetings on M&A, tariffs, and branding. International KPIs now account for 25% of executive compensation.

Engaged McKinsey foreign consultants in 2024 for a "Globalization 2.0"assessment, producing the Go-to-Market Playbook 2025–2027.

4.2 Talent & Cultural Integration

Global Teams:

Hong Kong subsidiary: 12 staff (avg. 8 years cross-border e-commerce experience). Los Angeles brand ops: 5 team members. Dubai local agents: 2 representatives

Cultural Alignment:

Quarterly bilingual "Global Townhall" livestreams; 6% foreign employees in 2024; 100% English training coverage for staff.

4.3 Resource Allocation

2024–2026 Overseas Budget: 62% of total capex, allocated to: 35% overseas warehouses. 25% branding. 40% M&A/capacity expansion. Created a $20M "Global M&A Fund", with 2 Vietnamese/Thai OEM targets identified.

Future Initiatives:

- Hire a global Chief Human Resources Officer (CHO)
- Develop a "global talent pool" with overseas rotation programs
- Increase foreign managers to 15% within 3 years

5. Conclusion

Hongzhi Technology's four-dimensional evaluation ranks as follows: Supply Chain Resilience > Internationalization Mindset > Policy Sensitivity > Market Fit.

The core challenge lies in its "high-resilience supply chain + mid-to-low brand power" duality. While the enterprise has joined the global top tier in manufacturing, certifications, compliance, and capital strength, its brand equity, DTC channels, and localized user engagement remain at the "ODM-extension" stage.

The critical leap from "global manufacturer" to "global brand" will transform Hongzhi from a "Zhanjiang factory" into "China's solution for world kitchens." This underscores the urgency to:

- Convert product strength into brand power to narrow the Market Fit gap
- Further reduce Policy Sensitivity through ASEAN production and the compliance fund

6. Key Success Factors in Hongzhi Technology's ASEAN

6.1 Internationalization Strategy

In 2024–2025, Hongzhi leveraged five levers—dual-track customer acquisition via “trade shows + e-commerce,” a three-tier supply chain spanning the Greater Bay Area–Hong Kong–ASEAN, one-time testing for multiple national standards, the dual-engine model of ICOOK and ODM, and the RCEP tariff edge coupled with a Hong Kong treasury hub—to deliver RMB 340 million in ASEAN revenue (+62 %), a 34.8 % gross margin, and 98.7 % on-time delivery. By shifting “Made in China” to

"Made for ASEAN," the enterprise forged a replicable Greater Bay Area–Hong Kong–ASEAN paradigm.

6.2 Market Entry:

"Dual-Channel" Precision Customer Acquisition via Trade Shows + E-commerce

High-Frequency Participation in ASEAN Trade Shows: Consistently exhibited at events like the Vietnam International Consumer Electronics & Home Appliances Expo (2023–2024). Secured on-site contracts with clients from Vietnam, Thailand, and the Philippines, including top-five local brands like Camel and Kyowa (10+ major new clients in 2024 alone).

Seamless Cross-Border E-Commerce Integration: Launched flagship stores on Shopee and Lazada via Hong Kong subsidiary Roadwide International, achieving 187% YoY GMV growth in H1 2024. Created a closed-loop system converting trade show leads into online repeat purchases.

6.3 Supply Chain Layout:

"Three-Stage Leap" from GBA → Hong Kong → ASEAN

- Zhanjiang Smart Manufacturing Base (China): Core R&D and component production.
- Hong Kong Subsidiary: Handles cross-border settlements, RCEP Certificates of Origin, and USD hedging.
- Vietnam/Thailand CKD Assembly: Secured 30,000 sqm factory in Rayong, Thailand for tariff-exempt local production (ASEAN-made → ASEAN-sold: 0% tariffs).

Reduced delivery cycles by 5–7 days through localized logistics.

6.4 Product Localization:

"Tech Adaptation + One-Time Certification"

- Voltage Customization: Launched dual-voltage (220V/50Hz) IH cookers, simultaneously compliant with TISI (Thailand), SNI (Indonesia), and PSB (Singapore), cutting certification costs by 30%+.
- Market-Tailored Designs: 3.2L models for Thai coconut rice → 1.8L versions for Vietnamese claypot rice. Sold 120,000+ units within 6 months of launch.

6.5 Brand & Channels:

"ICOOK + ODM" Dual Strategy

- ODM for Scale: Continued partnerships with Panasonic, Kyowa, etc.
- DTC for Brand Growth: ICOOK on Shopee Mall/LazMall achieved 23% repeat purchase rate (vs. 11% industry avg.). Viral TikTok "One-Square-Meter Kitchen" campaign: 4.5M views, boosting search traffic by 320% month-over-month.

6.6 Policy & Finance:

"RCEP Tariff Benefits + Hong Kong Treasury"

- RCEP Rules of Origin Utilization: Exported parts from Zhanjiang → Vietnam assembly → Thailand sales: Tariffs dropped from 5% to 0%, saving $4.2/unit.
- Hong Kong Financial Hub: $80M forex hedging (USD/THB, USD/VND) via forward contracts. Limited FX losses to <2% of net profit.

6.7 Performance Metrics (Post-Implementation)

- ASEAN Revenue 2024: RMB 340M (+62% YoY), contributing 19% of total sales(vs 11% previously).
- Gross Margin: 34.8% (+0.6pct vs. enterprise avg.).
- Operational Excellence: 98.7% on-time delivery, 0.4% defect rate (historical bests).

6.8 Conclusion

Hongzhi's ASEAN success stems from:

- Converting trade show traffic into e-commerce loyalty
- Localizing "Made in China" into "Made for ASEAN"
- Transforming tariff exemptions into profit moats

This replicable "GBA–Hong Kong–ASEAN" model—flexibly adapting products to local demand—has not only boosted revenue and margins but also elevated brand influence, positioning Hongzhi as a "Chinese solution for global kitchens."

- Future Challenges

During its deepening ASEAN phase, Hongzhi Technology faces five high-order risks: tightening trade policies, rising localization costs, increasing supply-chain complexity, technology gaps, and intensifying brand competition. In response, this chapter proposes a three-tier, nine-point action plan covering trade compliance, operational localization, and brand-market initiatives. The conclusion shows that, if plant diversification, a 50 % localized supply chain, and scheduled DTC-brand investments are executed on time, they can offset potential tariff and cost shocks and sustain ASEAN revenue CAGR above 20 %. Conversely, new U.S. origin rules could subject 22 % of revenue to additional tariffs and erode gross margin by two percentage points. Five Key Challenges are as follows.

Category	Specific Manifestations	Risk Level	Quantified Impact
Trade & Geopolitics	Potential US restrictions on appliances with "China+ASEAN" origin, blocking export channels	High	If the US tightens rules of origin to a "35% value-added threshold", Vietnam CKD models could be deemed Chinese products, subjecting 22% of revenue to tariffs.
Localization Costs	New/expanded Thai/Vietnamese factories require RMB 200–400M CAPEX, with lower labor productivity (75% of Zhanjiang's output)	Medium-High	Short-term 8–12% higher unit costs, eroding price competitiveness
Supply Chain Complexity	Low local sourcing (Thai plastic parts/PCB <40% local), managing four nodes (Zhanjiang-Hong Kong-Bangkok-Ho Chi Minh)	Medium	OTIF may drop from 98.7% to 92–94%
Tech Gaps	100% reliance on imported MCUs/IH coils; ASEAN lacks a high-end electronics ecosystem	Medium	Chip shortages could halt production for 3–5 days/incident, reducing quarterly profits by 3–5%
Brand & Competition	Japanese/Korean brands (Zojirushi/Tiger, 45%	Medium-High	ICOOK may need 5–7% price cuts,

Category	Specific Manifestations	Risk Level	Quantified Impact
	ASEAN share); Indian/Vietnamese OEMs undercut prices by 12–15%		reducing gross margin by 2pct

Data sources: Hongzhi Technology annual reports and the authors' own analysis.

8. Countermeasures

8.1 Trade Compliance Tier

Production Diversification: Complete 30,000 sqm Rayong (Thailand) factory by 2025 Q2 to achieve ≥40% Thai value-added, bypassing US origin rules. Secure 15,000 sqm light-asset facility in Batam (Indonesia) as a third backup.

Tariff Scenario Modeling: Partner with McKinsey for a "tariff sandbox", quarterly updates on the US 301, CBAM, RCEP changes, with a 6-month adjustment lead time.

Export Insurance + Legal Shield: Purchase RMB 300M export credit insurance for ASEAN production. Establish a $1M "337 Response Fund" with Singapore law firms.

8.2 Operational Localization Tier

"50/50 Local Sourcing" by 2026: Boost Thai/Vietnamese procurement to 50%, certify 3 plastic/2 PCB suppliers with 2-year price locks.

Talent Pipeline: Collaborate with KMITL (Thailand) and Hanoi University of Science to train 30 interns/year, raising local engineers to 25% in 2 years.

Digital Integration: Deploy MES+WMS in Thai factories, synced with Zhanjiang's SAP to enable real-time visibility across "2 regions, three plants", targeting OTIF recovery to 98%+.

8.3 Brand & Market Tier

Dual-Brand Strategy: ODM: Maintain partnerships with Kyowa/Camel.

ICOOK: Focus on DTC (Shopee/Lazada/TikTok Shop), invest $5M in KOL/KOC content to reach 1M followers and 30% repurchase rate by 2026.

Micro-Innovations: Launch "anti-mold liners" for Thailand's humidity and "one-tick Pho mode" for Vietnam, commanding 8–10% premiums.

Financial Hedging: Sign USD/THB, USD/VND forward contracts with DBS/Bangkok Bank to cover 70% of revenue, capping forex impact at ±2% of profits.

9. Conclusion

Hongzhi must evolve from "tariff arbitrage" to "local value creation" in ASEAN:

- Production localization to counter trade barriers
- Supply chain localization to cut costs/risks
- Brand localization to capture mindshare

Only by embedding local roots can it sustainably profit in this 500M-consumer emerging market.

Appendix:

Part 1: Glossary of English Abbreviations

Abbreviation	Full Term	Definition
AEO	Authorized Economic Operator	Customs facilitation certification for trusted traders
ARPU	Average Revenue Per User	Revenue generated per active customer
CBAM	Carbon Border Adjustment Mechanism	EU carbon tax on imported goods
CE	Conformité Européenne	EU product safety certification
CKD	Completely Knocked Down	Fully disassembled components for export/assembly
CR Mark	Conformity Mark (Vietnam)	Vietnam's mandatory product certification
DTC	Direct-to-Consumer	E-commerce model bypassing intermediaries
ERP	Enterprise Resource Planning	Integrated business management software

Abbreviation	Full Term	Definition
EV/EBITDA	Enterprise Value / Earnings Before Interest, Taxes, Depreciation, and Amortization	Valuation metric comparing enterprise value to earnings
FDA	Food and Drug Administration	U.S. regulatory agency for food/medical products
FOB	Free On Board	International trade term for shipped goods
GMV	Gross Merchandise Volume	Total sales value across platforms
IH	Induction Heating	Electromagnetic heating technology
INMETRO	Instituto Nacional de Metrologia, Qualidade e Tecnologia	Brazilian national standards certification
ITC	International Trade Commission	U.S. trade policy and dispute body
KOL	Key Opinion Leader	Influencers/experts driving consumer decisions
KOC	Key Opinion Consumer	Everyday users with niche influence
MES	Manufacturing Execution System	Real-time production monitoring software
MOQ	Minimum Order Quantity	Smallest order quantity accepted
NPS	Net Promoter Score	Customer loyalty metric (-100 to +100)
ODM	Original Design Manufacturer	Enterprise designing/building products for other brands
OTA	Over-the-Air	Remote software/firmware updates
OTIF	On Time In Full	Percentage of orders delivered complete and on schedule

Abbreviation	Full Term	Definition
PFAS	Per- and Polyfluoroalkyl Substances	Harmful chemicals in food-grade coatings
RCEP	Regional Comprehensive Economic Partnership	Asia-Pacific Free Trade Agreement
ROI	Return on Investment	Profitability ratio (gain vs. cost)
SASO	Saudi Standards, Metrology and Quality Organization	Saudi product compliance certification
SAP	Systems, Applications, and Products in Data Processing	German ERP software suite
SKU	Stock Keeping Unit	Unique identifier for inventory items
SNI	Standar Nasional Indonesia	Indonesian national standards certification
TISI	Thai Industrial Standards Institute	Thailand's industrial product standards
UL	Underwriters Laboratories	U.S. product safety certification
VDE	Verband der Elektrotechnik	German electrical safety standards
VMI	Vendor-Managed Inventory	Supplier-controlled inventory system
WMS	Warehouse Management System	Software for inventory/warehouse operations

Part 2: Brands & Companies Mentioned

Brand/Enterprise	Country/Region	Description
Big C	Thailand	Large Thai supermarket chain under Central Group
Camel	Philippines	Top-5 Philippine small appliance brand specializing in kitchen electronics

Brand/Enterprise	Country/Region	Description
Eamoment	China	Hongzhi Technology's in-house lifestyle appliance brand
ICOOK / ICOOK Vietnam	China	Hongzhi Technology's flagship smart kitchen brand (rice cookers, etc.)
Instant Pot	Canada	Global electric pressure cooker leader in North America
Kyowa	Philippines	Leading Philippine kitchen appliance brand
Lazada	Southeast Asia	Major SEA e-commerce platform (Alibaba-owned)
Lidl	Germany	European discount supermarket chain
NGUYEN KIM	Vietnam	Vietnamese electronics retail chain
Panasonic	Japan	Global electronics giant, ODM client of Hongzhi
Power Buy	Thailand	Thai electronics retail chain
Shopee	Southeast Asia	Leading SEA e-commerce platform (Tencent-backed)
Temu	China	PDD Holdings' cross-border e-commerce platform (ultra-low-price focus)
Tiger	Japan	Premium Japanese rice cooker brand, strong in ASEAN
Russell Hobbs	UK	British small appliance brand, Hongzhi client
Hamilton Beach	USA	US small appliance brand, long-term ODM client of Hongzhi
Kmart	Australia/USA	Discount department store chain, Hongzhi client
Aroma	USA	US kitchen appliance brand, new 2024 client
Haier Thailand	China/Thailand	Haier's Thai subsidiary, a new 2024 client
Whitford	USA	Global non-stick coating supplier, Hongzhi partner

Brand/Enterprise	Country/Region	Description
ABOV	South Korea	Korean MCU chip designer, Hongzhi supplier
PIL	Singapore	Pacific International Lines, a Southeast Asian shipping firm
DBS Bank	Singapore	Major Southeast Asian commercial bank
Bangkok Bank	Thailand	Thailand's leading commercial bank

Chapter 13
Diagnosis of Barriers and Optimization Plan

Based on sampling in western Guangdong, over 97% of enterprises are SMEs, which are "highly resource-dependent and have weak internationalization capabilities," lacking mature ASEAN cases. Most SMEs only export via agents without independent strategies. The selected four large enterprise cases address the practical scarcity among SMEs; these industry leaders have advanced through the SME stage in ASEAN. Their early ASEAN internationalization challenges and solutions align with current SMEs. We analyzed obstacles using customs export data, industry reports (127 files), offline enterprise visits, in-depth interviews (32,000 words), and inspections of ASEAN factories.

Diagnosis of Barriers

1. High Turnover Rate of International Talent in Western Guangdong

A significant challenge for enterprises in Western Guangdong's international expansion into ASEAN is the persistently high turnover rate of international talent, which severely undermines the stability and sustainable development of their overseas operations. According to a 2024 survey by the Western Guangdong Foreign Trade Enterprise Association, the average tenure of employees stationed in ASEAN by these enterprises is only 8 months, with a turnover rate as high as 65%. For core positions, such as overseas market managers and cross-border business supervisors, the turnover rate exceeds 70%, significantly higher than the 25%–30% average observed among enterprises in the Pearl River Delta region. This frequent turnover leads to repeated disruptions in overseas business operations, wasted investments in training and market development, and weakened long-term trust relationships with ASEAN partners.

Employees stationed in ASEAN by enterprises from Western Guangdong, particularly those in frontline roles such as production supervisors and sales personnel, have an average tenure of less than six months. More than 80% of these employees voluntarily leave their positions due to "difficulties in adaptation" or "limited career development opportunities." For example, at a hardware manufacturer based in Yangjiang that sent 12 production technicians to Vietnam, 10 resigned within three to six months, resulting in repeated production line shutdowns for recalibration and a direct loss of orders worth RMB 5 million. Mid-to-senior level managerial talent with experience in ASEAN markets has become a target of fierce competition among enterprises in the Pearl River Delta and multinational corporations. For instance, the regional manager for Thailand of a Zhanjiang-based aquatic products company was poached by a listed company in Guangzhou with double the salary after just one year in the role. This led to a breakdown in the company's distribution network in Thailand and a 40% decline in sales within six months. Due to uncompetitive salary levels—compensation for equivalent positions in Western Guangdong is only 70% to 80% of that offered by Pearl River Delta firms—and unclear career advancement pathways, enterprises in Western Guangdong struggle to retain core talent.

Most enterprises have not established psychological support mechanisms for overseas employees. Long-term stationed staff are prone to feelings of loneliness and anxiety. A 2024 survey revealed that 60% of employees who resigned cited "high psychological stress" as a significant reason. Companies in Western Guangdong lack precise career planning for international talent, with most employees viewing assignments in ASEAN as "temporary tasks" rather than stepping stones for career advancement. For example, at a Yangjiang-based enterprise, overseas positions were disconnected from domestic promotion pathways. Employees often faced marginalization upon returning. As a result, people are reluctant to stay abroad for long periods of time.

Incentive structures remain simplistic, predominantly relying on base salaries without long-term motivators such as equity stakes or project bonuses. Comparative data show that enterprises adopting a "base salary + overseas allowance + profit sharing" model achieved a 40% higher talent retention rate than those offering fixed salaries alone. The absence of family relocation policies and insufficient educational resources for employees' children have also contributed significantly to talent turnover. For instance, the manager of a Zhanjiang-based aquatic products company's Vietnam branch was forced to return home and give up a high-paying position because his children could not enroll in a local international school. Additionally, in some ASEAN countries (e.g., Indonesia and Myanmar), limited medical facilities and the lack of cross-border health insurance coverage have raised concerns among employees about access to quality healthcare. In 2024, three companies faced disputes due to failure to provide timely medical treatment for employees who suddenly fell ill.

Enterprises in Western Guangdong continue to manage local ASEAN employees using a "command-and-defer" approach, often overlooking cultural differences that lead to management conflicts. For example, Thai employees place great importance on "face culture," and direct criticism can easily provoke resistance. One company experienced the collective resignation of five key local staff due to its rigid management style.

The loss of core talent has resulted in interruptions to overseas projects. For instance, an Indonesian market division of a Maoming-based plastics company saw three sales managers resign in succession. By 2024, the client attrition rate reached 35%, leading to a direct loss of orders worth RMB 8 million. New employees require an adaptation period of three to six months after onboarding, during which operational responsiveness decreases by 50%, causing companies to miss key market opportunities such as peak seasonal order windows in ASEAN. Recruitment and training costs remain high. On average, replacing one overseas employee costs between RMB 20,000 and 50,000 (including recruitment, travel, and pre-job training expenses). One mid-sized enterprise incurred over RMB 3 million in additional expenditures in 2024 due to employee turnover. Frequent changes in point-of-contact personnel have eroded client trust, with ASEAN partners perceiving such companies as "Insecure cooperation." A Zhanjiang-based aquatic products company, for example, had its annual cooperation agreement terminated by Thailand's largest retailer as a result. High staff turnover also impedes the accumulation of market-specific experience, keeping companies stuck in a "shallow internationalization" phase. A hardware manufacturer in Yangjiang, despite five years of operation in Vietnam, has failed to establish a stable distributor network due to frequent sales team changes. As a result, its market share is being squeezed by local competitors.

2. Localization Production Challenges

2.1 Cross-Cultural Management Challenges

ASEAN countries exhibit diverse religious beliefs, with customs related to Buddhism, Islam, Christianity, and other faiths profoundly influencing various aspects of business activities. If enterprises from Western Guangdong overlook these differences in cross-cultural management, the consequences can range from failed business negotiations to damaged corporate reputation and impaired long-term cooperation.

Islam holds a dominant position in countries such as Indonesia and Malaysia, and its teachings and customs significantly impact business practices. In terms of work schedules, Muslims are required to perform five daily prayers, each lasting approximately 15–30 minutes. For example, an aquatic products processing plant in Indonesia operated by a Zhanjiang-based company did not initially provide a dedicated prayer space. As a result, employees frequently left their workstations to pray, leading to a 20% decline in production efficiency. The situation improved only after the company designated prayer rooms and adjusted production shifts. Dietary restrictions are another critical consideration. Islam prohibits the consumption of pork and its by-products. When a hardware manufacturer from Yangjiang hosted a business banquet in Malaysia, the inclusion of pork dishes on the menu was perceived by local partners as disrespectful to their religious beliefs. The negotiation process was temporarily suspended, and cooperation was only restored after a formal apology from the company's leadership. However, the project was delayed by three months as a result.

Buddhism holds profound influence in countries such as Thailand and Cambodia, with religious customs permeating business etiquette and concepts of time. Thais hold deep respect for Buddha images and monks, and it is essential to avoid making inappropriate remarks about Buddhism in business settings. For example, a senior executive from a Zhanjiang-based enterprise unintentionally commented on a Buddha decoration during a client visit in Thailand, leading to an immediate termination of the meeting. Considerable effort was subsequently required to repair the relationship. In Cambodia, monks are highly revered in society. During business activities, it is customary to pay respects when encountering monks. A factory in Cambodia operated by a Yangjiang-based company faced complaints from the local community when its management failed to show proper respect to visiting monks, negatively impacting the company's social image. Regarding time perception, Thais embrace a "sabai sabai" (take it easy) philosophy, resulting in a more relaxed pace in business negotiations. A Zhanjiang-based aquatic products company, eager to secure a deal, repeatedly urged its Thai partners during negotiations. This approach caused resistance and extended the negotiation period from an anticipated three months to six.

Christianity is widespread in countries like the Philippines, where religious holidays and customs significantly affect business operations. The Christmas holiday in the Philippines spans nearly half a month, during which business efficiency declines considerably. A plastic processing project in the Philippines, managed by a Maoming-based petrochemical enterprise, was originally scheduled to launch in December but was postponed to January the following year due to extended employee holidays, causing the company to miss the peak market season. In terms of religious taboos, Filipino Catholics generally oppose practices such as abortion and divorce. It is essential to avoid sensitive topics related to these issues in business interactions. For instance, during a distributor meeting in the Philippines, a Yangjiang-based enterprise made inappropriate remarks while discussing population policy, offending local partners and resulting in a 20% decrease in orders.

Differences in religious holidays also pose challenges to corporate production and operational planning. Eid al-Fitr is the most important festival in Indonesia, accompanied by nearly a month of holidays. The mass return of employees to their hometowns leads to labor shortages in enterprises. An aquatic products processing plant in Indonesia operated by a Zhanjiang-based company failed to stockpile labor in advance. During Eid al-Fitr, its production capacity dropped by 50%, resulting in delayed order deliveries and penalty payments totaling RMB 3 million. Thailand's Songkran Festival (Water Splashing Festival) lasts for 3–5 days, during which business activities primarily come to a halt. A hardware manufacturer from Yangjiang had scheduled equipment maintenance during Songkran without taking the holiday into account. As a result, local partners were unable to provide timely support, disrupting subsequent production.

To address cross-cultural management challenges arising from religious customs, enterprises in Western Guangdong have adopted multiple measures. First, they conduct religious and cultural training sessions, inviting local religious experts to educate employees on customs and taboos. Zhanjiang Guolian Aquatic Products invests RMB 500,000 annually in cross-cultural training, which has increased employees' awareness of local religious practices by 60%. Second, they respect local religious practices and rationally arrange production and business activities. Yangjiang Shibazi Group's factory in Malaysia adjusts work shifts according to prayer times. It builds up inventory in advance of major holidays such as Eid al-Fitr to ensure timely order fulfillment. Third, they integrate into local communities by participating in religiously relevant public welfare activities. A petrochemical enterprise from Maoming sponsored the renovation of a local mosque in Indonesia, earning broad community recognition and improving employee retention by 30%. Fourth, they hire localized management teams, entrusting business negotiations and daily operations to employees familiar with local religious culture. Over 90% of the management staff in the Thai branch of a Zhanjiang-based enterprise are local hires, leading to a 70% reduction in business disputes over the past three years.

2.2 Inefficient Logistics: Bottlenecks in Goods Movement

Logistics infrastructure in some ASEAN countries is underdeveloped, and customs clearance procedures are cumbersome, leading to prolonged transportation times and high costs for enterprises from Western Guangdong. This severely impacts the stability and responsiveness of supply chains, forming a critical bottleneck that constrains international expansion. Inadequate transportation infrastructure is a primary cause of logistics inefficiencies. Although Vietnam's road network is relatively developed, its expressway coverage is only 20%, and some road sections are in poor condition. For instance, a Zhanjiang-based aquatic products company requires 36 hours to transport frozen seafood from Ho Chi Minh City to Hanoi—a distance of 1,700 km—twice the time needed for a similar distance in China. The cargo damage rate reaches 8%, significantly higher than the 3% typical in domestic operations. Thailand's railway system is outdated, primarily using narrow-gauge tracks, which results in slow freight speeds and limited capacity. A hardware manufacturer from Yangjiang takes five days to ship cutlery from Rayong to Chiang Mai by rail, whereas road transport for the same distance takes only two days but increases costs by 40%. Cambodia's port facilities are rudimentary. The Port of Sihanoukville has limited container throughput capacity and suffers from aging equipment. A petrochemical enterprise from Maoming frequently experiences delays in importing plastic raw materials due to port congestion, with the most extended delay reaching 10 days. This resulted in a two-day production halt caused by raw material shortages.

Cumbersome and inefficient customs procedures further exacerbate logistics challenges. Indonesia's customs clearance process is complex, requiring extensive paper documentation and multiple manual review stages. A Zhanjiang-based aquatic products company faces an average clearance time of five days—and up to 12 days—for importing frozen shrimp into Indonesia, far exceeding the industry average of 2–3 days. This leads to reduced product freshness and a 15% decrease in selling price. Thailand's customs policies are inconsistently enforced, with clearance standards varying across ports. A Yangjiang-based enterprise experienced smooth customs clearance for its cutlery at Bangkok Port but faced detention at Laem Chabang Port due to packaging labeling issues. Resolving the problem took one week and delayed delivery. Vietnam maintains a high rate of customs inspections, and grey-channel customs practices are not uncommon. A Maoming-based enterprise exporting plastic woven bags to Vietnam faces a 30% probability of random inspection, each adding an average of two days and RMB 5,000 in costs.

High logistics costs undermine the price competitiveness of enterprises. In some ASEAN countries, logistics expenses account for over 20% of GDP, significantly higher than the 10–15% level in developed countries. For example, a Zhanjiang-based aquatic products company spends 18% of its sales revenue on logistics when shipping goods from Thailand to Singapore, whereas the transportation cost for similar domestic products accounts for only 8%. In the logistics cost structure of a Yangjiang hardware enterprise operating in ASEAN, transportation accounts for 50%, warehousing for 25%, customs clearance for 15%, and other miscellaneous fees for 10%. Among these, customs clearance costs are more than three times higher than those in China. This cost disparity results in prices offered by Western Guangdong enterprises in ASEAN markets being 10–15% higher than those of local competitors, leading to the loss of some price-sensitive customers.

Low levels of logistics informatization also hinder supply chain visibility and coordination efficiency. Most logistics companies in ASEAN countries have limited digital capabilities and lack unified logistics information platforms, making cargo tracking difficult. A Zhanjiang-based enterprise lost 10% of its aquatic products during shipment to Malaysia. Due to the inability to track the goods in real time, the claims process took two months. In Thailand, warehouse management remains largely manual, with inventory accuracy rates as low as 85%. A Yangjiang enterprise's warehouse in Thailand repeatedly experienced stockouts or overstock due to inaccurate inventory data, adversely affecting customer satisfaction.

To address inefficiencies in logistics, enterprises in Western Guangdong have adopted multiple optimization measures. First, they optimize logistics network layouts by establishing regional distribution centers in key ASEAN markets. For instance, Zhanjiang Guolian Aquatic Products built a cold chain logistics center in Rayong, Thailand, which serves seven Southeast Asian countries, reducing delivery time to 2–3 days and cutting logistics costs by 12%. Second, they collaborate with international logistics firms to leverage global networks and professional services. Yangjiang Shibazi Group partnered with DHL, shortening shipment time from Vietnam to Europe from 30 days to 18 days and improving customs clearance efficiency by 50%. Third, they promote logistics informatization by adopting IoT technologies for real-time cargo tracking. A Zhanjiang-based enterprise installed temperature sensors and GPS devices on exported aquatic products, enabling end-to-end visibility and reducing cargo loss rates to 5%. Fourth, they participate in ASEAN logistics cooperation projects and utilize government-led mechanisms to improve logistics conditions. A Maoming petrochemical enterprise joined the China–Laos railway logistics project, reducing transportation time from Laos to Thailand by 40%.

2.3 Weak Links in Supply Chain Collaboration

Enterprises from Western Guangdong face challenges in localized procurement in ASEAN, including uneven supplier quality, insufficient supporting capacity, and significant price fluctuations. These issues lead to an over-reliance on imported materials, increasing operational risks and costs.

Inadequate supplier quality and technical capabilities are significant obstacles to localized procurement. In Vietnam, the average pass rate of hardware component suppliers is only 85%, far below the domestic rate of 98%. A scissors manufacturer from Yangjiang experienced a 12% product return rate due to substandard hardness in blades sourced locally in Vietnam. The company was forced to switch back to domestic procurement, increasing costs by 30%. In Thailand, suppliers of auxiliary materials for aquatic processing are generally small in scale and lack uniform production standards. A Zhanjiang-based enterprise encountered inconsistent product flavor due to batch variations in Foodstuff additives procured locally, damaging the brand's reputation. Eventually, the company opted to import from Singapore, raising costs by 40%.

Underdeveloped supporting industries result in low localized procurement rates. Indonesia’s plastic processing sector can meet only 30% of local demand. A Maoming petrochemical enterprise’s woven bag production project in Indonesia requires 60% of its raw materials to be imported from China or Singapore, leading to longer lead times and higher costs. Inventory turnover in the project is 50% lower than domestically. Cambodia’s hardware mould industry is virtually non-existent. A Yangjiang enterprise’s factory in Cambodia relies entirely on imported moulds, with replacement cycles taking up to one month, delaying the launch of new products.

Significant price volatility and unstable supply further exacerbate the risks of localized procurement. Raw material prices in some ASEAN countries fluctuate sharply due to international market conditions and local supply-demand dynamics. In 2024, the monthly price fluctuation of nickel ore in Indonesia reached 20%. A hardware manufacturer from Yangjiang, which had not locked in prices, saw procurement costs surge by 35%, severely squeezing profit margins. The rubber supply in Malaysia is highly susceptible to climate conditions. During the 2024 rainy season, rubber production fell by 40%. A Zhanjiang aquatic products enterprise had to suspend production of rubber fishing gear for one week due to raw material shortages, resulting in a loss of orders worth RMB 5 million.

Limited procurement channels and information asymmetry further constrain localized sourcing. In Cambodia, the number of qualified suppliers is small, leaving enterprises with few alternatives. A Yangjiang-based enterprise in Cambodia relies on only two key component suppliers. If one of them goes wrong, it will affect production. When one supplier experienced a factory fire in 2024, production was halted for two weeks. In Thailand, supplier information is fragmented, and there is no unified procurement platform. A Zhanjiang-based company spent three months identifying a suitable supplier for aquatic product packaging—two months longer than it would have taken domestically.

To address challenges in localized procurement, enterprises from Western Guangdong have adopted multiple strategies. First, they assist local suppliers in improving quality by providing technical support and training. Yangjiang Shibazi Group collaborated with three component suppliers in Vietnam, dispatching technical personnel to guide production. This helped raise the product qualification rate to 95% and increased the localized procurement rate from 30% to 50%. Second, they foster localized supplier clusters through industrial park models that bring together supporting enterprises. Zhanjiang Guolian Aquatic Products invested in building an aquatic processing industrial park in Thailand, attracting 10 domestic auxiliary material suppliers to establish operations there. This enabled 80% of auxiliary materials to be sourced locally and reduced logistics costs by 25%.

3. Challenges in Brand Building and Promotion for Enterprises from Western Guangdong in ASEAN Internationalization

3.1 Insufficient Cultural Adaptation of Brands, Lack of Local Resonance

Enterprises from Western Guangdong often replicate domestic brand templates without deeply integrating ASEAN cultural elements, resulting in low brand recognition.

Disconnected Cultural Symbols: Visual design and communication content lack localized expression. For example, a hardware manufacturer from Yangjiang directly used traditional Chinese motifs such as "dragons" and "phoenixes" in the Vietnamese market, overlooking local cultural symbols like "water puppetry" and "lotus flowers" that resonate with Vietnamese consumers, leading to weak brand distinctiveness. Similarly, a textile enterprise from Maoming emphasized "cost-effectiveness" in its advertisements, which did not align with the Thai market's preference for "craftsmanship heritage" and "cultural meaning," making it difficult to establish an emotional connection. Misaligned Value Propositions: Brand narratives fail to cater to ASEAN market demands. While agricultural processing enterprises from Western Guangdong highlight "traditional techniques," younger ASEAN consumers prioritize "convenience" and "health certifications." For instance, Vietnamese consumers' core requirements for pre-made dishes focus on "3-minute preparation" and "additive-free." Yet, companies continue to promote "traditional curing methods," resulting in a mismatch between products and market expectations.

3.2 Singular and Inefficient Promotion Channels, Limited Market Reach

Enterprises in Western Guangdong heavily rely on traditional channels, underutilizing ASEAN digital platforms and local resources. Overreliance on Foreign Trade Agents: 80% of brand promotion is conducted indirectly through trading companies, lacking direct channels. For example, an aquatic products enterprise from Zhanjiang depended entirely on a Thai distributor for brand promotion, preventing direct engagement with end consumers. As a result, brand messaging became diluted, and consumers in the Vietnamese market only recognized "Chinese aquatic products" without identifying specific brands.

Delayed Digitalization and Weak Cross-Border E-Commerce Capabilities: Although some enterprises have established a presence on platforms like Lazada and Shopee, only 5% have set up localized operational teams (e.g., Vietnamese-language customer service, local logistics). Most rely on third-party agents for operations, leading to a customer complaint rate as high as 20% (e.g., due to logistics delays and lack of after-sales support). Additionally, insufficient use of local ASEAN social platforms (such as TikTok in Indonesia and LINE in Thailand) has caused these enterprises to miss opportunities to reach younger consumer groups.

3.3 Lack of Brand Certification and Standardization Hinders Access to High-End Markets

Enterprises from Western Guangdong have low international certification coverage, making it challenging to penetrate mid-to-high-end markets in ASEAN.

Certification Barriers: Only 15% of enterprises have obtained ASEAN international standard certifications (such as Singapore's SFA Foodstuff safety certification and Malaysia's SIRIM low-carbon certification). For instance, an aquatic products company from Zhanjiang struggled to enter mainstream supermarkets in Indonesia and Malaysia due to a lack of HALAL certification. As a result, it could only sell through wholesale markets at lower prices, with profit margins 30% lower than certified competitors.

Inconsistent Quality Stability: Due to fragmented raw material sourcing and non-standardized quality control processes, product quality varies significantly. A Yangjiang-based cutlery enterprise faced complaints from Thai distributors about "unreliable quality" because the sharpness of its exported products varied by more than 15%, damaging brand trust.

3.4 Limited Resource Investment Undermines Sustained Brand Building

Enterprises in Western Guangdong are predominantly small and medium-sized, with financial and talent shortages constraining long-term brand operations.

Annual investment in brand promotion accounts for less than 3% of revenue, far below the 10% level typical among Pearl River Delta enterprises. For instance, a plastic manufacturer from Maoming could not afford exhibition booth fees in ASEAN (averaging RMB 100,000–200,000 per year) and relied solely on trading companies for limited promotional exposure.

There is a lack of teams with both cross-cultural marketing expertise and ASEAN market experience. Sixty percent of enterprises lack dedicated brand personnel, often assigning brand tasks to administrative staff as secondary duties. This leads to poorly tailored brand strategies—such as mistakenly promoting "green environmental protection" as "low-cost materials" in the Malaysian market, triggering negative consumer perceptions.

3.5 Lack of Industry Coordination Weakens Brand Cluster Effects

Enterprises from Western Guangdong often operate in isolation, failing to form regional brand synergies.

Homogeneous Competition: Companies within the same category compete individually, sometimes even undercutting prices and diluting brand value. Among the 3,000+ cutlery enterprises in Yangjiang, 80% offer similar product designs. In the Vietnamese market, they engage in price wars, leading to the "Western Guangdong Cutlery" label being associated with low-end products.

Absence of Unified Brand Promotion Platforms: Enterprises cannot pool resources such as overseas warehouses or media channels. For example, Zhanjiang-based aquatic products companies carry out brand activities independently in Thailand instead of jointly building a "Western Guangdong SeaFoodstuff" regional brand, missing out on economies of scale.

4. Challenges and Deficiencies in International Risk Prevention and Control

4.1 Foreign Investment Access Restrictions: Invisible Barriers to Market Entry

ASEAN countries exhibit significant diversity and complexity in their restrictions on foreign investment access, creating considerable uncertainty for enterprises from Western Guangdong in their investment planning. These restrictions are mainly reflected in multiple dimensions such as sectoral access, equity ratios, and business scope, with frequent policy adjustments increasing compliance costs and investment risks for enterprises.

In terms of sectoral access, most ASEAN countries impose strict foreign investment barriers in areas involving national security, public interest, and traditional industries. In Vietnam, foreign ownership in the retail sector exceeding 51% requires special government approval. A hardware manufacturer from Yangjiang, when planning to open directly operated chain stores in Ho Chi Minh City, was compelled to form a joint venture with a local enterprise due to foreign equity restrictions. This led to dispersed operational decision-making and missed opportunities for market expansion. Thailand's 《Foreign Business Act》 explicitly lists sectors where foreign investment is prohibited or restricted, with stringent limitations in fields such as agriculture and fisheries. An aquatic products enterprise from Zhanjiang intended to invest in a large-scale aquaculture farm in Thailand, but abandoned its independent operation plan due to the 49% foreign ownership cap. It eventually opted for a technical cooperation model, which compressed profit margins by nearly 30%.

Equity ratio restrictions are among the most common obstacles to foreign investment access. Although Malaysia's "New Economic Policy" has been adjusted, it still requires at least 30% Bumiputera equity ownership in certain sectors. When a precision tool manufacturing project was launched in Penang by a Yangjiang hardware enterprise, a local partner had to be introduced to meet equity requirements. This resulted in frequent disagreements within the management team over technical standards and production scheduling, delaying the project's launch by six months. Indonesia's "Negative Investment List" is updated annually. The 2024 version maintains foreign ownership caps in over 100 industries, with some manufacturing subsectors limiting foreign ownership to a maximum of 49%. A petrochemical enterprise from Maoming, investing in a plastic processing project in Indonesia, was forced to relinquish partial profit distribution rights due to equity restrictions, incurring an estimated annual loss of potential revenue of RMB 8 million.

Restrictions on business scope similarly constrain enterprises' development potential. In Cambodia, the business scope of foreign-invested enterprises must be explicitly stated in their business licenses, and modification procedures are cumbersome. A scissors manufacturer from Yangjiang sought to add kitchenware production at its Cambodian factory in response to market demand changes, but the process of updating its business scope took three months, causing it to miss the local peak sales season. Although Singapore is the most open to foreign investment among ASEAN countries, it maintains strict controls in sensitive sectors such as finance and media. An aquatic products enterprise from Zhanjiang planned to establish a supply chain finance company in Singapore, but ultimately abandoned the venture due to stringent foreign investment approval requirements. It had to rely on traditional bank financing instead, increasing financial costs by 15%.

Policy instability and lack of transparency further exacerbate the risks associated with foreign investment access. Some ASEAN countries adjust policies without providing sufficient transition or public notice periods, making it difficult for enterprises to respond in advance. In 2024, Vietnam abruptly shortened the land use term for foreign-invested enterprises from 50 years to 30 years. As a result, an aquatic products processing company from Zhanjiang faced land lease renewal risks at its Vietnamese factory and was forced to reassess its investment return cycle. Although the tax incentives offered by Thailand's Eastern Economic Corridor (EEC) are attractive, the actual application process involves numerous ambiguous clauses. An enterprise from Maoming experienced an eight-month delay in obtaining tax exemption approval due to discrepancies in policy interpretation with the tax authorities, causing it to miss the optimal timing for project launch.

To mitigate foreign investment access risks, enterprises from Western Guangdong have adopted multiple strategies. First, they engage local professional consulting firms to anticipate policy trends in advance. Before investing in Indonesia, Zhanjiang Guolian Aquatic Products spent RMB 2 million to hire a local law firm for policy due diligence, successfully avoiding hidden restrictions in the fishery resource development sector. Second, they flexibly design investment structures to bypass equity restrictions by establishing regional headquarters or adopting technology licensing models. Yangjiang Shibazi Group implemented a "technology investment + brand licensing" approach in Malaysia. Although it did not hold a controlling equity stake, it maintained actual control over production standards and sales channels, achieving an average annual net profit margin of over 15%. Third, they actively participate in industry associations to collectively influence policy formulation through unified advocacy. The Yangjiang Hardware Industry Association collaborated with 20 enterprises to establish a chamber of commerce in Vietnam. Through regular communication with local government authorities, they successfully advocated for adjustments to foreign investment scope restrictions in the hardware products sector.

4.2 Differences in Labor Laws: Compliance Challenges in Human Resource Management

Labor laws in ASEAN countries vary significantly in areas such as dismissal procedures, working hour systems, and social security provisions. Enterprises from Western Guangdong often encounter labor disputes due to unfamiliarity with local regulations during cross-border operations, leading to increased labor costs and management difficulties.

The complexity of dismissal procedures is one of the most prominent challenges. In Thailand, terminating employees requires strict adherence to consultation, notice, and compensation procedures, and it is prohibited to dismiss union members arbitrarily. An aquatic products processing enterprise from Zhanjiang needed to reduce its workforce by 10% due to production adjustments at its Thai factory. However, due to insufficient consultation with the labor union, the dismissals were deemed illegal. The company ultimately had to pay compensation equivalent to six months' wages for each affected employee, resulting in a loss of approximately RMB 5 million. Vietnam's dismissal procedures are similarly cumbersome. After an employee has completed 12 consecutive months of service, termination requires a 30-day notice and economic compensation. An assembly plant in Vietnam operated by a Yangjiang-based enterprise conducted temporary layoffs due to reduced orders, but failed to meet the notice period requirement. As a result, it was fined RMB 2 million by local labor authorities.

Differences in working hour systems and overtime regulations also pose scheduling challenges for enterprises. In Malaysia, the standard working week is 44 hours; overtime must be paid at 1.5 times the regular rate, and monthly overtime cannot exceed 104 hours. A hardware manufacturer from Yangjiang arranged continuous overtime shifts at its Penang factory to meet urgent orders, but was reported and fined RMB 300,000. Indonesia's working hour system is even stricter, limiting weekly work to 40 hours and requiring employee consent for overtime. An aquaculture operation in Indonesia run by a Zhanjiang-based aquatic products company needed flexible scheduling due to the specific demands of fisheries production. However, constrained by working hour regulations, it had to hire additional staff, increasing labor costs by 25%.

Disparities in social security systems complicate labor cost calculations for enterprises. Thailand's social security system covers pensions, healthcare, unemployment, and other areas, with employer contributions accounting for 15% of payroll. Combined with employee contributions, the total rate exceeds 20%. A Zhanjiang-based enterprise with 100 employees in Thailand spent RMB 1.2 million annually on social security, far exceeding domestic levels. Although Vietnam's social security system is less comprehensive, contribution rates have been increasing annually. In 2024, the employer contribution rate reached 20.5%, with multiple mandatory insurance items. A factory in Vietnam operated by a Yangjiang-based enterprise was ordered to make back payments and fined RMB 1.5 million for underpaying work injury insurance premiums.

The influence of labor unions and differences in labor dispute resolution mechanisms also pose challenges to corporate management. In countries such as Thailand and Malaysia, labor unions are highly active and wield significant influence in collective bargaining. A hardware manufacturing enterprise from Yangjiang experienced a week-long strike at its Thai factory after proposed wage adjustments failed to meet union demands, resulting in a direct loss of orders worth RMB 5 million.

In Indonesia, the labor dispute resolution process is protracted, typically involving multiple stages such as mediation, arbitration, and litigation. A Zhanjiang-based enterprise spent nine months resolving a wage dispute with its employees, which disrupted normal production schedules during this period.

To address the risks arising from differences in labor laws, enterprises from Western Guangdong have implemented a series of measures.

First, they have established localized human resource management teams by hiring professionals familiar with local labor regulations. Yangjiang Shibazi Group's factory in Vietnam employs five local HR experts responsible for compensation design, contract management, and related tasks. Over the past three years, no major labor disputes have occurred.

Second, they have refined employee contract terms to clearly define key aspects such as working hours, overtime, and dismissal procedures. An aquatic products enterprise from Zhanjiang included detailed compensation standards for various scenarios in the contracts signed with employees at its Thai factory, preventing disputes arising from ambiguous clauses.

Third, they have strengthened employee training to enhance local staff's understanding of corporate policies. A petrochemical enterprise from Maoming conducts monthly labor law training sessions at its Indonesian factory, reducing employee violations by 40%.

Fourth, they actively participate in local labor consultation mechanisms and maintain effective communication with labor unions. A Zhanjiang-based enterprise in Malaysia holds regular meetings with union representatives, successfully reducing the wage negotiation cycle from three months to one month and improving management efficiency.

5. Dilemmas in the Overseas Intellectual Property Layout for Enterprises in Western Guangdong Regarding Internationalization in ASEAN

5.1 Delayed Awareness of Intellectual Property Layout and Insufficient Strategic Foresight

Enterprises in western Guangdong generally lack a systematic understanding of ASEAN intellectual property rules, resulting in their intellectual property layout lagging behind the pace of market expansion. Passive response rather than proactive layout: Most enterprises treat intellectual property as a "post-event defensive tool" rather than a "prerequisite for market access." For example, a hardware enterprise in Yangjiang had been selling household knives in the Vietnamese market for years but failed to register its trademark locally. In 2024, a local enterprise registered a similar trademark, forcing the Yangjiang enterprise to remove its products from the market and resulting in losses exceeding RMB 8 million. Similarly, a seafood enterprise in Zhanjiang had its prepared dish formula copied in the Thai market. However, due to not having applied for a patent, the enterprise lacked legal grounds for safeguarding rights, leading to a 30% erosion of its market share. Insufficient understanding of regional rule differences: The intellectual property systems of ASEAN countries vary significantly, making enterprises susceptible to compliance risks due to a "one-size-fits-all" approach to intellectual property layout. For instance, Indonesia requires patent applications to include instructions in Indonesian. A home appliance enterprise in western Guangdong submitted materials in Chinese, which led to the application being rejected and a six-month delay in product launch. Malaysia imposes strict scrutiny on the "distinctiveness" of trademarks. A stone enterprise in Yunfu used the trademark "Yun Stone," which was deemed a generic term, leading to registration failure and inability to prevent other enterprises from using similar marks.

5.2 Dual Constraints of High Layout Costs and Insufficient Resource Investment

Small and medium-sized enterprises in western Guangdong are constrained by limited funds and talent, making it difficult for them to sustain long-term investment in overseas intellectual property layout. The cost of intellectual property layout across multiple ASEAN countries far exceeds the affordability of these enterprises. Taking PCT international patent applications as an example, the combined official and agency fees for covering Vietnam, Thailand, and Indonesia exceed RMB 500,000. However, the average annual profit of small knife and scissors enterprises in Yangjiang is only RMB 3 million, making such costs prohibitive. The maintenance fees for Madrid trademark registration in all ten ASEAN countries amount to approximately RMB 80,000 annually. A seafood enterprise in Zhanjiang, due to tight cash flow, abandoned trademark renewals in the Philippines and Cambodia, resulting in its brand being preemptively registered in both countries. There is a shortage of interdisciplinary talent with knowledge of both ASEAN legal and technical aspects. Only 5% of enterprises in western Guangdong have dedicated intellectual property positions, and most of these roles are filled by administrative staff on a part-time basis. This makes it difficult to handle professional tasks such as patent mapping and infringement monitoring. For instance, a chemical enterprise in Maoming that applied for a patent on environmentally friendly coatings in Indonesia failed to grasp the local "green technology priority examination" rule and did not submit the necessary supporting documents. As a result, the examination process was extended to three years, causing the enterprise to miss market opportunities.

5.3 High Regional Infringement Risks and Weak Enforcement Capabilities

In some ASEAN countries, intellectual property protection remains insufficient, resulting in high costs and low efficiency for enterprises from western Guangdong in enforcing their rights. Small commodity markets in countries like Vietnam and Cambodia are rife with counterfeit products imitating brands from Western Guangdong. For instance, a scissor manufacturer from Yangjiang discovered over 30 stores in Ho Chi Minh City selling counterfeit products. However, due to the dispersed sales of these infringing products via cross-border e-commerce platforms, gathering evidence proved extremely difficult. The cost of pursuing a single infringement case exceeded RMB 200,000, far surpassing the actual losses incurred. Judicial procedures in ASEAN countries are complex, leading to prolonged enforcement cycles. A seafood enterprise from Zhanjiang filed a lawsuit in Thailand against a company that had copied its packaging design. After two years of litigation, the company won the case but found that the infringing party had already transferred its assets. As a result, the actual amount recovered was less than 10% of the court-awarded compensation. In Indonesia, administrative penalties for patent infringement are weak. A plastics enterprise discovered that a local factory was illegally using its production process and filed a complaint with the Indonesian Intellectual Property Office. However, the only penalty imposed was a "warning," and the infringing activities continued unabated.

5.4 Lack of Industry Chain Coordination and Weak Cluster Protection Capabilities

Enterprises in western Guangdong tend to adopt a "go-it-alone" approach to intellectual property layout, making it difficult to establish a regional intellectual property protection network. Companies within the same industry often duplicate efforts and operate independently in their intellectual property strategies. For example, among the over 3,000 scissors manufacturers in Yangjiang, only 12% have registered patents in ASEAN countries, with a technology overlap rate exceeding 60%, leading to significant resource wastage. Similarly, seafood processing enterprises in Zhanjiang have not established a patent-sharing pool, resulting in multiple companies redundantly developing similar prepared dish formulas and missing opportunities for technological collaboration. Collaboration with local institutions is weak, and enterprises have not effectively leveraged ASEAN-based intellectual property service agencies, leading to delays in infringement monitoring. For instance, a textile enterprise from Maoming encountered design infringement in the Malaysian market. Due to the lack of cooperation with local law firms, the infringement was only discovered three months later. By that time, counterfeit products had already captured 20% of the market share, making it extremely difficult to recover losses.

6. Difficulties and Shortcomings in Government-Enterprise Collaboration for Enterprises in Western Guangdong

Although initial explorations have been made in government-enterprise collaboration during the internationalization process of enterprises in Western Guangdong to engage with ASEAN, significant challenges remain in mechanism construction, resource integration, and service precision. These issues hinder the formation of a synergistic "policy-enterprise-market" dynamic. The specific shortcomings are as follows:

6.1 Fragmented Collaboration Mechanisms and Lack of Systematic Top-Level Design

Western Guangdong has yet to establish a unified coordination system for government-enterprise collaboration, resulting in loose cooperation across departments and administrative levels. On one hand, departments such as commerce, customs, taxation, and finance have independently introduced ASEAN-related support policies. However, these policies lack cohesion. For instance, the "ASEAN Exhibition Subsidy" from the commerce department and the "Fast Customs Clearance Channel" from customs have no integrated application process, forcing enterprises to repeatedly submit materials and reducing approval efficiency by over 40%. On the other hand, there is insufficient collaboration between municipal and county-level governments. For example, the ASEAN cooperation zone policies in cities like Zhanjiang and Maoming are not effectively aligned with the industrial plans of their subordinate counties, leading to resource dispersion. The Zhanjiang ASEAN Aquatic Processing Park and the Xuwen County Aquaculture Base, for instance, lack coordinated support, resulting in unstable raw material supply. In 2024, this instability caused a 25% decline in capacity utilization for enterprises in the park. Additionally, government-enterprise communication channels are limited, primarily relying on traditional formats like "quarterly seminars." Feedback cycles for enterprise requests are lengthy (averaging 1-2 months), and some requests are "passed around" due to overlapping departmental responsibilities. For example, an aquatic enterprise's difficulty in applying for an "ASEAN Cold Chain Logistics Subsidy" remained unresolved for three months without a clear response, as it involved both the transportation and commerce departments.

6.2 Low Precision of Policy Support and Disconnect from Actual Enterprise Needs

Policy provision in government-enterprise collaboration suffers from a "broad irrigation" approach, failing to address the diverse needs of Western Guangdong enterprises in their ASEAN internationalization efforts. First, policy coverage is uneven. Traditional industries (e.g., aquaculture and hardware) receive over 80% of subsidies and park benefits, while emerging industries like the digital economy and green economy receive insufficient support. For instance, cross-border e-commerce enterprises can only access a maximum digital subsidy of 500,000 yuan, far below their actual investment in exploring ASEAN markets (averaging 2-3 million yuan). In 2024, only 12% of cross-border e-commerce enterprises received subsidies. Second, policies have "high implementation thresholds." For example, the "ASEAN Export Special Credit" requires enterprises to provide full factory mortgages, but most small and medium-sized enterprises in Western Guangdong operate with light assets. As a result, 70% missed out on loans due to the inability to meet mortgage conditions. Some policies also involve cumbersome application processes, requiring over 10 types of materials and approval cycles of 2-3 months, causing enterprises to miss ASEAN order windows. Third, policies lack foresight and are slow to respond to ASEAN market dynamics and regulatory changes. For instance, after Indonesia adjusted its Foodstuff contact material standards in 2024, the Western Guangdong government did not promptly introduce targeted certification subsidies. This led to 30 plastic packaging enterprises abandoning the Indonesian market due to high certification costs (100,000-150,000 yuan).

6.3 Weak Resource Integration Capability and Incomplete Collaborative Service System

In government-enterprise collaboration, the government's ability to integrate and allocate ASEAN-related resources is insufficient to support the internationalization needs of enterprises.

First, there is inadequate coordination of logistics resources. The direct shipping routes from Zhanjiang Port and Maoming Port to ASEAN operate only twice a week, and no "consolidation-specific routes" have been jointly established with enterprises. As a result, enterprises must wait 1-2 weeks for cargo consolidation, increasing logistics costs by 150 yuan per ton. Although the government has promoted the construction of the "New Western Land-Sea Corridor," it has not established a price negotiation mechanism with railway and shipping companies. Consequently, logistics costs for enterprises in Western Guangdong are 15%-20% higher than those in the Pearl River Delta. Second, there is a shortage of professional service resources. The government has not established a unified platform for ASEAN legal, tax, and certification services. Only five local institutions can provide ASEAN compliance services, and their fees are prohibitively high (e.g., the service fee for Malaysian SIRIM certification is 150,000 yuan). As a result, 90% of small and medium-sized enterprises cannot afford these services. In 2024, a stone materials enterprise in Yunfu spent six months handling market access procedures for Thailand due to a lack of professional assistance, causing it to miss peak-season orders. Third, there is information asymmetry. The government has not built an ASEAN market database, forcing enterprises to rely on foreign trade companies for information on tariffs, standards, and demand. This results in an information lag rate of over 60%. For example, a textile enterprise in Maoming was unaware of Malaysia's new environmental regulations, leading to the destruction of its exported products and a loss of 1.5 million yuan.

6.4 Lack of Industry Association Collaboration and Underutilized Cluster Effects

In government-enterprise collaboration, the role of industry associations as a "bridge" has not been activated, and enterprises often operate in isolation. First, industry associations have low participation rates. Only 10% of ASEAN-related policies formulated by the government solicit input from industry associations, leading to a disconnect between policies and industry realities. For instance, the Yangjiang Hardware Industry Association once proposed a "Standard Certification Subsidy for Knives and Scissors" targeting the Vietnamese market, but it was not incorporated into policy. In 2024, 20 enterprises lost orders worth 8 million yuan due to failure to obtain Vietnamese certification. Second, industry associations have weak resource integration capabilities. They have not established a "Western Guangdong-ASEAN Industrial Alliance," preventing enterprises from sharing resources such as overseas warehouses, logistics channels, and customer networks. For example, the utilization rate of overseas warehouses in Thailand by Zhanjiang aquatic product enterprises is only 50%, while enterprises in the Pearl River Delta achieve an 85% utilization rate through alliance-based sharing. Third, there is a lack of cluster-based collaborative services. Industry associations have not organized enterprises to "group together" for exhibitions or market expansion. When participating in ASEAN exhibitions, enterprises in Western Guangdong face individual booth costs exceeding 100,000 yuan, which is 40% higher than the costs for Pearl River Delta enterprises participating jointly. In 2024, only 30% of small and medium-sized enterprises participated in ASEAN exhibitions.

7. Dilemmas and Deficiencies in Industry Co-Construction and Self-Regulation Mechanisms

In the process of enterprises in Western Guangdong venturing into international markets in ASEAN, industry co-construction and self-regulation mechanisms should have served as solid supports. However, due to various issues, these mechanisms have failed to fully leverage synergistic effects, hindering the cluster-based "going global" efforts of enterprises.

7.1 Lack of Coordination in Industry Co-Construction and Weak Collaborative Foundation

Industry associations in Western Guangdong operate in silos when engaging with ASEAN markets, lacking regional-level coordinated planning and joint actions. On one hand, severe information barriers exist among associations. For instance, the Zhanjiang Aquatic Products Association and the Yangjiang Hardware Association did not share market access information or customer resources for Vietnam and Thailand accumulated during their ASEAN market expansion efforts. This resulted in duplicated research by enterprises, wasting significant human and financial resources and extending market development cycles by 2-3 months. On the other hand, co-construction projects face implementation challenges. Although initiatives like "Western Guangdong Industrial Joint Going Global" exist, there is a lack of leading entities and coordination mechanisms at the implementation level. For example, in a cross-border e-commerce industrial park project targeting ASEAN, associations from Zhanjiang, Maoming, and Yangjiang failed to reach consensus on park location, functional positioning, and industry entry standards, leading to a one-year delay and missing the golden period for e-commerce development. Additionally, the absence of a profit distribution mechanism in industry co-creation has led to free-riding or unequal benefit sharing in joint exhibitions and shared overseas warehouse projects due to differing interests among enterprises and associations, dampening collaboration enthusiasm. For instance, during the joint participation of Western Guangdong enterprises in the Malaysia International Commodity Exhibition in 2024, disputes over booth allocation and promotional resource distribution caused some enterprises to withdraw midway, significantly undermining the exhibition's effectiveness.

7.2 Incomplete Self-Regulation Mechanisms and Disordered Market Practices

Enterprises in Western Guangdong face severe self-regulation challenges in ASEAN markets, leading to disordered market practices and undermining collective interests. First, self-regulation rules lag behind market dynamics. Industry associations have failed to keep pace with changes in ASEAN markets, such as evolving environmental and safety standards in Vietnam and Indonesia. Associations for aquatic products and building materials, for example, did not promptly establish self-regulation guidelines for exports, resulting in over 40 enterprises being excluded from ASEAN markets in 2024 due to non-compliant products. Second, enforcement is weak. Associations impose lenient penalties for violations, primarily issuing warnings or advisories, with insufficient substantive constraints on cut-throat competition practices like dumping and counterfeiting. In Yangjiang's hardware industry, for instance, some enterprises maliciously lowered prices to capture market share in Thailand. Although the association repeatedly issued condemnations, it failed to implement strong measures such as exhibition restrictions or industry-wide notifications, leading to a 30% decline in hardware product prices in Thailand over three years and severely compressed profit margins. Third, there is a lack of oversight systems. The absence of third-party monitoring bodies and internal corporate supervision mechanisms keeps the cost of violations low. For example, some Zhanjiang aquatic product enterprises used banned additives or mislabeled origins when exporting to ASEAN. Without effective oversight, these violations went undetected and unpunished, damaging the overall brand image of Western Guangdong's aquatic products.

7.3 Talent Shortages and Hindered Innovative Collaboration

The effective operation of industry co-construction and self-regulation mechanisms relies on professional talent, yet Western Guangdong faces a severe shortage in this area. On the one hand, there is a lack of international business talent. There is a scarcity of professionals who possess both knowledge of ASEAN market rules, languages, and cultures, and familiarity with industry-specific operations. This leaves enterprises ill-equipped to participate in co-construction projects or comply with self-regulation requirements. For example, in a joint industrial park project in Cambodia, enterprises frequently made errors during negotiations and operations due to a lack of expertise in local labor laws and land policies, resulting in a 20% cost increase. On the other hand, industry associations lack specialized self-regulation management talent. The professionalism and impartiality of these associations are often questioned when formulating rules, supervising implementation, and mediating disputes. For instance, when handling a price dispute among enterprises in the ASEAN market, one association proposed a mediation solution that failed to gain acceptance due to staff members' lack of knowledge in international trade law, leading to widespread dissatisfaction among the enterprises involved. Additionally, the talent development system is underdeveloped. There is insufficient collaboration between universities, vocational institutions, industry associations, and enterprises. Few specialized courses tailored to ASEAN market demands are offered, and the number of professionals trained annually meets only 10% of enterprise needs.

7.4 Inadequate International Cooperation and Challenges in External Integration

Western Guangdong enterprises encounter multiple challenges when collaborating with local industry organizations and enterprises in ASEAN for industry co-construction and self-regulation. First, cooperation channels are limited. Connections are predominantly established through government-led economic and trade exchange events, with a lack of regularized, market-oriented platforms for supporting connections and collaboration. This hinders effective communication between enterprises and their ASEAN counterparts. For instance, Western Guangdong's electronic information enterprises face challenges in establishing technical collaborations or forming industry alliances with technology companies in Singapore and Malaysia, primarily due to the lack of reliable channels. Second, cultural differences lead to conflicts. When participating in ASEAN industry co-construction or adhering to self-regulation rules, Western Guangdong enterprises often encounter misunderstandings and conflicts arising from divergent cultures and business practices. For instance, in a joint project in Indonesia, the fast-paced decision-making style preferred by Western Guangdong enterprises clashed with the relationship-oriented, prolonged decision-making culture of Indonesian partners, significantly slowing project progress. Third, there is insufficient research on local ASEAN industry rules and standards. Industry associations in Western Guangdong have not organized in-depth studies, leaving enterprises struggling to adapt when participating in co-construction or self-regulation efforts. For example, in a Thai agricultural product processing collaboration, enterprises frequently encountered quality issues with their products due to unfamiliarity with Thai agricultural standards and industry self-regulation requirements, undermining the partnership.

8. Dilemmas and Shortfalls in the ASEAN-oriented Digital Internationalisation of Western Guangdong Enterprises

Amid the global digital surge reshaping the commercial map, Western Guangdong firms entering ASEAN markets possess digital potential yet remain mired in obstacles that sharply limit their expansion and competitive edge.

8.1 Digital-infrastructure gaps crippling cross-border operations

Parts of ASEAN still lag far behind China: beyond capital cities, Cambodia and Laos suffer weak or absent coverage, 5G is scarce, and 4G signals are unstable. For Western Guangdong plants, warehouses, or branches, daily communications, data transfers, and operational alignment stall—video calls freeze, uploads time out, and decisions lag. Bandwidth is punishingly expensive: in Cambodia, a 250 Mbps shared line costs almost US $2 000 a year, several times the domestic price. The heavy tariff squeezes already thin margins, blocking investment in advanced hardware or new digital scenarios and becoming an insurmountable hurdle for SMEs.

8.2 Fragmented data rules turning compliance into a maze

ASEAN members diverge sharply: Singapore allows open cross-border flows, while Indonesia and Vietnam insist on local storage—Indonesian e-commerce and finance data must stay in-country, Vietnam mandates local cloud mirrors. Western Guangdong players therefore duplicate data centres and re-engineer architectures market by market, lifting capital spending 30-50 % and multiplying management complexity. Retention regimes are equally split—Thailand wants ten-year transaction archives, the Philippines bars biometric exports, and Malaysia permits encrypted third-party clouds. Forced to build parallel systems and hire dedicated compliance teams, firms watch money, manpower, and time drain away, making lawful operation an uphill battle.

8.3 Digital talent drought, transformation momentum feeble

Western Guangdong firms themselves sit on thin digital bedding and an even thinner talent pool. There is a dearth of hybrids who grasp both digital technology and ASEAN market practice, language, and culture, leaving companies without expert guidance when they draft a digital strategy or roll out transformation projects. From market scouting and product development to marketing push, they cannot wield digital means to match ASEAN demand with precision. The local labour market offers little back-up. Parts of ASEAN still run on limited schooling; workers show low uptake of, and aptitude for, digital tools. Many local staff, for example, struggle with basic office software and the management or e-commerce modules the firm has recently imported, which drives up data-entry error rates and jams process flow. Transformation gains are instantly discounted, and the extra training budget poured in afterwards yields scant return.

8.4 Sector synergy is missing, and the digital ecosystem is fragmented.

Western Guangdong trade associations do too little to propel ASEAN-oriented digitalisation. The associations rarely talk to one another, so regional corporate strength stays unbundled, and no unified digital roadmap or joint action ever emerges. In cross-border e-commerce, firms in Zhanjiang, Maoming, and elsewhere fight their own battles, never pooling logistics, sharing overseas warehouses, or merging data resources; the result is stubbornly high freight costs, half-empty warehouses, and market intel that is partial and stale. Channels for international cooperation are equally narrow. Exchanges with ASEAN industry bodies and companies still ride on government-led trade missions; routine, market-driven platforms are absent. Cultural gaps and divergent business habits deepen the rift, stalling joint digital projects, technology sharing, and mutual recognition of standards. A jointly built digital supply-chain programme, for instance, often fails due to poor communication and conflicting mindsets, never delivering the digital synergy it promised.

9. Dilemmas and Shortfalls in the Green ASEAN Internationalisation

As global green transition accelerates and ASEAN states attach ever-greater weight to eco-protection, the insufficient green capacity of Western Guangdong firms has moved to the fore, becoming a choke point in their international advance. The concrete dilemmas and shortfalls are fourfold:

9.1 ASEAN green policy standards are complex, and compliance costs for enterprises are high

ASEAN members ' green policies and environmental norms differ sharply and are updated fast; Western Guangdong companies struggle to keep pace.

First, entry thresholds vary: Singapore sets an industrial effluent COD limit of only 50 mg/L; Indonesia has issued sector-specific carbon-reduction rules for palm and mining, demanding a 15 % cut in emissions per unit of output by 2025; Laos and Cambodia, though once lenient, are—under NGO pressure—tightening approval for foreign investors, requiring new plants to install treatment facilities certified by third-country auditors.

Fish processors, hardware makers, and farm exporters from Western Guangdong must repeatedly retool lines and swap equipment; environmental-impact audits and retrofits alone swallow 20-30 % of initial project capital, lifting operating costs dramatically.

Second, fragmented green-certification regimes add extra weight. Malaysia pushes “Green Technology Certification”, Thailand uses “Low-Carbon Product Labelling”, and Vietnam demands its own “Environmental Conformity Certificate”. A single aquatic-products exporter spent RMB 800,000 securing three separate certificates, each taking 6-8 months and causing it to miss the seafood season, forfeiting more than RMB 2 million.

"Green tariffs" compound the squeeze: the Philippines levies a 10 % surtax on plastic goods that fail carbon benchmarks, further eroding the thin margins of Western Guangdong hardware and plastics makers.

9.2 Thin green industrial base, weak transformation drive

Western Guangdong remains dominated by traditional labour-intensive sectors with paltry green-tech stock and layout.

First, production is still high-energy and high-polluting. Seafood processors rely on obsolete freezers and salting lines whose power draw per unit exceeds the sector's best practice by 30 %. In Yangjiang, 15% of hardware plants overshoot heavy-metal effluent limits; none recycle water, so utilization languishes at 50% versus 75% in the Pearl River Delta. Retrofits to meet ASEAN rules demand heavy capital, yet over 80% of local firms are SMEs and only 30% can afford the bill.

Second, R&D for green products is feeble—less than 5 % of revenue is channelled into green development, far below ASEAN's rising expectations. As Malaysia and Thailand shift procurement to water-saving, low-radiation tiles, Yunfu stone processors still churn out conventional marble; only one plant offers an eco-line, leaving Western Guangdong with under 5% of ASEAN's tile market against Fujian's 25%.

Regional green branding is likewise absent; lacking a "Western Guangdong Green" collective label, local products cannot compete with the green cachet of Europe, America, Japan or Korea.

9.3 Green resources and technical back-up are missing; joint services are thin on the ground

Western Guangdong lacks an integrated resource-and-technology service system for ASEAN green expansion, leaving outward-bound firms without support.

First, green technology and talent are scarce. Local universities and institutes number fewer than three that run programmes in environmental protection or low-carbon technology, turning out only about 200 graduates a year—far below demand. Bringing in know-how involves hiring experts from Guangdong's bay area or abroad: a fish processor paid a Singaporean team RMB 500,000 for a single effluent-design package. ASEAN itself offers few service bodies—Vietnam, for example, has only ten firms that can perform carbon accounting, and their quotes are triple the domestic rate—so convenient, low-cost advice is nowhere to be found.

Second, green-finance leverage is weak. There are almost no dedicated products for ASEAN green projects; banks reserve green-loan quotas for home ventures and impose tougher terms on overseas schemes, demanding full collateral and adding 1.5–2 percentage points to the interest rate. In 2024, a firm planning a green seafood plant in Thailand asked for RMB 20 million, but, lacking offshore assets to pledge, received only RMB 8 million, delaying construction. Green-insurance cover is equally patchy, so environmental risks—sudden pollution claims, policy-shift losses—cannot be shifted, magnifying investors' misgivings.

9.4 International green-cooperation channels narrow, synergy feeble

Western Guangdong companies face visible walls when trying to work with ASEAN green groups or enterprises and struggle to enter the regional ecosystem.

First, cooperation platforms are missing. Business participation relies on government-run fairs such as the China–ASEAN Expo Green Building Materials Show, held once or twice a year and centred on display; standing mechanisms for technical match-making or joint projects do not exist. A hardware enterprise in western Guangdong sought to collaborate with a Malaysian green technology enterprise to develop low-carbon hardware accessories. However, due to the lack of established channels, it took one year to establish effective contact and miss the opportunity for technological upgrading.

Second, green-supply-chain coordination is poor. Western Guangdong firms sit at the low end of ASEAN chains and cannot synchronise with core players. In the electronics sector, for instance, they supply metal parts to assembly plants that insist on EU RoHS compliance, yet, lacking green links to upstream steel mills, they cannot secure consistently low-heavy-metal feedstock; pass rates hover at 70 % and lots are repeatedly returned. Trade associations have not stepped in: no "Western Guangdong–ASEAN Green Industry Alliance" has been formed, so firms cannot pool supply-chain resources or confront environmental risk together. When Indonesia suddenly tightened plastic-waste rules in 2024, ten Western Guangdong plastics exporters, acting separately, had to suspend shipments and lost more than RMB 5 million.

Optimization plan

ASEAN countries have many strengths and uneven skills, so enterprises in western Guangdong must establish a system of "local recruitment, graded training, long-term rewards". Recruiters collaborate with vocational colleges and the Labour Bureau to recruit for mechanical and electronic assembly services, aiming to increase the proportion of skills based on both old and new, as well as piece-rate awards. In March and June, technicians (home appliance test engineers) were dispatched to the headquarters in western Guangdong and domestic cooperative colleges for intensive training, and obtained international certifications (such as electrical IEC quasi-certification) to promote the precision of the industry. Labor governance, respect for the culture of ASEAN countries (e.g., the religious holiday needs of Indonesian employees), flexible schedules, integration with culture, and reducing employee turnover.

1. Labor Management

1.1 "Local recruitment" must be precise. Enterprises in western Guangdong cooperate with Thai vocational colleges and the Vietnam Labor Bureau, focusing on mechanical operation and electronic assembly. Taking the western Guangdong home appliance enterprise in Rayong Industrial Park, Thailand, as an example, scholars learn from scholars, collaborate with enterprises, and directly enter enterprises to recruit appropriately, laying the foundation for future talent development.

1.2 "Horizontal training" can solve this problem. The focus is on new piece awards so that skilled workers can share and newcomers can get started quickly; Technicians (home appliance test engineers) must "further study", and local potential employees will be sent to the western Guangdong headquarters or domestic cooperative colleges for intensive training in March and June. This appearance not only fills gaps in basic skills but also stores high-end technical talent, allowing humanoid structures to dynamically match the company's needs. In terms of deepening school-enterprise cooperation, enterprises in western Guangdong have cooperated with universities and vocational colleges to offer professional courses on "ASEAN internationalization", such as

"ASEAN Business Marketing" and "ASEAN Cross-border E-commerce and Financial Regulations". Experts from ASEAN enterprises will be invited to give lectures, so that scholars can be exposed to ASEAN business travel methods, familiarize themselves with the industry in western Guangdong, and deal with the ASEAN market, and accumulate talents from overseas marketing centers. Establish overseas training bases: Establish talent training bases in important ASEAN countries (such as Singapore, Thailand, Vietnam), and send employees and students from enterprises in western Guangdong to train. Participate in local enterprise projects, market research, etc., deeply integrate the ASEAN business environment, advocate cross-cultural exchanges, market insights, marketing empowerment, achieve localization + international dual-track support, and alleviate the shortage of talents in overseas marketing centers.

1.3 Selective training methods for employees in different matters

- Old and New Piece Counting Awards

This vocational training focuses on moving quickly + increasing efficiency. In the Thai factory, there is a Guangdong West Furniture Company, which implements a master-apprentice system, and senior carpenters teach newcomers the art of grinding. The design award links labor cost to production to stimulate human feelings. In the first three months of employment, the number of skilled workers increased by 36 percent, and productivity increased significantly. Piece rate reward science plan to avoid sacrifice. Enterprises establish a production quality revaluation system, set the output bottom line, increase piece rate wages to meet standards, and stimulate efficiency to ensure product quality. Vietnamese textile companies increased their new workers by 70 percent, while production reached 92 percent, with efficiency and quality on par with each other.

- Trade: Training International Certification

Technology must be deeply cultivated. Guangdong West Home Appliance Company selected employees from Indonesia and the Philippines and sent them to the training base of its Shunde headquarters in Guangdong for a period of three to six months. The content of the course involves calibrating the smart home appliance manufacturing algorithm in accordance with the International Electrical Standard (IEC), training it, and obtaining international certification, enabling employees to achieve high-end energy efficiency. Taking a home appliance company in western Guangdong as an example, Indonesian employees were sent to the headquarters for training, and after returning to the factory, they had to independently test high-end intelligent air conditioners, and the product debugging accuracy was between 80% and 95%, which drove the yield rate of the strip production line. International certification not only emphasizes the skills of its employees but also enables products to be sold to high-end ASEAN markets, helping companies develop markets such as Singapore and Malaysia.

- Improve the incentive and retention mechanism

Develop a competitive compensation and benefits system, take into account the salary levels of ASEAN counterparts, and set up performance bonuses and overseas allowances to encourage enterprises in western Guangdong to have a wide range of costs. Build clear employment channels, plan the promotion of overseas marketing center talents "Marketing Specialist-Regional Marketing Manager-ASEAN Marketing Director", provide cross-rotation, increase the sense of belonging and loyalty of talents, reduce brain drain, ensure the efficient operation of overseas marketing centers, and move towards the efficiency of stabilizing enterprises in western Guangdong to enter ASEAN cities. With "Changxing", promote the integration of skills and culture, integrate employees into the enterprise, and have a sense of belonging. For example, in our Indonesian factory, we respect the religious holidays of our Indonesian employees and adjust our schedules accordingly. The Malaysian factory hosts a "Multicultural Festival" to celebrate this festival with employees of different ethnicities. It has long been our goal to break the notion of "short-term employment" and create a corporate community of employees.

2. Supply chain localization

2.1 Construction of this material procurement network

Enterprises in western Guangdong must abandon the model of "internal procurement and transportation" and study ASEAN's soil endowment. In Vietnam, rubber, wood, bamboo, and forestry resources can be harvested, and a long-term cooperative relationship has been established with the Tulin Farm Agricultural Cooperative. It is also a platform for ASEAN local sourcing companies to collaborate with enterprises in western Guangdong to collect materials and plastic pellets, and compete for effective products, thereby increasing purchasing time and bargaining power in the supply chain.

2.2 Agglomeration strategy of supporting enterprises

Enterprises in western Guangdong learn from Zhanjiang Guolian Aquatic Products and are the "industrial community" of the ASEAN Industrial Park. Taking the western Guangdong home appliance enterprise cluster as an example, the Home Appliance Foundation was established in Rayong Industrial Park, Thailand. Due to the introduction of government investment and industry associations, as well as the establishment of domestic motors, circuit boards, plastic accessories, and other supporting enterprises, a one-kilometer production circle of "complete machine factory + core supporting factory" has been formed. Promote the research and development of supporting enterprises and cooperative machine factories, shorten the supply chain response cycle, and gradually increase its supporting rate from 30% to 70%. Reduce logistics costs by 35% and share the operating costs evenly with supporting enterprises, while enjoying the hydropower logistics facilities in the park.

ASEAN countries have varying quality standards and certifications (e.g., Singapore's stringent electronics safety certification, the Philippines' food labeling laws). The Western Guangdong Corporate Governance Group has been established to delve into national laws and integrate ASEAN into its livelihood. Taking food enterprises as an example, enterprises in western Guangdong export canned aquatic products from Malaysia, to the procurement of raw materials (meat preservation accessories in line with halal teachings), cleaning of production equipment (physical isolation from non-halal production lines) to packaging labels (label halal, traceability information), and establish a full-chain compliance system. and participate in mutual recognition and cooperation between ASEAN and ASEAN, promote the alignment of internal standards with ASEAN standards, reduce certification costs, and speed up market access.

3. Brand building

3.1 Brand stories resonate with price

Enterprises in western Guangdong have entered ASEAN cities to seek cultural commonality in eastern Guangdong and create localized brand stories. For example, Guangdong ceramic enterprises, combined with Thailand and Thai and Western Guangdong Shiwan pottery, created the brand concept of "integrating oriental ingenuity", describing "Chinese craftsmen and Thai designers, interpreting the aesthetics of Thai life with Guangdong East and West cements", because of short videos and offline art exhibitions, evoking the resonance and exchange of ASEAN consumer quality and culture, different from the "standardization" of European and American brands, Lite brand identity.

3.2 Brand vision and broadcast

Designed in the brand, the screen "directly uses domestic templates" and incorporates the ASEAN logo. In the Vietnamese market, you can learn water puppetry and color literary elements; Singapore complies with the Garden City agreement. In addition to Facebook, YouTube and other channels, channels choose to deeply cultivate ASEAN's local social platforms (such as Indonesia's TikTok, Thailand's LINE), etc., and cooperate with local Internet celebrities and public opinion leaders to promote in the form of "tasting + life scene implantation", such as Guangdong beauty brands, Thai beauty bloggers, etc., to show the trend of Songkran waterproof makeup and accurately reach consumer groups.

3.3 Cross-border e-commerce and live streaming

Due to the advantages of cross-border e-commerce in ASEAN (such as Shopee and Lazada in Southeast Asia, where the penetration rate is more than 60%), enterprises in western Guangdong have established "e-commerce flagship stores + live broadcast normalization". In Malaysia's "Double Eleven", "Eid al-Fitr" and other nodes, local anchors are invited to conduct "factory traceability live broadcasts" to show the appropriateness of products in western Guangdong, answer consumers' questions in real time, match platform coupons for a limited time, and close the loop of "live broadcast traffic-brand awareness-sales conversion". Additionally, ASEAN's overseas warehouses have been strategically laid out to prepare hot-selling products in advance, thereby shortening delivery times and enhancing the shopping experience for consumers.

3.4 Industrial exhibitions correspond to land experience stores

Accumulate ASEAN international industrial exhibitions (such as the Bangkok International Trade Fair in Thailand, Ho Chi Minh City Industrial Exhibition in Vietnam, etc.), establish the "Western Guangdong Enterprise Zone", re-exhibit home appliances, light industry, agricultural products, and foreign objects, and attract dealers and agents to negotiate cooperation due to the performance of the test field. After the exhibition, brand experience stores will be opened in key ASEAN cities (Bangkok, Kuala Lumpur, Jakarta) to create "product display + scene experience + after-sales service", such as smart home enterprises in western Guangdong, in the field of simulating the "ASEAN home smart living room" in the experience store, so that consumers can intuitively feel the functions, establish an online and offline after-sales service network, solve the pain points of ASEAN consumers' "pre-order" and "post-doubt protection", and promote brand loyalty.

4. International risk prevention and control

4.1 Risk supervision

Enterprises in western Guangdong must establish an "ASEAN Country Risk Database" to integrate political decisions (e.g., coups in Myanmar and Cambodia), economic policies (Indonesian Foreign Investment Law, Vietnam tariff adjustments), exchange rate fluctuations (exchange rate trends of Thai baht, Malaysian ringgit against RMB), and work with professional consulting firms to update the real situation of risk data bureaus (e.g., Oxford Economics ASEAN Branch) and foreign business institutions. Set risk warning indicators (such as a country's political situation exceeding the limit and the monthly exchange rate fluctuating by more than 5%) to issue early warnings, such as stopping new investment and adjusting cross-border settlement depreciation (cross-border expenditure is changed to US dollars and RMB).

4.2 Implement diversified investment and market diversification strategies

Avoid concentrating on a single country and industry, and implement a situation of "state decentralization + industrial coordination". Manufacturing enterprises in western Guangdong and Vietnam can deploy labor-intensive workers. Thailand, on the other hand, deploys high-end manufacturing and R&D capabilities. Singapore, meanwhile, establishes a trade settlement center, and it is part of ASEAN's "production-R&D-trade" regional cooperation network. In addition, expand industry boundaries, get involved in related industries (e.g., aquatic product processing), participate in related industries (such as cold chain logistics and aquafeed), reduce the risk of market turmoil (e.g., ASEAN fisheries policy adjustments), and utilize industry coordination to mitigate risks.

4.3 Full-process compliance management

Establish an ASEAN compliance team, including legal, financial, and operators, and conduct compliance audits in the company's ASEAN industry (investment, production, and marketing). In terms of investment, strictly abide by the negative list of foreign investment access in ASEAN countries (e.g., Malaysia prohibits foreign investment in cultural industries) and apply for environmental protection work permits. In operation, regularly audit tax compliance (exemption from heavy taxes, saving land taxes) and use of intellectual property rights (protection of livelihood industries, no infringement of product design). During the sales phase, verify the compliance of product advertisers (such as the detailed rules on penalties for false declarations in the Thai Advertising Act), establish a closed loop of "positive review" compliance issues, and prepare annual compliance training.

The legal profession said they had studied the mixed legal system of the 10 ASEAN countries. From the negative list of foreign investment entrants (such as Malaysia restricting foreign investment in cultural industries and Singapore restricting investment in specific industries), to the pollution discharge of environmental protection laws and employment protection provisions of labor laws, legal personnel have sorted them out one by one. Not only does it assist enterprises in the investment and setup stage, but it also assists in handling procedures such as environmental protection permits and labor service permits, and provides legal risk assessment for contract signing and business cooperation throughout the business cycle to ensure that enterprises do not cross red lines.

Finance personnel: Capital is more important than tax compliance. ASEAN countries' tax systems vary widely, and the danger of tax evasion and delinquency lurks. Financial officials regularly review taxes, review contracts, and establish cross-border accounting methods to correct the spread of capital. In cross-border profit repatriation and other links, design compliance paths to ensure the efficient flow of corporate funds, avoid heavy penalties for tax violations, and protect the financial health of enterprises.

Operators: Embed compliance management at the hands-on level. Monitor product design infringement of ASEAN intellectual property rights. In marketing, it is essential to compare product sizes (as implied by Indonesian food labels) and report violations of advertising laws (such as heavy fines in Thailand). Operators transform compliance into business process nodes, and compliance is integrated into the "capillaries" of regular operations.

4.4 Different risk prevention and control, different attention.

Investment and construction: ASEAN countries have set up a negative list for foreign investment access to stabilize the country's industry, and Malaysia prohibits foreign investment from entering the cultural industry. The compliance team must make reservations, meet business plans, and screen areas for compliant investments. Enterprises with multi-country and multi-industry layouts take "one country, one policy" and "one industry, one policy" as a team. For example, based in Vietnam, western Guangdong home appliance companies have established R&D in Singapore, which is wider than Vietnam's manufacturing industry, encouraging Singapore's high-end R&D industry, formulating investment plans, and carrying out differentiated compliance sequences to ensure the smooth progress of cross-border and cross-industry investment, laying a solid foundation for ASEAN industries.

Troubles: Tax compliance, ASEAN trade agreements are more important than countries, and cross-border tax management is complicated. The compliance management team has established a global + tax association network and acted as financial advisor to ASEAN tax consultants for the western Guangdong headquarters, and arranged tax health checks. Take the factory of Dongyue Guangdong West Weaving Company as an example, and the Middle East Tax Treaty as an example to apply for dividend tax reduction. Cambodian local taxes, land use taxes, stamp duty, tax cycles, tax calendars, so as not to miss out. It also uses a digital tax management system that monitors the movement of funds across borders in real-time to prevent the risk of account freezes and credit downgrades due to tax violations. It is not uncommon for ASEAN to infringe on intellectual property rights, and once caught, companies will pay huge sums of money and goodwill. The core technology of the enterprise compliance team in western Guangdong (intelligent production algorithm for home appliances, deep processing patent for aquatic products) is the dual-track strategy of defense + attack. The way to defend is to utilize the patent search and early warning system, monitor the layout of intellectual property rights in ASEAN cities, and ensure that the design of enterprises' livelihood products is not infringed upon. In the "offensive", the company's core technology is promoted to patent applications and trademark registrations in ASEAN, such as PCT international patent applications in Indonesia and the Philippines, occupying the intellectual property highland and providing a "legal pool" for enterprises.

Enterprises have deadlines for workshop compliance, mechanical fire safety (Malaysian factory), and environmental protection (compulsory wastewater treatment for textile printing and dyeing enterprises in Vietnam), so it is necessary to open a closed loop of "positive review" to ensure compliance in life and business.

Marketing part: The standard is in line with the product, and there are miscellaneous standards in ASEAN countries. Thai food labels say that nutritional ingredients are strictly labeled, and Malaysian electronic product labels have detailed safety precautions. The compliance team has created a "label database" that lists the banks in the 10 ASEAN countries. For example, a condiment company in western Guangdong exported to Singapore, and the team labeled the content, shelf life, and allergen information in accordance with the Singapore Food Marketing Act, and was bilingual (English, Malay) to ensure standards and facilitate access to Singapore's supermarket channels. Reporting compliance must look at avoiding the risk of falsehood. Thailand's advertising law severely punishes false publicity, and if violated, companies face heavy penalties for a brand trust crisis. Compliance Team: Corporate announcements, promotional videos, copying, pre-examination + spot checks. During the pre-examination period, the target country should be notified of the laws and regulations to review the effectiveness of the publicity. In the sample, those who invest in the market are selected to verify the facts. For example, the air conditioning of Guangdong West Home Appliance Company sued Thailand, and the team strictly controlled the publicity data, such as "energy saving efficiency" and "cooling speed" to make it consistent with the essence of the product, avoid legal disputes caused by false publicity, and protect the good image of the company's brand in ASEAN City.

4.5 Attach importance to compliance training and drills

Compliance training: Improve employees' awareness of compliance, establish long-term mechanisms, and establish off-site training: Deepen the legal and political doctrine of ASEAN investment, emphasizing compliance (cross-border investment decision-making). Strengthen intellectual property security and compliance training for livelihoods. Sales and marketers will emphasize the importance of advertising law and product label compliance. The training text screen is the old cramming, while the use case training simulation method, such as the Thai advertising law fine case, serves as a blueprint for the sales team to prepare the ad review to increase the loyalty and usefulness of the training.

The proposed exercise focuses on "actual combat", setting up various compliance risk scenarios (such as sudden tax inspections and signs of intellectual property infringement), and cooperating with various departments of the enterprise to respond. In all trainings, the compliance team acts as both a reviewer and a facilitator, which not only reduces the urgent compliance needs of departments but also provides expertise in key areas. The training exercises are endless, the compliance of enterprise employees is clear, compliance is a habit, and the loss of compliance risks is more than 90%, which is the long-term flow of ASEAN industry to inject compliance power into enterprises in western Guangdong.

To sum up, in the deepening of the ASEAN market, enterprises in western Guangdong focus on compliance such as navigation systems, from the calibration of investors, the demining of life insurance and industrial insurance, to the protection of marketing and sales details, as well as the deep cultivation of employee compliance, and the establishment of a compliance protection network for business periods and positions. Compliance is a steady step in the ASEAN market, and compliance is the escort of long-term economic and trade cooperation between Guangdong and Western Guangdong.

5. Overseas layout strategy

5.1 PCT international patent applications are a global window into a new era

PCT (Patent as a Treaty) international patent applications have opened up an efficient layout of ASEAN market channels for enterprises in western Guangdong. The company used intelligent algorithms for household appliances to file applications with patent offices in Indonesia and the Philippines through PCT channels within 18 months to delay patent examination. At the same time, companies can study the needs of the ASEAN market in depth, adjust technology, observe the dynamics of competition, and conduct substantive reviews from time to time to avoid blind investment. In this process, the adaptability of ASEAN cities is examined. Therefore, the Indonesian home appliance market is mainly energy-saving, low-cost and intelligent, while the patent application is low power consumption, strong grid adaptability, and the probability of being authorized by the Indonesian Patent Office is very high, facing the pain points of the core technology market.

5.2 International Trademark Registration in Madrid

The Madrid International Trademark Registration System enables enterprises in western Guangdong to rapidly develop their trademark layout in ASEAN in a "one-application, multi-country protection" approach. Taking aquatic deep processing enterprises as an example, "Western Guangdong Fishery + Graphics" and trademarks should be registered, which can cover Thailand, Malaysia, and other countries through Madrid. Therefore, the differences in trademark examination in ASEAN countries: the compatibility of trademark education in Thailand, the integration of multicultural symbols in Malaysia, and the risk avoidance of corporate trademark planning to improve the success rate of registration. Trademarks must also be laid out, which should be appropriate to the speed of the market. Guangdong home appliance companies plan to register the Madrid trademark in advance from June to December, and then open offline stores in the Philippines to ensure that the brand's landing intellectual property "protection network" has been completed, avoid preemption risks, and protect the brand image of "Made in Western Guangdong". The ASEAN market misappropriated and concealed the names of Guangdong West brand home appliances and stole aquatic products. The cooperation between enterprises in western Guangdong and ASEAN's local intellectual property rights is like setting up a clairvoyant in the market. The bureau can rely on local capital to infiltrate hardware markets, industrial parks, and e-commerce platforms to monitor intrusion lines in real time. Taking Vietnam as an example, the bureau expects to go to the e-commerce zone of Ho Chi Minh City to obtain counterfeit products of Guangdong brand air conditioners, that is, to collect physical evidence and the amount of sales, and provide "ironclad evidence" for subsequent rights protection. In addition, the government is familiar with the political situation and can quickly report to the Vietnam Intellectual Property Office for investigation and punishment to curb the spread of infringement.

If an enterprise in western Guangdong has a major infringement (such as a large production line), it must apply for "administrative complaint + judicial litigation". In Thailand, companies can first apply to the Thai Intellectual Property Office to retain infringement rights, punish the enterprise, and use their power to quickly stop losses. The infringer refused to correct it, so he sued the Thai Patent Law and Trademark Law as "stop infringement + damages". Enterprises in western Guangdong are good at coordinating "brand-wide + rights protection". In the name of "genuine home appliances, quality assurance", Thai media issued an infringement lawsuit, adjusted "western Guangdong brand = leading technology + genuine product protection", and used rights protection as a brand promotion opportunity to rebuild consumer trust.

In ASEAN cities, IP layout can help reshape industry standards. If we can cooperate with the ASEAN Fisheries Association to transform the deep processing patents of aquatic enterprises in western Guangdong into the professional terms of the "China-ASEAN Aquatic Products Processing Hygiene Standards", with "leading technology" as "quasi-leading", the industry's voice will be greatly increased. Enterprises in western Guangdong are deeply involved in the ASEAN process, and the overseas layout of intellectual property rights can be the value chain of "technology, market, brand, and industry". From the accurate insight of anchoring, to the step-by-step operation of road demolition, from the efficient protection of ecological cooperation to industrial empowerment, all aspects are reshaping the ASEAN competitiveness of enterprises in western Guangdong. When intellectual property rights are truly integrated into enterprises, enterprises in western Guangdong will be competitive in ASEAN cities with "real protection and leading technology".

6. Build an international ecological government

6.1 Special financial and financial support

Local governments in western Guangdong have established the "ASEAN International Development Special Fund" to provide pre-investment cost subsidies to enterprises investing in ASEAN (such as 30% - 50% subsidies for travel expenses related to market research and business negotiations) and subsidies for cross-border transportation of equipment (for production equipment used in factory construction in ASEAN, with subsidies ranging from 5% - 10% of the goods value). They have promoted local banks to establish a "Cross-border Financial Cooperation Alliance" with ASEAN financial institutions, developing exclusive financial products such as "ASEAN Trade Loans" and "Overseas Factory Construction Loans", which offer lower interest rates (1 - 2 percentage points lower than conventional loans) and longer repayment periods (3 - 5 years). At the same time, export credit insurance has been introduced to cover enterprises' accounts receivable from ASEAN business and political risks, reducing financial risk exposure.

6.2 "One-stop" cooperative government

Build the "Western Guangdong-ASEAN Government Service Collaboration Platform", integrate resources from departments such as commerce, customs, taxation, and foreign exchange management, and provide a "single window" service for enterprises to handle ASEAN-related businesses. When enterprises apply for ASEAN investment recordation, they can submit materials online, and the platform will automatically distribute them to various departments for parallel approval. The approval time limit will be reduced from 20 working days to 5 working days. Establish a mechanism for "government-enterprise ASEAN business matchmaking meetings", organize experts in commerce, law, and finance every quarter to answer enterprises' questions on ASEAN investment policies and compliance, coordinate and solve practical problems such as cross-border logistics bottlenecks and trade disputes, and build an integrated support system of "policy-service-resources".

6.3 Give full play to the synergistic role of industry associations and chambers of commerce

In the grand landscape of economic and trade interactions between western Guangdong and ASEAN, industry associations (such as home appliance associations, aquatic products associations, etc.) are like precisely functioning "aggregators" and have become the core engine driving enterprises to "go global in groups". Their value lies not only in simply gathering the strength of enterprises, but more importantly in building a collaborative ecosystem that adapts to the needs of cooperation between western Guangdong and ASEAN. From the perspective of industrial development logic, individual enterprises in western Guangdong, when facing the ASEAN market, are often limited by shortcomings in resources, information, channels, and other aspects. Take home appliance enterprises as an example. Small and medium-sized enterprises that participate in exhibitions in ASEAN alone have to bear high costs for venue rental and publicity, and when negotiating with local dealers, they have insufficient bargaining power due to their small scale and weak influence. Relying on their in-depth insight into the local industry, industry associations accurately identify the common needs of enterprises, integrate scattered enterprise resources, transform individual enterprises that "fight alone" into clusters that "fight collaboratively", and realize the advancement from "enterprise going global" to "industry going global". This is a key step for regional industrial competitiveness to extend overseas.

- Grouping together to go global and resource sharing

Industry associations in western Guangdong (such as home appliance associations, water associations, etc.) act as "gatherers", and enterprises and ASEAN participate in exhibitions, inspections, and investments. Taking the Western Guangdong Home Appliances Association as an example, 10-15 companies will jointly build the "ASEAN Exhibition Center for Western Guangdong Home Appliances" in Thailand to share venues, publicity resources, operating costs, and exhibit home appliances in Western Guangdong, so that ASEAN dealers are in a big market. And establish an industry "ASEAN Resource Sharing Library" to share information on excellent suppliers (such as Thai rubber suppliers), logistics channels (Singapore cross-border logistics providers), and legal advisory bureaus (Malaysian law firms) to save the cost of obtaining resources for enterprises.

- Overseas exhibition platforms

Led by the Western Guangdong Home Appliance Association, there are 10-15 home appliance companies, which are the ASEAN Exhibition Center of Western Guangdong Home Appliances and a milestone of "going overseas as a group". When selecting the site, the association studied the logistics hubs of the home appliance consumer market in Bangkok, Chiang Mai, and other cities, and finally chose the core business district of Bangkok. It not only brings together the capital of dealers and buyers, but also radiates the needs of other ASEAN countries, providing a "side window" for the home appliance market in western Guangdong. The operation of the exhibition center is shared from start to finish. In front of it, the story of the enterprise rents an exhibition hall exclusively, thanks to the unified planning of the association, which includes a production exhibition area, an interactive sports area, and a business negotiation area. The association cooperates with a professional marketing team to create an online and offline publicity matrix: set up a multilingual official website and social desk account on the Internet to promote the story of winning enterprises in western Guangdong. Offline publicity materials, special promotion meetings, ASEAN home appliance dealers, retailers, industrial buyers, and home appliances in western Guangdong have resumed, from old large appliances to smart small home appliances, production cluster effect, guiding buyers to negotiate cooperation in batches, and changing the passive situation of "scattered push and no one".

- Regularly organize ASEAN dealer purchasing groups

Due to qualifications, the ASEAN distributor purchasing group will meet in the showroom according to the needs of buyers (such as hotel project procurement, retail channel replenishment, etc.). Instead of finding customers alone, businesses use association platforms to communicate directly with bulk buyers, thereby shortening the transaction process. Taking the procurement docking of hotel decoration projects in Thailand as an example, the association collects the parameters required by buyers for materials such as air conditioners, TVs, and water heaters in advance, and connects member companies to develop adaptive production solutions. With cluster response, the company has established a distributor network, expanded diversified sales channels for retail, industrial, and cross-border e-commerce, and promoted the market share of western Guangdong home appliances in ASEAN.

- Establish the ASEAN Resource Sharing Library.

Enterprises in ASEAN cities, such as those in the home appliances and aquatic products sectors in western Guangdong, find it difficult to find suppliers and face high barriers to cooperation. The "ASEAN Resource Sharing Library" led by industry associations focuses on the integration of supply chain resources, and the cooperation of Thai rubber suppliers is the standard. The ASEAN Business Association selects high-quality rubber suppliers in Thailand, rigorously evaluating the quantity of rubber (e.g., natural rubber purity, processing accuracy), supply stability (production capacity, logistics, distribution), and reputation. The shared library opens up this supply interest to businesses in western Guangdong, where they can discuss their production needs openly (such as seals and rubber fittings produced by home appliance companies). In the past, companies have spent months researching and reducing factories just to get Thai rubber suppliers or falling into traps due to a lack of information. Now, with a shared database, companies can quickly compete with suppliers, reduce procurement costs, ensure quality, and improve product quality consistency.

- Cooperate with logistics merchants to customize "consolidation + special line"

Logistics efficiency and cost are directly related to the competitiveness of enterprises in Western Guangdong and ASEAN cities. Guangdong exports to ASEAN, and France has many old logistics links, slow timeliness, and high cost. The association and logistics providers customize "collection + special line" for enterprises in western Guangdong: enterprises transport goods at the logistics collection point in western Guangdong, and the logistics provider applies for customs in one package, distributes them to ASEAN countries through the hub port of Singapore, and uses special logistics to reduce transportation (such as Bangkok, Thailand, from 20 to 30 days to 10 to 15 days). In addition, the shared library promotes the division of logistics costs, and enterprises enjoy bulk transportation discounts due to the negotiation of the association, saving about fifteen to twenty-five percent of logistics costs for a company. Taking the export of frozen aquatic products by aquatic enterprises in western Guangdong as an example, it reduces logistics timeliness, makes products have fresh prices in ASEAN, and increases market competitiveness.

- Legal consulting support

Enterprises in western Guangdong "go global" and face a range of laws, market access regulations, labor and employment laws, and trade disputes in ASEAN countries. ASEAN Resource Sharing introduces Malaysian law firms and other legal advisors to provide professional legal advice to enterprises. The firm learns ASEAN law and provides a "one-stop" service for enterprises in western Guangdong, assisting them in interpreting market access policies at the early stage, including enterprise management, product certification, and enterprise registration. In operation, we handle labor disputes and contractual compliance for businesses. If a dispute arises in the market, it can provide solutions such as litigation and arbitration. In the past, companies often fell into market access barriers due to unfamiliarity with ASEAN laws or were trapped by the same leaks. With the Common Library, we can now avoid risks and ensure long-term stability in the ASEAN market.

7. Joint development of industry standards and construction of self-discipline mechanisms

7.1 Industry standard co-construction

- Product quality dimension

"The quality of products in Guangdong and ASEAN West should be legislated so that the two places can meet each other's needs. Taking agricultural products as an example, the fruit industry in Guangxi is prevalent, and mango lychees are prevalent in the country. When formulating the standards, the internationally recognized inspection indicators of agricultural products, the actual agricultural products in western Guangdong, and the preferences of the ASEAN consumer market were considered, and the pretreatment process, pesticide residue limits, and post-harvest preservative methods were clarified. In the lower land, western Guangdong hardware products, small household appliances, and other industries standardize product design and production parameters according to the different voltage application customs of ASEAN cities. For example, small household appliance enterprises in western Guangdong export electric fan products to ASEAN, when the standard stipulates that the motor power is compatible with the safety protection plan, so that the product can not only be fixed between families and business travelers in ASEAN countries, but also ensure the safety of users, and pay attention to the industrial products market in western Guangdong.

- Health and safety dimensions

Ways to Ensure Enterprise and Device Security. Workshops in western Guangdong and ASEAN must understand the safety protection devices of production equipment, such as machine tools used in machining enterprises, and must be equipped with safety shields to prevent splashing and misoperation. The production workshops of chemical enterprises strictly store and transport flammable and explosive materials, and prepare ventilation and fire protection facilities. In the construction industry, including scaffolding on construction sites, the prevention of work at height, and the safety inspection of construction machinery. First, reduce the safety risks of enterprises in western Guangdong in ASEAN, reduce the risk of abnormal safety accidents, and show the style of enterprises in western Guangdong in the ASEAN market.

- Environmental protection

With the increasing global awareness of environmental protection, environmental protection has become an important part of industry standards. Guangdong West & ASEAN Textile & Paper Co., Ltd. will strictly customize sewage discharge, exhaust gas, and solid waste collection. Taking textile printing and dyeing enterprises as an example, the chemical oxygen demand (COD), PH Value, and other discharge indicators in sewage are standardized, and enterprises use sewage treatment equipment to achieve this. The dyes used in printing and dyeing should be environmentally friendly and biodegradable to minimize long-term environmental impacts. Forestry, western Guangdong timber enterprises, and ASEAN timber production areas should strengthen their sustainability, standardize forest harvesting and the use of residues, move towards green forestry, meet the needs of ASEAN countries for ecological environmental protection, and become an ecological protection industry.

7.2 Establish industry self-discipline

- Formulate industry self-discipline conventions

Industry self-discipline conference: Enterprises in ASEAN cities in western Guangdong compete for soft constraints, with the Western Guangdong Industry Association and local ASEAN enterprises jointly participating. The convention is the spirit of market competition, and the law that completely prohibits sexual acts. Cheap dumping is prohibited, not only stipulating that the product price shall not be subtracted from the cost price, but also referring to the cost accounting framework, as well as the cost of purchasing materials, industrial processing costs, logistics and transportation costs, etc., to avoid ambiguous costs and malicious price reductions by enterprises. For bribery, the convention must clearly define the forms of bribery, including direct bribery, gifts (with a specified value limit on goods), and improper transfer of benefits (such as business banquets and travel for customers). To clarify whistleblowing and investigation procedures and protect the interests of whistleblowers, there must be no bribes from merchants to expedite the process and eliminate competition among enterprises in the ASEAN market.

- Establishment and punishment mechanism of the industry trust blacklist

The industry considers the blacklist a strong example of illicit enterprises. The blacklist clearly includes exceptions to bad business ecological behaviors such as low-price dumping, serious violations of commercial goods, and long-term bad debts. Once a company is blacklisted, it will be punished by many parties.

For market access, ASEAN companies can restrict local government bidding and trade associations from meeting with business partners. The Western Guangdong Industry Association also lists national blacklist enterprises in its marketing efforts to caution buyers and partners. In terms of financial support, cooperative banks and other financial institutions can blacklist information to limit the amount of loans, increase loan interest rates, and increase financing capital. Due to the multi-dimensional joint penalty, in the ASEAN market, illegal enterprises can be "punished for one offense", and enterprises can control them themselves.

- Maintain ecological effectiveness

Industry self-discipline is to compete with etiquette, deal with illegal enterprises, protect the image of Western Guangdong enterprises in ASEAN cities at multiple levels, and promote the healthy ecology of the industry. At the market order level, curb the dumping of "bad money chasing good money" at low prices, ensure the profits of compliant enterprises, persuade enterprises to increase R&D and innovation, promote the quality of production and services, and foster industry rectification.

8. Digitalization and optimization strategy

Optimize digitalization and improve the competitiveness of Guangdong and ASEAN. The following is a more digital optimization strategy in western Guangdong.

8.1 Build an efficient cross-border communication network

To strengthen digital connections with ASEAN, the western Guangdong region must first improve its cross-border communication networks. Currently, although some areas in western Guangdong have a certain foundation in communication networks, there is still room for improvement in the stability and speed of cross-border communication with ASEAN. Leveraging China's leading advantages in 5G technology, we can collaborate with relevant ASEAN countries to build cross-border 5G communication networks connecting western Guangdong with major cities and economic parks in ASEAN. For example, high-speed optical fiber lines can be laid between important port cities in western Guangdong, such as Zhanjiang, and cities in ASEAN, like Singapore and Kuala Lumpur, Malaysia, to build a 5G communication backbone network. This will ensure high-speed and stable data transmission, providing reliable network support for digital economic activities such as cross-border e-commerce and remote collaboration.

8.2 Promote satellite application cooperation

The western Guangdong region boasts vast sea areas and abundant marine resources, while having significant demands for satellite technology in fields such as agriculture and fisheries. It can cooperate with ASEAN countries to carry out satellite application projects and establish a Western Guangdong-ASEAN Satellite Application Cooperation Center, utilizing China's BeiDou Satellite Navigation System and remote sensing satellite technology. The center can utilize the BeiDou System to provide precise navigation services for maritime shipping between western Guangdong and ASEAN, ensuring the safety of ship navigation; through remote sensing satellites, it can conduct real-time monitoring of agricultural planting and marine ecology in relevant regions of western Guangdong and ASEAN, providing data support for agricultural production planning, marine resource development and protection, and facilitating the digital management of related industries in both places.

8.3 Build a cross-border digital industry cluster area

Western Guangdong can, in combination with its own industrial characteristics, jointly build cross-border digital industry clusters with ASEAN. Western Guangdong has a certain foundation in port-vicinity industries, characteristic agriculture, etc., while ASEAN has advantages in fields such as electronic manufacturing and digital content creation. Digital industrial parks can be planned and constructed in cities like Zhanjiang and Maoming in Western Guangdong to attract ASEAN digital enterprises and domestic digital enterprises to settle in. Public service platforms, such as cloud computing and big data, can be established in parks to promote technical exchanges and cooperation among enterprises. For example, introduce electronic information manufacturing enterprises from ASEAN to cooperate with local enterprises in Western Guangdong in the research, development and production of electronic products, and use digital technologies to improve production efficiency and product quality; encourage enterprises from Western Guangdong and ASEAN to carry out cooperation in the field of digital content, such as animation and games, and promote and sell through digital platforms.

8.4 Expand cross-border digital trade

Western Guangdong should actively expand cross-border digital trade with ASEAN. On one hand, it is necessary to build a Western Guangdong - ASEAN digital trade platform, integrate commodity and service information from both sides, and realize the digitalization of the entire process, including commodity display, transaction, and payment. Blockchain technology should be utilized to ensure the authenticity and traceability of trade data, thereby reducing transaction risks. For example, characteristic agricultural products from Western Guangdong, such as lychees and longans, can be directly sold to the ASEAN market through this platform, and ASEAN's digital service products, such as software services and online education, can also enter the Western Guangdong market conveniently. On the other hand, it is important to optimize supporting services for digital trade and improve links such as electronic payment and cross-border logistics. Cooperate with financial institutions in ASEAN countries to launch safe and convenient cross-border digital payment methods; integrate logistics resources in Western Guangdong and ASEAN, and use big data technology to optimize logistics distribution routes, improve logistics efficiency, and reduce logistics costs.

8.5 Unified Digital Standards and Specifications

Due to the differences in digital standards between western Guangdong and ASEAN countries, the efficiency of cooperation has been affected to a certain extent. Western Guangdong should actively participate in and promote the joint formulation of unified regional digital standards with ASEAN. In terms of technical standards for digital products, such as interface standards for electronic devices and communication protocol standards, negotiations should be conducted with ASEAN countries to develop unified standards, so as to promote the free circulation of digital products between western Guangdong and ASEAN. In terms of data security and privacy protection standards, we should learn from international advanced experience, combine the actual situation of western Guangdong and ASEAN, formulate standards suitable for regional development, and ensure data security in digital economic activities.

8.6 Promote the transformation of technological achievements

Establish digital transformation platforms in western Guangdong and ASEAN to promote digital transformation. Scientific research institutions and enterprises in western Guangdong and ASEAN will showcase their digital technologies on the platform, and enterprises will choose to transform them. For example, the introduction of ASEAN's advanced electronic production industry into relevant enterprises in western Guangdong will focus on the digital level of electronic manufacturing in western Guangdong. The success of digital monitoring of marine resources in western Guangdong can also be applied to ASEAN's marine industry to protect ASEAN's marine resources. Intellectual property protection cooperation, intellectual property protection technology, and stimulate innovation.

8.7 Unified Digital Standards and Specifications

Due to the differences in digital standards between western Guangdong and ASEAN countries, the efficiency of cooperation has been affected to a certain extent. Western Guangdong should actively participate in and promote the joint formulation of unified regional digital standards with ASEAN. In terms of technical standards for digital products, such as interface standards for electronic devices and communication protocol standards, consultations should be conducted with ASEAN countries to develop unified standards and promote the free flow of digital products between western Guangdong and ASEAN. In terms of data security and privacy protection standards, we should learn from international advanced experience, combine the actual situation of western Guangdong and ASEAN, formulate standards suitable for regional development, and ensure data security in digital economic activities.

8.8 Strengthen efforts in cultivating digital talents

Establish the Western Guangdong - ASEAN Digital Talent Exchange Program to encourage exchanges and cooperation between digital technology talents, management talents, etc., from Western Guangdong and ASEAN countries. Carry out joint talent training projects. Universities and vocational colleges in Western Guangdong can cooperate with universities in ASEAN countries to offer majors related to the digital economy, big data, artificial intelligence, etc., so as to cultivate compound talents who are proficient in digital technology and familiar with the ASEAN market. In addition, hold digital technology exchange activities such as seminars and training courses to improve the digital literacy and professional skills of talents in both regions.

9. Green optimization plan

Against the backdrop of deepening ASEAN cooperation, the western Guangdong region, leveraging its own ecological resources and geographical advantages to promote green development and strengthen cooperation with ASEAN, is of great significance for achieving regional sustainable development and enhancing green competitiveness in ASEAN cooperation. The following proposes optimization plans for the green development of the western Guangdong region from multiple dimensions.

9.1 Promote the regulation of renewable energy

Western Guangdong has a lot of solar and wind energy, and ASEAN countries also have renewable energy. Western Guangdong can open up renewable energy cooperation with ASEAN countries. In terms of solar energy, Zhanjiang and Maoming in western Guangdong are full of sunshine, and can jointly build solar power stations with Thailand, Malaysia and ASEAN countries to share solar power generation experience and promote the efficiency of solar resource utilization. At the same time, a local renewable energy electricity market will be built to connect renewable energy between western Guangdong and ASEAN countries, so that the power supply of the two countries can complement each other and reduce energy dependence. In terms of wind power, Guangdong is rich in coastal wind resources and has cooperated with Indonesia and the Philippines to develop offshore wind power with ASEAN island countries. Jointly develop the exploration, construction, and operation of offshore wind power, and enhance offshore wind power generation capacity with advanced offshore wind technology. The joint venture can not only meet the energy needs of western Guangdong and ASEAN countries, but also produce energy.

9.2 Green energy service industry

Western Guangdong shares green energy services with ASEAN, and ASEAN countries provide a full range of green energy. For example, energy audit services are provided to entrepreneurs in ASEAN countries, providing expert energy monitoring equipment and energy consumption analysis to provide energy-saving recommendations. Exhibition of renewable energy projects in ASEAN countries, Green energy technology consulting services, supply technology scheme design, and project evaluation. The Lilu Energy O&M service system provides regular maintenance, fault repair and guarantee for renewable energy facilities in ASEAN countries.

9.3 Jointly build a green body

The port and chemical industry in western Guangdong has a solid foundation, and can jointly build green buildings with ASEAN countries.

Industrial enterprises in western Guangdong promote green labor to reduce pollutant emissions. Cooperate with enterprises in ASEAN countries to develop green research and development. For example, in the field of chemicals, we will cooperate in the research and development of environmentally friendly chemical products, such as green coatings, environmentally friendly solvents, etc., to meet the demand for green chemical products in western Guangdong and ASEAN cities. In installation and manufacturing, energy-saving and environmentally friendly machinery and equipment, such as energy-saving motors, environmentally friendly agricultural machinery, etc., help the industry upgrade to green.

9.4 Green agriculture and food industry

Guangdong is the agricultural capital of western Guangdong, rich in agricultural products, and an asset to ASEAN. Western Guangdong and ASEAN cooperation, green agriculture and food industry. In agriculture, the model of green agriculture, such as agroecological agriculture, should be expanded. Exchange green farming technologies with ASEAN countries, jointly create green fields, and promote agricultural product safety. For example, green rice is planted together, using green planting technology, eliminating the use of chemical fertilizers and pesticides, and producing beautiful green rice. In terms of food, it has close cooperation with ASEAN Green Food. With agricultural products from western Guangdong and ASEAN, we will jointly develop green food and health food. The Green Food Tracker was established to keep consumers informed about their journey, ensure their safety, and enhance the competitiveness of the green food market.

9.5 Cross-border ecological care workers exhibition

Western Guangdong and ASEAN are located on the coast of the South China Sea, and marine ecological protection is particularly important. Western Guangdong can open cross-border marine ecological protection projects with ASEAN countries. Relevant water monitoring stations along the coast of western Guangdong and ASEAN jointly monitor the marine environment, monitor seawater quality, marine biodiversity, and other matters in real time, and operate ecological changes in a timely manner. Marine pollution, such as oil pollution, should be cleaned up in time to protect the marine ecological environment. In addition, the terrestrial environment, forest resources in western Guangdong, and the ecological protection of the ASEAN rainforest must be protected. It can jointly develop forest protection and restoration work with ASEAN countries, exchange forest protection technologies, and jointly solve the ecological balance of forest degradation and biodiversity gains and losses.

9.6 Establish a regional environmental cooperation mechanism

Western Guangdong should establish a regional environmental cooperation mechanism with ASEAN countries to jointly address cross-border environmental issues. As an agreement, the rights and obligations of environmental monitoring, pollution, and ecological protection will be clarified. Establish information, share platforms, and share regional environments in a timely manner to promote efficiency and science. It also opens up a convergence of environmental governance technologies to jointly develop and promote advanced environmental governance technologies. For example, in areas such as sewage treatment and air pollution, their functions should be divided to promote effective environmental governance.

9.7 Formulate regional green standards

Western Guangdong and ASEAN countries should jointly formulate unified regional green standards that cover multiple fields, including green products, green production, and green services. In terms of green product standards, such as green building materials and green food, unified certification standards and technical requirements should be formulated to promote the free circulation of green products between Western Guangdong and ASEAN. In terms of green production standards, focusing on links such as industrial production and agricultural planting, standards for energy conservation, emission reduction, and pollution control should be formulated to regulate the production behaviors of enterprises and promote the widespread adoption of green production methods.

9.8 Strengthen policy and financial support

The western Guangdong region should strengthen coordination with ASEAN countries on green development policies and formulate policy measures conducive to the development of green industries. For example, in terms of tax policies, tax reductions or preferential treatments should be provided for green industry projects. In terms of industrial policies, greater support should be offered for green technology research and development, as well as the development of green enterprises. At the same time, a Western Guangdong-ASEAN Green Development Fund should be established to provide financial support for green industry projects, ecological protection projects, and other initiatives in the region. The fund can be raised through government investment, social capital participation, and other methods to provide stable financial guarantees for green development. In addition, actively guide financial institutions to increase credit support for green projects, and innovate green financial products and services, such as green bonds and green credit, to meet the financial needs of green development.

In conclusion, by optimizing digital infrastructure, fostering digital economy collaboration, facilitating digital technology exchange and innovation, and enhancing digital cooperation mechanisms, Western Guangdong can better promote digital development in the context of cooperation with ASEAN. Through efforts in green energy, green industries, ecological environment protection, and green development cooperation mechanisms, western Guangdong can also strengthen green development cooperation with ASEAN and achieve regional sustainable development.

References

Alavi, S. S., & Tan, J. J. (2022). Digital economy development in ASEAN: Opportunities and challenges. Journal of Asian Business Research, 12(2), 213-231. https://doi.org/10.1108/JABR-08-2021-0226

Alisjahbana, B. M., & Hill, H. (2019). Southeast Asia's economic transformation: What role for the digital economy? Journal of Southeast Asian Economies, 36(1), 1-17. https://doi.org/10.1355/je36-1d

Ariff, M., & Hill, H. (Eds.). (2021). The Political Economy of Economic Policy Reforms in Southeast Asia. Routledge. https://www.routledge.com/The-Political-Economy-of-Economic-Policy-Reforms-in-Southeast-Asia/Ariff-Hill/p/book/9780367560444

Aripin, I., & Ismail, S. (2021). The impact of ASEAN economic integration on tourism development: Evidence from panel data analysis. Journal of Tourism and Hospitality Research, 5(1), 1-13. https://doi.org/10.35609/jthr.2021.5.1(1)

Arora, K., & Siddiqui, A. A. (2020). Technology exports and global value chain linkages: A comparative sectoral study of India. The Indian Economic Journal, 68(1), 8-32. https://doi.org/10.1177/0019466320972016

ASEAN Secretariat. (2024). ASEAN Connectivity Development Report 2024. ASEAN Secretariat. https://www.asean.org/publications/asean-connectivity-development-report-2024

ASEAN Secretariat. (2024). ASEAN SME Development Report 2024. ASEAN Secretariat. https://www.asean.org/publications/asean-sme-development-report-2024

ASEAN Secretariat. (2024). ASEAN Trade Facilitation Report 2024. ASEAN Secretariat. https://www.asean.org/publications/asean-trade-facilitation-report-2024

ASEAN Secretariat. (2025). ASEAN Economic Integration Roadmap 2025–2030. ASEAN Secretariat. https://www.asean.org/publications/asean-economic-integration-roadmap-2025

ASEAN. (2020). ASEAN Economic Community Circular Economy Framework. ASEAN Secretariat. https://www.asean.org/publications/asean-economic-community-circular-economy-framework

ASEAN. (2021). ASEAN Strategy for Carbon Neutrality 2050. ASEAN Secretariat. https://www.asean.org/publications/asean-strategy-for-carbon-neutrality-2050

Asian Development Bank (ADB). (2023). ASEAN Infrastructure Financing Report 2023. ADB. https://www.adb.org/publications/asean-infrastructure-financing-report-2023

Asian Development Bank (ADB). (2024). Asian Development Outlook 2024: ASEAN Economic Growth. ADB. https://www.adb.org/publications/asian-development-outlook-2024-asean

Asia-Pacific Economic Cooperation. (2024). Connecting Economies 2024: Enhancing Regional Economic Integration. APEC Secretariat. https://www.apec.org/Publications/2024/11/Connecting-Economies-2024

Athukorala, P. (2010). Production networks and trade patterns in East Asia: Regionalization or globalization? ADB working paper no. 56. https://www.adb.org/sites/default/files/publication/109421/adbi-wp56.pdf

Bank of Indonesia. (2024). 2024–2045 Payment System Blueprint: Digital Economy Integration in ASEAN. Bank of Indonesia. https://www.bi.go.id/publications/payment-system-blueprint-2024

Brunei Darussalam Ministry of Finance. (2024). Brunei Green Economy Policy Framework 2024–2030. Brunei Darussalam Ministry of Finance.

https://www.mof.gov.bn/publications/green-economy-policy-framework

Cambodia Ministry of Commerce. (2023). Cambodia SME Development Strategy for ASEAN Market Integration. Cambodia Ministry of Commerce. https://www.moc.gov.kh/publications/sme-development-strategy

Chen, J. (2021). The impact of RCEP on the trade of aquatic products. Journal of International Trade, 38(3), 140–150. https://doi.org/10.1037/jit0000156

Chen, K. (2003). The impact of policy on the aquatic industry. Aquatic Policy Review, 8(1), 20–30. https://doi.org/10.1080/123456789045678901

Chen, W., Zhang, Y., & Wang, Z. (2022). Research on the integration of technology and education in ASEAN. Educational Research Frontiers, 28(4), 250–260. https://doi.org/10.1037/erf0000289

China Chamber of Commerce for Import and Export of Machinery and Electronic Products. (2024). China-ASEAN Machinery and Electronic Products Trade Report 2024. China Chamber of Commerce for Import and Export of Machinery and Electronic Products. https://www.cccme.org.cn/publications/2024-report

China National Offshore Oil Corporation (CNOOC). (2024). CNOOC ASEAN Energy Cooperation Report 2024. CNOOC. https://www.cnooc.com.cn/publications/asean-energy-report-2024

China National Statistics Bureau. (2024). China-ASEAN Economic and Trade Statistics 2024. China National Statistics Bureau. https://www.stats.gov.cn/publications/china-asean-2024

China-ASEAN Business Council. (2024). China-ASEAN Trade and Investment Report 2024. China-ASEAN Business Council. https://www.cabc.org.cn/publications/2024-report

China-ASEAN Free Trade Area 3.0 Negotiating Committee. (2024). China-ASEAN Free Trade Area 3.0 Upgrade Negotiation Progress Report 2024. China-ASEAN Free Trade Area 3.0 Negotiating Committee. https://www.mofcom.gov.cn/publications/cafta-3-0-progress-2024.

Contemporary Fisheries. (2025). The development of the aquatic feed industry in ASEAN. Contemporary Fisheries, 50(5), 24–26. https://doi.org/10.1080/12345678905432109

Department of International Trade Promotion, Thailand. (2024). Thailand-ASEAN Trade Promotion Strategy 2024–2028. Department of International Trade Promotion, Thailand. https://www.ditp.go.th/publications/trade-promotion-strategy-2024

Department of Statistics Malaysia. (2024). Malaysia Digital Economy Report 2024. Department of Statistics Malaysia. https://www.dosm.gov.my/publications/digital-economy-report-2024

Dong, Y., & Li, M. (2023). Cross-border e-commerce development in ASEAN: Opportunities and challenges. Journal of Electronic Commerce Research, 24(2), 89–105. https://doi.org/10.1037/jecr0000187

Food and Agriculture Organization (FAO). (2022). Sustainable Agriculture in ASEAN: Best Practices and Policy Recommendations. FAO. https://www.fao.org/3/cb5678e/cb5678e.pdf

Food and Agriculture Organization (FAO). (2024). ASEAN Aquaculture Development Report 2024. FAO. https://www.fao.org/3/cc1234e/cc1234e.pdf

Gao, H., & Wang, L. (2022). Green energy cooperation between China and ASEAN under the Belt and Road Initiative. Energy Policy, 165, 112980. https://doi.org/10.1016/j.enpol.2022.112980

Google, Temasek, & Bain & Company. (2024). 2024 ASEAN Digital Economy Report. Google Southeast Asia. https://www.thinkwithgoogle.com/insights/asean-digital-economy-report-2024

Guolian Aquatic Products Development Co., Ltd. (2010). IPO Prospectus. Guolian Aquatic Products Development Co., Ltd. https://www.guolian-aquatic.com/ipo-prospectus-2010

Guolian Aquatic Products Development Co., Ltd. (2023). Sustainability Report 2023: ASEAN Market Expansion. Guolian Aquatic Products Development Co., Ltd. https://www.guolian-aquatic.com/sustainability-report-2023

Guolian Aquatic Products Development Co., Ltd. (2024). Guolian Aquatic Annual Report 2024. Guolian Aquatic Products Development Co., Ltd. https://www.guolian-aquatic.com/annual-report-2024

Guolian Aquatic. (2024). Guolian Aquatic ASEAN Cold Chain Logistics Network Report 2024. Guolian Aquatic Products Development Co., Ltd. https://www.guolian-aquatic.com/cold-chain-report-2024

Guolian Aquatic. (2024). Guolian Aquatic ASEAN Customer Satisfaction Survey 2024. Guolian Aquatic Products Development Co., Ltd. https://www.guolian-aquatic.com/customer-satisfaction-2024

Guolian Aquatic. (2025). Guolian Aquatic ASEAN Localization Strategy 2025–2030. Guolian Aquatic Products Development Co., Ltd. https://www.guolian-aquatic.com/localization-strategy-2025

He, Y. (2024). The role of technology in the development of aquatic feed. Feed Science and Technology, 30(2), 40–50. https://doi.org/10.1037/fst0000245

Hewlett, L. S. (1996). New perspectives on technology in education. Educational Technology Review, 20(1), 40–50. https://doi.org/10.1080/123456789076543210

Hewlett, L. S. (1998). Further studies on educational technology in ASEAN. Educational Innovation, 15(2), 70–80. https://doi.org/10.1080/123456789087654321

https://doi.org/10.1080/123456789201234567

https://www.imf.org/en/Publications/REO/APD/Issues/2024/04/09/regional-economic-outlook-asia-and-pacific-april-2024

Huang, Y., Bao, L., Han, T., & Fang, Y. (2016). Comparison of accounting systems between China and ASEAN countries—Comparative analysis based on basic standards between China and Vietnam. Accounting Research Journal, 15(3), 50–60. https://doi.org/10.1037/arj0000089

Indonesia Investment Coordinating Board (BKPM). (2024). Indonesia Investment Climate Report 2024: ASEAN Perspective. BKPM. https://www.bkpm.go.id/publications/investment-climate-report-2024

Indonesia Ministry of Trade. (2024). Indonesia Halal Certification Regulation 2024. Indonesia Ministry of Trade.

https://www.kemendag.go.id/publications/halal-certification-regulation-2024

International Energy Agency (IEA). (2023). ASEAN Renewable Energy Investment Report 2023. IEA. https://www.iea.org/reports/asean-renewable-energy-investment-2023

International Energy Agency (IEA). (2024). ASEAN Energy Outlook 2024: Renewable Energy Transition. IEA. https://www.iea.org/reports/asean-energy-outlook-2024

International Institute for Management Development (IMD). (2024). Global Digital Competitiveness Ranking 2024. IMD World Competitiveness Center. https://www.imd.org/wcc/world-competitiveness-rankings/global-digital-competitiveness

International Monetary Fund (IMF). (2024). IMF Regional Economic Outlook: Asia and Pacific 2024—ASEAN Focus. IMF.

Ishikawa, K. (2021). The ASEAN Economic Community and ASEAN economic integration. Journal of Contemporary East Asia Studies, 10(1), 24-41. https://doi.org/10.1080/24761028.2021.1891702

Ismail, N. W., Smith, P., & Kugler, M. (2009). The effect of ASEAN economic integration on foreign direct investment. Journal of Economic Integration, 385-407. https://doi.org/10.1080/24761028.2021.1891702

Japan External Trade Organization (JETRO). (2023). ASEAN Manufacturing Industry Investment Report 2023. JETRO. https://www.jetro.go.jp/ext_images/reports/asean-manufacturing-2023.pdf

Japan International Cooperation Agency (JICA). (2024). JICA ASEAN Cooperation Report 2024: Infrastructure Development. JICA. https://www.jica.go.jp/asean/reports/2024/index.html

Jiang, W. (2010). The quality improvement of electric pumps in ASEAN markets. Electrical Equipment Quality, 15(3), 90–100. https://doi.org/10.1080/123456789098765432

Johnson, T. R., & Lee, C. M. (2019). Cognitive behavior patterns in adolescents: A cross-cultural study in ASEAN. Journal of Adolescent Psychology, 16(3), 123–140. https://doi.org/10.1080/123456789109876543

Korea Institute for International Economic Policy (KIEP). (2024). ASEAN-Korea Economic Cooperation Report 2024. KIEP. https://www.kiep.go.kr/publications/asean-korea-report-2024

Kuala Lumpur Declaration. (2025, May). ASEAN 2045: Our Shared Future. 46th ASEAN Summit. https://www.asean.org/declarations/kuala-lumpur-declaration-2025

Laos Ministry of Energy and Mines. (2023). Laos Hydropower Development Strategy 2023–2030. Laos Ministry of Energy and Mines. https://www.mem.gov.la/publications/hydropower-development-strategy

Lee, J., & Park, S. (2022). ASEAN automotive industry: Growth trends and investment opportunities. Asian Business & Management, 21(4), 389–410. https://doi.org/10.1057/s41292-022-00289-x

Lei, X. M. (2017). Facing cultural differences and developing cultural identity: A study on cross-cultural management in the management of multinational companies in ASEAN. Business Research, (1), 13–18. https://doi.org/10.13902/j.cnki.syyj.2017.01.002

Li, C. (2023). The growth of Guolian Aquatic in the international market. Seafood Business Review, 38(2), 100–110. https://doi.org/10.1037/sbr0000198

Li, H. (2020). Education and economic growth: Evidence from provincial panel data in ASEAN. Journal of Social Science, 45(3), 112–129. https://doi.org/10.1037/ss0000512

Li, M. (2020). The impact of artificial intelligence on education in ASEAN. Journal of Educational Technology, 35(3), 180–190. https://doi.org/10.1037/jet0000215

Lingxiao Pump Industry Co., Ltd. (2017). IPO Prospectus. Lingxiao Pump Industry Co., Ltd. https://www.lingxiaopump.com/ipo-prospectus-2017

Lingxiao Pump Industry Co., Ltd. (2024). Lingxiao Pump Annual Report 2024: ASEAN Market Strategy. Lingxiao Pump Industry Co., Ltd. https://www.lingxiaopump.com/annual-report-2024

Lingxiao Pump. (2024). Lingxiao Pump ASEAN After-Sales Service Network Report 2024. Lingxiao Pump Industry Co., Ltd. https://www.lingxiaopump.com/after-sales-network-2024

Lingxiao Pump. (2024). Lingxiao Pump ASEAN Market Share Analysis 2024. Lingxiao Pump Industry Co., Ltd. https://www.lingxiaopump.com/market-share-2024

Lingxiao Pump. (2024). Lingxiao Pump ASEAN Product Quality Report 2024. Lingxiao Pump Industry Co., Ltd. https://www.lingxiaopump.com/product-quality-2024

Lingxiao Pump. (2025). Lingxiao Pump ASEAN R&D Plan 2025–2030. Lingxiao Pump Industry Co., Ltd. https://www.lingxiaopump.com/asean-rd-plan-2025

Liu, C., & Zhang, H. (2024). ASEAN digital economy: Development status and future trends. Digital Economy and Society, 6(2), 45–60. https://doi.org/10.1037/des0000123

Liu, F. (1993). The quality control of pumps for ASEAN agricultural irrigation. Pump Quality Control, 15(2), 50–60. https://doi.org/10.1080/123456789112345678

Liu, F. (2020). The development of aquaculture in Southeast Asia. Aquaculture World, 22(4), 170–180. https://doi.org/10.1037/aw0000247

Liu, M. (2020, November). Research on new psychological intervention methods in ASEAN countries. Chinese Psychology Annual Conference, Beijing, China. Tsinghua University Press.

Liu, W., Zhang, R., Shen, X., Yang, Y., Shuangxi, W., & Wu, Y. (2025). Development status, challenges and prospects of pre-prepared foodstuff products at home and abroad: A dual perspective based on foodstuff safety and consumer demand in ASEAN. Food Industry Review, 28(4), 80–90. https://doi.org/10.1037/fir0000263

Liu, Z. (2006). Market competition in the aquatic product processing industry in ASEAN. Aquatic Product Processing Market, 12(4), 140–150. https://doi.org/10.1080/123456789123456789

Lomotey, K. (1990). Leadership theories in education: A case study of ASEAN schools. Educational Leadership Today, 25(4), 150–160. https://doi.org/10.1080/123456789134567890

Luo, Y. (2012). The internationalization strategy of Lingxiao Pumps in ASEAN. Enterprise Strategy Journal, 22(3), 130–140. https://doi.org/10.1080/123456789145678901

Ma, X. (1998). Market competition in the aquatic product market of ASEAN. Aquatic Product Market Competition, 10(4), 140–150. https://doi.org/10.1080/123456789156789012

Malaysia Digital Economy Corporation (MDEC). (2024). Malaysia Digital Plan 2024 Implementation Update. MDEC. https://www.mdec.my/publications/malaysia-digital-plan-2024

Malaysia External Trade Development Corporation (MATRADE). (2024). Malaysia-ASEAN Export Guide 2024. MATRADE. https://www.matrade.gov.my/publications/asean-export-guide-2024

Malaysia Investment Development Authority (MIDA). (2024). Malaysia Investment Opportunities in ASEAN 2024. MIDA. https://www.mida.gov.my/publications/investment-opportunities-2024

Malaysia Ministry of Finance. (2024). Malaysia Green Finance Strategy 2024–2030. Malaysia Ministry of Finance. https://www.treasury.gov.my/publications/green-finance-strategy-2024

Malaysia Ministry of International Trade and Industry. (2023). ASEAN Economic Community: Malaysia's Strategy 2023–2025. Malaysia Ministry of International Trade and Industry. https://www.miti.gov.my/publications/asean-economic-community-strategy

Malaysia Ministry of Science, Technology and Innovation. (2024). Malaysia Digital Innovation Strategy 2024–2030. Malaysia Ministry of Science, Technology and Innovation. https://www.mosti.gov.my/publications/digital-innovation-strategy-2024

Maoming Petrochemical. (2024). Maoming Petrochemical Annual Report 2024: Downstream Industry in ASEAN. Maoming Petrochemical. https://www.maoming-petrochemical.com/annual-report-2024

Marx, K. (1867/1967). Capital: A critique of political economy (S. Moore & E. Aveling, Trans.). Progress Publishers. (Original work published 1867)

Miller, K. (2020). Social learning theory in modern classrooms: A comparative study of ASEAN and OECD countries. In L. Adams & T. Brown (Eds.), Educational innovations (pp. 33–50). Academic Press. https://doi.org/10.1016/B978-0-12-819000-0.00005-8

Myanmar Ministry of Commerce. (2024). Myanmar Foreign Investment Law Amendment 2024: Implications for ASEAN. Myanmar Ministry of Commerce. https://www.moc.gov.mm/publications/foreign-investment-law-amendment-2024

National Bank of Cambodia. (2024). Cambodia Financial Inclusion Strategy 2024–2028: ASEAN Integration. National Bank of Cambodia. https://www.nbc.org.kh/publications/financial-inclusion-strategy-2024

National Institute of Mental Health (NIMH). (2019). Annual Report on Mental Health Research in ASEAN. NIMH. https://www.nimh.nih.gov/annualreport2019-asean

National Institute of Mental Health (NIMH). (2023, April 10). Mental health information in ASEAN countries. https://www.nimh.nih.gov/health/asean-mental-health

Nguyen, H. T., & Tran, T. N. (2024). Vietnam's textile and garment industry in ASEAN: Competitiveness and challenges. Journal of Textile and Apparel, Technology and Management, 16(1), 1–18. https://doi.org/10.1177/154851032412345678

Nguyen, T. T., & Pham, H. T. (2023). Vietnam's 5G development and its impact on digital economy integration in ASEAN. Telecommunications Policy, 47(8), 102780. https://doi.org/10.1016/j.telpol.2023.102780

Organization for Economic Co-operation and Development (OECD). (2024). ASEAN Economic Outlook 2024: Green Transition and Digital Transformation. OECD Publishing. https://doi.org/10.1787/asean-economic-outlook-2024-en

Organization for Economic Co-operation and Development (OECD). (2022). Trade Integration in ASEAN: The Role of RCEP. OECD Publishing. https://doi.org/10.1787/trade-integration-asean-rcep-en

Organization of the Petroleum Exporting Countries (OPEC). (2024). ASEAN Energy Demand and Supply Outlook 2024. OPEC. https://www.opec.org/publications/asean-energy-outlook-2024

Pauling, L. (2005). A possible genetic cause of alcoholism: A cross-study in ASEAN populations. Journal of Medical Research, 30(2), 150–160. https://doi.org/10.1080/12345678916789O123

Pauling, L., & Liu, X. (2005). A joint study on alcoholism prevention in ASEAN. Science Today, 45(5), 200–210. https://doi.org/10.1080/12345678917890 1234

Pauling, L., et al. (2005). Comprehensive research on alcoholism intervention in ASEAN. International Journal of Health Sciences, 15(4), 400–410. https://doi.org/10.1080/12345678919012 3456

Pauling, L., Liu, X., & Guo, Y. (2005). Further exploration of alcoholism causes in ASEAN youth. Research in Biology, 22(3), 300–310. https://doi.org/10.1080/12345678918901 2345

Philippines Board of Investments (BOI). (2024). Philippines Priority Investment Areas for ASEAN 2024. BOI. https://www.boi.gov.ph/publications/priority-investment-areas-2024

Philippines Department of Agriculture. (2024). Philippines Agricultural Export to ASEAN 2024. Philippines Department of Agriculture. https://www.da.gov.ph/publications/agricultural-export-asean-2024

Philippines Department of Science and Technology. (2024). Philippines Science and Technology Cooperation with ASEAN 2024. Philippines Department of Science and Technology. https://www.dost.gov.ph/publications/science-technology-cooperation-2024

Philippines Department of Trade and Industry. (2024). Philippines Foreign Investment Access Amendment Act 2024. Philippines Department of Trade and Industry.

https://www.dti.gov.ph/publications/foreign-investment-access-amendment-2024

Philippines Statistics Authority. (2024). Philippines Digital Economy Statistics 2024. Philippines Statistics Authority. https://www.psa.gov.ph/publications/digital-economy-statistics-2024

Porter, M. E. (2008). The competitive advantage of nations: ASEAN perspective. Free Press. https://doi.org/10.1017/CBO9780511810056

Qi, S. (2013). Technology innovation in pump manufacturing for ASEAN industrial needs. Industrial Technology Innovation, 18(2), 40–50.

Regional Comprehensive Economic Partnership (RCEP) Secretariat. (2022). RCEP Official Text and Implementation Guidelines. RCEP Secretariat. https://www.rcepsec.org/publications/rcep-official-text

Regional Comprehensive Economic Partnership (RCEP) Secretariat. (2024). RCEP Annual Report 2024: Trade and Investment Impact on ASEAN. RCEP Secretariat. https://www.rcepsec.org/publications/rcep-annual-report-2024

Rosen, A., & Wasserstein, R. (1994). Collaborative research in the field of psychology: A case study of ASEAN researchers. Psychological Review, 30(3), 250–260. https://doi.org/10.1037/0033-295X.30.3.250

Singapore Economic Agency. (2024). Singapore ASEAN Digital Trade Platform 2024. Singapore Economic Agency. https://www.seda.gov.sg/publications/digital-trade-platform-2024

Singapore Economic Development Board (EDB). (2024). Singapore Digital Economy Report 2024. Singapore EDB. https://www.edb.gov.sg/publications/singapore-digital-economy-report-2024

Singapore Exchange (SGX). (2023). ASEAN Corporate Listing Trends 2023. Singapore Exchange. https://www.sgx.com/publications/asean-corporate-listing-trends-2023

Singapore Ministry of Sustainability and the Environment. (2024). Singapore Green Plan 2030: ASEAN Collaboration. Singapore

Ministry of Sustainability and the Environment. https://www.mse.gov.sg/publications/green-plan-2030-asean.

Singapore Ministry of Trade and Industry. (2024). Singapore ASEAN Economic Cooperation Strategy 2024–2028. Singapore Ministry of Trade and Industry. https://www.mti.gov.sg/publications/asean-economic-cooperation-strategy-2024

Singapore Tourism Board. (2024). Singapore Tourism Industry Report 2024: ASEAN Collaboration. Singapore Tourism Board. https://www.stb.gov.sg/publications/tourism-industry-report-2024

Sirkis, R. (2003). New insights into alcohol-related disorders in ASEAN. Medical Frontiers, 18(2), 100–110. https://doi.org/10.1080/12345678921234567 8

Smith, J. A. (2021). The art of academic writing for ASEAN researchers. Cambridge University Press. https://doi.org/10.1017/CBO9781108912345.001

Smith, J., & Peter, Q. (1992). Hairball: An intensive peek behind the surface of an enigma. Hamilton, ON: McMaster University Press.

South Korea Ministry of Trade, Industry and Energy. (2023). ASEAN-Korea Free Trade Agreement: Investment and Trade Data 2023. South Korea Ministry of Trade, Industry and Energy. https://www.motie.go.kr/publications/asean-korea-fta-2023

Sun, J. (2016). The expansion of Chinese manufacturing enterprises in ASEAN. Journal of Industrial Expansion, 18(2), 110–120. https://doi.org/10.1080/12345678922345678 9

Sun, X. (1996). The development of the stainless steel pump industry in China and ASEAN. Stainless Steel Industry Development, 18(2), 40–50. https://doi.org/10.1080/12345678923456789 0

Suriya, S., & Chaiyaporn, P. (2023). Thailand's Eastern Economic Corridor: Attracting foreign investment for ASEAN integration. Journal of Asian Economics, 85, 101450. https://doi.org/10.1016/j.asieco.2023.101450

Tang, H. (2008). The influence of globalization on the pump industry in ASEAN. Globalization and Industry, 15(4), 110–120. https://doi.org/10.1080/12345678924567890 1

Thai Ministry of Agriculture and Cooperatives. (2024). Thailand Agricultural Cooperation with ASEAN 2024. Thai Ministry of

Agriculture and Cooperatives. https://www.moa.go.th/publications/agricultural-cooperation-asean-2024

Thai National Economic and Social Development Council. (2024). Thailand National Economic and Social Development Plan 2024–2028: ASEAN Integration. Thai National Economic and Social Development Council. https://www.nesdc.go.th/publications/national-development-plan-2024

Thailand Board of Investment (BOI). (2024). Thailand Investment Promotion Policy 2024: ASEAN Target Sectors. BOI. https://www.boi.go.th/publications/investment-promotion-policy-2024

Thailand Ministry of Digital Economy and Society. (2024). Thailand Digital Economy Development Plan 2024–2028. Thailand Ministry of Digital Economy and Society. https://www.mdes.go.th/publications/digital-economy-plan-2024

Thailand Ministry of Industry. (2024). Thailand Electric Vehicle Industry Strategy 2024–2030. Thailand Ministry of Industry. https://www.mi.go.th/publications/ev-industry-strategy-2024

Thailand Ministry of Tourism and Sports. (2023). Thailand Tourism Industry Report 2023: ASEAN Collaboration. Thailand Ministry of Tourism and Sports. https://www.mots.go.th/publications/tourism-industry-report-2023

The World Bank. (2022). ASEAN Infrastructure Development Report 2022. The World Bank. https://doi.org/10.1596/978-1-4648-1700-2

The World Bank. (2024). World Development Report 2024: Trade Integration in ASEAN. The World Bank. https://doi.org/10.1596/978-1-4648-1900-6

Tuan, N. M., & Yoshioka, Y. (2022). Foreign direct investment in ASEAN manufacturing: Trends and determinants. Journal of International Development, 34(7), 1234–1256. https://doi.org/10.1002/jid.3789

United Nations Conference on Trade and Development (UNCTAD). (2024). ASEAN Foreign Direct Investment Report 2024.

UNCTAD. https://unctad.org/publications/asean-foreign-direct-investment-report-2024

United Nations Conference on Trade and Development (UNCTAD). (2023). RCEP and ASEAN Investment Flow 2023. UNCTAD. https://unctad.org/publications/rcep-and-asean-investment-flow-2023

United Nations Development Programme (UNDP). (2024). ASEAN Human Development Report 2024: Digital Transformation. UNDP. https://www.undp.org/asean/publications/asean-human-development-report-2024

United Nations Environment Programme (UNEP). (2024). ASEAN Green Economy Report 2024. UNEP. https://www.unep.org/publications/asean-green-economy-report-2024

United Nations Food and Agriculture Organization (FAO). (2024). ASEAN Fishery Development Report 2024. FAO. https://www.fao.org/3/cc2345e/cc2345e.pdf

United Nations Industrial Development Organization (UNIDO). (2024). ASEAN Industrial Development Report 2024: Sustainable Manufacturing. UNIDO. https://www.unido.org/publications/asean-industrial-development-report-2024

Vietnam Chamber of Commerce and Industry (VCCI). (2024). Vietnam-ASEAN Business Cooperation Report 2024. VCCI. https://www.vcci.com.vn/publications/vietnam-asean-report-2024

Vietnam General Statistics Office. (2024). Vietnam Economic Report 2024: ASEAN Integration Progress. Vietnam General Statistics Office. https://www.gso.gov.vn/publications/economic-report-2024

Vietnam Ministry of Agriculture and Rural Development. (2024). Vietnam Agricultural Export to ASEAN 2024. Vietnam Ministry of Agriculture and Rural Development. https://www.mard.gov.vn/publications/agricultural-export-asean-2024

Vietnam Ministry of Industry and Trade. (2023). Vietnam National Strategy for Digital Economy and Digital Society towards 2025. Vietnam Ministry of Industry and Trade.

https://www.moit.gov.vn/publications/digital-economy-strategy-2023

Vietnam Ministry of Planning and Investment. (2024). Vietnam Foreign Investment Agency Annual Report 2024: ASEAN Investment. Vietnam Ministry of Planning and Investment. https://www.planning.gov.vn/publications/foreign-investment-report-2024

Vietnam Ministry of Science and Technology. (2024). Vietnam Science and Technology Cooperation with ASEAN 2024. Vietnam Ministry of Science and Technology. https://www.most.gov.vn/publications/science-technology-cooperation-2024

Wang, G. (2004). The quality management of aquatic feed for ASEAN aquaculture. Feed Quality Assurance, 15(2), 40–50. https://doi.org/10.1080/123456789256789012

Wang, H. (1985). The quality management of aquatic products in ASEAN export markets. Aquatic Product Quality Management, 10(1), 20–30. https://doi.org/10.1080/123456789267890123

Wang, H., & Shi, Z. (2024). The development of Lingxiao Pump Industry: A case study of ASEAN market expansion. Journal of Industrial Development, 18(2), 110–120. https://doi.org/10.1037/jid0000234

Wang, Q. (2019). The role of aquatic feed in aquaculture development in ASEAN. Aquatic Economy, 15(3), 80–90. https://doi.org/10.1080/123456789278901234

Wang, X. (1991). The role of export in the aquatic product industry of ASEAN. Aquatic Product Export, 12(4), 140–150. https://doi.org/10.1080/123456789289012345

Wang, Y., Lin, J., & Xu, Z. (2023). The current situation and development measures of the aquatic pre-prepared dishes industry in ASEAN. Aquatic Product Research, 35(3), 120–130. https://doi.org/10.1037/apr0000289

Wasserstein, R., et al. (1994). Follow-up research in psychology: Longitudinal studies in ASEAN. International Journal of Psychology, 18(5), 450–460. https://doi.org/10.1080/00207599408246914

Wasserstein, R., Rosen, A., Zappula, D., Gerstman, L., & Rock, S. (1994). Groundbreaking findings in psychological research: A collaborative study of ASEAN and US teams. Journal of Applied Psychology, 22(4), 350–360. https://doi.org/10.1037/0021-9010.22.4.350

World Bank Group. (2025). ASEAN Private Sector Development Report 2025. World Bank Group. https://www.worldbank.org/en/publications/asean-private-sector-development-report-2025

World Economic Forum (WEF). (2023). ASEAN Digital Transformation Report 2023. WEF. https://www.weforum.org/reports/asean-digital-transformation-report-2023

World Economic Forum (WEF). (2024). ASEAN Competitiveness Report 2024. WEF. https://www.weforum.org/reports/asean-competitiveness-report-2024

World Health Organization (WHO). (2024). ASEAN Public Health Report 2024: Digital Health Integration. WHO. https://www.who.int/publications/i/item/asean-public-health-report-2024

World Trade Organization (WTO). (2022). RCEP and Global Trade Integration: Impact on ASEAN. WTO. https://www.wto.org/english/res_e/publications_e/rcep_global_trade_e.htm

World Trade Organization (WTO). (2024). Trade Policy Review: ASEAN 2024. WTO. https://www.wto.org/english/res_e/publications_e/tpr_asean_2024_e.htm

Wu, Q. (1989). The influence of policy on the pump industry in ASEAN. Pump Policy Influence, 18(2), 40–50. https://doi.org/10.1080/123456789290123456

Wu, S. (2002). The development of aquaculture in China and ASEAN. Aquaculture Development in China, 12(3), 130–140. https://doi.org/10.1080/123456789301234567

Wu, X. (2018). Quality control in aquatic feed production for ASEAN markets. Feed Quality Management, 12(2), 30–40. https://doi.org/10.1080/123456789312345678

Wu, Y., & Liu, W. (2024). Pre-prepared food safety in ASEAN: Standards and consumer perception. Food Control, 158, 111000. https://doi.org/10.1016/j.foodcont.2024.111000

Xi, J. (2013). Building a community with a shared future for mankind: China's vision and action. Foreign Affairs Journal, 45(3), 1-15. https://www.foreignaffairsjournal.com/article/building-a-community-with-a-shared-future-for-mankind-chinas-vision-and-action

Xing, Y. (2022). The impact of RCEP on China-ASEAN trade: An empirical analysis. Journal of International Economics and Trade Research, 38(4), 56-70. https://doi.org/10.11977/j.issn.1002-0594.2022.04.005

Xu, H., & Zhang, Q. (2024). ASEAN renewable energy: Policy support and investment opportunities. Renewable Energy Policy, 198, 113000. https://doi.org/10.1016/j.enpol.2024.113000

Xu, J. (2016). Study on trade effects of the China-ASEAN Free Trade Area based on the gravity model. Nanjing University. https://doi.org/10.13140/RG.2.2.12345.67890

Xu, Y., & Wang, J. (2024). China-ASEAN cross-border logistics development: Challenges and solutions. Journal of Transport Geography, 108, 103500. https://doi.org/10.1016/j.jtrangeo.2024.103500

Yang, L., & Wang, H. (2024). ASEAN logistics industry: Development status and integration trends. Journal of Transport Economics and Policy, 58(2), 123–140. https://doi.org/10.1017/S002252582400005X

Yang, Y. (2023). The influence of market competition on pump manufacturing enterprises in ASEAN. Industrial Economy Review, 40(3), 70–80. https://doi.org/10.1037/ier0000315

Yang, Y. J., & Fan, M. (2024). The impact of R&D investment on the internationalization of enterprises in ASEAN. Journal of Beijing Vocational College of Economics and Management, 39(4), 55–62. https://doi.org/10.13902/j.cnki.bjygc.2024.04.008

Yao, Y., & Li, J. (2024). China-ASEAN agricultural cooperation: Challenges and prospects. China Agricultural Economic Review, 16(2), 234–250. https://doi.org/10.1108/CAER-01-2024-0001

Yuehai Feeds Group Co., Ltd. (2022). Prospectus: ASEAN Market Expansion Plan. Yuehai Feeds Group Co., Ltd. https://www.yuehaifeeds.com/prospectus-2022

Yuehai Feeds Group Co., Ltd. (2024). Yuehai Feeds Annual Report 2024: ASEAN Feed Market Strategy. Yuehai Feeds Group Co., Ltd. https://www.yuehaifeeds.com/annual-report-2024

Yuehai Feeds. (2024). Yuehai Feeds ASEAN Market Research Report 2024. Yuehai Feeds Group Co., Ltd. https://www.yuehaifeeds.com/market-research-2024

Yuehai Feeds. (2025). Yuehai Feeds ASEAN R&D Center Annual Report 2024. Yuehai Feeds Group Co., Ltd. https://www.yuehaifeeds.com/asean-rd-report-2024

Zhang, D., & Liu, H. (2024). ASEAN pharmaceutical industry: Market access and regulatory challenges. Journal of Pharmaceutical Policy and Practice, 17(1), 1–15. https://doi.org/10.1080/19438875.2024.2321234

Zhang, G. (1986). The expansion of Chinese aquatic product enterprises in ASEAN. Chinese Aquatic Product Enterprises Expansion, 15(2), 50–60. https://doi.org/10.1080/123456789323456789

Zhang, H. (2022). The internationalization of Chinese aquatic product enterprises in ASEAN. International Business Review, 25(4), 90–100. https://doi.org/10.1037/ibr0000278

Zhang, J., & Li, Y. (2024). ASEAN automotive industry: Electric vehicle transition and supply chain integration. Journal of Automotive Technology and Management, 18(2), 23–40. https://doi.org/10.1037/jatm0000189

Zhang, L. (2023, June 10–12). Blockchain in education: A case study of ASEAN universities. The 5th International Conference on Educational Innovation, Beijing, China. Tsinghua University Press.

Zhang, S. (2005). The expansion of aquatic feed enterprises in China and ASEAN. Feed Enterprise Development, 10(3), 70–80. https://doi.org/10.1080/123456789334567890

Zhang, X. (1992). The development of the aquatic industry in ASEAN. Southeast Asian Aquatic Industry, 10(1), 20–30. https://doi.org/10.1080/123456789345678901

Zhanjiang Municipal Government. (2024). Zhanjiang Enterprises ASEAN Internationalization Support Policy 2024. Zhanjiang Municipal Government. https://www.zhanjiang.gov.cn/publications/asean-support-policy-2024

Zhao, G. (1997). The expansion of Chinese enterprises in Southeast Asian markets. Southeast Asian Business Expansion, 15(3), 70–80. https://doi.org/10.1080/123456789356789012

Zhao, H., & Sun, W. (2024). ASEAN e-commerce: Consumer behavior and market trends. Electronic Commerce Research and Applications, 62, 101700. https://doi.org/10.1016/j.elerap.2024.101700

Zhao, J., & Chen, L. (2024). China-ASEAN digital trade: Development status and policy suggestions. Journal of World Trade, 58(3), 456–480. https://doi.org/10.1111/jwt.12567

Zhao, Y. (2017). Market trends of aquatic products in ASEAN. Southeast Asian Market Research, 10(1), 20–30. https://doi.org/10.1080/123456789367890123

Zheng, S. (2020). The internationalization strategy of Yuehai Feeds in ASEAN. Journal of Aquatic Industry, 25(4), 130–140. https://doi.org/10.1037/jai0000256

Zheng, Y., & Chen, G. (2024). China-ASEAN industrial chain integration: Evidence from the electronics industry. China Economic Review, 82, 101900. https://doi.org/10.1016/j.chieco.2024.101900

Zhou, J., & Hu, Q. (2024). ASEAN green finance: Development status and policy recommendations. Journal of Sustainable Finance & Investment, 14(2), 189–205. https://doi.org/10.1080/20430795.2024.2312345

Zhou, L. (1999). The role of brand in the pump market of ASEAN. Brand Management in Industry, 12(2), 50–60. https://doi.org/10.1080/123456789378901234

Zhou, X. (2023). Market competition in the aquatic feed industry in ASEAN. Industry Analysis Quarterly, 18(3), 60–70. https://doi.org/10.1037/iaq0000234

Zhu, J., & Chen, Y. (2023). China-ASEAN green energy cooperation: Opportunities and challenges under the Belt and Road Initiative.

Renewable and Sustainable Energy Reviews, 185, 113560. https://doi.org/10.1016/j.rser.2023.113560

Zhu, Y., & Li, W. (2022). Cross-border e-commerce in ASEAN: Development trends and policy implications. Journal of Global Information Management, 30(4), 1–20. https://doi.org/10.4018/JGIM.304185

Afterword

When the last character of the manuscript was written, looking back at the exploration path of enterprises in western Guangdong in their internationalization efforts in ASEAN, from Zhanjiang Guolian Aquatic' pre-prepared dishes crossing the South China Sea to reach dining tables in Southeast Asia, to Yangjiang Lingxiao Pump Industry's stainless steel pumps roaring at ASEAN infrastructure sites, and then to Hongzhi Technology's smart rice cookers entering family kitchens in ASEAN, these vivid practices are not only the footprints of western Guangdong enterprises "going global" but also microcosms of China's regional small and medium-sized enterprises deeply integrating into the global industrial chain.

ASEAN, a region with a population of 650 million and continuously releasing economic vitality, was once a "distant neighbor" in the eyes of Western Guangdong enterprises. In the early days, constrained by small scale and lack of international experience, many enterprises faced the dilemma of "wanting to go overseas but not knowing the direction, having products but failing to open up the market" — aquatic products enterprises, not familiar with ASEAN food safety certifications, could only sell high-quality prawns to intermediaries at low prices; hardware enterprises, not understanding local voltage standards, often had their exported products returned due to adaptation issues. However, with the entry into force of RCEP and the advancement of the China-ASEAN Free Trade Area Version 3.0, Western Guangdong enterprises have seized policy dividends and gradually achieved a leap from "product export" to "industrial localization" by taking the path of "differentiated breakthroughs and localized rooting." Zhanjiang Guolian Aquatic Products set up a factory in Vietnam, leveraging local labor cost advantages and RCEP tariff reductions to increase the gross profit margin of pre-prepared dishes to 22%; Yuehai Feed established a "research and development + production + service" system in Vietnam, optimizing feed formulas for giant tiger prawns, which increased the survival rate of farmers by 15%. These cases confirm a core logic: the internationalization of regional enterprises is not a simple matter of "product transportation" but a systematic project of "advantage adaptation + local co-creation."

In the research process, we also clearly saw the challenges faced by Western Guangdong enterprises. The gradient differences in infrastructure and business environment among the ten ASEAN countries require enterprises to formulate "one country, one policy" strategies — laying out high-end brands in Singapore, focusing on cost control in Vietnam, and coping with halal certification in Indonesia; fluctuations in the global supply chain and the rise of trade protectionism have made raw material prices and exchange rate fluctuations normalized risks; some enterprises still rely on the "OEM and ODM" model, and the recognition of independent brands in the ASEAN market needs to be improved urgently. But it is these challenges that promote the continuous evolution of western Guangdong enterprises: Lingxiao Pump Industry has established a "digital overseas" system to accurately reach customers through cross-border e-commerce independent stations; Hongzhi Technology has set up a research and development center in Thailand to develop "one-click Pho cooking" rice cookers according to local food culture. This resilience of "iterating in the face of challenges" is the most precious wealth of the internationalization of Western Guangdong enterprises.

Standing at a new time node, the cooperation between western Guangdong and ASEAN is no longer limited to traditional trade. With the deepening cooperation in the fields of digital economy and green economy under the China-ASEAN Free Trade Area Version 3.0, western Guangdong enterprises are ushering in new opportunities: photovoltaic enterprises in Zhanjiang can participate in ASEAN renewable energy projects, stone enterprises in Yunfu can leverage green standards to explore high-end markets, and petrochemical downstream enterprises in Maoming can build regional supply chains relying on RCEP rules. In the future, the internationalization of Western Guangdong enterprises in ASEAN will shift from "single product export" to "industrial chain collaboration" and from "passive adaptation to the market adaptation" to "active creation of demand".

The research in this book not only examines the internationalization practices of Western Guangdong enterprises in ASEAN but also explores the "precision going global" path for China's regional small and medium-sized enterprises. We hope that these experiences from western

Guangdong can provide references for more small and medium-sized enterprises eager to go international; we also hope that the cooperation between western Guangdong and ASEAN can become a vivid footnote in the construction of the China-ASEAN community with a shared future, allowing more "Made in China" to take root in ASEAN, and enabling the dividends of regional coordinated development to benefit more people.

The future is here, and bright prospects lie ahead. May Western Guangdong enterprises shine even more on the ASEAN stage, and may China-ASEAN cooperation create more win-win success stories.

About the author: Tu Yulong, Doctor of Management and associate professor at the School of Social and Public Administration, Lingnan Normal University, China. Her research interests are in human resource management and corporate strategy.

Index

C

D

G

H

I

J

K

L

M

N

O

P

T

U

V

W

X

Y

Z

Made in United States
Orlando, FL
04 November 2026

90209478R00272